RESEARCH METHODS FOR EVERYDAY LIFE

Blending Qualitative and Quantitative Approaches

SCOTT W. VANDERSTOEP
DEIRDRE D. JOHNSTON

JOSSEY-BASS
A Wiley Imprint
www.josseybass.com

Published by Jossey-Bass
A Wiley Imprint
989 Market Street, San Francisco, CA 94103—www.josseybass.com

Jossey-Bass books and products are available through most bookstores. To contact Jossey-Bass directly call our Customer Care Department within the United States at (800) 956-7739, outside the United States at (317) 572-3986, or via fax at (317) 572-4002.

Jossey-Bass also publishes its books in a variety of electronic formats. Some content that appears in print may not be available in electronic books.

Library of Congress Cataloging-in-Publication Data

VanderStoep, Scott W.
    Research methods for everyday life : blending qualitative and quantitative approaches / Scott W. VanderStoep, Deirdre D. Johnston.
        p.   cm.
        ISBN 978-0-470-34353-1 (alk. paper)
            1. Social sciences—Research—Methodology.   2. Psychology—Research—Methodology.
3. Qualitative research.   4. Social sciences—Research—Statistical methods.   5. Psychometrics.
I. Johnston, Deirdre D.   II. Title.
    H62.V323   2008
    001.4'2—dc22

                                                                            2008037380

Printed in the United States of America
FIRST EDITION

PB Printing   10 9 8 7 6 5 4 3 2 1

TABLE OF CONTENTS

LIST OF TABLES, FIGURES, AND EXHIBITS

CHAPTER 4

CHAPTER 5

CHAPTER 6

CHAPTER 7

CHAPTER 9

CHAPTER 10

CHAPTER 11

ABOUT THE AUTHORS

SCOTT W. VANDERSTOEP is Professor of Psychology, Chair of the Psychology Department, and Director of Academic Assessment at Hope College, Holland, Michigan. He has a PhD in education and psychology from the University of Michigan. He is published extensively in the area of college student learning and thinking. His recent research appears in *Teaching of Psychology, Encyclopedia of Classroom Learning,* and *Journal of Educational Psychology.* He is the author (with Paul Pintrich) of *Learning to Learn: The Skill and Will of College Success,* published by Prentice-Hall (2008), and the editor of *Science and the Soul: Christian Faith and Psychological Research,* published by University Press of America (2003). His current research focuses on the development of psychological profiles of young athletes who suffer from overuse injuries. He teaches courses in developmental psychology, psychology and religion, and advanced data analysis.

DEIRDRE D. JOHNSTON is Professor of Communication and Chair of the Communication Department at Hope College, Holland, Michigan. She has a PhD in communication studies from the University of Iowa. She is published extensively in the area of work-family research and was nominated for the 2005 and 2007 Rosabeth Moss Kanter Award for Excellence in Work-Family Research. Her most recent research appears in *Sex Roles: A Journal of Research, Mass Communication and Society, Human Communication Research,* and *Sociological Focus.* She is the author of *The Art and Science of Persuasion,* published by McGraw-Hill, and is currently working on a book entitled *Global Communication Ethics: An Exploration of Nonviolent Communication and Sustained Dialogue in Cross-Cultural Engagement.* She teaches courses in research methods, communication theory, intercultural and gender communication, and persuasion.

To our children
Amy, Mark, & Alli
Ellie & Anneka

PREFACE

Both of us came of age in our respective social science disciplines (VanderStoep in psychology and Johnston in communication) in an era when quantitative techniques dominated the research landscape. Both of us were well trained in experimental design and advanced statistical techniques. Although we still hold these research strategies in high regard, a new generation of social science students is learning an eclectic approach to social science methodology that includes both qualitative and quantitative methods. By the time you reach the end of this book, we hope you will feel comfortable attempting all of the methodologies we describe. Research can be intimidating, and some of the techniques we describe are complex. Even long-time researchers do not feel completely comfortable with all of the techniques in this book; instead, they specialize in certain techniques. Nonetheless, we believe the hands-on approach of this book—highlighted mostly through the Your Turn activities—will make you feel more comfortable with actually doing research as opposed to simply reading about it.

■ ■ ■

ACKNOWLEDGMENTS

At Hope College, we received support from our colleagues in the departments of psychology and communication, respectively. John Shaughnessy in Hope's Psychology Department was particularly helpful. As an author of an enduring research methods textbook, he was able to give keen insight and good counsel when it seemed like the project would never get finished. We are also particularly grateful to our long-time Dean of Social Sciences, Nancy Miller. She hired both of us at Hope College and provided extra encouragement for this project. She will retire in 2008 after serving as dean for 24 years.

We are also grateful to two of Hope's best students, Jessica Gartner and Anne Hoekstra. They read the entire manuscript from cover to cover and provided great feedback that only students can give. Their honesty kept us humble and made the book better. Our office managers, Linda Koetje from Communications and Kathy Adamski from Psychology, provided support for many aspects of the book, including reference checking, formatting, and preparation of the materials.

We were friends long before we were co-authors. Thus, our families have endured endless conversations at social gatherings regarding this book. Our children stay busy when our attention turns away from them and toward the pages of this book. Our spouses, Jill VanderStoep and Jim Dumerauf, balance their own professional lives and provide testimony to what it means to be great spouses.

We are grateful to Andy Pasternack at Jossey-Bass, who first met us through an unsolicited manuscript that was dropped off at his booth at the American Psychological Association. He was willing to take a chance on this project when other publishers were not. Associate Editor Seth Schwartz provided guidance in bringing the book to publication standards.

To all students or faculty who want to comment, correct, or suggest ideas for future editions, please contact us at vanderstoep@hope.edu or johnston@hope.edu.

Scott VanderStoep
Deirdre Johnston

INTRODUCTION

The purpose of this book is to help you become effective consumers and producers of research. We live in a world where the amount information available increases exponentially each year. One of the most important skills that you can bring to the workforce in the 21st century is the ability to interpret and evaluate existing data. In addition, the 21st-century workforce needs people who can produce valid and reliable data, accurately interpret trends and patterns, and summarize findings in a way that others can understand. We take the title—*Research Methods for Everyday Life*—seriously; we will introduce you to a variety of everyday examples that highlight the need to understand social science research.

This book will help you develop your quantitative and qualitative research techniques by exploring questions about human social behavior that will provoke your curiosity and connect with the experiences of your life. Throughout the book you will find real-life examples of practitioners using various research methodologies to answer questions in various lines of work, including psychology, sociology, education, business, political science, kinesiology, anthropology, and communication studies. You will also have the opportunity to engage in hands-on applications in which you actually do research. This is accomplished with numerous Your Turn boxes inserted in each chapter. The Your Turn exercises provide the opportunity to practice and apply the research methods and concepts presented in a chapter. The skills that you will practice during the exercises in the Your Turn boxes include sampling, naturalistic observation, surveying, coding, analysis, and report writing. In addition, you will have the opportunity to work with actual data and learn to analyze data statistically using SPSS (*Statistical Package for the Social Sciences*).

Research Methods for Everyday Life: Blending Qualitative and Quantitative Approaches is an introductory undergraduate text that highlights and explains the essentials of research methods. We focus on the essentials of research methods to help undergraduates understand and engage the research in their social science disciplines, to instruct students in conducting their own primary research, and to prepare students for advanced or graduate study. We reduce students' anxiety about research methods by presenting the essentials of research in a way that is easy for students to read and understand. We include stories, examples, real-life applications, and skill-development exercises. We include the essentials necessary for a solid undergraduate grounding in research methods; however, we exclude advanced terminology, difficult theoretical issues, and complex data analysis procedures.

This textbook features both quantitative and qualitative methods. Each approach receives four chapters of coverage. The chapters on quantitative methods cover measurement, correlational designs, basic experimental designs, and advanced experimental designs. The qualitative chapters cover introduction to qualitative methods, design and analysis, qualitative methods (ethnography, phenomenology, case study, textual analysis, and applied research), and qualitative research tools (focus groups, interviewing, observation). In addition, the first chapter gives the reader a general overview of the research process.

The second chapter of the book covers the "who, how, and why" of research designs. Specifically, it introduces: (1) sampling techniques, (2) choice of a research design, and (3) determination of a research question that will inform public opinion and direct future studies. The book takes you chronologically through all stages of the research process, with ample opportunity along the way to practice the necessary skills.

The most complex material is found in Chapters 5 and 6. Students and instructors may find that portions of those chapters do not fit into their course in research methods. However, given the variety of approaches to teaching an introductory methods course, we include it and encourage you to engage with this more difficult material. The final chapter describes ways to disseminate your research findings through writing and public presentations.

Regardless of your major, your goals for life after graduation, or the level of affection (or contempt) you have for social science research, we hope that the material found in these pages will make difficult concepts easier to understand, and also increase your appreciation for and interest in being a competent researcher.

RESEARCH METHODS FOR EVERYDAY LIFE

CHAPTER

UNDERSTANDING RESEARCH

LEARNING OBJECTIVES

- Understand theories, hypotheses, and where research questions come from.
- Understand the fundamental research distinctions of qualitative vs. quantitative, basic vs. applied, and traditional vs. action research.
- Understand the elements and importance of a research proposal.
- Understand the elements and importance of research ethics.
- Obtain an introduction to basic SPSS terminology and operations.

Some students do not like research. Those who pursue degrees in social sciences such as psychology, communication, sociology, anthropology, or education do so with a passion for understanding the human condition, and often with a desire to be of service to human-kind. For some of these energetic students, a course in how to conduct social research is not a top priority. Why should students care about a research class, especially if they have no plans to become researchers after college?

It is crucial to remember that research is, for social scientists, the fundamental way the people in their field understand human beings. Furthermore, the practical applications of that research and those understandings by teachers, social workers, and therapists are also based on research. For example, why do facilities that treat substance abusers use one kind of therapy instead of another? Because research on the treatment of substance abuse has demonstrated that certain techniques are more effective than others (Kaminer, Burleson, & Goldberger, 2002). Why might it be ineffective for grade-school teachers to rely too heavily on rewards and reinforcements to motivate students? Because research suggests that extrinsic rewards cause children to choose less difficult academic tasks (Harter, 1978). How do parents decide whether spanking is an effective form of discipline? Most likely they read books on parenting—and it is hoped that those books are informed by research. Research suggests that spanking results in higher immediate compliance with parents' demands, but also more aggression on the part of the spanked children in the long run (Gershoff, 2002). Such conclusions in research are not always straightforward, however; other researchers have looked at the use of spanking as a discipline technique and found it not to be as detrimental as supposed (Baumrind, Larzelere, & Cowan, 2002). As you will discover through this book, research involves the collection, analysis, and interpretation of data, and not all researchers agree on the meaning of the same research evidence.

Whether or not you ever conduct your own research study, whether you need to make crucial decisions at your place of employment, or whether you are dealing with a family member who needs psychological help, understanding and interpreting social science research is crucial to effective and informed citizenship. This book will help you develop the skills you need. It will do so in two ways.

First, this book will make you a *consumer* of research. Some of you may become professional social researchers, spending most of your work lives actually engaged in social science research. (Remember, though, that even the most active professional researchers only spend their time doing research on a very narrow area of social inquiry.) However, most of you will spend the majority of your professional lives reading research rather than doing it. In fact, people trained in the social sciences use their research skills in life domains other than their chosen professions. Researchers use their research skills when they read the newspaper, discuss politics, and parent their children. After reading this book, you will have the tools necessary to critically evaluate the claims of advertisers, educators, pollsters, and others who assert that statements are factually correct. Being an informed consumer of research is vital to competency in an information-rich world.

Second, this book will also teach you to be a *producer* of research. If your interests are in human services, you may not think you will ever conduct a research study. However, being able to conduct research will make you extremely valuable to your organization. We firmly believe that practitioners who can conduct research will be highly prized by social service organizations. In real-life employment settings, research skills are greatly needed yet underutilized; this book is an attempt to make future practitioners more comfortable with consuming and producing research. If you can market yourself as the "research person" on your staff, you will be highly valued in your workplace—and you will save your organization a lot of money in outside research services.

Many of you may also pursue advanced study in psychology, communication, education, sociology, or some other social science field. Most master's degrees require a research-based thesis, for which the skills covered in this book are fundamental. Those who pursue terminal degrees in social science, particularly doctoral degrees, will spend a significant portion of their professional lives engaged in research. In short, this book will speak to many different students at many different levels. We hope that you find this book helpful to your current academic inquiry, but also that the skills you learn from this book will stay with you for years to come.

This chapter covers five fundamental topics essential to the research enterprise. First, we describe the traditional understanding of the research process. Second, this book focuses on both quantitative and qualitative approaches to social science research, and we discuss the basic distinction between the two methods of inquiry. Each approach is expanded upon in subsequent chapters (quantitative methods are covered in Chapters 3 through 6 and qualitative methods are covered in Chapters 7 through 10). Third, we discuss the purpose of and strategies for writing a research proposal. Planning out intentions for research prior to data collection is essential to ensuring quality. Fourth, we explore the issue of research ethics. This concept is often overlooked by the general public, but as a member of the research community it is incumbent upon you to become familiar with the ethical standards to which researchers must adhere. Finally, we introduce the elements of using a statistical-computing software package (SPSS). We will cover more advanced techniques in subsequent chapters. In this chapter we simply identify the preliminary techniques needed to get started with a research project.

THE RESEARCH PROCESS

The classic research-process model involves starting with a theory, generating hypotheses, testing the hypotheses, and interpreting your results. As Figure 1.1 illustrates, the research process is cyclical, not linear. The results of one study feed back into the system and inform future research. Researchers will tell you that the process is actually not that clear-cut. Often researchers will get an innovative idea about what to study and not be very informed about what theories might support it; however, after some initial investigations, they may go back and explore what other related research says.

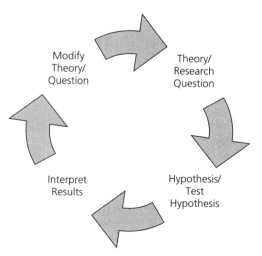

FIGURE 1.1. *Classic research process model*

For those just beginning in research, however, starting with theory and hypothesis generation is probably the most secure method for starting a research project. Having a good idea is important, but it is just as important to know how your idea fits in with other related ideas and research that has been done previously in the area. An idea that is not grounded in a previous theory is often not very useful to the larger research community.

Consider one practical example of the idea of starting with theory. One dissertation advisor always gave students who had an interesting research idea the following suggestion: Go learn as much as you can about what other people have already done. Getting familiar with previous research begins the process of becoming an expert in the field and helps you figure out where your idea fits into the overall theory. It also allows you to make sure you are asking a question that is consistent with methods that others have used before.

Theories and Research Questions

Theories are sets of organizing principles that help researchers describe and predict events. When non-scientists use the word *theory*, they are making a claim about the knowledge they have of a particular phenomenon. Non-scientific theories usually consist of a statement or set of statements that describe something, explain why something happens, and/or predict what will happen in the future. A scientific theory has the additional feature of allowing testable hypotheses to be generated from the theory. A scientific theory must have enough specificity and clarity for the theory to be testable.

Consider an example. One theory in the field of social psychology is the theory of cognitive dissonance, which states that when we feel tension between what we believe and what we do, we will justify our actions or change our beliefs to make our attitudes and beliefs consistent (Festinger, 1957; Myers, 2008). From this theory, a researcher can make predictions about what people will do when faced with conflict between what they do and what they believe. Theories gain support if experiments, surveys, or other techniques (discussed throughout this book) provide evidence that the theory is accurate. Thus, a theory in science will survive if the evidence supports it. The viability of theories is not based on popularity contests. Rather, if the collective research evidence supports a theory, the theory will survive. If the evidence does not support the theory, the theory fades from the collective scientific dialog (or perhaps gets modified).

Students commonly ask, "Where do theories come from?" Sometimes theories come from reading the existing literature in an area of interest (as discussed earlier). Sometimes theories come from our intuitions and observations. Perhaps you are a social worker with a full client load of pregnant teenagers. You notice that those young women who function better differ from those who struggle, and you come to believe that their better functioning is a result of social support from extended family. With this intuition, you can begin to develop a theory that social support positively influences pregnant teenagers.

Theories are tied closely to a **research question**, which is a clearly articulated statement about the topic of interest. Some research questions come from theory. Some come from observation. Some come from intuition. In terms of specificity, a research question rests in the middle between a theory, which is very broad, and a hypothesis, which is very precise. Asking a research question serves to narrow your focus on the topic of interest.

For example, you may be interested in the relationship between political beliefs and attitudes toward sexuality. Your theory might be that political beliefs inform sexual attitudes (or perhaps vice versa). Your research question, in turn, might be: "Is there a difference between people with socially conservative political beliefs and people with fiscally (money-related) conservative political beliefs with regard to attitudes toward sexuality?" The research question brings you one step closer to testing your theory. From this research question, you can construct a hypothesis to test.

Hypotheses

Whereas theories are general statements and research questions are mid-level statements, **hypotheses** (plural of hypothesis) are specific predictions about what will happen according to the theory. As we will learn throughout this book, a theory can be tested in several ways (which we will teach you in the book). In the preceding example of pregnant teenagers, the theory could be tested by constructing a questionnaire measuring the teens' social support, interviewing the pregnant teenagers themselves, or interviewing the teens' family and friends. The results of the investigation will confirm or refute the hypothesis that social support from extended family promotes healthy functioning in pregnant teens.

As another example, consider the cognitive dissonance theory discussed previously. A researcher might generate the hypothesis that when people are forced to act in a certain way, they will show more positive support for the attitude that aligns with the behavior. For example, cognitive dissonance theory would say that if you *force* someone to wear a seatbelt, eventually that person's attitude toward wearing the seatbelt will become more positive. This hypothesis stems directly from the theory, but is phrased in terms that are specific enough to be tested. What distinguishes a theory from a hypothesis is that a theory is stated in general terms and a hypothesis is stated in a specific, testable form.

This proposed hypothesis, generated from cognitive dissonance theory, must be tested to determine if the evidence confirms or refutes it. Notice we say that evidence confirms or "supports" the hypothesis. The reason researchers say *support* (rather than *prove*) is because social science by its nature is a probabilistic endeavor. As you will learn in this book, we make research claims based on a belief that there is a high probability that we are correct. We never have 100% certainty in social science, but the more research studies that support a hypothesis, the more likely it is that the scientific community will accept the theory and hypothesis as true.

Even if researchers find support for a hypothesis in one research study, they are careful not to conclude that such findings will *always* occur. Thus, social scientists tend to avoid using the word *prove*. Rather, researchers express their findings in terms of probabilities: it is likely that the findings of a particular study are true, and therefore the hypothesis is supported. For example, Steinberg and Dornbusch (1991) hypothesized that teenagers who participated in for-pay employment would suffer negative consequences in other aspects of life. They collected data on adolescents' work behavior and their social and academic functioning. The data supported their hypothesis: greater amount of paid work *was* related to lower grades, less participation in positive behaviors, and increased experimentation with drugs and alcohol. Because the hypothesis was supported with empirical evidence, we can be confident that the relationship between adolescent work and negative adolescent behaviors probably exists and that the theory is true. However, unlike other disciplines, such as formal logic and many types of mathematics, which have hard-and-fast rules that apply in *all* cases, social scientists do not claim that findings from a particular study will hold true in all circumstances and contexts.

Such an approach may sound tentative, but it actually adds to the integrity of the research process. Social science researchers seek **replication**—demonstration of the same findings of a study in a different place or with a different group of people. That is, they hope to repeat their findings in their own research and that of other researchers who are exploring the same question. As evidence that confirms, disconfirms, or modifies the initial findings is discovered or collected, researchers shape their understanding of what they are studying.

This illustrates an important element of social science research, the fact that it is self-correcting. Just as ballots are counted on election night, scientific theories continue to be updated as more evidence is gathered from the field (research labs in the case of social science, voting precincts in the case of elections). Whereas elections eventually end, the self-correcting nature of research allows evidence to be gathered without a restriction on time. In science, the polls never close. This allows the scientific community to change its collective mind based on the evidence. Through the integrity of researchers, an emphasis on replication of research findings, and reliance on independent verification from other researchers, researchers modify their theoretical claims in ways that most honestly, accurately, and fully account for the evidence.

A good example of this self-correction comes from research in education and psychology on what motivates people. Research in the 1950s on operant conditioning illustrated the power of reinforcements in increasing desirable behavior and punishments in extinguishing undesirable behavior (Skinner, 1997). To this day, reinforcements are seen as powerful ways to motivate people. Tools such as increased pay, increased praise, and increased recognition are all ways in which teachers, employers, and athletic coaches motivate their staffs. Later research, however, demonstrated situations in which people were not motivated by reinforcements. For example, Lepper, Greene, and Nisbett (1973) asked children to play with toys in a laboratory. Randomly selected children were told that they would receive a reward for playing with the toys; these children actually played for less time with the toys than children who were *not* told that they would get a reward. The idea that children who anticipate a reward engage in the rewarded behavior *less* than those who do not get a reward for doing so is in direct conflict with the prediction from operant conditioning that rewards increase behavior. These researchers concluded that the reward actually served as an explanation for the children of *why* they were playing with the toy (that is, "I must play with this toy because I am getting a reward"), which served to decrease the children's intrinsic motivation (engaging in a behavior for its own sake) for playing with the toy. Such modifications of previous research findings serve to delineate the boundaries of the theories being explored. In other words, does a certain theory explain behavior in all situations, or only under certain conditions? Operant conditioning can explain behavior under many circumstances, but not under the conditions set forth in the experiment by Lepper and his colleagues. This example illustrates that after a theory is proposed, and a hypothesis is tested and supported, science always keeps the door open to modification of our existing understanding based on new evidence.

TYPES OF RESEARCH

Once a researcher understands the basic research model (described in the preceding section), he or she needs to choose an approach to investigate the topic of interest. Although this is a broad-brush distinction, most research is best understood as being either quantitative or qualitative in nature. In general, **quantitative research** specifies numerical assignment to the phenomena under study, whereas **qualitative research** produces narrative or textual descriptions of the phenomena under study. Although we describe each approach in detail in following chapters, it is helpful to outline the general advantages and disadvantages of both types at the outset. As you will see, the upsides and downsides of each approach are inverses of each other (Figure 1.2).

The advantage of quantitative research is that the findings from the sample under study will more accurately reflect the overall population from which the sample was drawn (more will be said about this in Chapter 2). For example, the Institute for Social Research at the University of Michigan conducts annual surveys of adolescent drug use (www.monitoringthefuture.org). In 2007, the Institute found that 16% of eighth-graders, 33% of tenth-graders, and 44% of twelfth-graders reported using alcohol at least once in the 30 days prior to being surveyed. This finding is based on reports from more than 40,000 teenagers. With such a large sample, we can be fairly confident that these figures accurately portray the status of adolescent alcohol use in America.

Characteristic	Quantitative Research	Qualitative Research
Type of data	Phenomena are described numerically	Phenomena are described in a narrative fashion
Analysis	Descriptive and inferential statistics	Identification of major themes
Scope of inquiry	Specific questions or hypotheses	Broad, thematic concerns
Primary advantage	Large sample, statistical validity, accurately reflects the population	Rich, in-depth, narrative description of sample
Primary disadvantage	Superficial understanding of participants' thoughts and feelings	Small sample, not generalizable to the population at large

FIGURE 1.2. *Quantitative versus Qualitative Research*

The disadvantage of the quantitative approach is that, because the study contains so many participants, the answers research participants are able to give do not have much depth. They have to be superficial, or else the researchers would be overwhelmed by information that cannot adequately be analyzed. In the University of Michigan study, we know what percentage of teenagers have used alcohol, tobacco, and other drugs, but we know very little else. Although the survey is interesting, consider a few questions the survey does *not* answer:

- Why do these teenagers drink?

- What are their thoughts and feelings while they drink?

- Do adolescents ever talk about alcohol use with their parents, and if so, what do they discuss?

These more narrative questions (and answers) could be very revealing, but are not easily handled with a quantitative study. As we will see throughout this book, each approach has its own advantages and disadvantages. Ideally, a two-pronged approach that employs both quantitative and qualitative techniques can be employed. However, practically speaking, limitations of resources and time often prohibit such an exhaustive endeavor. Therefore, it is best to match the particular research goal to the research strategy that will help achieve that goal. If a large, accurate sample that will generalize to the larger population is desired, quantitative research would be preferred. If a detailed narrative account of a particular subgroup is desired, then qualitative research is recommended. The goal of this book is to help you match method to problem. Throughout this book, we provide details on the advantages and disadvantages of each approach to help you better understand which method would be the best match for your research question.

If a researcher desires a more narrative understanding, then a qualitative strategy would be preferred. The main advantage of qualitative research is that it provides a richer and more in-depth understanding of the population under study. Techniques such as interviews and focus groups allow the research participants to give very detailed and specific answers. For example, imagine that you are hired by a hospital to explore people's experience with holistic (also called alternative or complementary) medicine. In such a project, conducting a focus group with patients who suffer from chronic pain and asking them to respond to several questions would provide a rich description of these people's experiences. Questions might include what symptoms they have (for example, migraine headaches), what alternative treatment modalities they have tried, and what effects those treatments have had on their symptoms. The results of these interviews could produce an interesting narrative that would reveal insights into the benefits of holistic medicine that a quantitative study could not.

The main disadvantage of qualitative research is that sample sizes are usually small and non-random, and therefore the findings may not generalize to the larger population from which the sample was drawn. Furthermore, the samples are often non-random, and thus the people who participate may not be similar to the larger population. In the preceding example regarding holistic-medicine use, you can imagine that most of the focus-group participants would praise or give anecdotal evidence of the benefits of holistic medicine, but it would not be possible to know whether these few people are representative of others who were not interviewed. If the participants are more likely to suffer from chronic pain, it is also likely that they believe traditional medicine has been inadequate for them and therefore they are more likely to embrace alternative techniques.

Another distinction often made by professional researchers is between **basic research**, an investigation that adds to the knowledge of a particular area of study, but may not have obvious and immediate applications to real-world settings; and **applied research**, an investigation that does have obvious and immediate applications. Research that is done in laboratories or via computer simulation is most often basic research. Applied research more often takes place in real-life settings such as schools, hospitals, or nursing homes. Survey research (discussed in detail in Chapter 4) is often applied research, as it has immediate application regarding drug use, customer satisfaction, or whatever topic is being addressed in the survey.

Educational researchers make yet another distinction between traditional research and action research (Mills, 2003). **Traditional research** tries to describe, predict, and control the area being investigated. According to Mills, traditional research is conducted by professional researchers (for example, university professors) in controlled environments using mainly quantitative methods, with the goal of generalizing to the larger population. **Action research** is conducted by educational practitioners, with the goal of improving the particular institution at which they work. Action research is conducted by teachers and principals with students in that school as participants. Action research has as its focus the improvement of the organization in which the research is being conducted.

Below is the first Your Turn box. You will find several of these in each chapter. We offer these as homework problems, in a sense. We strongly encourage you to jot down the answers to the Your Turn exercises in your text or on a separate sheet of paper. We firmly believe that it will deepen your understanding of the material presented in this book.

YOUR TURN

Qualitative or Quantitative Research

For each of the settings listed below, describe in one or two sentences two interesting research topics that could be performed at that site. Select one research topic that could be studied using qualitative methods and one that could be studied using quantitative methods. Explain why a qualitative or quantitative study is appropriate for that problem. The sites are:

1. School playground
2. Hospital
3. Supermarket

RESEARCH PROPOSALS

Once a general strategy has been selected (either quantitative or qualitative), the next step is to describe in as much detail as possible the process by which the research will be completed. The document that describes the planned research process is called a **research proposal**. Research will be successful only when it is carefully planned. When the authors first started doing research for our master's theses and doctoral dissertations, we both found research proposals boring. We now realize that research proposals are necessary to execute the project effectively, we require our students to prepare them in research methods classes, and we even view writing research proposals as enjoyable. They are enjoyable because writing a research proposal allows you to mentally explore ways in which the study could be conducted. For those who like doing research, such mental exploration is invigorating.

Components of Research Proposals

A research proposal has several features. It should clearly explain why the study you are proposing is a vital component of discovery in the field. In other words, the proposal should make a compelling case as to why your study is the "next best" study to conduct. The proposal should also be very specific about methodology: the research participants you will study, what instruments or techniques you will use to study them, and how you will analyze the data collected. Finally, the proposal should answer the "so what" question: Assuming the study goes forward, how will the findings from this study make a difference to other researchers (basic research study) or practitioners in the field (applied research study)? By the end of the proposal, the reader should have a clear idea of how the study will be conducted and why it is important (Table 1.1). Your goal should be to make the reader as excited about reading the results of the research as you are about conducting the research.

Literature Reviews   Almost all proposals require some review of previous research literature. The extent of the required review varies by the type of proposal. A doctoral dissertation will require a nearly exhaustive review of the relevant literature. A response to a **request for proposals (RFP)**, which is a call from an organization for researchers to submit a plan to conduct research on a specific question unique to that organization, may not require much literature review at all. A grant application to a government agency or an undergraduate honors thesis would usually fall somewhere in the middle of these two extremes.

The literature review serves two purposes. First, it should convince the reader that the researcher is familiar with the literature and competent to conduct investigations. Second, it should convince the reader that the proposed study fits into the existing body of knowledge and explain how the proposed study is needed to fill a gap in the literature.

It is important to know your audience with respect to reviewing the literature. Organizations involved in the delivery of social services may only care that you are competent to conduct their specific study. For example, from 2001–2004, author VanderStoep conducted an evaluation for a church organization that was interested in determining the beneficial effects of its homelessness interventions. This proposal needed very little in the way of literature review. In fact, for very specialized research projects there may not be any existing literature. In contrast, if you are proposing your doctoral dissertation or

TABLE 1.1 Elements of a Good Proposal

Component	Possible Technique
Compelling reason why the study should be conducted	Describe previous research and why it is incomplete. Explain why your study will fill in this gap in knowledge.
	Make it your goal to convince readers that yours is the next-best study.
	Present a sufficient literature review; this will depend on the study being proposed and the audience reading the proposal. The review should convince readers that the researcher is knowledgeable and that the study is needed to fill a gap in the existing literature.
Specification of the methodology	Identify the sample of participants you want to study.
	Describe the instruments or techniques you will use to observe these participants.
	Specify particular data analysis techniques that match the type of data you will obtain.
Convincing argument for the reader that the outcomes of the study will be important	Assume that the reader is skeptical—anticipate a "so what" question in response to your proposal.
	Tell pure researchers how your study will add to the body of knowledge.
	Tell applied researchers and practitioners why your findings will be important to those working in the field.
	Aim to get the reader as excited about the study as you are.

master's thesis, part of demonstrating your research competency is showing that you have read and understood the existing literature. Thus, a thorough literature review is advised. You should know more about your topic than anyone else on your thesis committee.

YOUR TURN

Literature Review

Lists of possible articles to read for a literature review can be built quite quickly using keyword searches of electronic databases. There are several social science databases. The most common are PsychINFO, EconLit, SocINDEX, and JStor.

Do a *keyword search* in each of these four databases using some combination of *two* of the following terms: *children, religion, poverty, family.* Did the searches in the four different databases yield different articles? What might explain the differences?

RESEARCH ETHICS

Research ethics deals with how we treat those who participate in our studies and how we handle the data after we collect them. Each discipline will have its own ethical guidelines regarding the treatment of human research participants. The general principles that we outline here largely cut across disciplinary boundaries. Many of the current ethical guidelines have their origins in the Belmont Report, a report prepared by the National Commission for the Protection of Human Subjects of Biomedical and Behavioral Research. (A copy of this 1979 report is found on the National Institutes of Health website.) Prominent and leading organizations, such as the American Psychological Association, post their ethical guidelines on their websites and in printed materials (for example, Sales & Folkman, 2000). Regardless of your specific area of study, you will need to be familiar with ethical issues.

According to the Belmont Report, researchers must be concerned with three ethical issues:

▦ *Respect for Persons*: Researchers must recognize research participants as autonomous agents, and those who have diminished autonomy (for example, the young, the disabled) must be granted protection.

▦ *Beneficence*: Researchers will secure the well-being of participants by not harming them and, further, maximizing possible benefits and minimizing possible risk.

▦ *Justice*: There must be fairness in the distribution of benefits and possible risks across all research participants. The iniquitous Tuskegee experiments, in which research participants were infected with syphilis and subsequently not given treatment, is an example from the bad old days before ethical guidelines. That the research participants were poor, black men who were not informed of the nature of the study made this research endeavor particularly villainous and a clear violation of the justice guideline.

Institutional Review

Most colleges and universities have institutional review boards, often referred to as IRBs. These committees oversee research projects conducted on campus. Proposals must be approved by the IRB before data collection begins. Most committees require researchers to submit a thorough plan for data collection, a copy of the informed consent sheet you will give participants (see, for example, Exhibit 1.1), and a description or sample of any instruments you will administer to participants or stimuli to which they will be exposed. For research conducted with or on animals, there is often a separate committee for animal care, which usually consists of several professors, one off-campus member, an ethicist, and a veterinarian.

Although the preponderance of the burden for ethical conduct lies with the researcher, the participants also have an implicit ethical obligation to be honest as they answer questions and to avoid sabotaging the research process. For example, completing a paper-and-pencil survey by filling in random survey bubbles or by answering the opposite of one's true feelings is also an ethical violation. Unfortunately, there is little a researcher can do

EXHIBIT 1.1 Informed Consent Document

Informed Consent Form
Epistemic and Religious Beliefs among College Students
Fall 2005

This study examines students' beliefs about learning and knowing, and the relationship of those beliefs to learning and problem solving.

This research is being conducted by Scott VanderStoep, a professor at Hope College. He hopes to obtain normative, descriptive data about students' beliefs about learning, and how those beliefs relate to students' thinking about contemporary problems. **All your responses and scores will be confidential. We will not describe or identify any individual responses, only responses across groups of people.**

Completing these questionnaires and answering the open-ended questions should take 40–50 minutes and should be done **in one sitting in a quiet environment.**

You have certain rights as a participant. They include:

1. Voluntarily agreeing to participate in this research.
2. Refusing to participate (in part or in full) with NO penalty to you whatsoever.
3. Withdrawing from participation at any time without penalty.

If you begin the experiment and then choose not to participate, please notify the experimenter.

By agreeing to participate you verify that:

1. You are 18 years of age or older.
2. You have read and understand the information written above.
3. You voluntarily agree to participate in this research.
4. You agree to complete this task by yourself and that you will answer the questions honestly.
5. You understand that you are free to withdraw from participation at any time without penalty.

If you have any questions about this study or comments/suggestions about your participation in this research, please contact Dr. Scott VanderStoep in 243 VZH (ph. 395-7417). This study has been approved by Hope College's Institutional Review Board. If you agree to the terms noted above, please sign and print your name below:

_____
Signature

_____
Printed Name

to combat such deception. Much social research is predicated on the assumption that research participants are behaving ethically and telling the truth.

Informed Consent

People who participate in a research study usually have the right to know that they are part of that study. Informed consent involves several components:

- Describing the details of the research study to the participants (or their legal representatives, in the case of children or others who are not able to give informed consent).

- Identifying any potential risks, such as informing participants that they have the right to withdraw from the study at any time.

- Identifying any potential costs to withdrawing. If college students are participating as part of course requirements, the researcher should alert them to an alternate assignment of equivalent time commitment and expected educational value as research participation. In the field of psychology, for example, it is implicitly assumed that psychology students who take part in a research study will gain some knowledge about psychological research by serving as participants. If the student does not participate in, or withdraws from, a research study, an alternative educational assignment should be given.

The exception to informed consent would be with naturalistic observation (see Chapter 4) in which the people "participating" are anonymous to the researcher. Because their behavior is naturally occurring and no identification of the person is made, informed consent is not required.

Opportunity to Withdraw

Participants who volunteer for a study must also be allowed to discontinue participation. If research participants feel stressed, tired, or otherwise unable to continue the study to completion, there should be no implied or stated threat of penalty for withdrawing. The informed consent should make it clear what the results of terminating will be, even if the probability of withdrawal is low. One approach to this problem is to provide participants with prorated compensation based on the percentage of the study they completed. If participants are being paid $25 for participating in a focus group, and the focus group begins to explore issues that make the participant uneasy (for example, a focus group for a hospital that asks sensitive questions about private behaviors), a withdrawing participant should be paid for the part of the focus group that she or he completed. For college students who participate for course credit, such partial credit could be harder to construct—but you should have a plan, especially if you think participants might not finish the study. As with many parts of the research process, it is wise to prepare for low-probability events. They are easier to deal with in advance than after they occur.

Offering Incentives

Although participation in research is technically voluntary, it is also the case that research participants should be compensated for their time and effort. Such compensation should vary depending on time, task complexity, and risk. Researchers at universities very commonly offer course credit as the main incentive. Researchers might also give financial incentives of varying amounts. A minimal-risk interview or experiment would yield a low incentive. For example, a group of undergraduates (Balmer, Siler, & Sorenson, 2004) conducted hour-long interviews with graduating seniors as part of their work on college students' cognitive and motivational development. Each student subject was paid $15 for his or her time. Researchers at hospitals will pay much more, as much as $100, for studies involving positron emission tomography (PET). A PET study would be considered higher-than-normal risk, because the participant must be injected with radioactive material that attaches to a naturally occurring body compound (such as glucose). The general rule is: the higher the risk, the higher the incentive.

On the other end of the continuum, incentives are not always needed. Debra Swanson and I (Johnston & Swanson, 2004) interviewed full-time working mothers, part-time working mothers, and at-home mothers about parenting and marriage. Because we were well known in our small community, we were able to recruit participants who participated for free. Because we did not have sufficient funds to pay participants, we recruited interviewees without offering any financial incentives. In such situations, researchers should make it clear to the participants that no incentive will be offered or granted.

Using Deception

For some areas of social science, particularly certain areas of experimental social psychology, deception is a crucial issue on which reasonable people will likely disagree. At its core, **deception** is the practice of giving false information to research participants about some aspect of the study. The purpose of deception is to get participants to reveal their true thoughts, feelings, or behaviors, which they would not otherwise provide if the true nature of the experiment were made known to them. As soon as possible following the study, the researchers need to inform participants that the information they received during the experiment was in fact a ruse. This is done in the debriefing (see below).

An example of a deception experiment is a study published in the *Journal of Personality and Social Psychology*, the leading journal in social psychology (Baumeister, Twenge, & Nuss, 2002). In their experiments, these researchers asked participants to take a test that they claimed measured people's propensity to end up alone later in life. Some of the participants were randomly assigned to receive the following statement from the researchers from the "results" of this so-called test:

> *You're the type who will end up alone later in life. You may have friends and relationships now, but by your mid-20s most of these will have drifted away. You may even marry or have several marriages, but these are likely to be short-lived and not continue into your 30s. Relationships don't last, and when you're past the age where people are constantly forming new relationships, the odds are you'll end up alone (p. 819).*

These researchers were interested in studying social exclusion. They wanted to test whether being socially excluded (by being given the preceding feedback) would produce more aggression, retaliation, and depression among the participants. The researchers did indeed find that those who were given this feedback were more aggressive, retaliatory, and depressed than others who were given another type of bad news.

The irony of such false-feedback experiments is that to be effective, they have to be believable, and to be believable they have to be very obvious; the more obvious they are, the more potentially hurtful they could be. Those who believe that deception is a necessary component of some social research argue that it is the only way in which true thoughts and behaviors will be demonstrated. The decision to use deception is made by weighing the potential benefits of the research findings against the risk of the deception.

Those researchers who feel that deception should not be used see the collateral damage of deception studies as, at the very least, inestimable and maybe even quite harmful. It is fair to say that most deception research is done in psychology, and also to say that most psychology researchers at a university share the same participants (college undergraduates). So imagine students who participate in a deception experiment first, then go to a non-deception experiment later in the semester. Now that these students have been told they were in an experiment in which they were deceived, there are several possible negative consequences. For example, students might be on guard for another deception experiment, and thus concentrate not on the task at hand but rather on trying to discern the expected deception in the current experiment. Or, they could harbor hostility about research in general after having been fooled and in turn try to sabotage the current experiment. To the best of our knowledge, no one has ever tried to calculate any possible ill effects that deception experiments have on participants' behavior in subsequent non-deception research.

On the other side of the fence, some argue that researchers can combat the negative effects of deception with thorough debriefing, which is discussed in the next section (Blanck, Bellack, Rosnow, Rotheram-Borus, & Schooler, 1992). The purpose of this section is not to convince you that deception is always wrong or even sometimes wrong. Rather, the goal is to alert you to the fact that any decisions regarding research must be made against the backdrop of the ethical criteria discussed earlier.

Debriefing

Debriefing of participants takes place at the conclusion of the study, and it involves revealing the purposes of the research. It should be done as soon as possible after completion of the study, preferably immediately after participation. It is important to provide a written debriefing so that participants leave the research experience with a tangible description of the activities they just performed. An oral debriefing is also recommended if the research participation was stressful or the research design was complicated.

Debriefing serves at least two purposes. First, it clears the air about the rationale of the study. Participants can hear, in the researcher's own words, why she conducted the study. Second, it can educate participants about the topic at hand, thereby increasing the community's collective knowledge about the issue. The debriefing can be done in person, upon completion of the study, or it can be done via correspondence (surface mail or email) after the researchers have completed some of their analyses. Waiting until this point has the disadvantage of providing delayed rather than immediate feedback, but it has the advantage of providing the participants with interesting, first-hand knowledge of the study findings.

Exhibit 1.2 is a letter that Debra Swanson and I sent after the motherhood study described earlier. Mothers who participated in this study were very interested in the rationale for the study. They were also interested in the results, so after we completed the study we sent the participants another letter summarizing our findings from the study. Providing this information created goodwill among the participants because it showed them that they were an important part of the project.

EXHIBIT 1.2   **Debriefing Letter from Researchers Sent to Interviewees**

July 25, 2002

Dear Friend:

Thank you for your participation in our research study on the Social Construction of Motherhood. For some of you, your interview took place over two years ago! We have been busy transcribing the over 100 interviews that we did, cleaning and organizing the data, and reading all of the interesting stories. We have enjoyed learning more about you and about your thoughts on mothering.

We wanted to share a couple of our preliminary findings with you and to give you a chance to respond. We found that work decision had a major impact on how a woman constructed her ideas of good mothering. (For this letter, I will use the distinction of employed, part-time worker, and stay-home for stylistic purposes. We know that all mothers work.)

- Stay-home mothers are not conflicted about their decision to stay home—they have consciously decided to be with their preschool children—but many of them miss having adult interaction. Those stay-home mothers that have adequate access to good outside support (parents, a spouse with flexible hours, neighbors at home) enjoy being home more than stay-home mothers who don't (far from family, spouse who works long hours, neighbors who are all gone during the day). This may sound too obvious, but what it says is that we could be more supportive as a community by helping isolated families with organized play groups, mom support networks, and built-in flexibility for the spouse's job.
- Employed mothers are not conflicted about their decision to work—many of them trained for their positions or want to work to maintain a certain lifestyle—but miss time with their families. They often spend just as much time doing one-on-one activities with their children as stay-home mothers, at the expense of time with spouse or housework. These women would like to have more flexibility built into their jobs while their children are young without sacrificing their careers. Another solution would be a shorter work week for all full-time workers, men and women. These extra hours could be used for family activities, care for elderly, parents, or community volunteer services.

■ Part-time working mothers were the happiest on life satisfaction and mood inventories. Part-time working mothers believed they had the best of both worlds, but tended to compartmentalize their lives between work and home. Likewise, they tended to quantify their time with children: counting up the number of craft activities, sports, or lessons their children were able to participate in. These part-time working mothers note that adequate home help from their spouses was a problem more than other moms.

You may find that your story doesn't really fit your category, and that is true of research that is done on people. Not everyone fits the pattern. But we were surprised at the number of women who did fit. As you can see, there are strengths, and weaknesses, to all of the decisions.

We are planning on using this research to write a book. Our overall goal is not to suggest that one decision is better than the other, but rather what it is that we can do to support families and all the choices they make about their children. Mothers do what they do because they want the best for their kids.

We will send you a postcard to update you in the future when the book has a publication date. In the meantime, please feel free to contact us with your comments.

Sincerely,
Deirdre D. Johnston
Associate Professor of Communication
Hope College

Debra H. Swanson
Associate Professor of Sociology
Hope College

Plagiarism

Research ethics prohibit an investigator from presenting the ideas or data of others as his or her own. A breach of this ethical dimension could be manifested in several ways:

■ Theoretical or conceptual ideas generated by one researcher are presented in a paper, presentation, or grant proposal by another researcher.

■ Data collected and presented by one researcher are presented by another researcher. It would not be considered plagiarism, however, if a publicly available dataset (such as from the U.S. Census Bureau) were used by multiple researchers. In fact, it is likely that this will happen among researchers exploring the same line of investigation. Furthermore, it is expected that researchers will make their data available to, in the words of the American Psychological Association, "other competent professionals" to verify the findings. What one should avoid is using previously published data and presenting it as original. This is perhaps most likely for researchers within the same research program. For example, consider a researcher who submits for publication a paper that uses data he already used in a previous paper. If the second paper merely references the previous paper, there is no problem. However, if the same data are used as the focus of the second paper, this ethical line has been crossed. In theory, the same should be true of conference presentations. However, anyone who has attended research conferences and has seen the same people present from year to year knows that often a presentation in one year looks a lot like the presentation made in a previous year. The standard is probably not as strict for conference presentations, because conferences are often times for researchers to "demo" their newest ideas, and sometimes the whole story of the new data cannot be told without the context of old data that were presented at an earlier conference.

An egregious example of plagiarism, or what might be better labeled fraud, is the generation of fraudulent data. A rising star in the field of social psychology, Karen Ruggiero, had her work cited in such highly visible places as *Psychology Today*. In 2001, Ruggiero was forced to admit that she had fabricated data in studies while she was at Harvard University. She was forced to retract four published studies and was banned from receiving federal funding for five years. Although such tragic examples are rare, they highlight both the pressure that some researchers feel to produce publishable results and also the personal integrity that is absolutely essential in scientific inquiry. Above all, social scientists need to be truth-tellers, and they must put truth-telling in front of any personal preferences or pressures.

Ethics Example

In 2001, author VanderStoep was approached by people who were interested in children's safety, particularly with respect to children's ability to manipulate car trunk-release devices. The company gave me the following question to answer: At what age could children successfully manipulate different types of trunk-release devices? I enlisted the help of my social psychologist colleague Mary Inman to determine the best design for the study. Before we could write the proposal, we had to answer several questions, among them:

■ Where should the experiment take place?

■ Should the children be in the dark (like in a car trunk)?

■ Should the parents be in the room with the children (unlike a trunk)?

■ How much about the study should children be told? (We feared that making the experiment too much like a game would fail to signal the dangers of playing near or in open car trunks.)

After many hours of discussion, we decided on a plan (Inman, VanderStoep, & Lynman, 2003). From that plan we wrote a proposal.

What you will likely find as you determine what method to use is that each decision has certain advantages and certain disadvantages. These advantages and disadvantages have to be filtered through the ethical considerations such as respect for persons, beneficence, informed consent, and opportunity to withdraw. As you prepare your proposal, you should make those decisions based on maximizing the advantages and minimizing the disadvantages *as they relate* to your particular research questions.

Consider the solutions to the ethical dilemma we faced:

1. We proposed to conduct the experiment in a psychology laboratory room rather than a real-life setting like a dark room in the child's house, or even more realistically, in the trunk of a car. We chose this because we wanted the control of a lab setting to cut down on any unwanted variance that different locations might produce. We were also worried about the ethical implications of actually putting children in a real-life setting. Even though we could guarantee their safety by having adults present and not completely closing the trunk, we did not feel comfortable giving children the actual experience of being in a trunk, for fear that, on the one hand, they might find it novel and exciting; or, on the other hand, be so traumatized by the experience that they had long-lasting negative effects.

2. We decided to conduct the experiment in a darkened room. Although we lost **mundane realism**—making the research setting simulate actual life events—with this approach, we found the ethical concerns about the clearly more realistic setting of an automobile trunk to be sufficiently troubling that we opted for the less realistic setting. The disadvantage of the approach we took is that we might not get an adequate assessment of the children's performance.

3. We decided to have the parents accompany the children during the experiment. Again, the loss of mundane realism was a concern, but we did not want the situation to become overly frightening for the children.

4. We decided not to tell the children it was a study about car trunks. We did this partly to avoid scaring them, and partly to avoid giving them any ideas that being in a trunk might be fun. At the conclusion of the experiment, we spoke with children about the importance of having parents always know their whereabouts, and stressing that they should never go anywhere without their parents knowing where they are headed.

As is probably obvious from the ethics-related decisions we made, the study became more a study of children's manual dexterity in the dark than about their ability to open a trunk-release device in a real-life setting. Because the experimental situation was more optimal than what a child locked in a trunk would encounter, we saw the success rates in the experiments as "upper bounds" of actual performance in a real-life trunk situation. We were clear in our discussion and interpretation of the data, for we did not want our data to be misinterpreted by people who might someday make decisions about the manufacturing of such products.

GETTING ACQUAINTED WITH SPSS

In Chapters 2 through 6, many of the Your Turn boxes will involve performing data-analysis procedures using a statistical-computing program called SPSS (Statistical Package for Social Scientists). This is a user-friendly and powerful statistics package that is available on most university campuses. There are various options for statistical computing, however, and much of what we teach in this book could be performed with the spreadsheet program Microsoft Excel. In this section we show you a variety of SPSS operations. These are the basic operations, and may look familiar to anyone who is proficient with spreadsheet programs. We will introduce the more advanced statistical operations when we cover each particular topic in the text. We include only the information on SPSS necessary to teach the topics we intend to cover. There are excellent texts specifically dedicated to SPSS if you want to learn more (for example, Green & Salkind, 2005).

Getting Started

After you open SPSS, you are asked which of several things you would like to do. Most of the time you will want to select either *Type in data* (if you need to create a dataset) or *Open an existing data source* (if you have already entered data or were given a dataset). If you type in data, the interface is almost identical to that of a spreadsheet program (with one added feature, discussed next). If you want to edit an existing dataset, it is easy to browse for your file. You can also open other types of documents, including Excel, Lotus, or SAS files. Because using SPSS is similar to using a spreadsheet, common operations, such as Copy, Cut, Save As, and others, can be used in both Mac and Windows platforms.

Variable View versus Data View

SPSS allows you to view your spreadsheet in one of two ways: Data View or Variable View. *Data View* arranges the names of the variables in the columns (down) and the cases (participants who filled out or completed your data) across the rows. This is the standard way in which most spreadsheets are viewed. *Variable View* allows you to see the list of variables and their features but not the actual cells of the spreadsheet. To select this option, click on the *Variable View* button in the bottom left-hand corner of the screen. *Variable View* is convenient if you have a dataset with hundreds of variables. Instead of scrolling across the screen to find the name of the variable you need, *Variable View* shows all of the variables in the first column.

Types of Variables

The two most common types of variables in SPSS are *string variables* and *numeric variables*. You should specify a numeric variable for quantitative variables and a string variable for variables that include text (for example, male, female). The variable name can have a maximum of eight characters, regardless of whether it is string or numeric. String variables can have a maximum of 32,760 characters as the data input. Numeric variables have a maximum of 40 numeric values in front of the decimal place and 16 values beyond the decimal point. *Numeric variable* is the default selection, but the type of variable can be changed by left-clicking the gray box inside the variable type column (the second column in *Variable View*).

To enter data, go to *Data View* and begin typing as in any other spreadsheet. You can also cut and paste data from a text file or spreadsheet file. For numeric variables, simply enter the values from your computer's numeric keypad. For string variables, type the characters (for example, *male*) in the appropriate cell.

Labels and Values

After you have entered the data, SPSS allows you to enter variable labels (called *Labels*) when in *Variable View*. Because the name of the variable can be only eight characters, the label is very helpful in identifying the variable. Imagine a survey question that asks, "All things considered, how happy would you consider your life to be?" The name of the variable must be less than eight characters; perhaps you could call it *lifesat*. The *Label* field, however, allows you to type in the whole survey question. This is particularly helpful when you have many variables or when your collaborators use the data but do not know or remember the exact items.

The *Values* field allows you to use words to describe your numeric values. Imagine a survey that has a five-point scale with 1 = strongly disagree, 2 = disagree, 3 = neutral, 4 = agree, and 5 = strongly agree. In the cells of the data file you would enter the appropriate numbers. To help you and other researchers identify what those numbers correspond to, you would enter the descriptive words (for example, "strongly agree") in the *Label* column (see Figure 1.3). This assists the researchers in identifying what the numbers mean. These values also get printed on any output that is produced, making it easier to read the results.

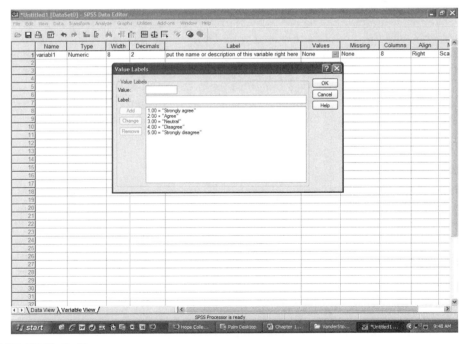

FIGURE 1.3. *SPSS screen showing labels*

YOUR TURN

SPSS

1. Open SPSS.
2. Select *Type in data.*
3. Go to *Variable View.*

Enter the following variable names: ID (numeric), gender (string), act (numeric), gpa (numeric), yearsch (numeric), satis (numeric).

Enter the following labels for the six variables: student ID number, student gender, ACT score, cumulative college GPA, year in school, satisfaction with school measure.

Enter the following as values for the variable *satis:* (1 = I'm very dissatisfied with this university, 2 = I'm fairly dissatisfied with this university, 3 = I'm undecided with this university, 4 = I'm fairly satisfied with this university, 5 = I'm very satisfied with this university). Enter the following as values for the variable *yearsch:* 1 = freshman, 2 = sophomore, 3 = junior, 4 = senior.

Enter the following data as sample entries:

ID	gender	ACT	GPA	yearsch	satis
001	male	23	3.2	1	3
002	female	24	3.4	3	4

SUMMARY

Research can begin with an intuition that you want to subject to scientific scrutiny. It can also begin with a business's or organization's need for a specific answer to a specific question. The research process involves generating a question (hypothesis), collecting data to test that hypothesis, then analyzing and interpreting the results of your investigation. Research can be quantitative or qualitative in nature, depending on whether you want to collect statistical information or narrative information. Whatever the purpose or strategy of research, it all must be conducted and understood through an ethical lens, which sees research participants as worthy of respect and protection, and considers that the purpose of the research is ultimately to try to benefit humankind. Researchers can analyze quantitative data with statistical-computing packages such as SPSS, the basics of which were shown in this chapter. More advanced techniques are shown in subsequent chapters.

KEY TERMS

action research

applied research

basic research

debriefing

deception

hypotheses

mundane realism

qualitative research

quantitative research

replication

request for proposals (RFP)

research proposal

research question

theories

traditional research

CHAPTER

2

THE WHO, HOW, AND WHY OF RESEARCH

LEARNING OBJECTIVES

- Understand various sampling procedures and be able to match a sampling strategy to a particular research question.
- Understand various research strategies and research designs, and be able to match a strategy and design to a particular research question.
- Identify the purpose of a particular research study with respect to its contribution to the scientific enterprise or to the solution of a unique problem.

From 1999 to 2004, when I (author VanderStoep) was the director of a college's social science research center, I met with more than 20 organizations a year to discuss possible research projects. My standard approach in that first meeting was to ask three questions:

- *Who* should you study?
- *How* should you study them?
- *Why* should you conduct the research?

This chapter focuses on these three questions, which we consider foundational to any good research project. This chapter explores a variety of approaches to answering these questions. One lesson you will learn from this chapter (and this book in general) is that there is seldom only one answer to a question in social research methodology. Rather, each approach or technique carries with it costs and benefits; the best methodology is the one that maximizes benefits and minimizes costs for that particular project. With respect to sampling, this means trying to select participants who are best suited for your study and will allow you most effectively to accomplish your research goal. Often the goal is to obtain a **representative sample**—a group that is similar to a larger population. If your goal is to get a representative sample of a population, a random sample is probably best. If your goal is to know as much as you can about a particular organization or subgroup, in-depth interviews of a non-random sample will be the best approach.

In this chapter we discuss a variety of strategies for generating a sample, collecting data, and designing a study. However, one important lesson in this chapter (and several other chapters in this book) is that there is no one *perfect* research methodology. Each strategy has advantages and disadvantages. The goal of researchers is to select the strategy that maximizes the benefits and minimizes the costs of their particular research approach. We first address how to gather people who are willing to participate in a research study.

WHO: SELECTING A SAMPLE

Researchers make the distinction between a **population**, the universe of people to which the study could be generalized, and a **sample**, the subset of people from the population who will participate in the current study. The **sampling frame** refers to the eligible members of the population. For example, suppose you are interested in surveying citizens of McCracken County, Kentucky. The estimated 65,514 county residents make up the population, a randomly selected list of those residents (we discuss later in the chapter how to obtain or generate such a list) makes up the sampling frame, and the residents who actually complete the survey make up your sample. Because some people will choose not to participate or will not be available when the researchers try to contact them, the sampling frame must be bigger than the sample.

Why Is Sampling Important?

Sampling is important because, in almost all cases, it is not practical to study all the members of a population. The rare exception is small populations, such as the U.S. House of Representatives, the U.S. Senate, or perhaps a very small town or village. For example, Settlers Township of Sioux County, Iowa, has a population of 131, so we might be able to collect data from the whole population if we used the right methodology. In most instances, though, we do not—and cannot—sample the whole population. In some studies the researchers would like to make some claim about **generalizability**—that is, how much, how well, or how closely the findings from the current sample apply to the entire population. However, differences exist regarding the extent to which a study is generalizable. Researchers who are mostly concerned about evaluating the effectiveness of a particular program might not worry much about whether the findings are generalizable to people who are not in the program. For example, a school principal who surveys the parents of her students is probably not concerned about whether those parents' beliefs generalize to (are common to) parents of children in other schools or districts. In contrast, a hospital that is conducting a community-wide citizen survey measuring health behaviors and attitudes would be very interested in having its findings generalize to the population as a whole. One of the hospital's goals might be to develop a health "report card" that will help it connect with all of the people in its service area. Given this organizational goal, it would be important to know how research findings generalize beyond the sample in the current study.

In general, there are two ways to select members for a study: randomly or non-randomly. A **random sample**, sometimes called a *probabilistic sample*, is a sample in which each member of the sampling frame has an equal chance of being selected as a study participant. A **non-random sample** is a sample in which each member of the sampling frame does not have an equal chance of being selected as a participant in the study. We discuss each of these approaches in the following sections.

Non-Random Sampling

In **non-random sampling,** participants are selected based on characteristics they possess or their availability to participate. Therefore, each population member is not equally likely to be selected to participate. Imagine a jar containing 60% white marbles and 40% blue marbles; random sampling (discussed below) would maintain the same percentages in the sample over a long period of time. A non-random sample does not use this probabilistic aspect of selection. Instead, non-random samples are collected in one of two ways.

Convenience Sampling Convenience sampling involves selecting people for your research who are available (or convenient) for study. Selecting people simply because they are available is clearly not a random sample, as not all people in the population have an equal chance of being selected. Convenience samples often involve people whom the researcher knows or people who live close to the research site. The advantage of convenience sampling is the ease with which participants can be recruited. Placing an ad in the paper or posting flyers in neighborhoods are two ways to recruit convenience samples. The disadvantage, as with all non-random sampling techniques, is the lack of representativeness of the general population. For example, researchers may select people who live or work near a major university where the researcher is employed. Such people may possess different characteristics than the population to which the researcher would like to generalize, and therefore the results from this sample may not generalize well to the larger population.

Snowball Sampling In **snowball sampling**, a core group of participants is initially sampled for the research project. These participants are then asked to identify others who might be eligible to participate. This second generation of participants is then contacted. These people, in turn, identify other participants. The sample, like a rolling snowball, begins to build on itself and increase in size. One advantage of snowball sampling is the ability to grow a network of participants by taking advantage of your relationship with the current participants. This is helpful for hard-to-reach groups such as those who are marginalized by society (for example, the homeless). Another related advantage of snowball sampling is that it allows the researcher to focus on people who have particular characteristics of interest to the project. To conduct a large-scale study on certain low-base-rate topics would be very expensive, because the number of people in the general population who have the characteristic you are studying is quite small. For example, suppose that you are interested in studying the psychological effects of chronic pain. You could start by contacting chronic pain clinics and asking for volunteers. Using this initial list, you invite these people to share names of others they know who have or had similar medical concerns. This is more efficient than simply taking a random sample of people and selecting only those who have chronic pain. If you did this, you would end up "throwing out" most of the people in your sample, after wasting a lot of time and effort to find appropriate participants.

Atkyns and Hanneman (1974) provide an example of snowball sampling from the research literature. The focus of their research project was identifying the motivation and other behaviors of dealers of illegal drugs. The researchers presented questionnaires to current and former drug users. The users were then asked to deliver the questionnaire in a sealed envelope to any drug dealers they knew. Occasionally a drug dealer was identified to the researchers, in which case the researchers delivered the questionnaire directly. In this study, researchers relied on drug users and dealers to create their sample.

The obvious disadvantage of snowball sampling is the same as with the convenience sample: the sample will probably not be representative. Because the "snowball" of participants contains many people who have interrelationships, they are likely to share similar interests and values. These people will be similar to each other, but they may not be similar to the larger population. For example, in a chronic-pain study, the initial participants will know the second-generation participants because of their shared experience of chronic pain. This will create similarity among the participants and possible dissimilarity between this group and other people. In the Atkyns and Hanneman drug-dealer study, it is clear that snowball sampling did not provide a random sample, and thus it is not possible to know how the results from this sample of drug dealers generalize to the overall population. Nevertheless, given the anticipated reluctance of drug dealers to participate in surveys and the difficulty university researchers would have in identifying and locating or contacting them, snowball sampling in this case seems the best choice for selecting participants.

YOUR TURN

Non-Random Sampling

Identify three groups of people or three behaviors that are unique or rare and for which snowball sampling might be needed. Identify how you might make the initial contact with these groups to start your snowball rolling.

Group One: _____

Method for snowball sampling: _____

_____

Group Two: _____

Method for snowball sampling: _____

_____

Group Three: _____

Method for snowball sampling:_____

_____

Random Sampling

In contrast to the strategies discussed in the preceding section, in random sampling each member of the sampling frame has an equal chance of being chosen to participate in the study. Imagine 10,000 beans in a well-shaken jar. Each bean in the jar (theoretically) has an equal chance of being selected any time a bean is taken from the jar. For example, Charlotte Witvliet, Tom Ludwig, and Kelly VanderLaan (2001) conducted a study of the physiological effects of either granting or not granting forgiveness to a perpetrator who had caused harm. In this study, the population was college undergraduates, the sampling frame was students enrolled in introductory psychology at their institution, and the sample was those who were selected to participate. Of the approximately 180 students enrolled in introductory psychology that semester, each one had an equal chance of being selected. Similarly, large-scale surveys of middle- and high-school students' drug use (described in Chapter 1) involve national populations from which, in theory, every teenager enrolled in school is equally likely to be selected. The notion of equal likelihood is the principle underlying all forms of random sampling.

Simple Random Sampling Simple random sampling involves picking a certain number of participants out of the total number of possible participants in the sampling frame. In simple random sampling, a fixed percentage of the total sampling frame is selected for participation. Figure 2.1 shows the mechanics of drawing a simple random sample. In most cases, the population and sampling frame are so large as to make exhaustive sampling of the population impossible. The beauty of random sampling is that the larger the sample, the more closely it will mirror the percentages in the overall population. Assessing how close the sample is to the population is done by computing the **margin of error**. Margin of error represents the extent to which repeated random samples will deviate from the population. As demonstrated in Table 2.1, margin of error decreases as the sample size increases and/or the number of response alternatives increases. For example, in a presidential poll with two candidates, a sample size of 500 will yield a margin of error of 4.4%. This means that if a pre-election poll showed McCain had 52% support and Obama had 48% support, we can be 95% confident that McCain's actual level of support is between 47.5% and 56.5%. In this particular case, if a candidate needs 50% to be elected, the estimate of 52% is not large enough to be confident that McCain will be elected prior to the actual election.

As can be seen from Table 2.1, margins of error diminish with increasing sample size. A large increase in precision is achieved by moving from a sample of 100 to a sample of 500 respondents. However, moving from a sample of 500 to a sample of 1,000 provides a smaller increase in precision. Researchers must weigh the added costs of expanding the sample size against the benefit of the increased precision from that larger sample size. Why must researchers sample so many people and why is there always a degree of uncertainty? The answer lies in the inherent variability of people. If everyone had the same opinion on an issue (for example, everyone in a particular county will vote for Candidate A), then we would have perfect precision in our measurement and our margin of error would be zero. However, because people differ, researchers have to account for this variability by building some uncertainty into their measurements and calculations. The more people in the sample, the more the sample will "look like" the population and thus the variability (margin of error) will be reduced.

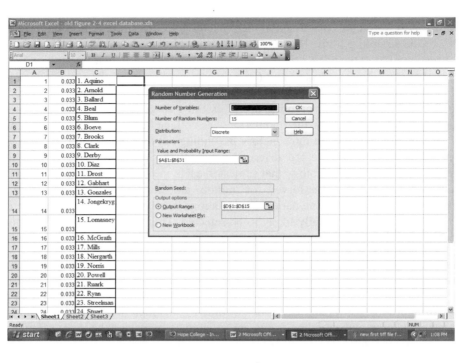

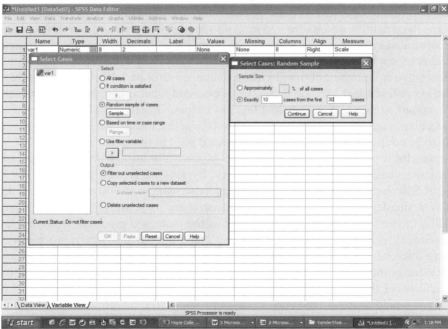

FIGURE 2.1. *Selecting a simple random sample*

TABLE 2.1 **Margin of Error as a Function of Sample Size**

Size of Sample	Two Response Alternatives (for example, McCain or Obama)	Four Response Alternatives (for example, Strongly Agree, Agree, Disagree, Strongly Disagree)
100	9.8%	8.5%
400	4.9%	4.2%
500	4.4%	3.8%
1,000	3.1%	2.7%
10,000	1.0%	0.8%

These margins of error are for 95% confidence.

Simple random sampling is often used, both by experimental researchers in laboratories (selecting from a sampling frame of eligible participants, such as undergraduate students) and by survey researchers. However, just because someone is selected to participate in a research study does not guarantee that he or she *will* participate in the study. In experimental research, students may forget to show up for their experimental session or choose not to go. In survey research, many people do not participate. We all have received surveys in the mail or been called on the telephone and have forgotten, refused, or otherwise failed to complete the survey. This problem of randomly selected participants not completing the research is called *non-response*. A researcher is faced with a **response bias** when those who do not participate differ from those who do participate in ways that are integral to the research. If respondents do not differ from non-respondents on variables that are relevant to the study, then a researcher need only send out more surveys or schedule more experimental sessions to build up the sample size. However, if non-response is related to an important variable in the study, the results from the sample will be different from the larger population being studied. An example of response bias comes from a study of alcohol consumption by Lahaut, Jansen, van de Mheen, and Garretsen (2002) of the Addiction Research Institute in the Netherlands. After the researchers sent out a mail survey, the researchers made house visits to those people who did not complete the survey. They found that among those who did not respond (but completed the survey when the researchers visited their home), there were higher percentages of both "abstainers" and "excessive" drinkers. Drinkers identified as "occasionally excessive" and "moderate" were overrepresented in the original sample and underrepresented in the follow-up study. This study suggests that when studying alcohol use via a mail survey, researchers are likely to get lower numbers of abstainers *and* heavy drinkers in the sample.

Solving the problem of non-response bias is difficult. One strategy is to perform aggressive follow-up data collection, as Lahaut and others did by making house visits to non-respondents. Other strategies for solving this problem involve complex statistical corrections. One example is to check the demographic makeup of your respondees to make sure you are getting good representation for variables such as gender, race, and age. For example, if a researcher finds that there are fewer African American males in the sample than in the population, then the researcher can "add" more African American responses to the dataset by **statistical weighting** of the African American males who did respond. Statistical weighting involves overcounting the returned surveys of the underrepresented group. For example, if a researcher received only half as many surveys as desired returned from African American males, then each of the returned surveys from this group would be counted two times (100% ÷ 50% = 2). If the sample represented only 80% of the population, then each returned survey from this group would be counted 1.25 times (100% ÷ 80% = 1.25).

Stratified Random Sampling Stratified random sampling involves selecting research participants based on their membership in a particular subgroup or **stratum**. The technique allows the sample to look more like the population in terms of mirroring the different subgroups. Unlike simple random sampling, stratified random sampling involves selecting research participants based on their membership in a stratum. Dividing the sampling frame into strata (plural of stratum) allows the researcher to sample people proportionately based on the size of each stratum. For example, according to the 2000 census, 3,694,820 people live in the city of Los Angeles and 1,719,073 (46.5%) are Hispanic or Latino. In a stratified sample of 1,000 city residents, researchers would make sure that 465 of the 1,000 sample residents were Hispanic/Latino. Stratified sampling improves the accuracy of the sample because it ensures that any differences between the strata are controlled by making sure that each stratum is proportionately represented. Imagine a presidential poll that sampled a larger number of voters from large cities than are actually represented in the population. If big-city voters usually vote Democratic and rural voters usually vote Republican, the sample would not accurately reflect the population, and would overestimate the support for the Democratic candidate. Stratified sampling is one tool to reduce **selection bias**—unintentional yet systematic differences between the people in the sample and the people in the population. If one group is either overrepresented or underrepresented in a sample, selection bias has occurred. If this group differs on the variable of importance, the sample will not accurately reflect the larger population.

Systematic Sampling In **systematic sampling**, a researcher moves through the sampling frame list and selects one out of every fixed number of entries. For example, if a phone survey needs 400 respondents out of 10,000 people from a phone book or purchased calling list, then in systematic sampling the researcher will pick every 25th person (4% of 10,000 is 400). This is a form of random sampling, but because selection is based on where one is in the list, not everyone has an equal chance of inclusion. For example, if we randomly decide to start at the 10th person on the list, then the 11th through 34th people will not be included, even though selection *began* with a random process. Exhibit 2.1 provides practice in systematic sampling.

EXHIBIT 2.1. **Selecting a Systematic Sample**

Systematic sampling is a form of random sampling. We demonstrate this technique using the sampling frame from Figure 2.1. First, identify the number of people desired in your sample (say, 8) and the number of people in your sampling frame (24). This means that one out of every third person in the sampling frame will be in the study.

Using a random number table as before, select a two-digit number between 1 (01 in the random number table) and 24. This is the first person in your sample. Since you need every third person, move down the row of participants (then back up to the top), selecting every third person until you reach 8 people. For example, if the number from the random table was 17, you would select the following people: 17, 20, 23, 26, 29, 2, 5.

Cluster Sampling **Cluster sampling** involves randomly selecting or assigning groups of people, rather than individuals, based on membership in a group, geography, or some other variable. For example, if a large metropolitan school district has 35 elementary schools, you could assign students to receive a certain type of experimental instruction based on their school. You could randomly select 15 schools to receive instruction in English Language Arts (ELA) using the 6 + 1 Trait Writing program, while the other schools would continue to teach ELA as they have been (standard program). One disadvantage of this approach appears in this example: if students *within* a certain school are very different, it might be hard to detect differences in students *between* different schools because of the variations in the schools. In other words, if the schools teaching 6 + 1 have parents with higher levels of education than parents at the schools teaching the standard program, any differences in writing performance may be due to parent-education differences rather than differences in the writing program. The Your Turn box provides a chance for you to try using a computer to select a sample.

YOUR TURN

Generating a Random Sample

A researcher rarely collects data from everyone in the sampling frame. Figure 2.2 shows how to randomly select participants from a sampling frame of size 31 using SPSS. Enter the data shown on Figure 2.2 and randomly select your own participants using the technique described.

1. Open a data file in SPSS.

2. Under *Data,* select Select Cases.

3. Select Random Sample of Cases, click Sample.

4. Select either the proportion of cases or an exact number of cases.

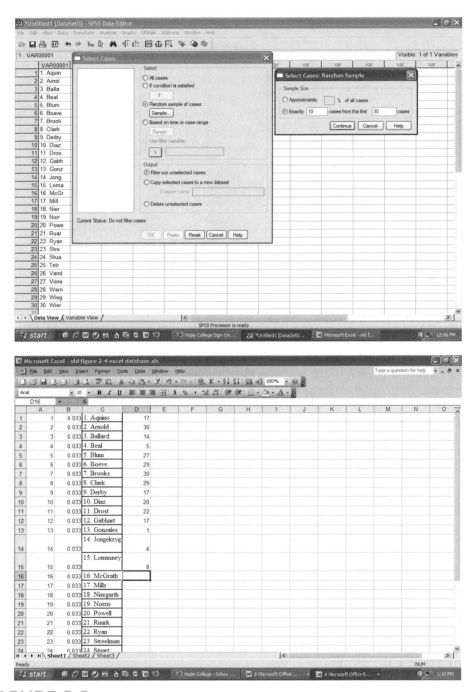

FIGURE 2.2. *Generating random numbers using SPSS*

HOW: SELECTING A RESEARCH STRATEGY

After you have identified the group of people to participate in your study, and a method for deciding how to include them in the study (sampling), you are ready to collect data. Hence, the next decision you must make is what strategy you will use for collecting data. In this section we discuss two parts of that question. First, where will the study take place (for example, laboratory versus survey)? Second, how frequently will you collect data from your participants (one time versus multiple times)? As with the *who* question, there is no perfect solution or single correct answer for decisions about the *how* question. Rather, answering this question involves weighing the costs and benefits of various strategies.

Experimental Research

Experimental research takes place in laboratory settings. An example is the Witvliet, Ludwig, and VanderLaan (2001) study discussed earlier, which took place in a psychology laboratory. The major advantage of the experimental study is the degree of control it provides. In an experiment, every participant is exposed to the same environment—including the characteristics of the room, the experimenters, and the instructions the participants receive. The one aspect of the study that is not the same is the **independent variable**, that is, the variable that is systematically controlled by the researcher to determine the effect of that variable. By systematically changing the independent variable and holding all other variables constant, the researchers can be confident that any change in the **dependent variable**—the outcome the researchers are measuring—is actually due to the effect of the independent variable. Such control cuts down on random variation that makes it difficult to interpret the results. Laughlin, VanderStoep, and Hollingshead (1991) compared the problem-solving performance of four-person groups to the performance of four single individuals. In this experiment, the dependent variable was problem-solving performance. The independent variable was group size, and it had two *levels*: individual versus group. The purpose of the experiment was to determine how group performance compared to the best-performing individual working alone, the second-best-performing individual working alone, the third-best working alone, and the fourth-best (worst) working alone. Because the study was an experiment, all of the participants attempted to solve the *same* problems in the *same* setting under the *same* circumstances. This minimized the effects of external factors that could affect problem-solving performance.

One important disadvantage of experimental studies is that the nature of the experiment may be very unlike what people actually experience in the real world. In the Laughlin et al. (1991) experiment, the problem-solving tasks the participants attempted were artificial and unlike what people might actually do in everyday life. In this way, what experiments gain in control they lose in *mundane realism* (described in Chapter 1). So, although experimental studies benefit from exerting control, they suffer from being conducted in artificial settings. Chapters 5 and 6 describe the advantages and disadvantages of experiments in greater detail.

Descriptive and Correlational Research

Descriptive research is just what it sounds like: it describes the attitudes and behaviors observed during the investigation. This approach to research is in many ways the converse

YOUR TURN

Experimental Research

Identify the independent variable, the levels of the independent variable, and the dependent variable from the abstract printed here:

This experiment assessed the emotional self-reports and physiology of justice outcomes and forgiveness responses to a common crime, using a three Justice (retributive, restorative, no justice) × 2 Forgiveness (forgiveness, none) repeated-measures design. Participants (27 males, 29 females) imagined their residence was burglarized, followed by six counterbalanced justice-forgiveness outcomes. Imagery of justice—especially restorative—and forgiveness each reduced unforgiving motivations and negative emotion (anger, fear), and increased prosocial and positive emotion (empathy, gratitude). Imagery of granting forgiveness (versus not) was associated with less heart rate reactivity and better recovery; less negative emotion expression at the brow (corrugator EMG); and less aroused expression at the eye (lower orbicularis oculi EMG when justice was absent). When forgiveness was not imagined, justice-physiology effects emerged: signs of cardiovascular stress (rate pressure products) were lower for retributive versus no justice; and sympathetic nervous system [response] (skin conductance) was calmer for restorative versus retributive justice.

Source: Witvliet, C. V. O., Worthington, E. L., Root, L. M., Sato, A. F., Ludwig, T. E., & Exline, J. J. (2008). Retributive justice, restorative justice, and forgiveness: An experimental psychophysiology analysis. *Journal of Experimental Social Psychology, 44*, 10–25. Reprinted with permission.

of experimental research with respect to advantages and disadvantages. Whereas experimental research exhibits much control over the setting in which the participants' behavior is observed, descriptive research take place in natural, real-life settings. A common descriptive research technique is **naturalistic observation**, which involves collecting data where people are ordinarily found. For example, Hawkins, Pepler, and Craig (2001) studied bullying among first- through sixth-grade students. To do this, they observed elementary school children involved in playground activities. They collected measures such as the frequency of bullying, the amount of time bullying was done alone versus in the presence of peers, and the types of interventions peers used to stop bullying. Such a study allows authentic understanding of bullying in a particular, real-life context. The researchers would not have gained such a realistic assessment of bullying if they had pursued an experimental approach to studying this issue.

In this study of school bullies, the researchers did not create or monitor any independent variables. Rather, they simply noted the behavior of the children on the playground and constructed measures related to bullying and subsequent intervention. In general, when deciding between experimental research and descriptive research, one must choose between the benefit of control in experimental studies versus the benefit of realism in field studies. Chapter 4 describes strategies for descriptive research and Chapter 5 describes strategies for experimental research in greater detail.

In terms of control, a **quasi-experiment** falls somewhere between naturalistic observation and experimental research. A quasi-experiment involves conducting an experiment, usually in a real-life setting, without the benefit of random assignment of participants to conditions or other controls. Because quasi-experiments are usually done in real-life settings rather than in laboratory settings, they are often considered not truly experimental research, but rather **correlational research**, which involves identifying statistical relationships between two variables rather than causal relationships. Thus, while the researchers have control over the independent variable in a quasi-experiment, they do not have control over other factors in the environment. An example of a quasi-experiment is a study on the effects of noise on female residence halls conducted by Cheuk Ng (2000). The independent variable in this study was how close dorm residents lived to a noisy construction site. The results of the study showed that those living closer to the noise had higher rates of sleeplessness, speaking louder, and keeping windows closed. A quasi-experiment involves some control in that the independent variable is monitored by the researcher. However, it occurs in a naturalistic setting and the experimenter may not have control over when the independent variable occurs. In this way, a quasi-experiment falls between an experimental study and a naturalistic observation. Chapter 6 describes quasi-experimental designs in detail.

Survey Research

Surveys provide the advantage of sampling a large group of randomly selected people to measure their attitudes and behaviors. For a relatively low cost in time and money, a researcher can collect self-reported attitudes and behaviors about virtually any social issue. Furthermore, with the data analysis training provided in this book or in a more comprehensive data analysis class, even undergraduate students can download survey data or perform analyses right at the websites of major survey organizations, such as the University of Michigan's Institute for Social Research, the National Opinion Research Center, or the U.S. Census Bureau. This means that researchers may not need to collect original survey data; rather, they can perform **secondary data analyses**—data analysis on previously collected data—as part of their investigations. If researchers do indeed construct and administer their own surveys, they have several options for administering them. Like most decisions regarding research designs, each option has both advantages and disadvantages. We describe these options in detail in Chapter 4.

Researchers who design and administer their own surveys should use the techniques for randomly selecting participants described earlier in this chapter. After a sample has been selected, the researcher must make a decision about how to gather the data. The most common survey methods are telephone surveys, mail surveys, email surveys, and face-to-face interviews. Telephone surveys produce a relatively high response rate, but there is some risk of selection bias regarding those without land lines or those who have caller ID and screen calls. Mail surveys are inexpensive and efficient, but are even more likely to suffer from low response rates or non-response bias than phone surveys. Email surveys are even less expensive, but have a sampling bias toward those with greater computer access. Face-to-face interviews produce the highest response rates, but are the costliest in money and researchers' time. As with most decisions regarding research, each technique has advantages and disadvantages. In Chapter 4 we provide more details about the administration of these different techniques.

In field research and in survey research, most investigations involve studying correlations. A **correlation** is a statistical measure of association between two variables. The measure of association that is used to assess the association between variables is called the **correlation coefficient**. A correlation coefficient has both a direction and a magnitude. The direction can either be *positive* or *negative*. A positive correlation indicates that high scores on one variable co-occur with high scores on another variable in the study. An example is the relationship between shoe size and height. In general, people who wear large shoes tend to be taller, and those who wear small shoes tend to be shorter. A negative correlation indicates that high scores on one measure co-occur with low scores on another variable in the study. For example, Christine Smith and Irene Frieze (2003) sought to develop a scale that would measure rape empathy—understanding of the perspective of a victim of sexual assault. They developed an 18-question scale, and found a negative relationship between participants' scores on victim empathy and beliefs about victim responsibility. In other words, participants who were high on victim empathy tended to believe that a victim was *not* responsible for the crime. Throughout this book, we make frequent references to positive and negative correlations, and in Chapter 4 we show you how to compute the numerical values of correlation coefficients.

Types of Designs

Now that we have answered the first part of the *how* question—the type of study design—we are now ready to answer the second question: the frequency of data collection. Whereas the first question concerns the settings for data collection, this section talks about the different setups available for data collection.

One-Shot Design   The most common research design is the **one-shot design**—one group of participants is studied only one time. This can be done with surveys, experiments, or field studies. An example of a one-shot longitudinal study, conducted by Mary Inman and colleagues (Inman, McDonald, & Ruch, 2004), asked participants to complete a creativity test; participants then were given one of three randomly assigned feedbacks about their creativity. In other words, the independent variable was type of feedback, and it had three levels. One-third of the participants were in the *failure condition* and were told:

> *The test revealed that you consistently gave uncreative answers. That is, in terms of other college students who have taken this test, your score fell in the 20th percentile on the scale (where low scores = very uncreative, high scores = very creative).... [Y]our*

score indicates that you gave uncreative, original (common) answers. That is, your answers were very consistent with the people who have taken this test before.

One-third of the participants were in the *success condition* and were told:

The test revealed that you consistently gave creative answers. That is, in terms of other college students who have taken this test, your score fell in the 80th percentile on the scale (where low scores = very uncreative, high scores = very creative). . . . [Y]our score indicates that you gave creative, unique answers. That is, your answers were novel, very rarely similar to those offered by people who have taken this test before.

The final third of the participants were in the *ambiguous condition* and were told:

The test revealed that you frequently bounced across the scale. Sometimes you gave unique and creative answers, other times you gave common and uncreative answers. . . . Sometimes your score fell around the 20th percentile on the scale . . . other times your score fell around the 80th percentile. In short, the test strongly predicts that for any given problem, you may be creative or uncreative and there are no systematic predictors determining when you will be one or the other.

(The information students received was false, and thus this procedure involves the delicate ethical issue of deception, discussed in Chapter 1.)

The dependent variable was the participants' emotional reactions after they received the feedback. As hypothesized, those in the failure condition had the most negative reactions and those in the success condition had the most positive reactions.

This study is characterized as a one-shot study because the researcher collected data from one group of participants only one time. The advantage of this design, which is clearly the most common approach in both experimental and correlational research, is its efficiency and the low cost in time and resources needed to conduct the study. The researcher has to access the participants only one time (through a survey, experimental session, or observation). There is no need to follow the participants over time and conduct the experiment or survey again.

As mentioned earlier in this section, with respect to type of study design, the advantages and disadvantages of a one-shot design are inverses of each other. One-shot designs do not allow comparisons of age differences, nor does this design allow researchers to track participants over time. In the Inman et al. (2004) study, for example, she found that those in the negative condition had more negative reactions *immediately following* the feedback they received. With a one-shot design, there is no way of knowing how long-standing such negative emotions might be. To answer this question, other approaches are required.

Longitudinal Design A **longitudinal design** studies the same people over multiple data-collection periods. The advantage of a longitudinal study is that the true effects of time or your intervention can be assessed through changes observed in the sample. A researcher who is studying drug treatment can monitor changes over time to assess the effectiveness of a drug therapy. Without the ability to follow the same people over time, it is difficult to make claims about a drug's effectiveness. A disadvantage of the longitudinal study is demonstrated by a study by Angie Fagerlin, Jennifer Feenstra, and me (VanderStoep, Fagerlin, & Feenstra, 2000). We studied a group of introductory psychology students, at the end of the course, to determine what they remembered. We then tracked down those same students two years later to ask them again what they remembered. We found that the percentage of course-relevant concepts that students remembered (as opposed to non-course material, such as stories or anecdotes) dropped significantly over the two-year period. Testing the same students at both time intervals made it possible to make inferences about the deterioration of students' memory over a two-year period following a college course. However, the disadvantage is that the researchers had difficulty tracking down the former students two years later, and many of those students did not complete the questionnaire they were sent. The dropping out of participants over time in a longitudinal study is known as **attrition**.

A larger and better-known longitudinal study that spans a much longer time period is the Framingham Heart Study (www.framingham.com/heart). Concerned about the rapid rise of cardiovascular disease, in 1948 the U.S. Public Health Service commissioned a study in Framingham, Massachusetts. The first cohort of participants consisted of 5,209 healthy residents aged 30 to 60. The study of the next generation of participants (5,124 children of the original study participants) was commissioned in 1971. The Framingham Heart Study has been the basis of more than 1,000 scientific papers, and is responsible for groundbreaking findings related to the relationship between behavior and disease. In fact, the term *risk factor* was coined in the Framingham study. What makes the Framingham study a longitudinal study is the fact that data were collected from the same people over repeated samplings. In this study, researchers collected data from participants every two to four years; participants were given extensive medical exams and underwent behavioral assessments.

An advantage of the longitudinal study is that, by using the same people over time, one can be quite confident that the independent variable is at least partly causal on the dependent variable (although without an actual experiment there is always some potential for other causal explanations). For example, the Framingham study was the first to discover that blood pressure and cholesterol were predictive of heart disease. Because heart disease takes years to develop, it would have been more efficient to study a group of 20-year-olds, a group of 40-year-olds, and a group of 60-year-olds. (This would be a cross-sectional study, discussed later in this chapter.) Studying people of different ages allows the study to be completed more quickly. If your organization is pressed for time and needs results immediately, the one-shot study (or cross-sectional study, discussed next) is probably the best alternative. However, if your organization can lay the groundwork for a long-term study that others can carry forward, a longitudinal study is preferred. One advantage of the longitudinal study is that it is less likely to be victim of **cohort effects**. A cohort effect arises when the finding that is thought to be due to the independent variable is in fact due to some generational differences in the sample. In the example of heart disease and cholesterol, it may be that 60-year-olds (raised in a different generation) had different life experiences that caused them to have both higher cholesterol and more heart disease. By studying the same group over time in a longitudinal study, researchers can gain more confidence that the changes that occur over time are not due to cohort effects.

A disadvantage of the longitudinal design is its immense cost in terms of time and money. Most organizations are unable to fund or sustain such a long-term research endeavor. Another disadvantage is the long time required to yield any results. Most organizations or researchers want their results right away. These researchers or these organizations simply cannot wait many years for a longitudinal study to yield research results.

Cross-Sectional Design A **cross-sectional design** studies several different groups of people of different ages to compare whether age differences exist in the behavior or attitude being studied. An example of a cross-sectional study is one by Lorna Jarvis and her colleagues (Jarvis, Merriman, Barnett, Hanba, & VanHaitsma, 2004). They studied two- and four-year-olds' understanding of novel words. Previous research had shown that preschool children, when confronted with a novel word that sounds like a familiar word, will think that the novel word is a novel object. For example, if asked what a "japple" is and given a choice between a picture of an apple and a picture of a pencil, they will pick the pencil. Jarvis and her colleagues attempted to extend these findings to different ages. They hypothesized that very young children (two-year-olds) would think that a japple is an apple more often than older children (four-year-olds), who would think that a japple is something other than an apple. Consistent with their hypothesis, the researchers found that two-year-olds thought a japple was an apple 44% of the time and four-year-olds thought a japple was an apple only 15% of the time.

An advantage of a cross-sectional design is that it is the most efficient way to identify the age at which certain social and psychological factors occur. The Jarvis study demonstrated that two-year-olds focus on phonological similarity. That is, a two-year-old might think, "japple sounds like apple, so a japple must be a kind of an apple." Sometime between two and four years of age, though, children stop paying attention to such sound similarity. That is, a four-year-old might think, "I know what an apple is, so a japple must be something else." Cross-sectional studies allow the discovery of such changes.

One disadvantage of a cross-sectional study appears when differences between the age groups exist not because of maturation but because of cohort effects. For example, imagine a researcher is interested in determining whether reaction times decrease as people age. To answer this question, a researcher could employ a cross-sectional study in which 20-year-olds, 50-year-olds, and 80-year-olds have their reaction time measured by executing keystrokes on a computer. The researcher will likely find that the 20-year-olds show faster reaction time than the 80-year-olds (with 50-year-olds in the middle). However, the youngest group is likely more familiar with computers because of generational differences (familiarity with computers being the cohort effect); thus, such a task is not an appropriate way to measure reaction time. Such cohort effects are more often a problem when the age differences between the groups are large. It is unlikely that cohort effects would be present with age differences as small as those in the Jarvis study.

Repeated Independent Samples Design Studies using a **repeated independent samples design** investigate a different sample of people over repeated trials to track changes in behaviors or attitudes. Because it is costly and the attrition is high in longitudinal designs, it is often better to employ the repeated samples type of design, so that the researchers can track changes over time but do not have to worry about tracking the *same* people each sampling period. A nationally known repeated independent samples design is the Monitoring the Future project at the University of Michigan. This study shows that alcohol use by twelfth-graders dropped from near 90% in the early 1990s to 72% in 2007 (Figure 2.3).

One advantage of a repeated samples design is that you can get a type of longitudinal data without keeping track of all the original research participants. A repeated samples design can track trends over time without the risk of attrition. Conversely, one disadvantage of the repeated samples design is that it does not track the same people over time. For example, the Monitoring the Future study studies eighth-, tenth-, and twelfth-graders, but it does not have data on how drug and alcohol use changes as these students become adults.

Table 2.2 displays the advantages and disadvantages of these designs. Researchers should pick a research design based on the needs of the study and the resource limitations they must work under. For example, it would often be desirable to initiate a longitudinal study, but limits on time and money make this difficult. Read the Your Turn box to explore ways in which a particular topic can be studied with multiple methods.

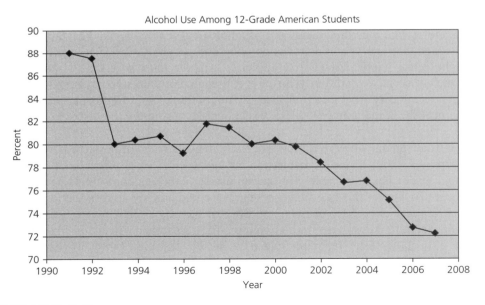

FIGURE 2.3. *Data from a repeated independent samples study*
Source: www.monitoringthefuture.org

TABLE 2.2   **Benefits and Drawbacks of Various Research Designs**

	One-Shot	**Longitudinal**	**Cross-Sectional**	**Repeated Independent Samples**
Advantages	Efficient; get results fast	Track changes over time	Obtain age differences without waiting for longitudinal results	Longitudinal effects without having to wait
Disadvantages	Cannot assess long-term effects	Time; money; attrition of participants over time	Possible cohort effects	Narrow age range; cannot discern participants' changes over time

YOUR TURN

Types of Designs

Consider the research topic of the relationship between extracurricular activities and school achievement. Identify how this topic could be studied with a longitudinal design, a cross-sectional design, and a repeated independent samples design.

WHY: DOING RESEARCH THAT MAKES A DIFFERENCE

Now that you have answered the *who* question and the *how* question, you must finally answer the *why* question. You can think of the *why* question as the "so what" question. This final step involves identifying why your research is important to other researchers or to practitioners in the field. In this section we describe two ways to express the importance and meaning of research. The first way applies mostly to basic research and the second applies mostly to applied research, although some overlap is possible.

Basic Research: Inform Future Research

One way in which basic research shows its importance and meaning is that it adequately tests the hypothesis in question. A developmental psychologist who is interested in the age at which children develop understanding of the passive voice will want to collect data that tests passive-voice comprehension of children of different ages. Simply identifying when children learn the passive voice helps the researcher (and others researchers) learn more about this topic. A second way in which basic researchers justify basic research is by contributing to the larger body of research knowledge. In our roles as professors, we have reviewed hundreds of undergraduate research papers. Many of them are potentially intriguing stand-alone investigations. However, most of these proposed studies do not fit into a larger theoretical framework through which other researchers can better understand the topic under investigation. In other words, these studies fail to answer the question "who cares?" One way to help answer that question is to read the previous literature more carefully. The findings of a current study must be interpreted in light of those previous findings, and the present study should suggest directions for future research.

The lesson is this: This problem can be avoided if you first ask yourself the question that a reviewer will ask: "Why should I be interested in this topic?" If you cannot think of a good theoretical or practical answer to this question, the study is not worth doing.

Applied Research: Inform Policy and Planning

Applied researchers (see Chapter 1), especially those doing research for specific organizations, ask a slightly different "who cares" question. An organization must be sure, prior to conducting or commissioning the research, that the results will be important to the organization. The best research actually helps to solve a real-life problem. Far too often the results of these studies go largely unused by organizations. When I (author VanderStoep) was the director of a social research center, one way I would help organizations solve this problem was to have specific organizations respond to the following scenario(s):

> *Imagine that the study turned out exactly how you expected it. In other words, the results were as you intuitively believed they would be (call this Outcome A). Now imagine that the study turns out exactly the opposite of what you expected. In a phone survey, for example, the subgroup of people you thought would strongly agree with certain survey questions in fact strongly disagreed, and vice versa (call this Outcome B). Given these two potential outcomes of the study, how would the organization respond differently to Outcome A than to Outcome B?*

If the members of the organization cannot articulate how organizational decision making would be different under Outcome A than under Outcome B, chances are the organization will not be well served by conducting a research study. Rather, the organization should do some more planning about its mission and vision first. Then, when they feel like they have developed their strategic thinking enough to benefit from a research study, the leaders should revisit the possibility of conducting a research study. The lesson for applied researchers is this: Sometimes the best research study is the one that is delayed. Research is costly and time-consuming, so the decision to conduct research should be made cautiously.

SUMMARY

Selecting a sample (who), deciding on a data-collection and research-design strategy (how), and knowing why the proposed study will be important (why) provide the essential foundation for moving forward with any research project. If you have learned one thing from this chapter, we hope it is this: There are many research options, and none of them is perfect. Each decision about research strategy brings with it both advantages and disadvantages. The task of the researcher is to identify which technique will maximize the advantages and minimize the disadvantages for the particular research problem and target population.

We are now ready to move forward to discuss the details of quantitative and qualitative designs. We begin with quantitative strategies. The next four chapters describe how to conduct various quantitative studies and potential advantages and disadvantages of these studies.

KEY TERMS

attrition
cluster sampling
cohort effects
convenience sampling
correlation
correlation coefficient
correlational research
cross-sectional design
dependent variable
descriptive research
generalizability
independent variable
longitudinal design
margin of error
naturalistic observation
non-random sample
one-shot design

population
quasi-experiment
random sample
repeated independent samples design
representative sample
response bias
sample
sampling frame
secondary data analyses
selection bias
simple random sampling
snowball sampling
statistical weighting
stratified random sampling
stratum
systematic sampling

CHAPTER

3

QUANTITATIVE RESEARCH: MEASUREMENT AND DATA COLLECTION

LEARNING OBJECTIVES

- Identify types of data that researchers collect and the appropriate type for a particular research question.
- Understand what constitutes an effective and high-quality measure.
- Identify the various strategies for collecting data, and be able to match the collection strategy to a particular research question.

To conduct good research, it is vital to construct meaningful variables and to measure the variables properly. In this chapter we describe the measurement of variables as a three-step process. First, a researcher must turn abstract concepts into measurable events. We show the different types of variables and the properties of each of those types. Second, a researcher must determine that a measure is of high quality. We show the criteria by which the quality of measures is determined. Third, a researcher must gather the information from the potential participants in the study. We describe different techniques for accomplishing this task.

MEASUREMENT: TURNING ABSTRACTIONS INTO VARIABLES

The first step in data collection is to figure out how to measure what you are interested in studying. This is easy for physical measurements such as weight and height, but harder for concepts in social science. Social science research involves abstract concepts: aggression, achievement, attraction, and so on. A social science researcher must move from an abstract concept to one that can be measured. She does this by creating variables. A **variable** is a construct that can take on two or more distinct values. A collection of variables from a sample make up what researchers call **data**. [*Note:* Data is a plural noun, so you will see statements such as "data are" in this text.]

Researchers use an **operational definition** to capture the meaning of the abstract concept they are trying to measure. Specifically, an operational definition defines how a variable will be measured or assessed. Some operational definitions are straightforward, such as gender, year in school, or college major. Others variables are more difficult to define, such as aggression. One possible operational definition of aggression might be "physical or verbal behavior intended to cause harm" (Myers, 2008, p. 345). However, some people might have a different definition of aggression, such as "an intentional physical or verbal act toward another person that *actually does* cause harm." Because there can be different definitions for the same variable, it is important for researchers to be clear about the operational definitions they are using.

In the following sections we describe different kinds of variables. Each variable can be analyzed in different ways, some of which we will describe in this chapter and others in Chapters 4 through 6. Researchers need to anticipate what type of analysis they will use before they select the variable in the study. In this section we discuss four types of variables/data that social scientists collect. Table 3.1 summarizes the characteristics of these four different types.

Nominal Data

Nominal data divide responses into two or more distinct categories. In nominal data, each response is assigned to only one category, and thus responses differ only in kind, not in degree or amount. Measurement usually refers to dependent variables, but independent variables can also be classified according to these four types. Independent variables are often nominal data, especially in experimental designs (Chapters 5 and 6). For example, male/female, treatment group/placebo group, and first-year/senior are examples of nominal independent variables. Another nominal variable would be responses to the question: "For whom did you vote in the 2008 presidential election?" The two main response alternatives would be *Obama* or *McCain*.

Once you collect your nominal data, you need to represent it in a tabular or visual form. A common way to display nominal data is with a **frequency distribution**, which shows how often the different possible values of the variable were selected. For example, Table 3.2a shows the voting percentages in the 2004 presidential election. Another way to display nominal data is with a cross-tabulation. **Cross-tabulation** is a method to show how the responses of one nominal variable relate to the responses of another nominal. For example, Table 3.2b shows the results of the 2004 presidential election for different racial/ethnic groups. The Your Turn box gives you an opportunity to perform a cross-tabulation on nominal data.

TABLE 3.1 Types of Data

Measurement Scale	Definition	Logical Property	Example
Nominal/ Category	Discrete response alternatives	$A \neq B$	Did you vote in the last presidential election? (Yes, No)
Ordinal	Response alternatives increasing/ decreasing in value (ordered responses)	$A > B > C$	What is your highest level of education? (Less than high school, high school graduate, some college, college graduate); in what place did a runner finish a race?
Interval	Response alternatives increasing/decreasing in equal increments	$A > B > C$ where the distance between A and B is the same as between B and C	Achievement test such as ACT
Ratio	Measure contains an absolute zero	If $A = 2B$, then B actually possesses half the quantity as A (and A contains two times the quantity as B)	Physical measurements; agricultural production measures

TABLE 3.2a Frequency Distribution of Nominal Data (One Variable)

2004 Election Results	Percentage
Voted for Bush	51%
Voted for Kerry	48%

TABLE 3.2b Cross-Tabulation of Nominal Data (Two Variables)

2004 Election Results by Demographic Group	White	African American	Latino	Asian
Voted for Bush	58%	11%	44%	44%
Voted for Kerry	41%	88%	53%	56%

Source: CNN exit poll.

YOUR TURN

Your Turn: Nominal Data

This exercise involves producing a cross-tabulation. The data show college students' beverage preferences (beer, wine, or nonalcoholic) for men and women. Follow the steps here to enter the data in SPSS and produce a cross-tabulation of gender and drink preference.

Gender (M = male, F = female)	Preference
M	beer
M	wine
M	beer
M	beer
M	na
M	wine
M	beer
M	wine
M	na
M	na
M	na
M	beer
M	wine
M	beer
M	beer
M	wine
M	beer
M	na
M	beer
M	wine
M	wine
M	beer
M	na
M	beer
F	wine
F	wine
F	wine
F	beer
F	na
F	na
F	wine

F	wine
F	na
F	na
F	beer
F	beer
F	wine
F	na
F	beer
F	wine
F	beer
F	na
F	beer
F	wine
F	wine
F	beer
F	na
F	beer

1. Open SPSS; select *Type in data*. Select *Variable View* at the bottom left of the screen.
2. Create two variables. Under *Name*, call one variable *gender* and the other one *pref*. Under *Type*, make the *gender* variable a String variable and make *pref* a Numeric variable.
3. Conduct a cross-tabulation in SPSS by selecting *Analysis/Descriptive Statistics/Crosstabs*.
4. Select *gender* to go in the *Row* box and *pref* to go in the *Column* box and click *OK*.
5. Using a calculator, indicate the percentage of men who preferred beer and the percentage of women who preferred wine.

You can also do this without the calculator by selecting either *Row Percentages* or *Column Percentages* from the *Cells* option in SPSS. Try both (one at a time) and see if you can determine which one gives you the correct answer for Step 3. The output you should get from Step 3 is as follows.

			PREF		Total
		Beer	Na	Wine	
GENDER	F	8	7	9	24
	M	11	6	7	24
Total		19	13	16	48

Ordinal Data

Whereas nominal data recognize differences in the *kind* of response alternatives, **ordinal data** make a further distinction by *quantity* of response alternatives. Ordinal variables show numerical differences between response alternatives. Consider the following response alternatives to the question, "What is your highest level of education?": (1) less than high school, (2) high school graduate, (3) some college, (4) college graduate, (5) beyond college. These response alternatives show increasing amounts of schooling and are an example of ordinal data. As Table 3.1 indicates, the comparison is no longer simply A ≠ B, but rather A < B. The word *ordinal* refers to the ordering of responses, such as from smallest to largest, hottest to coldest, or highest intelligence to lowest intelligence.

Ordinal data are often summarized in the same fashion as nominal data, specifically with frequencies and percentages of each response alternative. Table 3.3a shows ordinal data on educational attainment from a survey of South Dakota residents. In addition, ordinal data can be cross-tabulated with another variable. Table 3.3b shows the education variable cross-tabulated with respondents' gender. The Your Turn box shows how to tabulate ordinal data from an existing data source, in this case a large national database called the General Social Survey.

TABLE 3.3a **Frequency Distribution of Ordinal Data**

From the State of South Dakota	Less than High School	High School Graduate	Some College	College Graduate or Beyond
Frequency	581	2021	1742	1783
Percentage	7.9%	33.0%	29.7%	29.2%

TABLE 3.3b **Cross-Tabulation of Ordinal Data with a Nominal Variable**

From the State of South Dakota	Less than High School	High School Graduate	Some College	College Graduate or Beyond
Male	8.9%	34.1%	27.4%	29.5%
Female	7.0%	32.0%	31.9%	29.0%

Source: Behavioral Risk Factor Survey (www.cdc.gov/brfss).
Note: Frequencies were determined by multiplying the percentages by the total sample size reported on the Centers for Disease Control website.

YOUR TURN

Ordinal Data

The General Social Survey is conducted each year by the National Opinion Research Center (NORC). The NORC website contains an interactive data analysis tool that allows production of frequencies and cross-tabulations.

1. Go to the following website: http://www.norc.org/GSS+Website/

2. Click the *Data Analysis* tab, then click the plus sign next to the phrase *NORC Public Use Data Catalog*. Then click the plus sign next to *GSS*. Then click the icon next to the phrase *General Social Surveys, 1972–2006*.

3. Near the top of the page, you will see a tab entitled *Browse GSS Variables*. Click on this tab and then select *Subject Index*. You can select any variable you want. As a demonstration, we selected the letter P, then Political, then *Political ideology*. There are three questions under political ideology, and we selected *THINK OF SELF AS LIBERAL OR CONSERVATIVE*.

4. This will display the following distribution:
   EXTREMELY LIBERAL 2.6%
   LIBERAL 11.2%
   SLIGHTLY LIBERAL 13.0%
   MODERATE 38.7%
   SLIGHTLY CONSERVATIVE 16.6%
   CONSERVATIVE 14.8%
   EXTREMELY CONSERVATIVE 3.1%

5. Using this technique, create a frequency distribution for the question "MARRIED PEOPLE HAPPIER THAN UNMARRIED," which is found under *M* and then *Marriage*.

Interval Data

Interval data are similar to ordinal data in that both reflect increases in quantity. With interval data, however, the quantity between the different responses of the variable is the same. A good example of an interval variable is grade point average. The difference between 2.50 and 3.00 is considered to be the same mathematical difference as that between 3.00 and 3.50. Most other achievement measures are considered interval data as well. Thus, the mathematical distance between a 24 and a 26 on the ACT is the same as the mathematical distance between a 26 and a 28.

Another example from athletics illustrates how ordinal and interval data are different. Imagine a cross-country race with 50 participants. Ordinal data would be the place in which the runners finished. We know that first place is faster than second place, but we do *not* know if the distance between first and second place is the same as the distance between second place and third place, and so on. So, order of finish is, as the name implies, an ordinal variable, but the actual finish times would be interval data.

A very popular type of scale in the social sciences is the **Likert scale**. A Likert scale is a type of response alternative in which participants indicate their degree of agreement with a stated attitude or judgment. An example would be: "A marriage between two people of the same gender should be legal." The Likert-scale response alternatives could be: strongly agree, agree, neutral, disagree, and strongly disagree.[1] Strictly speaking, Likert scales are ordinal. However, researchers usually treat Likert scales as interval because *it is assumed* that the distances between the scale values are equal; this is how we discuss them in this section. Interval data can be displayed using a scatterplot. A **scatterplot** is a way to graphically represent the relationship between two variables, and is commonly used with interval data. The Your Turn box gives you an opportunity to create a scatterplot. Interval data are analyzed using a correlation coefficient, which we discuss in Chapter 4.

YOUR TURN

Interval Data

If you have data from two variables measured on an interval scale, you can plot the values from those variables on a scatterplot using SPSS.

1. Type in the data shown here (*Note:* Save this dataset for the next Your Turn box as well):

Grade	Selfconf
3.3	6.5
3.7	6.5
3.3	4.0
3.0	4.0
2.7	2.5
4.0	6.0
4.0	7.0
3.3	5.3
2.3	3.3
4.0	5.3
3.7	6.3

---

[1] Not all scales are Likert scales. A specific procedure is used to create a Likert scale, which we do not describe here (see Shaughnessy, Zechmeister, & Zechmeister, 2006).

1.7	2.8
4.0	6.0
4.0	6.5
2.3	3.3
2.3	4.5
3.3	6.2
3.3	6.6
3.0	5.0
3.0	4.3

2. These are data from a class called "Science and Technology for Everyday Life." The first variable is final grade (on a 4-point scale) and the second variable is students' mean score on a five-item self-confidence index. Name the first variable *grade* and the second variable *selfconf*. Make them both numeric variables (under *Type*).
3. Select *Graphs/Scatter*.
4. Select *Simple*, and click *Define*.
5. Put *grade* in the Y axis field and *selfconf* in the X axis field. You should get something resembling Figure 3.1.

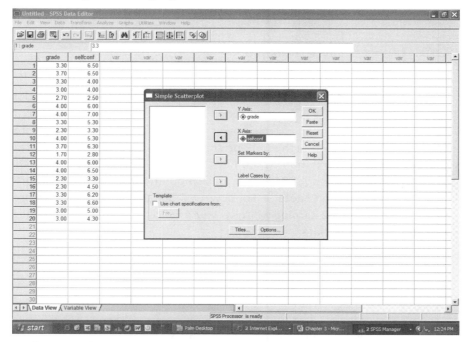

FIGURE 3.1. *Simple scatterplot screen in SPSS*

Clicking *OK* will produce a scatterplot that looks like Figure 3.2.

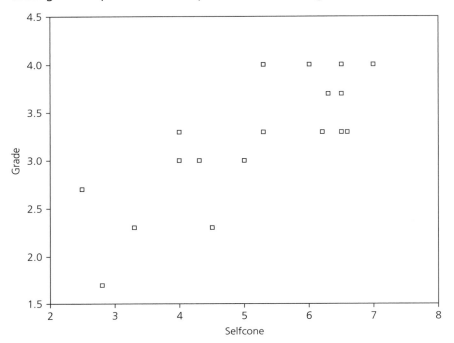

FIGURE 3.2. *Simple scatterplot*

Each dot represents the two scores for one student. This figure shows that the dots are concentrated in the lower left and the upper right of the scatterplot. This pattern indicates a positive correlation: low scores on one variable occur with low scores on the other variable (lower left of scatterplot), and high scores on one variable occur with high scores on the other variable (upper left of scatterplot). A negative correlation would have a scatterplot that moves from the upper left to the lower right. We describe computation of correlation coefficients in greater detail in Chapter 4. For now, we hope showing you how to produce and interpret a scatterplot will give you a better understanding of how researchers use interval data.

We can also use interval data to compare scores across different groups. The data from the next Your Turn box address the question of whether men and women differ in self-confidence. This exercise demonstrates how to create a bar graph to display the differences between the two groups.

YOUR TURN

Mean Differences with Interval Data

This exercise uses the data from the previous Your Turn box to create a bar graph. We have added a third variable, *gender*, so that we can compare males and females on the self-confidence measure.

1. Enter another variable called *gender* and place it in the third column with the following values:

Male
Male
Male
Female
Female
Male
Male
Female
Female
Female
Male
Female
Female
Female
Male
Male
Female
Female
Male
Male

2. Under *Graphs*, select *Bar*.

3. Select *Simple* as the type of graph and click *Define*.

4. Under *Bars Represent*, select *Other Summary Function*.

5. Select the variable *selfconf* as the variable to go in the top variable box.

6. Put the variable *gender* in the *Category Axis* variable box. Your screen should look like the one in Figure 3.3.

FIGURE 3.3.   *Creating a bar graph in SPSS*

7. Click *OK*. These steps should produce a bar graph.

8. What conclusion do you draw from these data?

Ratio Data

Ratio data are set apart from ordinal (increasing order) and interval (equal spacing) data by having the additional property of an absolute lower value that corresponds to the absence of the measure. In other words, ratio data have an absolute zero. Physical measurements are often ratio data. For example, consider an agricultural research study that has fruit production as the dependent variable. A plant that produces zero pieces of fruit would receive a score of zero—the absence of that entity. Such data are not as common in the social sciences as they are in the physical or biological sciences.

Ratio data, as the name implies, allow numerical values to be placed in ratios. In our agricultural example, if Plot A produced an average of 40 pieces of fruit and Plot B produced an average of 20 pieces of fruit, we could claim that Plot A produced two times as many pieces of fruit as Plot B (a 2:1 ratio). We could not make a similar claim with interval data. For example, if Student A rated himself a "1" on a seven-point self-confidence scale (interval measure) and Student B rated herself a "7" on the same scale, we could not claim that Student B is seven times as self-confident. Nor could we claim that the lowest score on self-confidence implies the complete absence of self-confidence.

Now that you have an understanding of the different measurement scales that can be created, we will turn to a discussion of the criteria researchers use to determine that their measures are of high quality.

CHARACTERISTICS OF GOOD MEASURES

Quantitative social science research involves creating measures of behaviors, thoughts, or attitudes. This involves assigning numeric values to these constructs. Some measures (speed, distance) are inherently quantitative. Other measures may not be inherently quantitative. For example, depression may not be an inherently quantitative construct, but researchers could create measures of depression that make it a quantitative construct. In the case of depression, a common assessment is done with the Beck Depression Inventory. Patients complete a 21-item questionnaire to determine if they have symptoms of depression. If a patient has a score above 30, he is considered to suffer from "severe depression" (Beck, Ward, Mendelson, Mock, & Erbaugh, 1961).

It is not enough simply to create a numeric measure. The measure must be *truthful*— it must accurately reflect the construct. If researchers create a measure of intelligence, they must be sure that this measure actually reflects intelligence. They must also create a measure that is *consistent*—it must yield the same results across time, circumstances, and groups of people. Creating a truthful (valid) and consistent (reliable) quantitative measure is the focus of the next subsections.

Validity

Validity is about truthfulness. A measure shows **validity** if it actually measures what it claims (or is intended) to measure. To illustrate, consider a study by Good, Aronson, and Inzlicht (2003). They developed an intervention designed to improve female, minority, and low-income students' mathematics achievement. The intervention was a mentoring program in which college students encouraged the young people in this study to view intelligence as changeable rather than fixed and to attribute academic difficulties to the novelty of the educational environment rather than to personal inadequacies. The results showed that the middle-school students who took part in the mentoring program showed significant improvement on a standardized mathematics achievement test. This study made an important contribution to understanding how to improve mathematics achievement among groups that have traditionally not done well in math.

The results of this study would have been meaningless without valid measures. The key measure in this study was mathematics achievement, and these researchers needed to show that their measure of mathematics achievement indeed measured that construct. We will describe different types of validity and how it can be established.

Content Validity Content validity refers to the extent to which the items or behaviors fully represent the concept being measured. A straightforward example of this is a teacher who is preparing an examination for a class on research methods that uses this text. If the

test covers the first three chapters of this book, the professor will have a test with high content validity if the questions on the test adequately cover concepts from those three chapters. The test will have low content validity if it fails to cover adequately the important information from these chapters, or if the test covers material that is not included in the first three chapters.

You can determine content validity by asking an expert or group of experts to review your instrument. Glenn Gamst and his colleagues (Gamst et al., 2004) constructed the California Brief Multicultural Competence Scale (CBMCS). This instrument consisted of 21 self-report items measuring components such as multicultural knowledge, awareness of cultural barriers, and sensitivity to multicultural consumers. To establish content validity, the researchers asked a panel of experts to review the items and to judge the extent to which the items in the instrument sufficiently measured multicultural competence.

Construct Validity **Construct validity** refers to the extent to which the measure is on target to measure the construct being studied. An example is intelligence. An intelligence test has high construct validity if the scores on the test actually measure what the researchers believe is "intelligence." In other words, if those who get high scores on an intelligence test are recognized as "smart," then the intelligence test has high construct validity. Construct validity is slightly different from content validity. Content validity is concerned with whether the instrument is *broad enough* to capture the concept being measured. An intelligence test might have good construct validity if "smart" people scored high on the test, but the same test might not have extremely high content validity if it measured only some aspects of intelligence and ignored others. "Smart" people would still score high on the test (construct validity), but certain aspects of intelligence would not be considered (content validity).

There are two ways to determine construct validity. One is by evaluating **convergent validity**, which is the extent to which other measures of the same behavior are similar to your measure. For example, suppose we give the (hypothetical) VanderStoep-Johnston Test of Intelligence (VJTI) to a group of fifth-grade students. Our test will be high in construct validity if our test is similar to another test that has construct validity, such the Wechsler Intelligence Scale for Children, 4th edition (WISC-IV). If the students' scores on the VJTI and their scores on the WISC-IV are similar, then we have established convergent validity. In other words, researchers use convergent validity to assess construct validity. (This is done by examining the correlation between the two tests; we discuss the computation of correlation coefficients in Chapter 4.)

Research by Dinger, Oman, Taylor, Vesely, and Able (2004) provides an example of convergent validity. They studied 56 elderly individuals (average age = 75 years) as a way to establish convergent validity of the Physical Activity Scale for the Elderly (PASE) instrument. Participants wore activity monitors to document their movement for one week. At the conclusion of the week, trained interviewers asked participants about their activity using the PASE interview protocol. The results of this study indicated that participants with high scores on the PASE also had high activity as measured by the monitors. In this case, the electronic monitor served to validate the validity of the self-report PASE instrument. Similarity between the two measures allowed the researchers to claim convergent validity.

One might ask: If the measurement device used to validate the instrument currently being studied is already good, why do researchers need to create another one? One answer is that science advances with a better and wider assortment of measuring instruments from which to choose. Another answer is that sometimes newer instruments make research more precise or easier to conduct. In the Dinger et al. (2004) study, having a self-report instrument that is just as valid as an electronic device could save time and money and allow researchers who do not have access to electronic devices to conduct valuable research. All of this activity advances the collective scientific enterprise.

A second way to establish content validity is by way of **discriminant validity**. One achieves discriminant validity when the instrument being examined is *uncorrelated* with another measure that is presumably unrelated. For example, we would want an intelligence test like the VJIT to be uncorrelated with other psychological constructs such as motivation. If intelligence and motivation are correlated, then our measure that we think is measuring intelligence may also be measuring motivation. If the two instruments are uncorrelated, we cannot be certain that the VJIT measures intelligence, but we can be certain that the instrument is not getting confused with motivation.

Predictive Validity **Predictive validity** refers to the extent to which a measure is related to some other measure that you would be interested in predicting. (This is sometimes called *criterion validity*.) For example, suppose a school principal is interested in predicting which students will get in trouble. He wants to find a way to predict what types of students will receive in-school detentions. An educational researcher proposes developing a measure of school bullying as a way to predict in-school detentions. The researcher will measure bullying with observational methods and give each child a score on the Bullying Index. To establish predictive validity, those Bullying Index scores will be compared to the number of in-school detentions. If the scores on the Bullying Index are positively correlated with detentions, then the Bullying Index has high predictive validity and the principal would have a good way to predict which students are likely to get detentions. If there is no relationship between detentions and bullying, then the Bullying Index would have low predictive validity, and the principal would need to look for another way to figure out which students will likely get detentions.

Researchers can also establish predictive validity by showing a negative correlation with a measure that is thought to be the opposite of bullying. For example, high predictive validity would exist if scores on the Bullying Index were *negatively* correlated with students' scores on a conflict-avoidance scale. Notice that predictive validity is slightly different from convergent validity. Convergent validity shows a relationship between two measures designed to measure the same construct (intelligence, bullying). Predictive validity shows a relationship between the construct in question (bullying) and a related measure, but not one that measures the same construct (detentions).

A study by Xu and colleagues (Xu, Siegrist, Cao, Li, Tomlinson, & Chan, 2004) provides a good example of predictive validity. They were interested in the predictive validity of a questionnaire measuring job stress in women. In their study they surveyed 421 working women from Beijing, China. They selected blood pressure, sleep trouble, tiredness, and feeling nervous as variables to test the predictive validity of their job-stress scale. Because these negative symptoms are physiological manifestations of job stress, a job-stress questionnaire that correlated with these negative symptoms would have predictive validity. The researchers found that scores on their questionnaire did indeed correlate with these symptoms.

Schwab-Stone and colleagues (Schwab-Stone et al., 1996) evaluated whether the National Institutes of Mental Health Diagnostic Interview Schedule for Children (DISC) predicted childhood psychopathology. They conducted the DISC interview with 247 children and then rated the children for the presence of symptoms of five different behavior disorders. They found that the results of the DISC correlated with the psychologists' assessment of behavior disorders. In other words, the DISC had predictive validity for childhood disorders.

We have illustrated several different types of validity in this section. In the Your Turn box, you have the opportunity to explore how you might establish validity for a social science construct.

YOUR TURN

Validity

Your task is to develop a valid measure of classroom misbehavior among elementary school students.

1. Provide an operational definition for your dependent variable (see beginning of chapter) _____

2. Describe ways you could demonstrate the following for your measure:

   a. Content validity

   b. Construct validity

   c. Predictive validity

Reliability

Reliability is the extent to which a measure yields the same scores across different times, groups of people, or versions of the instrument. Reliability is about consistency. If a person takes an intelligence test several times, and each time the test produces a similar intelligence test score, that intelligence test has high reliability. Most commercially produced instruments (for example, ACT, SAT) have high reliability. Interestingly, a measure can have high reliability but low validity. Imagine we decide that a measure of intelligence should be the length of one's ear lobe. Although this measure clearly has no validity, it will have high reliability—ear-lobe length will be consistent upon repeated measurements. Here we discuss different ways to determine the reliability of a measure.

Cronbach's Alpha **Cronbach's alpha** is the most common way to assess the reliability of self-report items. Cronbach's alpha measures the degree to which the items in an instrument are related. It has a maximum value of 1.0. Values closer to 1.0 reflect a stronger relationship between the test items. For an instrument with a high alpha, participants who score high on one item on the test would also score high on other items on the test. Similarly, participants who score low on one item of the test would also score low on the other items on the test. Tests with low alphas would indicate that there was little similarity of responses. The steps for computing Cronbach's alpha using SPSS are shown in the Your Turn box.

YOUR TURN

Cronbach's Alpha

Below are scores from 10 different people on 5 questions measuring intrinsic motivation for school (that is, learning for its own sake). Each question is on a 7-point scale with higher values reflecting greater intrinsic motivation.

1. Double-click the SPSS icon. Select the *Type in data* button.

2. Create five variables, calling them *motivat1* to *motivat5*.

3. Type in the following data into SPSS for the 10 students:

7	6	6	5	6
6	6	6	7	7
6	7	7	7	7
5	5	7	5	5
6	6	6	6	5
7	7	6	6	5
2	3	2	3	2
1	2	2	2	2
3	4	3	4	3
5	5	4	4	4

4. Click the *Analysis* pull-down menu, drag down to *Scale*, and select *Reliability Analysis*. The word *Alpha* should appear in the bottom left of the dialog box next to the word *Model*.

5. Select the variables *motivat1* through *motivat5* by clicking on them and then moving from the left box to the right box. Your screen should resemble Figure 3.4.

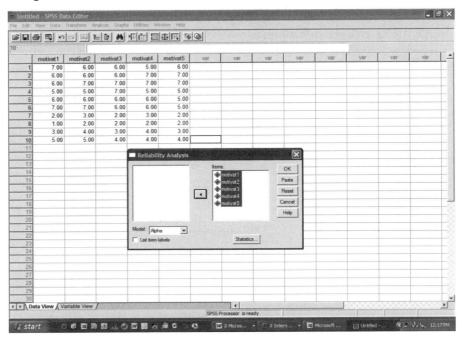

FIGURE 3.4.   *Reliability analysis screen in SPSS*

6. The output should produce an alpha of .9754. What does this tell you about these five measures of intrinsic motivation?

7. Change the scores on the motivation items to investigate ways in which the alpha could be lowered. How could you get a value close to zero?

Test-Retest Reliability **Test-retest reliability** measures the similarity of participants' scores at two different times. The greater the similarity between the two sets of scores, the higher the test-retest reliability. This method of determining reliability is often used for measures of achievement and other types of performance. For example, educators would want intelligence test scores to remain similar over time. Tests on which students' scores were similar across repeated testing sessions would have high test-retest reliability. This procedure can be time-consuming because it requires you to administer the instrument two times. Also, if the questions are very memorable or if only a short amount of time has passed between the two test administrations, the test-retest procedure might not work. Instead, two versions of the test may be needed.

Parallel-Forms Reliability An instrument has high **parallel-forms reliability** if similar, but not identical, versions of the same instrument have the same measurement characteristics. The parallel-forms approach solves the problems associated with assessing test-retest reliability. If people's scores on the two different versions are similar, the measure has parallel-forms reliability. This method of determining reliability is often used when you are trying to determine if a measure changes over time. For example, if you assess student achievement at the beginning and end of a semester with two different achievement tests, the forms will have to be parallel.

Inter-Rater Reliability Inter-rater reliability is often used for behavioral observations. A measure has high **inter-rater reliability** if two people who are observing a behavior agree on the nature of that behavior. Donaldson, Hill, Finch, and Forero (2003) developed a sports safety audit tool to be used by amateur sports clubs in Australia. Because individual clubs would be using this instrument, it was important to demonstrate inter-rater reliability, for without it the different clubs could not be confident that the ratings would be meaningful. In this study, they asked 24 different observers from 8 different sports clubs to use the instrument. There was a high degree of agreement among these 24 individuals when they assessed the safety of these sports clubs using this instrument. Thus, these results support the claim that there is high inter-rater reliability in this study.

In the case of low inter-rater reliability, possible remedies include revising the instrument or behavioral checklist, providing clearer operational definitions, or providing better training of the observers. Perry, VanderStoep, and Yu (1993) classified classroom observations from U.S., Japanese, and Chinese mathematics classrooms using six categories to describe classroom activity (for example, rote recall, problem solving). To achieve high inter-rater reliability, the three researchers selected 30 lesson transcripts, which they coded together. They discussed each lesson until they agreed on the coding of that event. Next, two different raters coded an additional 45 lessons. The two raters agreed on the coding of the lessons 87% of the time. With this high inter-rater reliability, the researchers thus felt comfortable having the remaining lessons coded by only one of the raters. The next Your Turn box exercise asks you to practice determining inter-rater reliability.

YOUR TURN

Inter-Rater Reliability

The following exercise involves working with a partner. Find a behavior or activity that you can observe and on which you can make judgments. Examples could be estimating speed of traffic, judging a televised athletic or performance event, or evaluating the friendliness of a clerk in an ice-cream store. (Yes, we are encouraging research at the ice-cream store, all for the sake of science!). Your tasks are:

1. Operationally define the variable you are observing (speed, quality, friendliness).

2. Pick a response scale (miles per hour, yes-no, very nice/medium nice/not nice). Put the data you and your friend collect on the sheet below.

Rater	1	2	3	4	5	6	7	8	9	10
You
Friend

3. Determine how you will score high reliability. For example, for a categorical variable such as fast-slow or present-absent, reliability should be measured by percent agreement between the two raters. For a numerical variable such as speed, Cronbach's alpha would be a good measure of agreement (see the previous Your Turn box).

4. Estimate of inter-rater reliability: _____

COLLECTING DATA

Now that you have an understanding of what constitutes a high-quality measure, we turn to the techniques that researchers use to obtain these measures in their studies. These techniques differ in terms of who records the data and what gets recorded (see Table 3.4). Each technique brings with it certain costs and benefits, which you must take into account as you plan your data collection.

Self-Report

A technique that social scientists commonly use to collect data is self-report. **Self-report data** are collected by asking participants to answer questions on their own. This is done by completing a survey or questionnaire, either via phone, mail, email, Internet, or group setting. The main advantage of the self-report strategy is the efficiency with which data

TABLE 3.4 Data-Collection Methods

	What Gets Recorded?	
Who Records Data?	Actual Behavioral Record	Judgment of Attitude or Behavior
Research Participant	Performance measure	Self-report data
Researcher	Physiological measure	Behavioral observation

can be collected. Self-report data collection can be done with copies of the questionnaire, pencils, and a group of randomly selected participants. More advanced versions of self-report data collection involve other techniques, including telephone interviewing and Web surveys. Websites such as surveymonkey.com and zoomerang.com provide survey construction and analysis in a user-friendly interface. Online surveys save on copying, postage, and data-entry costs. Whatever the delivery method, self-report data collection is a robust approach to collecting attitudinal and behavioral data.

Thousands of examples of self-report data, from all fields of social science research, are published in journals or presented at conferences each year. Undergraduate student Michelle Anne Williams (2004) asked 73 undergraduate students to complete several questionnaires developed by previous researchers, including the Desire for Control (DC), Achievement Motivation (AM), and Future Time Perspective (FTP) questionnaires. The Desire for Control questionnaire consisted of 20 statements on which students evaluated their degree of agreement on a scale from 1 (*disagree very much*) to 7 (*agree very much*). Williams then correlated participants' scores on the DC, AM, and FTP scales. Self-report data are very useful for this type of research.

The main disadvantage of all self-report measures is that the researcher must rely on the participants' reports of their own attitudes, perceptions, or memories. Social psychologists have known for a long time that people have a **self-serving bias**, a tendency to report their behaviors and attitudes in a positive light. As noted by social psychologist and author David Myers (1996), people think that they are more intelligent, better workers, better drivers, friendlier, and more ethical and honest than their peers. Researchers are thus faced with the possibility that self-reports will produce inaccurate responses. At the same time, self-reporting is a powerful and flexible way to collect data that allows you to measure many aspects of human activity. We hope this will become clear to you as you work on the Your Turn box.

YOUR TURN

Self-Report

For this exercise, working with a partner will be helpful.

1. Construct a five-item self-report questionnaire on a topic of interest to both of you. Topics could include athletics, music, television viewing habits, or attitudes/behaviors related to school and studying. Of the five items, attempt to make one nominal response, one ordinal response, and one interval.

2. After you construct the questionnaire, you and your partner should each administer the questionnaire to 10 different individuals.

3. You can tabulate your responses manually, with SPSS, with Excel, or with another software package.

4. Create a frequency distribution or graph showing the percentage of each response category.

Behavioral Observations

Behavioral observations differ from self-report data in that behavioral observations come from the researchers rather than from the study participants. The main advantage of behavioral observations is that they provide a third-party account of people's activities. This avoids the self-serving bias that might occur when people evaluate their own behaviors and attitudes. Although third-party judgments are still subject to bias, such bias is less likely in behavioral observations as compared to self-report data. Another kind of bias, however, can appear with behavioral observations. **Self-presentation bias** is when participants in the study know they are being observed and behave differently because of it. If participants do not know they are being observed, this bias should not be present.

There are two main cautions when using behavioral observation as a data-collection technique. The first is the extra cost, particularly in terms of researchers' time, compared to collecting self-report data. The second disadvantage is that behavioral observations can take place only in certain situations. Unlike self-report data, which can be collected on even private matters, behavioral observations are confined to mostly public events. For more private thoughts and behaviors, we must rely on self-report data. This is ironic, because reporting of private behaviors is probably more subject to the self-serving bias.

An example of use of behavioral observations is a study by Robert Coplan and Kenneth Rubin (1998). These researchers used the Preschool Play Behavior Scale (PPBS) to evaluate nonsocial play in young children. The PPBS is completed by teachers based on observations of their students. It is a behavioral checklist to measure children's solitary play and includes activities such as onlooker behavior, reading and listening, and active conversation (Guralnick, Hammond, & Connor, 2003). Based on these behaviors, children were classified into three subtypes of solitary play: solitary-reticent, solitary-passive, and solitary-active. The behavioral observations formed the basis for a classification of the children. For example, children classified as engaged in solitary-passive play tended to show healthy emotional regulation (Rubin, Coplan, Fox, & Calkins, 1995).

When conducting behavioral observations, it is important to have a good categorization scheme for classifying the behaviors you observe. Most researchers prefer to have behavioral classifications that are both mutually exclusive and mutually exhaustive. *Mutually exclusive* means that each behavior can be classified into only one category. *Mutually exhaustive* means that every behavior gets classified. Developing a mutually exclusive behavioral observation scheme can be difficult, because people are often observed performing more than one activity at once, or a behavior could fit into more than one category. For example, in the Perry, VanderStoep, and Yu (1993) study described earlier, each classroom lesson was coded as belonging to only one category (mutually exclusive). However, classroom behavior is complex, and sometimes a behavior does not fit neatly into a preexisting category (not mutually exhaustive). To develop a mutually exhaustive behavioral observation scheme, researchers can create a category called "other" into which researchers put all behaviors that do not fit the preexisting categories. Researchers strive to categorize as few observations as possible as "other." If this category becomes too large, researchers will occasionally take a subset of the "other" responses that are similar to each other and make a new category. For example, suppose you are observing playground behavior and your original categories were large-group play (more than 6 children), small-group play (2–6 children), and solitary play. After a couple hours of observation, you noticed there were many two-person groups, which seemed to have different play patterns from the groups of size 3–6. If you had recorded the exact number of participants in your observations, you would then be able to go back to your data sheet and create a fourth play-group size (two-person group).

As this example illustrates, collecting behavioral observations may appear easy, but there can be layers of complexity to such data collection. The Your Turn box provides an exercise by which you can gain experience collecting behavioral observations.

YOUR TURN

Behavioral Observations

You can conduct behavioral observations anywhere there are people. Here is one example.

Go to the main undergraduate library at your university. Use the following procedure to gain experience collecting behavioral observations:

1. Site 1: Walk through the main floor of the library and make observations of the people working in a high-traffic area on the main floor. Record their behavior using the following coding scheme of mutually exclusive and exhaustive behaviors. (You may modify the coding scheme as you wish, but make sure you use the same coding scheme for both parts of this exercise.)

   - Studying quietly alone
   - Engaged in conversation/nonacademic (talking with friends, cell phone)
   - Engaged in conversation/academic (group learning)
   - Working on computer/academic
   - Working on computer/nonacademic
   - Other

Also record the student's gender.

Remember that these are judgments you will need to make as a researcher. You will have to judge whether the conversation is academic or nonacademic. (*Hint:* Developing clear *operational definitions* will help.) You could link this Your Turn exercise to the inter-rater reliability exercise earlier in the chapter and compare your behavioral ratings to others'.

2. Site 2: Collect the same observational data on one of the quiet floors of the library (sometimes called "the stacks"). After you complete your observations, your data sheet should look something like this:

Behavioral Observation	Main Floor Men (%)	Main Floor Women (%)	Quiet Floor Men (%)	Quiet Floor Women (%)
Studying quietly alone				
Engaged in conversation/ nonacademic				
Engaged in conversation/ academic				
Working on computer/ academic				
Working on computer/ nonacademic				
Other				

This display of behavioral observations will allow comparisons of differences in library behavior based on differences in location, and also will reveal any gender differences that might exist.

3. Summarize your findings by making comparisons based on any differences by location or differences by gender.

Physiological Measures

Self-reports rely on participants' own attitudes and judgments. Behavioral observations rely on researchers' judgments of participants. Physiological measures provide bodily measures much like those found in the life sciences. One advantage of using physiological measures is the *precision* of data-collection instruments. Most instruments designed to measure physiological data (for example, blood pressure, heart rate) possess a degree of measurement sophistication that other social science measures do not. Furthermore, physiological data are far less likely to be subject to the bias of self-report data.

An example of using physiological measures in social science research comes from Charlotte Witvliet and her colleagues (Witvliet, Ludwig, & VanderLaan, 2001). The researchers asked participants to imagine either a hurtful life event (grudge-holding condition) or to imagine forgiving the perpetrators (forgiveness condition). The researchers found that those in the grudge-holding condition showed higher heart rate and blood pressure than those in the forgiveness condition.

The main disadvantage of collecting physiological measures is the expense and expertise required to collect these data. The training often comes either from graduate school or from working directly in a particular research lab where physiological data are collected. Most social scientists do not possess the capability or training to collect data of this nature. However, with the proper equipment and training, physiological measures can be very valuable to many areas of social science.

Performance Measures

Performance measures are similar to physiological measures in that they contain an actual behavior record. Performance measures are also similar to self-report measures in that the participant is the one providing the record of the data (Table 3.4). Performance measures are often used in the fields of organizational behavior and educational studies. Organizational researchers might use skills tests or worker performance as the dependent variable. For example, consider a researcher who is interested in the relationship between salespersons' job satisfaction and their job performance. One way to conduct this study would be to measure worker job satisfaction (self-report data) and gross sales revenue (performance measure). In education, students take various achievement tests or other measures of student performance. In the state of Pennsylvania, for example, all elementary school students take the Pennsylvania System of School Assessment (PSSA) tests in fifth, eighth, and eleventh grades. District administrators can then correlate the PSSA scores with other educational data they have collected.

Researchers sometimes use commercially produced performance instruments to measure various behaviors. This is particularly true in education, where tests to measure student achievement that have demonstrated reliability and validity are available for purchase. In general, these instruments vary on two main dimensions. First, they differ on whether they measure absolute performance or relative performance. A **normative measure** determines a person's performance relative to the performance of others. A common normative instrument is a test of school learning called the Terra Nova. This test gives each student a percentile score. This test focuses not on what the student learned, but rather on how the student performed relative to other students. The opposite is true for a **criterion measure**, which gives a measure of how much a student has learned in a particular subject. If a mathematics achievement test has 10 objectives on it, a criterion instrument would indicate what percentage of the problems for each objective the student successfully completed. With a criterion measure, the focus is on what the person has learned, not on a relative comparison to others.

Another dimension on which performance measures differ is whether they measure progress or potential. An **achievement measure** assesses the amount of material a person has mastered. The ACT, taken by many college-bound students, is an achievement instrument, measuring student performance in mathematics, science, and other content areas. An **aptitude measure** measures a person's potential for success in a given area. An intelligence test given to young children, measuring their reasoning and problem-solving skills, is an example of an aptitude instrument. Both achievement and aptitude measures are used primarily in educational and organizational research.

Performance measures are advantageous when productivity and achievement have to be quantified. In the area of student achievement, researchers can collect self-report data asking a survey question such as, "On a scale from 1 to 10, please indicate how much you learned in this course." In the area of worker performance, an analogous question could be asked by replacing "produced at your job" for "learned in this course." Although these self-report data are helpful, they are subject to the self-serving bias mentioned earlier. Performance measures are usually free of this bias. Measuring a student's memory for course material is a more accurate gauge of what he learned than a self-report item asking him to judge his memory for course material.

There are two potential disadvantages of using performance measures in social science research. The first potential disadvantage is cost. Performance measures are more costly than self-report measures. Performance measures take longer to collect and probably cost more because the instrument designed to measure performance must usually be purchased from a for-profit testing company. A second potential problem with performance measures deals with the validity of the measure of performance. This is especially true if research participants know they are being evaluated. If they know they are being evaluated, they may behave differently than they ordinarily would. For example, participants may become nervous and therefore underperform relative to their usual performance or achievement level. Some people just "don't test well," because of anxiety or other factors. Conversely, some people may perform even better if they know their performance is being evaluated. One can imagine workers who are regularly quite lazy becoming very productive during the periods when they know their performance is being measured. Despite these potential disadvantages, we see a big push in the field of education to produce performance measures. Terms like "accountability," "outcomes-based assessment," and "results-oriented" all desire performance measures in research. It is unlikely that this trend will change, so future researchers must be familiar with using this type of measurement.

SUMMARY

The goal of this chapter was to describe the different characteristics of measures and the techniques used to collect data. The different characteristics of measures—nominal, ordinal, interval, ratio—correspond with different ways of displaying and analyzing data. Regardless of the type of measurement you select, it is essential to have valid and reliable measures of your variables if you are to conduct meaningful social science research. Without validity and reliability, research findings are not useful. Social science data can be collected in several ways: self-report, behavioral observation, physiological measure, or performance measure. We noted that each strategy brings with it advantages and disadvantages. The decision on type of data-collection strategy should be based on which method best matches the goals of the study and on which method is most affordable.

KEY TERMS

achievement measure

aptitude measure

construct validity

content validity

convergent validity

criterion measure

Cronbach's alpha

cross-tabulation

data

discriminant validity

frequency distribution
inter-rater reliability
interval data
Likert scale
nominal data
normative measure
operational definition
ordinal data
parallel-forms reliability
predictive validity

ratio data
reliability
scatterplot
self-presentation bias
self-report data
self-serving bias
test-retest reliability
validity
variable

CHAPTER

4

QUANTITATIVE RESEARCH: DESCRIPTIVE AND CORRELATIONAL DESIGNS

LEARNING OBJECTIVES

- Understand the basic elements of correlational data.
- Produce effective survey questions using strategies described in this book.
- Identify the various strategies for collecting data using correlational studies, and be able to match a strategy to a particular research question.
- Conduct data analysis of correlational research.

In this chapter we explore descriptive and correlational research designs. These techniques are considered nonexperimental because they generally involve only the measurement of variables and not the manipulation or control of variables. Although some of these techniques were mentioned in Chapter 2 in the context of selecting a methodology, in this chapter we explore the details of executing those techniques—the "nuts and bolts" of doing research using these techniques.

BASIC CONCEPTS

Correlational research involves identifying relationships between two variables. As was mentioned in Chapter 2, a **correlation** is a statistical measure of association between two variables. A correlation has a direction and a magnitude. With respect to direction, a correlation can be either positive or negative. A **positive correlation** exists when, as one variable increases (or decreases), the other variable also increases (or decreases). Figure 4.1 shows a scatterplot (see Chapter 3) of a positive correlation between college students' scores on a critical-thinking scale and scores on a self-regulation scale (goal-setting, planning, monitoring). These data were collected from 49 students enrolled in a "Science and Technology for Everyday Life" course. Each dot represents a person's score plotted on the two-dimensional space on the graph. Notice the shift in clusters of points from lower left to upper right. Such a trend is indicative of a positive correlation. In other words, as critical thinking goes up, self-regulation also goes up, and vice versa.

A **negative correlation** is the opposite of a positive correlation; two variables are negatively correlated when, as the value of one variable increases, the value of the other variable decreases (and vice versa). Figure 4.2 shows a scatterplot of a negative correlation from the same "Science and Technology for Everyday Life" dataset. The variable on the X axis is *Test Anxiety* and the variable on the Y axis is *Self-Efficacy* (that is, self-confidence). Notice the shift in clusters of points from upper left to lower right. Such a trend is indicative

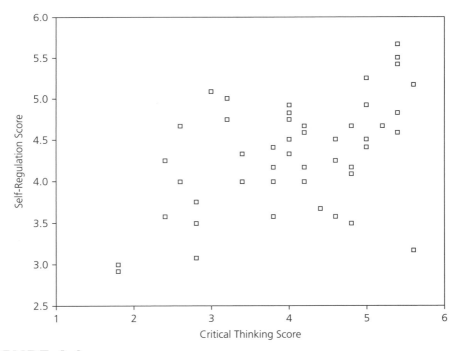

FIGURE 4.1.   *A scatterplot of a positive correlation*

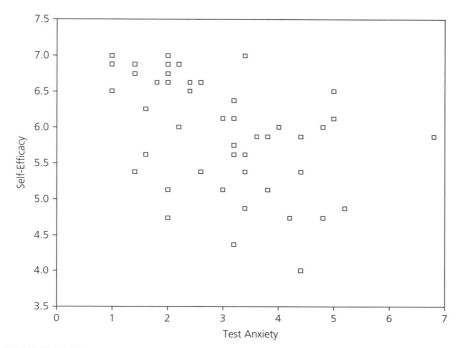

FIGURE 4.2.   *A scatterplot of a negative correlation*

of a negative correlation. In other words, as test anxiety goes up, self-confidence goes down (and vice versa). A zero correlation occurs when there is no statistical relationship between two variables. Instead of a scatterplot that has points moving from lower left to upper right (positive correlation) or upper left to lower right (negative correlation), a zero correlation will show no trend on the scatterplot: the points will seem randomly placed.

CAUSATION AND PREDICTION

Prediction means that if a researcher knows a person's score on one measure or variable, the researcher will have a good guess about what the person's score is on another measure. For example, a significant predictor of how someone will vote in an election is how often they attend church. The more often people attend church, the more likely they are to vote Republican. The less often people attend church, the more likely they are to vote Democratic. In this case we would say that church attendance predicts voting behavior. In contrast (and as an extreme example), knowing someone's shoe size would tell us very little about voting behavior. In this case we would say that shoe size is a poor predictor of voting behavior and that there is zero correlation between the two variables.

One of the goals of social science research is prediction. In an effort to understand and improve human affairs, social scientists believe that the more they know, the more they can predict; the more they can predict, the more they can intervene to increase positive outcomes or prevent negative outcomes. For example, research by officials at a county health department discovered that teenagers' main source of alcohol (before they were old enough to buy it legally) was taking it from their parents without the parents' knowledge. This was contrary to an intuition that teenagers were obtaining alcohol illegally from rogue store owners who were selling to underage people. With this information in hand, public health officials de-emphasized efforts to work with law enforcement on illegal sales and began a program entitled "Attitudes Matter . . . Parents, Alcohol, and Youth." Among other interventions, the program sought to educate parents on being aware of the alcohol they have in the house, being at home when teenagers have friends over, and encouraging parents to call other parents when their children are going over to a house to ensure that alcohol will not be available. In short, a big predictor of teen drinking was found to be availability of alcohol from parents. From this knowledge, researchers and practitioners came up with a plan to reduce teen drinking.

Prediction is not the same as **causation,** which in social science refers to the claim that a change in one variable (independent variable) *creates* a change in another variable (dependent variable). The burden of proof for causation is higher than for prediction, and the designs discussed in this chapter offer predictive power but do not offer causal proof. (Chapters 5 and 6 discuss causal designs.)

In short, social scientists believe three components must be present to infer causation. First, there must be *covariation*. In other words, as one variable changes, another variable must change. This is the same criterion for inferring prediction, and so the designs discussed in this chapter satisfy this criterion. Second, there must be *time order*. Specifically, cause must precede effect. In surveys, we often do not know which came first. Returning to our church/voting example, it is not clear which came first: church attendance or voting. In other words, does church attendance cause one to become Republican? Or does voting Republican set a complex causal system in place that creates church-going people? Correlational designs cannot determine this causal connection. Finally, other plausible causal variables must be eliminated. Elimination of other potential causes is best done in experimental research. Experimental research, as we will see in Chapter 5, most often eliminates other causal variables by randomly assigning participants to different experimental conditions. This random assignment will, over a large enough number of participants, make the effects of any other possible causal variables balance out. Such balancing is not possible with correlational research, because we cannot randomly assign people to different conditions. For example, in the Behavioral Risk Factor Surveillance Survey from the Centers for Disease Control, there is a positive correlation between reported health status (excellent, very good, good, fair, or poor) and level of education. In other words, as your level of education goes up, so too does your self-reported health status. Using level of education as the predictor variable and health status as the criterion variable, we can say that education predicts health status—but we cannot say that education *causes* increased health status. There was no random assignment of people to education levels. We do not know which came first, health status or education. Also, we cannot eliminate other plausible causal variables. For example, there is also a positive correlation between health status and number of vegetables consumed per day. Thus, number of vegetables consumed becomes a plausible alternate explanation for overall health.

Such a situation, in which one variable is correlated with two other variables, is common in correlation research. Because of the lack of experimental control, most correlational researchers look for predictive relationships and stop short of making claims about causation. The next Your Turn box provides some entertaining correlation/causation exercises. Read these and try to determine what factors might explain the correlations.

YOUR TURN

Correlation and Causation

Can you come up with causal explanations for these correlations?

1. People who ate Frosted Flakes as children had half the cancer rate of those who never ate it. Conversely, those who often ate oatmeal were four times more likely to develop cancer than those who did not. Does this mean that Frosted Flakes cereal prevents cancer and oatmeal causes it?

2. Scientists have linked obesity with television watching. What are some possible explanations for this correlation? What causes what?

3. Divorce is not good for your health, claims a best-selling book. Divorced males under the age of 70 are much more likely to die from heart disease, lung cancer, and stomach cancer. Their suicide rate is five times as high; their fatal car accident rate is four times as high. Is divorce the cause of these maladies?

4. There is a positive correlation between milk consumption and incidence of cancer. Does drinking milk cause cancer?

5. The amount of body lice was *positively* correlated with good health. That is, the more body lice people had, the healthier they were. Does this mean you should hope to get infested with body lice as soon as possible? What explanation could exist for this correlation?

Source: These problems were compiled by Bolt (2001) and also appear in VanderStoep and Pintrich (2008).

DATA GATHERING

Surveys

Surveys are the best way to collect a large amount of data from a large number of people in a short amount of time. Surveys are very robust and can be used in many life domains. Author VanderStoep spent five years directing a social research center, which conducted surveys for local agencies. Consider the following examples of when the research center used surveys for these organizations:

1. A sheriff's department conducts a survey of residents on their familiarity with the hazards of methamphetamine use in their community.

2. A U.S. landscape furniture company conducts a survey of potential customers in Canada to determine what particular needs these international clients might have.

3. Public school administrators survey voters to gauge citizens' willingness to vote for a $50 million bond proposal to build a new high school.

Constructing Survey Items—You Only Get One Chance   Once a survey is produced, the train has left the station, and you as a researcher must live with whatever decisions you made during preparation. Thus, it is crucial to pay attention to detail *before* you send out the survey. The two most important details that will ensure a successful survey are proper sampling and construction of quality items. We discussed the different sampling strategies for all methodologies in Chapter 2, so we will not revisit them here. In general, because the goal of a survey is to draw conclusions about the underlying population from which the sample was drawn, it is usually best to employ a random-sampling technique in survey research.

A survey is only as good as the items of which it is made. There are several keys to constructing good survey items:

1. *Have a symmetric set of response alternatives.* **Response alternatives** are the choices of answers on a survey from which respondents select. For example, a national restaurant chain used to invite customers to complete an automated telephone survey after their meal. The questions asked about relevant issues such as taste of food, appearance of food, and quality of wait staff. The response alternatives were: Excellent, Very Good, Good, Fair, and Poor. Although subject to individual interpretation, one could certainly make the argument that there are three positive response alternatives, one neutral, and only one negative alternative. We recommend an equal number of positive and negative responses. In this survey, the response alternatives could be Excellent, Good, Fair, Poor, and Very Poor. Alternatively, to keep the words similar on both sides of this attitude continuum, you could use Very Good, Good, Fair, Poor, and Very Poor.

2. *Avoid double-barreled questions.* A **double-barreled question** is a survey item that has two distinct components in the stem of the question; for example, the question "Do you support increasing the state sales tax and increasing funding for K-12 schools?" A respondent might support increasing the sales tax but not increasing funding for schools; conversely, a respondent might oppose increasing the sales tax but support increasing school funding. Either way, the results are difficult to interpret because it is not possible to know whether the respondents supported only one (and if so, which one) aspect of the question or both. The best solution to this problem is to ask separate questions about increasing sales tax and increasing school funding.

3. *Make the stem of the question unbiased.* Researchers should avoid cuing respondents that one answer is seen as more desirable than another, or leading respondents toward a particular way of thinking. Examples of (fictitious) biased survey questions are: (a) "Do you support liberating the Iraqi people from a vicious dictator by supporting the War in Iraq?" and (b) "Do you support funding America's most precious national resource, our children, by fully funding the Head Start preschool program?" (You may have noticed that these are also double-barreled questions.) Of course, one person's bias may be another person's objectivity. The best way to ensure that you are being unbiased is to ask someone else (preferably someone who is not familiar with the research and someone who does not share your values and opinions) to review the items to check for possible wording bias.

We mentioned previously that making the response scale symmetric is important, but it is important to select the proper *type* of response scale for your survey item. Surveys most often measure one of two phenomena: attitudes or behaviors. The response scale for attitude questions usually contains one of the following:

Strongly support	Support	Neutral	Oppose	Strongly oppose
Strongly agree	Agree	Neutral	Disagree	Strongly disagree

These response scales are *five-point* Likert scales (Likert scales were discussed in Chapter 2), but researchers also use three-point, seven-point, and sometimes even nine-point scales. We recommend five-point scales for attitude questions, because it provides enough response alternatives to reflect the various opinions, yet is not so large as to make it cumbersome for the respondents. With a seven-point response scale, it will be more difficult to find a descriptor to go with each response alternative. For seven-point scales, researchers usually add the word *very* to the two ends of the continua shown earlier. Occasionally, and more often with multipoint response scales, researchers will attach descriptors only to the **anchors,** the two endpoints of a response scale.

Another decision that will have to be made about the response scale is whether a midpoint should be included. The preceding examples—with an odd number of response alternatives—include a midpoint, usually identified by "neutral." Sometimes researchers do not want respondents to fence-straddle, and so will change a five-point scale to a four-point scale or a seven-point scale to a six-point scale by eliminating the midpoint. This is recommended if the survey is serving a very specific real-world purpose. For example, if a public school district surveys voters about whether they will support a bond proposal for a new high school, it might want people to give a clear answer. The disadvantage of having no midpoint is that there might be respondents who genuinely are neutral. Perhaps these people agree with some aspects of the issue and disagree with others, but the net result is a middle-of-the-road opinion. In the school example, knowing that there are people who are neutral or undecided (the midpoint of a survey question) might also be helpful because the district could target an aggressive marketing campaign to the undecided respondents. A related disadvantage of not including a midpoint is that some people mistake "neutral" for "no opinion," "not applicable," or "unsure."

We urge people to think of a midpoint as the response for people who are knowledgeable about an issue and are undecided. In addition, we recommend including a separate response alternative for those who have no opinion, are unaware of the issue, or are unsure. This extra response alternative helps clarify the issue for respondents and makes it easier for the researchers to interpret the results. In data analysis, we recommend excluding the "no opinion" responses from analysis and including the midpoint responses.

The response scales for behaviors are not usually different, because instead of asking a respondent to identify a point on a continuum that most closely responds to their attitudes, respondents are asked to estimate how often they engage in a certain behavior. This can be done by asking them to estimate the frequency of their behavior, such as:

Very frequently	Frequently	Occasionally	Rarely	Very rarely
Always or almost always	Frequently	Occasionally	Seldom	Never or almost never

As you can probably see, it is difficult to build the same kind of symmetry into behavior estimates as into attitude items. One difficulty lies in determining the inverse of a word such as "frequently." We chose *rarely* in the first example. It is also difficult to identify what the midpoint of the response scale should be. In attitude items, it is usually "neutral." In behavior items, we picked "occasionally" in our preceding examples, but that decision was arbitrary. Perhaps "sometimes" is a better midpoint. A third problem with this approach to measuring behavior is simply deciding which descriptors to use and in what order. For example, the word "frequently" implies more occurrences than "occasionally," but what about "occasionally" versus "sometimes"?

These problems can be avoided by asking participants the actual *number* of times they engaged in the behavior of interest. For example, author VanderStoep consulted with an outdoor furniture manufacturer, which conducts an annual customer-satisfaction survey of architects and facilities managers. One survey item asks "How often do you purchase outdoor furniture for your company?" The response alternatives are:

Once a month or more	Every 1–6 months	Every 6–12 months	Less than once a year

The clear advantage to this approach is it provides a more precise quantitative estimate—a numerical range—of the behavior. Another related advantage is that it removes the need for respondents to interpret the question; this cuts down on variability due to different people's understanding of words like *occasionally*. One potential disadvantage arises if researchers do not know enough about the behavior and therefore do not provide the proper numerical ranges. For example, if 95% of architects in the outdoor-furniture survey only purchased furniture once a year or less, there would be little variance in responses, and the results of this item would not be helpful. A solution to this problem is simply to create an open-ended question: "How often in the past two years have you purchased outdoor furniture?" The researchers can then group responses into categories that meet their needs.

Whether one collects attitudinal or behavioral data from surveys, it is worth remembering our discussion from Chapter 3 of the self-serving bias. In general, we think a lot more of ourselves than is actually true, and this comes out in surveys. Surveys are very helpful for lots of real-life social research needs, but as with any technique discussed in this book, they have disadvantages. Always keep in mind that people's self-reports are subject to both memory error and intentional distortion.

YOUR TURN

Constructing Survey Items

Following is an exercise developed by Laura Madson at New Mexico State University (2005). Identify the problem with each of the survey questions, and suggest modifications.

1. I oppose raising taxes.
2. How often do you have sex?
3. I exercise often.
4. Although I know it is important, I don't always practice safe sex.
5. I make it a practice to never lie.

Telephone Surveys Contacting potential survey respondents via telephone is very common. One advantage of a phone survey is that most people have phones. A second advantage is that the participation rate is much higher than surveys sent through surface mail.

Of course, there are disadvantages to phone surveys as well. Although most people still have land lines, there is a trend for people to disconnect their land telephone lines and use only a cellular telephone. Currently, cellular telephone numbers are usually not available through the normal channels for constructing a sampling frame (see below). Although the Federal Communications Commission announced Local to Wireless Number Portability (LWNP) in 2004, allowing customers to change a former land line into a cellular number, it remains to be seen whether people will actually do this. Although the land line-cellular issue will change over time, for now most cell phones are not available for inclusion in a sampling frame.

A second disadvantage of phone surveys is the increasing popularity of caller ID. People are far less likely to answer a phone call from an organization that they do not recognize (even if it is a reputable scientific organization). Fairly obviously, this will reduce participation rates. Also, if those with caller ID are different from those without caller ID, it could create a response bias (Chapter 2).

A third disadvantage of telephone surveys is that phone-survey samples are not always representative. For example, more females complete phone surveys than males. This may be because females are more often at home, or perhaps because men are more likely to refuse to participate once contacted. In phone surveys, furthermore, younger residents are more likely to be underrepresented in the sample. This may be because younger residents are more likely to have cell phones, but this was true even before cell phones became popular. Young people may simply be in their homes less.

In addition, researchers must be selective about when to contact potential respondents, and how the contact time affects who gets included in the sample. Calling during the day will oversample those who are home during the day, such as those who stay at home with young children (mostly women) or those who work evening or overnight shifts. Calling in the evening tends to oversample those without evening commitments outside of the home, such as elderly persons or those with limited mobility. A further consideration is that residents often confuse telephone surveys with telemarketing. This is further muddied because some telemarketers disguise their sales intentions by falsely indicating that they are conducting a survey. (In the political arena, this is called "push-polling." If you live in Iowa, New Hampshire, or a state with an early presidential primary, you have probably received at least one push-poll.) It is not long before the true purpose of that call is revealed. Such chicanery among non-researchers hampers the honest efforts of actual researchers.

In 2003, the Federal Trade Commission (FTC) passed the Amended Telemarketing Sales Rule, colloquially known as the national Do Not Call Registry. This policy allows households to register their phone number with the FTC, after which telemarketers are prohibited from making unsolicited sales phone calls. Nonprofit and research organizations are exempt from the do-not-call restrictions. In one way, this is a benefit to researchers because for those who are registered there will be less incoming phone traffic, which might in turn increase participation rates. However, the intense popularity of the registry (more than 100 million Americans registered as of August 2005) suggests that perhaps citizens have grown weary of intrusions into their homes. It is difficult to know whether citizens distinguish between for-profit, nonprofit, and research telephone calls.

Telephone numbers for survey research are available for purchase from companies that specialize in creating sampling frames, such as Survey Sampling, Inc. There are two approaches to sampling for telephone surveys. One is **directory-listed sampling.** This procedure randomly selects households with listed telephone numbers. Households that have unlisted phone numbers or families that have recently moved will not be included in any sample developed using directory-listed samples.

The other procedure is **random-digit dialing.** From a technical aspect, this procedure can take several forms, which are beyond the scope of this book. The actual production of these random numbers is a daunting task. Fortunately, there are for-profit companies that specialize in exactly this type of work, so you will not need to know how to do this randomization yourself. However, it is important to be aware of two aspects of random-digit dialing. First, because nonlisted numbers are included, the sample will be more representative. For example, random-digit dialing increases the percentage of minority respondents. This is a good strategy to use if the researcher places high importance on reaching subgroups that would otherwise not be accessed with directory-listed sampling. A second consideration is that random-digit dialing is more expensive. It is more expensive because some of the numbers will not be working phone numbers, so you will have to pay callers more money and they will have a lower number of completed calls per hour. The extra financial cost involved in using random-digit dialing must be weighed against the advantage of increasing the representativeness of the sample.

Mail Surveys Paper-and-pencil surveys delivered through surface mail are effective for reaching a large group or geographical area. With minimal costs for survey production, the major financial cost is postage. The standard process is to create a survey using survey-production software. Such software produces a survey with response "bubbles" that respondents fill in to indicate their answers. These surveys can then be scanned by a related software product. These surveys are printed at a printing shop (photocopying on an office copier usually does not work) and mailed to respondents with a cover letter and a return envelope enclosed with the survey. Many colleges and universities have the survey-production software and optical scanner needed for such projects. If such technology is not available in house, there are for-profit companies that will perform this service. If these options are not viable for your project, we recommend photocopying the survey and hand-entering the data (Chapter 1). This will not look as professional as an optically scannable survey, and thus this option is chosen less commonly, but the approach is perfectly acceptable and is still frequently used.

Here are several practical tips to make your mail survey user-friendly and increase response rate.

1. *Include a cover letter that is only one page long.* The cover letter should be long enough to tell potential respondents how important the survey is and how much their opinions are valued, but short enough so that they do not become bored or overwhelmed.

2. *Put a return date in bold.* If respondents are not given a specific date by which to return the survey, it will continue to drop to the bottom of the stack and will never get completed.

3. *Send a reminder email or postcard.* Although a postcard will add postage cost, we have found that such a follow-up increases the response rate. Reminder emails are easy, and can be done without cost or inconvenience. However, with a mail survey it is unlikely that the researcher will also have access to the sampling frame's email addresses.

4. *Don't make your survey too long.* How long is too long? There is no one answer to this question. In general, shorter is always better. Surveys conducted for organizations that have lots of departments or constituencies tend to grow because each group wants its own items included. We encourage you always to strive for a one-page survey (front and back). This may seem short, but if you use survey-production software, you can fit much more on one page than you can on one page of a

Microsoft Word document. Also, it is better to print on the front and back of one page than to put two pages collated or stapled together.

5. *Look professional.* Survey-production software often gives a more "scientific" appearance to a survey than a document produced in Microsoft Word, although with the *Table* function and special characters like boxes and circles Word documents can also be made to look professional. In most cases we recommend using survey-production software if it is available to you. Still, in our consulting, some clients have told us that they believe their potential respondents prefer the more informal-looking Word documents. The customer is (almost) always right.

6. *Consider putting surveys on heavier-than-usual paper.* This adds to sturdiness and professionalism. If you are using survey-production software, you will need to consult the manual to determine how thick the paper can be and still be read by the scanner.

7. *Timing is everything.* Avoid sending surveys out between the middle of November and early January. People get very busy at this time of the year and surface mail surveys, in particular, are likely to get ignored amidst heavy holiday mail. We also urge caution during peak vacation times of July and August. If you are doing work for educational institutions, the time leading up to spring recess is also a less-than-optimal time.

After the initial mailing, allow approximately one month for respondents to complete the survey. This gives people sufficient time to return it. If time and money are sufficient, send a follow-up postcard (see Step 3) two weeks after the initial mailing. Respondents do not usually identify themselves on the survey, so follow-ups will have to be sent to everyone in the sampling frame. The postcard should indicate the following:

■ Because the responses are anonymous, there is no way of knowing who has already completed the survey. Therefore, everyone is receiving this note. Thank those who have completed the survey and ask those who have not completed it to do so.

■ Remind respondents of the importance of the survey.

■ Remind people of the due date (printed in bold).

■ Give respondents a telephone number to call or an email address to contact if they have lost the survey and would like a new copy.

The main advantage of a mail survey is that it allows the researcher to sample a large group of people in a large geographical region. Because almost everyone has a mailing address, it is not required that respondents have a telephone or computer. Furthermore, respondents do not have to be home when the survey is administered (as in a telephone survey), which allows respondents to answer the questions at their own pace, to think carefully about their responses, and to offer more in-depth written comments that are difficult to capture in a phone interview.

The biggest disadvantage of a mail survey is the response rate. A "cold" survey from an organization with which the respondents have no relationship is going to yield a response of only about 10% to 15%. In terms of absolute size of sample, this might not be problematic with large sampling frames.

The biggest problem with a low response rate is that it is very likely that those who completed the survey will differ significantly on various characteristics compared to those who did not complete the survey. Imagine a survey on attitudes regarding the constitutionality of same-sex marriages. If you sent a survey to 100,000 randomly selected Americans, chances are you would get 10,000 to 15,000 of them back. That sample size is large enough to draw conclusions from; however, if those who returned the survey were different from the 85,000 people who did not respond, you would not have a representative picture of what the entire population believes. In this case, those who returned your survey may be either strongly supportive of same-sex marriages or highly condemning of them. This could paint a picture of a very polarized citizenry on this issue, because the moderate people in the middle or those with no opinion at all were not included in the sample.

In general, mail surveys can sample a broad range of people who might not be easily reachable through phone or email. They also allow respondents to answer questions on their own time at their own pace. They also allow researchers to ask questions in more depth, which could produce a richer, more meaningful dataset.

Web/Email Surveys At a very fast pace, Web/email surveys are becoming extremely popular. Web surveys have evolved quickly in the past ten years, and they are very user-friendly. Anyone with access to a computer can produce a survey using a website such as zoomerang.com or surveymonkey.com, which allows production and distribution of Web surveys. This is a great tool for college students doing independent research projects.

The advantages of Web surveys are several. First, the financial savings are compelling, as there are no printing or postage costs. In fact, one estimate is that an email survey costs an average of $1.32 per completed response, compared to $10.97 for each completed response using surface mail (Kaplowitz, Hadlock, & Levine, 2004). Second, response times are faster. Mail surveys tend to sit on a pile of other papers for up to several weeks. In contrast, respondents tend to complete Web surveys quite quickly. At our institution, for example, approximately 90% of total responses from Web surveys are completed within the first 48 hours after the initial email notification is sent. Third, the response rate is higher than a survey sent via surface mail. Responding to Web surveys is more convenient and hassle-free, which increases the response rate.

One disadvantage of Web surveys is that the sample is biased toward those with more technological training or greater access to the Internet. If a large portion of the sampling frame is wired to the Internet, this is not an issue, and it will become less of an issue as greater numbers of people obtain Internet access. Conducting Web surveys with college students is a very good idea. College students have high-speed Internet access and check their email frequently.

A second possible disadvantage, which may become a greater disadvantage over time, is that Web surveys are so easy and inexpensive to administer that respondents to whom the surveys are mailed may become weary or overloaded. Just as people became overwhelmed with unsolicited surface mail, people may eventually begin to see Web surveys as spam that they immediately delete in the same way they throw away paper surveys that come in the mail. This will be less of a problem if the email directing respondents to the URL containing the survey is from someone familiar to them and the issues are important to the respondents.

Face-to-Face Interviews   Another method for collecting self-report data is to speak with people in person. Surveys completed using this technique are often similar to telephone or mail surveys in terms of content. Face-to-face interviews allow a wider channel of communication. For example, the in-person situation may be more amenable to asking participants to repeat their answers, or may give interviewers more time to write down responses.

Furthermore, this technique may offer the opportunity to ask follow-up questions based on participants' responses to previous questions. This allows deeper exploration of issues. For example, imagine an interview question on an exit survey by a restaurant that asked, "On a scale of 1 to 5, with '1' being very dissatisfied and '5' being very satisfied, how would you rate the quality of food?" Interviewers could be instructed to ask follow-up questions of those who answered 1 or 2. For example, follow-up questions could be, "What did you order?"; "What specifically was dissatisfying—temperature, presentation, promptness of service?" This is also possible with a phone survey, but the personalized nature of the interaction may produce more detailed responses from the participants, thus giving researchers more in-depth data. This is difficult to do in a mail or Internet survey.

The major disadvantage of the face-to-face interview is that it is quite costly in terms of time and money. Prescheduled interviews can take a long time to set up. A university research organization teamed up with the students enrolled in an adult-development class to conduct care-satisfaction interviews with adult children of elderly residents living in a nursing home. Because there were undergraduate students from the class who could conduct the interviews, it was cost-effective to do such a project. Without these volunteers, the project would have been much more expensive.

Face-to-face interviews can be useful when researchers know that potential respondents will be located at a particular place. For example, at amusement parks or shopping centers, you may be approached by an employee armed with a PDA and a set of questions. The researchers ask a variety of demographic questions: how many in your party, how many days are you staying, how many stores did you visit, how many times have you visited the park, what is your home zip code, and so on. This type of face-to-face interview is actually quite inexpensive because the participants are already present. These questions allow business owners to develop a profile of their customer base and to fashion marketing and advertising to improve sales. The response rate of face-to-face interviews is also very high. It is far more difficult for someone to turn down a researcher in person than to refuse to participate over the phone, on the Web, or via surface mail. Also, people at places like amusement parks are usually in a good mood, and research in social psychology shows that happy people are more helpful (Myers, 2008).

Researchers, then, have several options for survey data collection. Like most decisions in social research, there is no single perfect solution. Rather, each choice comes with advantages and disadvantages. Table 4.1 summarizes the benefits and drawbacks of different survey options.

TABLE 4.1   Advantages and Disadvantages of Various Options for Administering Surveys

Data-Collection Option	Advantages	Disadvantages
Telephone	Most people have telephones, creating a large sampling frame Higher response rate than surface mail Little work for respondents	People may confuse survey researchers with telemarketers, resulting in lower participation rate Caller ID and call-screening lower participation rate Selection bias: those with unlisted numbers and those who use only cell phones are not in sampling frame
Surface Mail	Addresses are easy to purchase through database company, creating a large database that is the most representative of all sampling frames (but see disadvantage of low response rate) Respondents can complete the survey at their own pace, providing long, written, narrative answers and therefore thorough data Because respondents can complete on their own time, can likely conduct a slightly longer survey than by telephone without lowering response rate	Low response rate, unless incentives are involved or population has vested interest in survey Expensive in terms of labor and postage More work for respondents than telephone survey The longer the survey, the more persuasion (for example, financial incentives, postcard follow-ups) must be used to improve response rate
Internet/Email	Low cost; minimal set-up costs and no sending charge Less work for respondents than surface mail (but more than telephone), provided respondents have access to the Internet Larger sampling frame than other techniques	Response bias: those with technological resources and knowledge or computers are more likely to respond
Face-to-Face Interview	Very thorough data, both quantitative and qualitative Allows for probes and follow-up questions to tailor interviews based on respondents' unique knowledge or experience	Expensive in terms of labor costs Smaller sample size than other techniques

YOUR TURN

Face-to-Face Interviews

This project is best completed with another student from the class. Interview people as they leave the university cafeteria after dinner, asking them these questions:

1. On a scale from 1 to 5, with 1 being very poor and 5 being very good, how would you rate the quality of the meal?

2. What part of the meal was the LEAST satisfying?

   a. Main course

   b. Vegetables

   c. Fruit

   d. Dessert

   e. Drinks

Also record the student's gender. Save these responses. We will use them to demonstrate data analysis later in the chapter.

Observations

Whereas surveys ask for people's self-reported behavior or attitudes, observations collect actual occurrences of behavior. One type of observational technique is called **participant observation.** In such an investigation, the researcher enmeshes himself or herself in the community under study. As a participant in this community, the researcher also makes records of behaviors of the other members of the group. One advantage to such an investigation is that observations of behavior tend to be more reliable than self-reported survey data (recall the self-serving bias from Chapter 3). Another advantage is that behaviors that can be observed by a participant might not be as amenable to survey-style data collection. A disadvantage of participant observation is the expense in time and salary to employ researchers to perform the observations. A famous example of a participant observation is from Rosenhan (1973). In his article "On Being Sane in Insane Places," he documented the reactions of hospital workers to patients with mental illness. This was a participant observation because the researcher was housed in this hospital as a patient, so the researcher was able to gain first-hand experience of the people being studied.

With a **non-participant observation** technique, the researchers observe a group of people from outside of the group and thus do not embed themselves in the community under study while they conduct their investigations. For example, a researcher observes children's behavior on the playground. An advantage of the non-participant observation is that the observer can remain detached, and therefore might be less prone to bias. The disadvantage is the inverse: not being enmeshed in the community does not allow the intimacy and depth of observation that a participant observation can achieve.

The actual data collection can be done in the form of either event sampling or time sampling. **Event sampling** involves recording all or a proportion of the specific instances of the behavior of interest. A behavioral scientist interested in studying aggression may choose a certain number of the aggressive acts she observes (say, every fourth), and code those acts for content, such as: (a) to whom the aggression was directed, (b) whether it was instrumental or hostile aggression, (c) type of aggression (verbal, physical, or both), and (d) gender configuration (girl aggressing against girl, boy against boy, girl against boy, or boy against girl).

If behavior is very frequent and recording of every episode (or even every fourth episode) becomes unmanageable, **time sampling** could be used. This involves recording behavior by taking systematic observations at preset intervals. These intervals could be fixed, such as for 2 minutes every 15 minutes; or random, such as for 2 minutes 4 times an hour at randomly selected time periods. All of the aggressive acts that are observed during those eight minutes (for example, 10:08–10:10 A.M.; 10:23–10:25 A.M.; 10:38–10:40 A.M.; 10:53–10:55 A.M.) each hour are recorded and classified just as in event sampling.

Deciding how to classify observational data is crucial to a meaningful observational study. A common approach is to develop checklists. A checklist provides a set of descriptors that transform the data into quantifiable components. The checklist provides a description of the type of aggression, the aggressor, and the victim. The researcher could also complete a **rating scale** for each behavior—an observational record in which the observer records his or her own judgment about the nature of the aggressive act.

YOUR TURN

Non-Participant Observation

This observation should take place in a living room of a college apartment or house where there is a television with a remote control. For this observation, you need to be sitting in the room when at least one other person is watching TV and using the remote. Situate yourself in the room and pretend to do your homework or other activity with a clipboard and recording sheet and a timing device. Try not to draw attention to yourself. Record the amount of time people watch one channel before they change channels. Also record the gender of the person doing the channel surfing. Your data sheet should look something like this:

Amount of Time Watching Channel Before Changing	Gender	
_____ (sec)	M	F
_____ (sec)	M	F

Take the average of the men's and women's average time watching a channel. Do you see a difference? In the next chapter we will show you how you can perform a statistical test to determine if the two means are significantly different.

DATA ANALYSIS

Descriptive Statistics: Central Tendency and Spread

The most common measure of central tendency is the **mean:** the arithmetic average of a set of numbers. Means are important for descriptive studies because they provide information about the average participant's score on a measure. College admissions officers are interested in an incoming class's mean GPA and SAT scores. The mean of the current year can be compared to the means of previous years, or the mean of males can be compared to that of females, and so forth. The two other measures of central tendency are the **mode,** the most frequently occurring number in a dataset; and the **median,** the middle score of numbers in a dataset. (With an odd number of observations, the middle score is the median; with an even number of observations, most people and computer programs select the average of the two middle scores as the median.)

A measure of spread measures how much variability there is among the observed scores on a variable. A straightforward measure of spread is the **range:** the lowest score in the dataset subtracted from the highest score. Two common but more complex measures of spread that quantitative researchers use are variance and standard deviation. The *variance* of a sample is the sum of the squared difference between each observation and the mean value, divided by one less than the number of observations (that is, if your sample has 100 people in it, you would divide by 99).

The variance is best computed by following these steps.

1. Create a table as shown here, which contains the GPAs of incoming college first-year students. For this example, the mean GPA is 3.1

Column 1: GPA	Column 2: GPA Minus Mean GPA	Column 3: Square of Column 2
3.4	0.3	0.09
3.1	0	0
3.9	0.8	0.64
2.0	−1.1	1.21
Total	*0*	*1.94*

2. Now divide the total of Column 3 (called the sum of squared deviations) and divide by the number of observations minus 1. In this case, $1.94 \div 3 = 0.647$. Column 2 (called the sum of the deviations) should always equal zero. This serves as a good check on your math. Every number in Column 3 should be positive, because each entry is squared, thus making all values positive numbers.

The **standard deviation** of a sample is the square root of the variance, and is defined as the average amount any one observation will differ from the mean. The standard deviation is used more often than the variance because it is on the same metric as the original values. Remember that the variance is created by squaring the values, so taking the square root returns the number to its original metric. In the preceding example, the square root of .647 is .804.

Statistics texts can provide more detail on how to compute measures, but these values are computed very easily using statistical software. More important than how to compute these is knowing that the more varied a set of numerical responses, the higher the measure of spread. When the variance is too big, the mean is not as informative. For example, if the variance of the GPA of an entering class is large, then knowing the mean does not tell the admissions department much about the entering class, because the students are so varied. Figure 4.3 shows the mean, median, mode, variance, and standard deviation for a Test Anxiety scale for a group of students in a college science course (produced using SPSS). Figure 4.4 shows the frequency distribution: the numerical scores and the number of times that a score appears. The Your Turn box shows you how to produce descriptive statistics and a frequency distribution using SPSS.

YOUR TURN

Descriptive Statistics

1. Either create a new dataset by typing in new data (see Chapter 1), or use an existing dataset. For this exercise, type in the four GPAs used previously: 3.4, 3.1, 3.9, 2.0.

2. To obtain descriptive statistics, select Analyze/Descriptive Statistics/Descriptives. Clicking on the Options button will allow you to select mean, range, variance, and standard deviation. Click OK.

3. To obtain a frequency distribution, select Analyze/Descriptive Statistics/Frequencies. Clicking on the Statistics button will also allow you to generate descriptive statistics, just as the *Descriptive* function does. Click *OK*. Figure 4.3 shows the output from the descriptives command and Figure 4.4 shows the output from the frequencies command.

N	Valid	49
	Missing	8
Mean		2.9306
Median		3.0000
Mode		2.00[a]
Std. Deviation		1.33638
Variance		1.78592

[a]Multiple modes exist. The smallest value is shown.

FIGURE 4.3. *Descriptive statistics of test anxiety scores for students in "Science and Technology in Everyday Life" class*

Inferential Statistics: Understanding Statistical Significance

Besides using the descriptive statistics just described, researchers are also interested in determining if there are differences in their data. This is done using **inferential statistics,** which are statistics used to draw conclusions about significant relationships between variables. To understand inferential statistics, we refer back to our discussion of sample and population from Chapter 2. Because research is not done on populations (entire groups of people), but rather on samples (subsets of populations), there is a component of uncertainty attached to researchers' conclusions. This uncertainty stems from not being completely sure if the sample accurately represents or estimates the true nature of the population. For example, consider the example of channel-changing frequency in the Your Turn box earlier in this chapter. If we found that men changed channels more often than women, we would use inferential statistics to make a claim as to whether our sample of men and women were similar to the entire population of men and women. How would we do that?

We do it by making a claim about how likely the relationship between variables (in this case, gender and channel-changing) is to be true. This claim is made in terms of a probability, and is called a **level of significance.** The level of significance is the probability that a relationship between variables is *not* real, but rather due to chance factors. Most social science researchers use .05 as the level of significance to decide if a relationship is **statistically significant.** A finding is deemed statistically significant if the level of significance surpasses a threshold such that researchers are willing to conclude that the finding is a "real" relationship rather than an artifact of chance factors. For example, if the difference in channel-changing behavior between men and women had a level of significance of less than .05, then the researchers would conclude that men and women differ on this variable. (Often the phrase used is: "The finding is statistically significant.")

TEST ANXIETY POSTTEST

		Frequency	Valid Percent	Cumulative Percent
Valid	1.00	5	10.2	10.2
	1.40	3	6.1	16.3
	1.60	2	4.1	20.4
	1.80	1	2.0	22.4
	2.00	6	12.2	34.7
	2.20	2	4.1	38.8
	2.40	2	4.1	42.9
	2.60	2	4.1	46.9
	3.00	2	4.1	51.0
	3.20	6	12.2	63.3
	3.40	4	8.2	71.4
	3.60	1	2.0	73.5
	3.80	2	4.1	77.6
	4.00	1	2.0	79.6
	4.20	1	2.0	81.6
	4.40	3	6.1	87.8
	4.80	2	4.1	91.8
	5.00	2	4.1	95.9
	5.20	1	2.0	98.0
	6.80	1	2.0	100.0
	Total	49	100.0	

FIGURE 4.4. *Frequency distribution of test anxiety scores for students in "Science and Technology in Everyday Life" class*

It must be made clear that with such claims of a "real" relationship between variables comes the possibility that the researchers are wrong and that the relationship does not really exist. This possibility is quantified by the *p* **value**, which refers to the likelihood that the difference between two variables that was found in the current study would be this large or larger if you assumed that there was no difference. In other words, if it is assumed that men's and women's channel-changing behavior does not differ, and it is discovered that they do, what is the chance that such a difference is only due to chance? The smaller the *p* value, the less likely it is that such a finding is due to chance and that the difference is "real."

The larger the difference, the smaller the *p* value, and the smaller the chance that the researchers are wrong to claim that the difference is real. Even so, the study could be wrong—if the researchers found that men and women differ and they actually do not, the researchers' inference would be incorrect. The idea of researchers "being wrong" is called a **Type I error:** a researcher believes that a relationship is true when in fact it is due only to chance factors. To reiterate, the lower the *p* value, the lower the chance of a Type I error. If an inferential statistic has a *p* value of .02, a researcher would say that, if she conducted this study 100 times, approximately 2 times out of 100 a statistically significant difference would *not* be found. The opposite of a Type I error is a **Type II error:** believing there is *not* a difference between two variables when there really is one. You can think of a Type I error as a false positive and a Type II error as a false negative.

Remember that all of this only makes sense when we return to our original point at the beginning of this section: drawing conclusions in social science research involves a degree of chance. As researchers, we make claims in terms of the likelihood that the claim is true. Table 4.2 will help clarify this issue. Next, we illustrate the idea of statistical significance by showing how it applies using different statistical techniques.

TABLE 4.2 **Summary of Type I and Type II Errors**

	What Really Is True in the Population (Unknown)	
	There is a relationship between two variables	There is *not* a relationship between two variables
What Is True in the Sample of Our Study (Known) — There is a relationship between two variables	Study accurately demonstrates what is true in the population	Type I error
There is *not* a relationship between two variables	Type II error	Study accurately demonstrates what is true in the population

Correlation

As stated at the beginning of this chapter, correlations have a direction and a magnitude. The most common statistical measure of correlation is the **Pearson correlation**. The Pearson correlation measures the relationship between two interval variables, and most social scientists use it for ordinal data as well (see discussion in Chapter 3). Its range is from −1.0 to +1.0. The magnitude of a correlation increases as the absolute value of the correlation increases. In other words, the closer a correlation is to +1.0 or −1.0, the greater its magnitude. The Your Turn box shows how to compute correlations using SPSS.

YOUR TURN

Correlation

1. For this exercise, you can collect your own data or use the dataset provided here. This dataset shows height in inches and shoe sizes of 10 adults. Enter these data into SPSS.

Height	Shoe Size
74	11
71	9.5
72	10
72	10.5
73	12
78	13
68	10
74	12
70	10
73	11

2. Select *Analyze/Correlate/Bivariate.*

3. Select the *Pearson* box under the *Correlation Coefficient* section of the dialog window.

4. Move the two variables from the left panel to the right panel. Click OK. Your screen should resemble Figure 4.5.

5. What is the correlation between height and shoe size?

6. How do you interpret this correlation?

7. You can modify the dataset to see how changing some of the values will make the correlation either stronger or weaker.

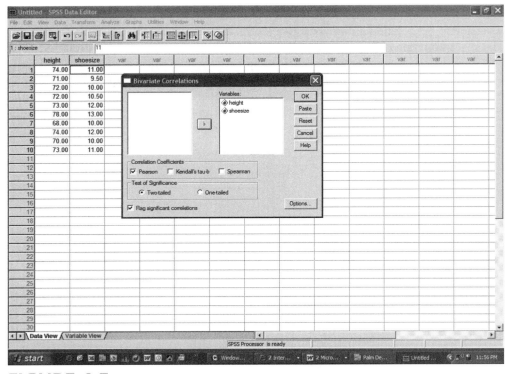

FIGURE 4.5. *Bivariate correlations screen in SPSS*

Figure 4.6 shows output for Pearson correlations using SPSS for a study of college student motivation. This **correlation matrix** (set of correlations among variables in a study) shows the relationship between intrinsic motivation (motivated by the task or challenge itself) and extrinsic motivation (motivated by reward, praise, or other incentive) at the beginning (pretest) and end (posttest) of a college semester. Figure 4.6 shows a statistically significant *positive* correlation between the pretest and posttest measures of intrinsic motivation and the pretest and posttest measures of extrinsic motivation (the SPSS output shows a p value of .000, which means that the probability of making a Type I error is less than .001). How would you interpret these findings? These correlations indicate that people who score high on either intrinsic or extrinsic motivation at the beginning of the semester (pretest) also score high on that measure at the end of the semester (posttest). Likewise, those with low scores at the beginning of the semester were also likely to have low scores at the end of the semester.

Figure 4.6 also shows a statistically significant (if one uses .05 as the acceptable level of significance) *negative* correlation between intrinsic and extrinsic motivation at both pretest and posttest. How would you interpret this finding? This correlation indicates that lower pretest scores on intrinsic motivation are related to *higher* pretest scores

CORRELATIONS

		Intrinsic Motivation Pretest	Intrinsic Motivation Posttest	Extrinsic Motivation Pretest	Extrinsic Motivation Posttest
Intrinsic Motivation Pretest	Pearson Correlation	1	.671**	−.321*	−.275
	Sig. (2-tailed)		.000	.018	.065
Intrinsic Motivation Posttest	Pearson Correlation	.671**	1	−.200	−.309*
	Sig. (2-tailed)	.000		.183	.031
Extrinsic Motivation Pretest	Pearson Correlation	−.321*	−.200	1	.658**
	Sig. (2-tailed)	.018	.183		.000
Extrinsic Motivation Posttest	Pearson Correlation	−.275	−.309*	.658**	1
	Sig. (2-tailed)	.065	.031	.000	

*Correlation is significant at the 0.05 level (2-tailed).
**Correlation is significant at the 0.01 level (2-tailed).

FIGURE 4.6.   *Pearson correlation coefficients using SPSS*

on extrinsic motivation (p value of .018). The same is true for posttest scores (p value of .031).

Cross-Tabulation and Chi-Square

If the research study involves nominal data, it is most helpful to display the data as a *cross-tabulation*. As we mentioned in Chapter 3, cross-tabulation is a method to show how the responses of one nominal variable relate to the responses of another nominal. Figure 4.7 shows SPSS output for a cross-tabulation of gender with the answers to a question regarding sexual abstinence. These data come from a sexual education program for seventh-graders implemented by a nonprofit organization. The inferential statistic used in cross-tabulations is the **chi-square**: a measure of association between two nominal variables. If a chi-square is statistically significant, it means that there is a relationship between the two nominal variables, in this case gender and self-reported future sexual activity. Just as a Pearson correlation shows a relationship between two interval variables,

			Male	Female	Total
During the next year:	I probably will have sex	Count	1	0	1
		% within Question 1	.9%	.0%	.4%
	I am not sure whether or not I will have sex	Count	8	2	10
		% within Question 1	7.2%	1.5%	4.1%
	I probably will not have sex	Count	15	7	22
		% within Question 1	13.5%	5.2%	8.9%
	I am sure I will not have sex	Count	87	126	213
		% within Question 1	78.4%	93.3%	86.6%
Total		Count	111 100.0%	135 100.0%	246

Chi-Square Tests

	Value	df	Asymp. Sig. (*p* value)
Pearson chi-square	12.42	3	.006

FIGURE 4.7. *Cross-tabulations and chi-square statistics using SPSS*

a chi-square shows a relationship between two nominal variables. In this case, the chi-square has a *p* value of less than .05, and so we can conclude that there is a significant difference between males' and females' responses to this question. Looking at the actual values in the cross-tabulation table, it appears that boys are more likely to indicate that they are unsure of their future sexual behavior in the upcoming year and girls are more likely to indicate that they will be abstaining from sexual activity in the upcoming year. Specifically, 7.2% of males and only 1.5% of females indicated that they were "unsure" of whether they would have sex. In contrast, 93.3% of females and 78.4% of males indicated that they were sure they would not have sex in the next year. The chi-square statistic tests whether this relationship is statistically significant.

YOUR TURN

Cross-Tabulation and Chi-Square

1. Enter the following (hypothetical) nominal data of gender and major. In this dataset, m = male, f = female, a = art major, n = natural science major, s = social science major, h = humanities

m	a
m	a
m	n
m	n
m	n
m	n
m	n
m	n
m	n
m	n
m	n
m	n
m	n
m	n
m	s
m	s
m	s
m	s
m	s
m	s
m	h
m	h
m	h

m	h
f	h
f	h
f	h
f	h
f	h
f	h
f	h
f	h
f	h
f	a
f	a
f	a
f	a
f	a
f	a
f	a
f	a
f	n
f	n
f	n
f	n
f	s
f	s
f	s
f	s

2. Under *Variable View,* make sure you select *string* under *Type*. Cross-tabulation/ chi-square is the only data analysis technique covered in this text that can be done on string data. We could also assign numeric values to each string value and get the same result.

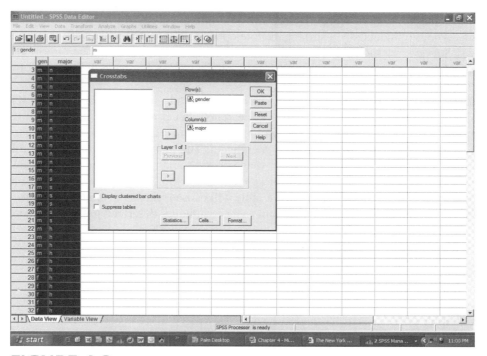

FIGURE 4.8. *Crosstabs screen in SPSS*

3. After you enter the data, select *Analyze/Descriptive Statistics/Crosstabs.* Your screen should resemble Figure 4.8.

4. Select the *Statistics* button and click on *Chi Square.*

5. Select the *Cells* button and click on *Percentages: Column.*

6. Click *OK.*

7. What is the chi-square value? The *p* value?

8. Looking specifically at the output table, what conclusion do you make about the relationship between declared major and gender?

SUMMARY

Correlational research provides descriptions of relationships between interval variables. The nature of correlational research allows for prediction among variables—knowing the score on one variable gives information about the score on the other variables.

Correlational studies do not, however, allow investigators to make claims about causal connections between variables. Data from descriptive studies are most often collected using surveys (conducted via surface mail, telephone, or Internet), observations, or interviews. Surveys are the most cost-efficient, but do not provide rich or deep information about behavior and attitudes. Observations are the costliest, but have the potential to be the richest source of data.

Analyzing data from descriptive and correlational studies involves computing descriptive statistics such as mean and variance. Researchers can also make claims about the relationship between variables by determining if certain statistical measures (Pearson correlation, chi-square) are statistically significant. The techniques in this chapter allow researchers to describe relationships between variables and to make predictions based on those relationships. As stated earlier, these techniques do not allow researchers to make claims about whether a change in one variable will cause a change in another variable. To make claims about causality, we must turn to the techniques described in the next chapter.

KEY TERMS

anchors	level of significance	prediction
causation	mean	random-digit dialing
chi-square	median	range
correlation	mode	rating scale
correlation matrix	negative correlation	response alternatives
correlational research	non-participant observation	standard deviation
directory-listed sampling	p value	statistically significant
double-barreled question	participant observation	time sampling
event sampling	Pearson correlation	Type I error
inferential statistics	positive correlation	Type II error

CHAPTER

5

QUANTITATIVE RESEARCH: BASIC EXPERIMENTAL DESIGNS

LEARNING OBJECTIVES

- Identify the different types of validity in experimental research.
- Identify the different types of variables in experimental research and understand how to manipulate, measure, or control them.
- Conduct data analysis of experimental research.

The correlational designs described in Chapter 4 allow scientists to make claims about relationships between variables. Whereas correlational designs allow descriptions of relationships among variables, experimental designs allow researchers to make claims about **causal inference**; that is, to make statements about which variable is the cause and which variable is the effect. This chapter describes what makes an experimental design different from a correlational design and what characteristics of experimental research must be present if the researchers are to make claims about causation.

EXPERIMENTAL VALIDITY

Internal Validity

Whereas validity (discussed in Chapter 3) refers to the truthfulness of a measure, internal validity refers to the truthfulness of the experiment being conducted. Specifically, **internal validity** refers to the extent to which the claim of changes in the independent variable causing changes in the dependent variable is accurate. For example, an experiment by Burton, Wilson, Cowan, and Bruce (1999) showed participants various video clips of people with whom the participants were familiar. The independent variable was how much of the person's body the participants could see. Participants saw one of three types of photos: full-view, body-obscured, and face-obscured. Participants correctly identified more than 90% of the full-view photos, nearly 90% of the body-obscured photos, and only 30% of the face-obscured photos. The researchers' hypothesis that recognizing familiar people seems to be mostly a function of viewing the face appears to be supported.

Internal validity is established by conducting an experiment that has certain characteristics and is free of certain biases. In other words, can we confidently conclude that seeing facial information is actually the cause of this change in recognizing people? This question is answered by asking two other questions. First, is the independent variable *truly* the cause of the dependent variable? Second, can other possible explanations for the relationship between the independent variable and the dependent be logically eliminated? If the answer to these questions is yes, then the researchers can claim that the experiment has internal validity.

External Validity

External validity refers to the extent to which the findings from one investigation will generalize to other samples, populations, or settings. Although this chapter is on experimental research, the concept of external validity refers to all types of social science research. Barbara Hofer (1994) developed an instrument to assess college students' *epistemic beliefs*—beliefs about the nature of learning and knowing. In developing the instrument, she determined the construct validity (Chapter 3) of the instrument by administering her instrument and a similar epistemic-beliefs instrument to a sample of students at the University of Michigan. After assessing construct validity, she sought to determine external validity by administering the instrument to a different population (Hofer, VanderStoep, & Pintrich, 1996). Specifically, she and her colleagues administered the questionnaire to a group of students at a small, religiously affiliated private college. She got similar results from the two studies; because the populations at the two institutions were very different, this provided evidence of external validity. Additionally, Karabenick and Moosa (2005) extended these findings to a sample in Oman, Jordan. This effort also represents an attempt to determine the external validity of the research on epistemic beliefs.

TYPES OF VARIABLES

As noted in Chapter 2, *variables* are constructs that can take on two or more distinct values. (This is opposed to a *constant*, which always takes on the same value.) We also noted in Chapter 2 that there are four kinds of variables: nominal, ordinal, interval, and ratio. Ordinal, interval, and ratio data are considered **numeric variables**, because they take on quantitative values on increasing value. Examples include grade point average (GPA), SAT score, or score of a job-satisfaction survey. Nominal variables are considered **categorical variables**, because they take on values that represent discrete groups rather than quantitative values. Examples of categorical values include gender, birth country, and ethnicity. We explore this distinction in greater detail later in this chapter. For now, the general distinction between a categorical variable and a numerical variable is relevant as we discuss independent variables.

Independent Variables

As mentioned in Chapter 3, *independent variables* are variables that are systematically controlled by the researcher to determine the variable's effect on the outcome (dependent variable). In experimental research, we refer to independent variables as factors. A **factor** is an independent variable controlled by the researcher. Independent variables in experimental research have two or more *levels:* distinct amounts of an independent variable. Independent variables in experimental research are usually randomly assigned by the researcher such that research participants will receive a particular level of the independent variable. In a hypothetical experiment measuring the effect of caffeine consumption on reaction time, a researcher might have caffeine as the independent variable with three levels: 200 mg, 100 mg, and 0 mg. One-third of her participants would receive 200 mg of caffeine, another one-third would receive 100 mg of caffeine, and the other one-third would receive no caffeine. The no-caffeine condition is known as a **placebo**; this is a nonactive or zero-level version of an independent variable, often used in drug trials. In this case the placebo would be a product that looked similar to what the other conditions received (for example, a pill), but which contained no caffeine.

A real-life example of an independent variable from experimental research is from Share (2004). He presented third-grade Israeli children with unfamiliar Hebrew words. One of his independent variables—presentation frequency—was how many times he showed the children these words. The independent variable had three levels: one time, two times, or four times.

Independent variables exist in correlational research as well, although in correlational research they are usually called *predictor variables*. Predictor variables are not systematically varied by the researcher. Rather, correlations between the predictor variable and dependent variable are measured with the data analysis techniques described in the previous chapter. We will not reexamine these techniques in this chapter, but we mention it here to draw the parallel between the independent variable of experimental research and the predictor variable of correlational research. Each is a measured variable, and the relationship between it and the dependent variable is examined.

An example of a predictor variable from correlational research comes from a study of test anxiety by Thomas Gross (1990) of the University of Redlands. He collected test scores from students in three different college courses, and also asked students to complete the Test Attitude Inventory designed to assess general test-taking anxiety. Using test anxiety as his predictor variable, he found that as total test anxiety increased, the students' performance on the exam questions decreased (recall negative correlation from Chapter 4).

As is the case in this example, many predictor variables in correlational research are individual-difference variables. An **individual-difference variable** is a measure of some inherent trait, disposition, or personality difference. An individual-difference variable can be numeric or categorical. One of the most common categorical individual-difference variables is gender. Race and ethnicity are also commonly used as categorical independent variables in social science research. Examples of numeric individual-difference variables are income, SAT score, or score on a political-conservatism scale. These variables are considered predictor variables because participants are not assigned to a level of that variable; rather, their score is part of the dispositional, historical, or cultural makeup of a research participant.

In summary, whether the research is experimental or correlational, the independent variable is on the front end of the research study, with the goal of determining its relationship to the dependent variable, which we discuss next.

Dependent Variables

As mentioned in Chapter 2, a *dependent variable* is the outcome measure in which researchers are interested. In correlational research, a dependent variable is sometimes called a *criterion variable*. To collect measurements of dependent variables, researchers observe, test, or survey the research participants. The dependent variable is what is measured by the observation, test, or survey. As we discuss later in this chapter, dependent variables can be collected in a variety of ways, including performance measures (for example, school grades, total sales), self-report measures (for example, attitudes, depression inventory), or physiological measures (for example, heart rate).

Critical to effective research is a clear understanding of the variables in your study. Whatever term is used, these variables are the outcomes of interest in a research study. One way this goal is achieved is by providing *operational definitions* of your dependent variables, as discussed in Chapter 3. An operational definition defines how a variable will be measured or assessed. Having a clear operational definition is important for many reasons. As we mentioned in Chapter 3, clear operational definitions are valuable because other researchers can *replicate* your research; that is, conduct a similar study to determine if similar results can be obtained. Another reason a clear operational definition is important is because unlike in the physical sciences, where agreements about measurements are commonly understood, consensus on measurement is not as easily achieved in the social sciences. For example, researchers may differ on what constitutes school achievement, juvenile delinquency, depression, or political conservatism. By being clear about operational definitions, other researchers can determine how their operational definitions are different or the same, and how differences in the definitions may affect research findings. If one educational researcher defines "gifted" as scoring above the 95th percentile on a nationally normed *achievement* test and another researcher defines "gifted" as scoring above the 98th percentile on an *aptitude* test (recall the distinction between aptitude and achievement from Chapter 3), these researchers will have different samples in their study and may get different results.

Another important component of dependent-variable measurement is consistency in data gathering. In surveys, for example, it is important to collect the information from all respondents during roughly the same time period. Distributing some of the surveys in the spring and others in the summer may produce different results. An example of this once occurred on a network newsmagazine show, in which some type of "question of the week" was posed, and viewers were asked to respond online. The question was "How do you like to spend your free time?" One of the response alternatives was "working in the yard."

Putting aside the sampling and response problems of having people respond to polls online, with no control over who responds or how many times, what was interesting about this example was that the question was asked in April. It seems quite likely that after a long, cold winter, many people would be eager to "work in the yard." Indeed, that was the most popular response. Asking that question in December or January may have yielded a very different result.

In addition to collecting data at the same time, it is also important to be consistent in your data-gathering protocol (process). Returning to the study by Share (2004), in which he showed third-grade Israeli children 18 unfamiliar words, one dependent variable was word recognition, specifically the ability to distinguish between the words the students saw and other words that looked very similar. To measure this dependent variable, he read the following to the children:

> Here are two words that both look very much alike, but if you look carefully you'll see that they're different. One of these words, and only one, is the same as the name of the [word] you read. . . . Make sure to look very carefully at each word and then tell me which one is the right one (p. 273).

This precision in collecting data on the dependent variable (reading the exact same script to all the participants) is typical of experimental research. Even in applied and quasi-experimental studies, clear operational definitions and data-collection procedures are important, even if the research setting does not allow as much control as is afforded in experimental research.

In summary, the dependent variable is on the back end of the research study. It is the outcome of interest, and the relationship between it and the independent variable is the focus of any particular study. Researchers must take care to measure and collect the dependent variable with precision and consistency.

Extraneous Variables

An **extraneous variable** is a rival explanatory variable that could also explain the relationship between the independent and dependent variables. The presence of an extraneous variable makes it difficult to make claims about the relationship between the independent and dependent variables. Extraneous variables can be eliminated in experimental research by employing several techniques, which we describe later in this chapter. In experimental research, the presence of extraneous variables creates what is known as a **confound**: a situation in which it is not known whether changes in the dependent variable were caused by the independent variable or by an extraneous variable. By eliminating potential extraneous variables in experimental research, investigators can make more confident claims that changes in the independent variable produce changes in the dependent variable. It is more difficult to eliminate extraneous variables in correlational research.

One example of an extraneous variable is time. Consider a survey to evaluate a professor's performance. If a survey is completed early in the semester, the ratings of professors might be high. If students complete ratings at the end of the semester, the ratings might be lower.

An extraneous variable might also be another variable in the study. Consider the relationship between nutrition and body weight. In many studies, obesity is operationally defined as a body mass index (BMI; weight in kilograms divided by height in meters squared) of 30 or greater. According to the Centers for Disease Control (www.cdc.gov/ brfss), the median percentage of obese adults (across all states) was 11.6% in 1990 and 22.1% in 2002. Using BMI as a dependent variable, researchers could investigate, for example, the relationship between body weight and the frequency of leisure-time activity. Suppose investigators conducted a telephone survey in which they collected, among other things, information on adults' height and weight (for computing BMI) and exercise habits. If it were discovered that people who exercise infrequently have higher BMI, then the researchers would have support for their hypothesis that exercise frequency is related to weight. A possible extraneous variable in this study is eating habits. It may well be that people who exercise little also eat foods that are high in sugar, which could also contribute to increased BMI.

In correlational research such as this, the best way to handle the presence of an extraneous variable is to measure the potentially extraneous variable as part of the original investigation. This will allow the researchers to account for changes in both the predictor variable (exercise) and the extraneous variable (eating habits) and to determine if exercise is related to BMI above and beyond any relationship it has with eating habits. Without measuring potential extraneous variables, researchers have no way of assessing the impact of these variables on the dependent variable.

Extraneous variables can also occur in experimental research. One way in which this occurs is through the **placebo effect**, which arises when participants behave differently because they *believe* that the independent variable is having an effect rather than because the independent variable is *actually* having an effect. If a researcher gives undergraduates a beverage and tells them that it contains alcohol, the expectation of what alcohol will do may make the participants behave as though they are consuming alcohol. If this occurs, you have an example of an extraneous variable in an experiment. We will say more about controlling potential extraneous variables later in this chapter. The Your Turn box tests your knowledge of different types of variables.

CHARACTERISTICS OF EXPERIMENTS

Several features separate experiments from other quantitative research designs. These features allow researchers to make the claim that the independent variable causes the dependent variable. In this section we describe six characteristics of experimental studies: covariation, time order, elimination of rival variables, presence of a control group, random assignment, and balancing of unwanted variables.

Covariation

As stated earlier, the main feature of experimental designs is that they allow researchers to make claims about causality. Inherent in a claim about causality is a claim about **covariation**. Covariation occurs when scores on two variables change at the same time. If researchers find that increased studying results in increased achievement, they are

YOUR TURN

Types of Variables

Below is an abstract reprinted from the *Journal of Experimental Child Psychology.* Using this abstract, identify:

1. The independent variable(s).
2. The dependent variable(s).
3. Any individual differences that the researchers measured.
4. Any possible extraneous variable(s) that may produce a confound.

Working memory has been implicated in the early acquisition of arithmetic skill, but the relations among different components of working memory, performance on different types of arithmetic problems, and development have not been explored. Preschool and Grade 1 children completed measures of phonological, visual-spatial, and central executive working memory, as well as nonverbal and verbal arithmetic problems, some of which included irrelevant information. For preschool children, accuracy was higher on nonverbal problems than on verbal problems, and the best and only unique predictor of performance on the standard nonverbal problems was visual-spatial working memory. This finding is consistent with the view that most preschoolers use a mental model for arithmetic that requires visual-spatial working memory. For Grade 1 children, performance was equivalent on nonverbal and verbal problems, and phonological working memory was the best predictor of performance on standard verbal problems. For both age groups, problems with added irrelevant information were substantially more difficult than standard problems, and in some cases measures of the central executive predicted performance. Assessing performance on different components of working memory in conjunction with different types of arithmetic problems provided new insights into the developing relations between working memory and how children do arithmetic.

Source: Rasmussen, C., & Bisanz, J. (2005). Representation and working memory in early arithmetic. *Journal of Experimental Child Psychology, 91,* 137–157. Reprinted with permission.

claiming that there is a relationship between time spent studying and performance on achievement tests. Although it is true that all causal relationships are correlational relationships, it is *not* the case that all correlational relationships are causal. Thus, covariation is necessary but not sufficient for an experimental study; it is just the first step. Several other criteria must be considered.

Time Order

Simply because two events are correlated does not necessarily mean that they are causally connected. Imagine a correlation between two variables, fancily named X and Y. There are at least three possibilities for a correlation between these variables: X causes Y, Y causes X, or some other third variable (dare we call it Z!) causes both X and Y. To determine a causal connection, a researcher must also establish a time-order relationship. Experiments allow time order to be established because the researcher controls the independent variable and purposely puts it before the dependent variable to establish the desired time order (that is, cause comes before effect).

Perhaps your parents were like ours and told you, "Wear a warm coat outside or you'll catch a cold." Implicit in that statement is that catching a cold is caused by exposure to inclement weather. Such a causal claim can be made only when the cause precedes (in time) the hypothesized effect. In experimental research, if the hypothesis is that caffeine affects reaction time, the researcher is careful to administer the caffeine prior to measuring reaction time. Such a luxury is not present in correlational research. For example, suppose researchers find a positive correlation between amount of funding a school district spends on academic programs and students' scores on standardized tests. It is possible that the increased money caused increased student achievement, but one cannot be sure. One reason there is doubt is because time order has not been established. It is impossible, in this research design, to determine if the increased funding came first. Increased funding could lead to increased achievement, or it could be the other way around. A second reason for the impossibility of making a claim about causality is because there are other extraneous variables that could explain the relationship, a topic to which we now turn.

Elimination of Rival Hypotheses

As mentioned earlier, causality is difficult to determine in the presence of rival variables that could also explain the relationship. For example, imagine that college admissions officers find a correlation between high school GPA and SAT scores. It is unlikely that either one of these variables *caused* the other to happen. Rather, it is likely that both SAT scores and GPAs are caused by a variety of other variables, such as cumulative hours spent studying and doing homework, genetics, school attendance, and other variables that cannot practically be considered in an experimental design.

Experiments are able to eliminate rival variables because researchers are able to exert control over the experimental situation. For example, they control the experimental situation to ensure that the independent variable occurs prior to the dependent variable. In experiments, researchers go to great lengths to make sure that the groups that comprise the different levels of the independent variable are as equal as possible in every way except the independent variable. The logic of this approach is this: If the groups differ only in terms of the independent variable, then any difference in the dependent variable must be due to differences in the independent variable. Therefore, a researcher could conclude that the independent variable caused the change in the dependent variable. For example, if the independent variable is caffeine with three levels (200 mg, 100 mg, and 0 mg) and the dependent variable is reaction time, researchers will seek to have the only difference between the three groups be the amount of caffeine they receive. Experimental researchers do this by creating a control group, randomly assigning participants to the levels of the independent variable, and balancing unwanted variables.

Presence of a Control Group One of the main ways in which experimental researchers eliminate rival variables is by creating a **control group**: a group of participants in an experiment who receive either no exposure to the independent variable or the same exposure that would otherwise occur in everyday life. Imagine that researchers are interested in studying the effects of violent video games on children's aggression. In this case, the video game is the independent variable and aggression is the dependent variable. To conduct this study, researchers would randomly assign (see below) half of the participants to play a violent video game. After the children played the game for a period of time, the researchers would then need to observe the children someplace where aggression might occur (for example, in a free-play situation). If the researchers observed only the children who played the violent video game, they would not be able to determine if any aggressive behavior was actually due to the violent video game, or whether it was due to those children simply being aggressive. To determine if the amount of aggression is due to the video games or some other factor, they must compare the score from the aggressive-video-game group to the control group. The goal of experimentation is to make the **treatment group**—the group that received the independent variable—similar in all ways to the control group except for the presence of the independent variable. Since the treatment group played a video game, it is also advisable to have the control group play a video game, but one that is nonviolent. Why? It may be that simple exposure to video itself causes violent behavior. Giving the control group a nonviolent video game eliminates this rival variable. If the difference between the violent group and the nonviolent group is statistically significant (see Chapter 4), the researchers could conclude that exposure to the violent video game *caused* changes (increases) in aggressive behavior.

What is important in this section is to note that the researchers would not be able to infer causality without the presence of a control group. Without a control group, there would be no way of knowing if the amount of aggression observed in the treatment group was different from what normally occurs with this group of children. The control group provides an estimate of the amount of aggression that might occur in the absence of the violent content.

Simple Random Assignment Another way in which researchers can eliminate rival variables is by randomly assigning participants to the different levels of the independent variable. **Random assignment** means that all participants have an equal opportunity to be placed in any of the conditions of the experiment. (You may remember random sampling from Chapter 2, in which all members of the sampling frame have an equal opportunity to be selected. Random assignment is the analogous tactic for experimental research.) For example, imagine an experiment designed to measure students' motivation for learning. The independent variable is *motivation*, and it has three levels: (1) a video of a motivational speaker, (2) the written text of the motivational speaker's talk, or (3) a nonmotivational video. With random assignment, each participant would have a one-third chance of being placed in the motivational-video condition, a one-third chance of being placed in the motivational-text condition, and a one-third chance of being placed in the nonmotivational-video condition.

The purpose of random assignment is to ensure that any difference that might occur between the groups is a result of the independent variable and not some extraneous variable. In our motivation example, imagine that instead of randomly assigning participants (say, 30 total) to the three groups, the researchers instead simply assigned the first 10 people to arrive to the motivational-video condition, the next 10 to the motivational-text condition, and the next 10 to the nonmotivational-video condition. Such non-random assignment creates a rival variable: perhaps those who show up early for experiments are more motivated than those who show up late. If all the latecomers are in one group and all the early arrivers in another group, we would have a confound.

Even with random assignment, one experimental condition may have more of one type of person than another condition. For example, one group may have more males, more athletes, or a higher group GPA. However, with random assignment the chance of this occurring diminishes and, *over the long run*, becomes less and less likely. Why is "over the long run" important? Imagine assigning 20 people—10 men and 10 women—to one of two experimental groups. Although assigning an equal number of males and females to the two groups is desirable, it is still possible that, even with random assignment, one of the experimental groups could end up with 8 males and 2 females. However, with a larger number of participants, such an imbalance becomes unlikely. Specifically, statisticians tell us that there is a 1.4% chance of assigning 8 males/2 females or 8 females/2 males by chance. However, it is virtually impossible (on the order 10^{-23}) to get 80 males/20 females or 80 females/20 males by chance.

Why does this occur? It occurs because of a fundamental law of statistics known as the **law of large numbers**. Simply stated, this law holds that as the size of a sample increases, the more likely it is that the sample will approximate the overall population. In this case, if there are 50% females and 50% males in the population, one may not get 50% of each gender with a small number of participants. However, with a larger number of participants—say, 100 males and 100 females—the probability of getting close to 50% of each gender is very high. In other words, the random assignment of participants to conditions becomes an important tool for balancing out individual differences as the number of participants increases. The Your Turn box allows a demonstration of the statistical principle underlying the logic of random assignment and a chance for you to do a random assignment for yourself.

YOUR TURN

Law of Large Numbers and Random Assignment

1. *Girls and Boys.* Consider three hospitals. At Hospital X, 10 babies are born each day; at Hospital Y, 50 babies are born each day; and at Hospital Z, 100 babies are born each day. At which hospital is it more likely that more than 60% of the babies born will be girls? (Assume that 50% of babies born are girls and 50% are boys.)

_____ Hospital X

_____ Hospital Y

_____ Hospital Z

2. *Heads and Tails*

Flip a coin 10 times and record the number of heads: _____

Flip a coin 50 times and record the number of heads: _____

Flip a coin 100 times and record the number of heads: _____

   Which of these flip sessions differed the most from 50%? Compare your flip outcomes to those of your classmates. Why do you think this happened? Did this exercise help you answer the hospital question? _____

_____

_____

3. *Random Assignment.* Listed here are 31 names of potential participants. If we were assigning participants to the motivation experiment described earlier, we would randomly assign the participants to one of three experimental groups using two different methods. First, move down the list and place a 1, 2, or 3 next to each person. For example, Breen would be in Condition 1, Breuker in Condition 2, Buck in Condition 3, Buyze in Condition 1, and so forth. Because there are 31 people, there will not be equal numbers in each condition. If you correctly did the random assignment, there should be 11 people in Condition 1 and 10 people each in Conditions 2 and 3. A more complex method is to use a random number table from a statistics textbook. If you have such a book from a statistics class, move along the random number table. When you encounter the first number that is either a 1, 2, or 3, you should put the first person in that condition. For example, if you first find a 2, then put Breen in Condition 2, then move on to Breuker and look for the next 1, 2, or 3. Place the condition numbers next to each student's name and compare how different the two randomization procedures are. Did Method 2 result in roughly equal numbers of participants per condition?

Name	Randomization Method 1	Randomization Method 2
Breen		
Breuker		
Buck		
Buyze		
Crowder		
De Jong		
De Petro		
Edwards		
Fineout		

Frantz
Graves
Gray
Greenland
Haines
Haulenbeek
Heneveld
Izenbaard
Kerkstra
Konny
Le
Meek
Merlihan
Northuis
Oosterink
Southard
Timmins
Ummel
VanTimmeren
Vinas
Weingartner

4. Why do you think we put an exercise on law of large numbers with an exercise on random assignment in the same Your Turn box? _____
_____
_____

Stratified Random Assignment An even more precise way to assign participants to experimental groups is with **stratified random assignment**. This technique is based on the same rationale as the stratified random sampling covered in Chapter 2. Specifically, people are assigned to conditions based on a preexisting trait. This ensures that the trait is equally likely to be present in all of the experimental groups. If the researcher wants to guarantee equal proportion of genders in each condition, she would employ stratified random sampling.

Why would this be important? After all, we just learned that (over the long run) gender will balance out if you use simple random sampling. One reason would be to avoid a potential confound. To conduct stratified random sampling, a researcher would use the same random-assignment method described earlier, but do it separately for males and females. Researchers need to use stratified random sampling only if they think the stratification variable will possibly affect the dependent variable. Otherwise, simple random assignment will work just fine. Possible variables used in stratified random sampling include gender, year in school, or race/ethnicity. The Your Turn box offers an opportunity to do the same random assignment you did in the previous Your Turn box, but this time stratifying by gender.

YOUR TURN

Stratified Random Assignment

Here is the same list of participants shown in the previous Your Turn box, with the gender of the participants indicated next to the names. Using the same techniques as in the previous Your Turn box, construct a stratified random sample by gender.

Name	Randomization Method 1	Randomization Method 2
Breen (M)		
Breuker (M)		
Buck (F)		
Buyze (F)		
Crowder (M)		
De Jong (F)		
De Petro (F)		
Edwards (F)		
Fineout (F)		
Frantz (M)		
Graves (F)		
Gray (F)		
Greenland (F)		
Haines (M)		
Haulenbeek (F)		
Heneveld (F)		
Izenbaard (F)		
Kerkstra (F)		
Konny (F)		
Le (F)		
Meek (F)		
Merlihan (F)		
Northuis (M)		
Oosterink (F)		
Southard (M)		
Timmins (M)		
Ummel (F)		
VanTimmeren (F)		
Vinas (F)		
Weingartner (F)		

Matching An alternative to random assignment that also achieves the goal of eliminating unwanted differences between experimental groups (and therefore reducing the risk of rival variables) is a technique called matching. **Matching** involves making the experimental groups as similar as possible on a potential rival variable. For example, imagine a study in which researchers construct two instructional conditions for learning probability problems: a standard problem-solving instructional condition (standard learning) and a condition in which you teach people how the probability principle being learned is different from other probability principles (comparison learning). You are interested in determining whether these teaching methods affect students' problem-solving performance. So, the independent variable is instructional condition (two levels) and the dependent variable is problem-solving performance. One rival variable that could affect the interpretation of your results is overall intellectual ability. In other words, people with more advanced education or more advanced intellectual skill might be likely to do better on the dependent variable. One way to solve this is to match participants based on their intellectual skill and assign them to conditions so that each experimental condition has people with the same level of intellectual skill.

For example, suppose you use ACT score as your measure of intellectual skill. In matching, you would take a student with an ACT score of, say, 26, and assign him to the Standard condition. You would then search for another student in your sampling frame with an ACT score of 26 and assign him to the Comparison condition. You would continue this matching through the entire sampling frame, trying as much as possible to match each person on ACT score and assigning people with similar ACT scores to *different* conditions. This can be done with gender, race, or any other variable that might be related to the independent variable. As the Your Turn box indicates, it is not always possible to find an exact match on the matching variable. If matching is not possible because there are not enough sets of similar scores, then we recommend using random assignment or stratified random assignment.

YOUR TURN

Matching

Here is a list of students' last names and (fictitious) ACT scores. Assign participants to one of two experimental conditions—standard instruction or comparison instruction—matching them on ACT scores as closely as possible. Make sure that you still randomly assign the matched pairs to conditions. After you have done this, compute the mean ACT score for each of the two experimental groups. If the means are very similar, then you have done a successful job of matching on ACT score.

Name	Act Score	Instructional Condition (1 = Standard, 2 = Comparison)
Adams	26	
Burgess	23	
Dekkenga	28	
Doupe	31	
Evenhouse	31	
Fortney	32	
Heeringa	22	
Isherwood	26	
Kaliszewski	31	
Kirsch	23	
Koopman	24	
Kuiper	22	
Langshaw	22	
Lynch	23	
Marshall	24	
Matre	22	
Meeusen	25	
Mittelstaedt	25	
Morden	28	
Murphy	25	
Pedigo	26	
Purtee	25	
Schneider	32	
Specht	27	
Thompson	26	
Vilmann	25	
Walkowicz	32	
Wolters	30	
Yonker	32	
Zoellner	24	

Mean ACT score of Condition 1: _____

Mean ACT score of Condition 2: _____

Balancing Unwanted Variables No matter how hard we, as experimenters, try to eliminate extraneous variables, we cannot control all aspects of the experimental setting. It is not practical to match or stratify on every possible variable, so the next best strategy for dealing with these variables is to balance them equally across all the experimental conditions. This equal distribution of *nuisance* variables makes it less likely that one experimental group will be disproportionately affected by such a variable. For example, if we were to conduct the problem-solving experiment described earlier with the two conditions of standard instruction and comparison instruction, and we were further to use two experimenters—Michael and Sonja—to conduct the experiment, we would want to make sure that the two experimenters administered the two conditions equally often. In other words, it would be a potential confound if Michael conducted the experiment for the standard condition and Sonja conducted it for the comparison condition. With each experimenter doing each condition equally often, any differences between the experimenters would balance out over time. Potential nuisance variables include age, gender, or race of experimenter. They could even be as subtle as voice tone, dress style, or likeability. Other possible nuisance variables that must be balanced across conditions include experimental setting (if researchers are using multiple rooms), time of day, and day of week. All of these factors should be balanced.

TYPES OF EXPERIMENTAL DESIGNS

Although we have referred, at least indirectly, to the different types of experimental designs available to you, in this section we formally describe different types of experimental designs that can be employed. These designs are considered basic designs. We refer to basic experimental designs as those in which there is only one independent variable and in which each participant is assigned to only one level of that independent variable. In Chapter 6, we discuss other experimental designs that are referred to as *complex*, meaning that they employ more than one independent variable and/or participants are assigned to more than one level of the independent variable. For now, though, our focus is on basic experimental designs.

Random-Groups Design

The most straightforward way to design an experiment is to employ a **random-groups design**, in which participants are randomly assigned to one of the experimental conditions. The process of randomly assigning research participants to experimental conditions was discussed in detail previously in this chapter. The assignment to groups can be completely random, or selectively random based on some characteristic of the participants such as age or gender (stratified random sampling). An example from earlier in the chapter described an experiment testing the effect of caffeine on reaction time. The independent variable of caffeine had three levels: 200 mg, 100 mg, or 0 mg (placebo). A random-groups design would randomly assign one-third of the participants to the 200-mg condition, one-third to the 100-mg condition, and one-third to the placebo.

Matched-Groups Design

In lieu of randomly assigning participants to groups, researchers can employ a **matched-groups design**. In a matched-groups design, participants are placed into groups based on some preexisting characteristic. This characteristic should be a variable that you as a researcher believe is correlated with the dependent variable. As described earlier, the matching takes place by finding a number of participants equal to the number of experimental groups (that is, select two participants for a two-group design, three participants for a three-group design) who have the same or nearly the same score on the matching variable. The matched-groups design controls for any differences that might be created, even after random assignment, between the experimental groups based on this variable.

Natural-Groups Design

In a **natural-groups design**, some difference already present among the participants is used in assigning the groups. In other words, researchers use an individual-difference variable (described earlier in this chapter) to make up the levels of the independent variable. Common individual-difference variables include gender, race/ethnicity, year in school, or political or religious affiliation. An undergraduate student recently conducted a study in which he asked people to self-identify as either religiously conservative, religiously moderate, or religiously liberal (VanderStoep & Norris, 2005). He used answers to these questions to compare the groups on a variety of dependent measures, including political beliefs, beliefs about learning, and beliefs about various aspects of religious behavior and practice.

Such studies are powerful because they take people just as they are and attempt to identify how they differ on a variety of dependent measures of interest. The major weakness of this design is that there is no way to assess the internal validity or causality. In other words, did the independent variable *really* cause the dependent variable? The VanderStoep and Norris study found that those who identify themselves as religiously conservative believe that knowledge is more certain and less complex than those who identify themselves as religiously liberal. Because there was no random assignment of participants to experimental conditions, it cannot be claimed that religious conservatism *caused* these differences in beliefs about knowledge. It could be that a whole set of personal and cultural factors that accompany religious conservatism are at work in creating these differences.

DATA ANALYSIS

In the previous sections of this chapter we described experimental designs and basic strategies for implementing them. In this final section we discuss how to analyze the data that you would get from a basic experimental design. These statistical techniques are used whether you have used a random-groups design, a matched-groups design, or a natural-groups design. Our experience is that students are often anxious about conducting data analysis. We believe that competence in data analysis will be an important way in which you can set yourself apart from candidates and competitors for prized positions in graduate school. Besides, if you never analyzed the data from your experiment, you would never know if your theories were supported!

t Tests

A *t* **test** is used to determine if two groups or levels of an independent variable differ on a dependent variable. In the basic experimental designs described in this chapter, where each group receives only one treatment of the independent variable, the type of *t* test used is called an independent-samples *t* test. An **independent-samples *t* test** compares mean scores from a study in which each participant receives only one level of the independent variable. (This will be contrasted with another form of *t* test in which each participant receives both levels of the independent variable. We cover this *t* test in Chapter 6.) If a *t* test is found to be statistically significant, we would say that the two groups differ on the dependent variable. Recall from Chapter 4 that most social scientists use a *p* value of less than .05 as the cutoff for statistical significance. If the *t* test is not statistically significant (*p* value greater than .05), we would say that the two groups do not differ on the dependent variable. For example, if you wanted to compare whether males differed from females on first-year college GPA, you would employ an independent-samples *t* test. As another example, in the experiment described earlier comparing standard instruction to comparison instruction on problem-solving performance, an independent-samples *t* test is the proper statistical technique to employ. Computation of *t* tests is fairly complicated, but is covered in most college statistics classes. For our purposes, it is more important to know the conditions under which a *t* test is used (comparing means of two groups), how to execute them in SPSS, and how to interpret the output. The Your Turn box gives you the opportunity to conduct a *t* test using SPSS.

YOUR TURN

Independent-Samples *t* Test

Enter the following data into an SPSS dataset. Call the first variable *RELIGION* and the second variable *BELIEF*. Make them both numeric variables. *RELIGION* is coded "1" for those who self-identified as religiously conservative and "2" for those who self-identified as religiously liberal. (The actual study had a response for religiously moderate, but is not included in this example.) Using the *Value Labels* column, code a "1" as *conservative* and a "2" as *liberal*. The variable *BELIEF* is the participant's answer to the following question: "In most social conflicts, I can easily see which side is right and which is wrong." Participants responded to this question on a five-point scale, with 1 being "strongly disagree" and 5 being "strongly agree." In other words, high scores indicate that a person believes he or she can tell which side of a social conflict is right or wrong with great certainty.

Religion	Belief
2	2
1	3
2	3
1	3
1	4
1	2
2	3
1	4
2	3
1	3
2	3
2	2
1	4
1	3
1	4
1	3
2	2
2	1

To perform the *t* test, pull down the *Analysis* menu. Select *Compare Means*, then *Independent-Samples t test*. Place the *BELIEF* variable in the upper box by selecting it and clicking the arrow. This is where the dependent variable goes. Place the *RELIGION* variable in the lower (smaller) box by selecting it and clicking the arrow. This is where the independent variable goes. Below the independent variable, click on *Define Groups*. Enter the two numeric values that your independent variable has. Most of the time the values are 1 and 2, but they can be any two integers. Click *OK*.

The output should look like this:

GROUP STATISTICS	RELIGION	N	Mean	Std. Deviation	Std. Error Mean
Belief	1	10	3.3000	.67495	.21344
	2	8	2.3750	.74402	.26305

INDEPENDENT SAMPLES TEST	Levene's Test for Equality of Variances		t test for Equality of Means				
	F	Sig.	t	Df	Sig. (2-tailed)	Mean Difference	Std. Error Difference
EQUAL VARIANCES ASSUMED	.175	.681	2.762	16	.014	.9250	.33489

We want to know if there is a significant difference between the religious conservatives and the religious liberals on this question.

The first component of the output with which you should be concerned is the t value and *p* value (written as *Sig. 2-tailed* in the output) shown under *t-test Equality of Means*. Is the finding significant? If so, the component of the output that says *Group Statistics* contains the means of the two groups. Based on this output, do conservatives score higher or lower on the response to this variable?

_____

How would you interpret this result? _____

_____

Analysis of Variance

An **analysis of variance (ANOVA)** is used to determine if three or more groups or levels of an independent variable differ on a dependent variable. Analysis of variance is the logical extension of a *t* test; a *t* test is for two groups and analysis of variance is for three or more groups. The test statistic produced by ANOVA is the *F* statistic, and like the *t* test, a *p* value is associated with the *F*. If the *p* value is less than .05, researchers conclude that the ANOVA is statistically significant and therefore the three (or more) groups differ from each other. For example, the caffeine-reaction time experiment described earlier would be analyzed using an ANOVA comparing the mean for the three levels of the independent variable (caffeine) on the dependent variable (reaction time).

ANOVA is more complicated than the *t* test, because if a *t* test is statistically significant we know that one group is significantly higher/lower than another group—because there are only two groups. By looking at the means, it is obvious which group is higher. However, with ANOVA there are three or more groups, so even though we know that there is a statistically significant difference, we cannot know for sure where those differences are. For example, in the experiment described earlier examining the effects of a motivational video on motivation for learning, suppose we found a statistically significant difference between the three levels of the independent variable—motivational video, motivational text, and nonmotivational video. The ANOVA will only tell us that the means differ, but not which means are different. To determine this, we need to conduct **post-hoc tests**: statistical tests performed on statistically significant ANOVAs to determine how the means differ from each other.

Consider three levels of the independent variable—A, B, and C—and a statistically significant F statistic from the ANOVA. There are three possibilities: A is different from B, B is different from C, and A is different from C. A post-hoc test will indicate which of the three means are different from one another. The Your Turn box allows you to try conducting an ANOVA and a popular post-hoc test, the Tukey HSD test.

YOUR TURN

Analysis of Variance

Enter the following data into an SPSS file. These are hypothetical data from the experiment described earlier comparing the effect of a motivational video, motivational text, or nonmotivational video on participants' motivation for learning.

Condtion	Motivate
1	5
1	4.2
1	3.8
1	3.6
1	3.6
1	4
1	2.8
1	3.4
1	3.8
1	3.6
2	3
2	3
2	2.2
2	2.4
2	2.2
2	3.2
2	2.4
2	2.4
2	3
2	2.6
3	4.8

3	2
3	2.2
3	3
3	3.2
3	3.2
3	4.2
3	1.8
3	2
3	2.2

The variable *CONDTION* is the independent variable. Using the *Value Labels* column, code the three levels with a "1" for *motivational video,* a "2" for *motivational text,* and a "3" for *nonmotivational video.* The variable *MOTIVATE* is the participant's mean score on a five-item motivation scale, with a range of 1.0 to 7.0. To conduct the analysis of variance, pull down the *Analysis* menu and select *Compare Means* (just like the *t* tests) and then *One-Way ANOVA.* Your screen should resemble Figure 5.1.

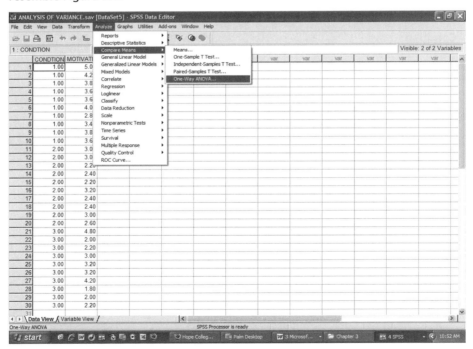

FIGURE 5.1. *Conducting an ANOVA in SPSS.*

Place *MOTIVATE* in the Dependent List box and *CONDTION* in the *Factor box*. Click *Options* and select *Descriptive*. This will provide the means scores for the three conditions. Then click *Post-Hoc* and select *Tukey*. If the overall *F* statistic of the ANOVA is significant, the Tukey follow-up test will examine if any of the means are different from one another. Click *OK* and your output should look like this:

Descriptives

MOTIVATE

	N	Mean	Std. Deviation	Std. Error	95% Confidence Interval for Mean	
					Lower Bound	Upper Bound
Motivational Video	10	3.7800	.56921	.18000	3.3728	4.1872
Motivational Text	10	2.6400	.37476	.11851	2.3719	2.9081
Nonmotiva-tional Video	10	2.8600	1.01566	.32118	2.1334	3.5866
Total	30	3.0933	.84647	.15454	2.7773	3.4094

ANOVA

MOTIVATE

	Sum of Squares	df	Mean Square	F	Sig.
Between Groups	7.315	2	3.657	**7.334**	**.003**
Within Groups	13.464	27	.499		
Total	20.779	29			

Multiple Comparisons
Dependent Variable: MOTIVATE
Tukey HSD

| (I) CONDTION | (J) CONDTION | Mean Difference (I–J) | Std. Error | Sig. | 95% Confidence Interval | |
					Lower Bound	Upper Bound
Motivational Video	Motivational Text	1.1400*	.31581	.003	.3570	1.9230
	Nonmotivational Video	.9200*	.31581	.019	.1370	1.7030
Motivational Text	Motivational Video	−1.1400*	.31581	.003	−1.9230	−.3570
	Nonmotivational Video	−.2200	.31581	.767	−1.0030	.5630
Non-motivational Video	Motivational Video	−.9200*	.31581	.019	−1.7030	−.1370
	Motivational Text	.2200	.31581	.767	−.5630	1.0030

*The mean difference is significant at the .05 level.

The middle box is where you should look first. This shows an *F* value of 7.334 with a *p* value of .003. Because the *p* value is less than .05, we conclude that the analysis of variance is statistically significant. From this you know that the three means are statistically different. You should next look at the top box that says *Descriptives*, which shows the means of the three experimental conditions. You see that the highest mean is for Motivational Video, then Nonmotivational Video, then Motivational Text. The Tukey follow-up test is shown in the bottom box that says *Multiple Comparisons*. This tells you which of the three means are statistically different from one another. Moving to that final box, in the first line of that box you will see a comparison of Motivational Video to Motivational Text. The first value in the column *Mean Difference (I–J)* is 1.14. This is the difference between the Motivational Video mean (3.78) and the Motivational Text mean (2.64) shown in the first box. The box labeled *Sig.* is the *p* value for this Tukey follow-up test. It is .003, which is less than .05. Therefore, we conclude that the Motivational Video mean is statistically higher than the Motivational Text mean. Doing this for the other two comparisons, we find that Motivational Video is significantly higher than Nonmotivational Video (*p* = .019), but that Nonmotivational Video is not significantly different from Motivational Text (*p* = .767).

This is how you do ANOVA. It is the statistical tool to use whenever you have a study that compares the means of three or more groups.

SUMMARY

This chapter outlines the essential elements of experimental design. Successful experiments have internal validity, which allows researchers to claim that the independent variable caused changes in the dependent variable. Experiments that have internal validity have certain characteristics, including covariation, cause preceding effect in time, elimination of extraneous variables, random assignment or matching of participants to conditions, the presence of a control group, and balancing of unwanted variables. Data from experiments are analyzed with either a *t* test, which compares mean differences of two groups, or an analysis of variance (ANOVA), which compares mean differences of three or more groups.

KEY TERMS

analysis of variance (ANOVA)
categorical variables
causal inference
confound
control group
covariation
external validity
extraneous variable
factor
independent-samples *t* test
individual-difference variable
internal validity
law of large numbers

matched-groups design
matching
natural-groups design
numeric variables
placebo
placebo effect
post-hoc tests
random assignment
random-groups design
stratified random assignment
t test
treatment group

CHAPTER

6

QUANTITATIVE RESEARCH: ADVANCED EXPERIMENTAL DESIGNS

LEARNING OBJECTIVES

- Identify the three different types of complex designs, and be able to match a design to a particular research question.
- Identify how to control or eliminate pitfalls that accompany repeated-measures design.
- Conduct data analysis of complex designs.

In this chapter we move from one-variable experimental designs to more complicated designs. To lay the groundwork for what we cover in this chapter, it helps to make a distinction between repeated-measures designs and between-groups designs. A **between-groups design** is an experiment in which participants receive only one level of an independent variable. This is the design that we studied in Chapter 5. We covered various ways to create the between-groups design—random assignment, matched groups, and natural groups—but the common element was that each participant was in only one group/level of the independent variable.

In this chapter we modify this model of experimental design in three ways. First, we cover experiments in which participants in the experiment receive all levels of the independent variable rather than just one level. These are known as **repeated-measures designs**. In this chapter we describe methods for implementing these designs. A second variant on the model discussed in Chapter 5 is experiments with more than one independent variable. These are called **complex designs**. A third way that experiments become more complex is if they are conducted outside of a standard laboratory setting. Most experiments that take place in schools, hospitals, or other real-life settings are almost always *quasi-experiments*. We introduced quasi-experiments in Chapter 2, and we describe the details of conducting them in this chapter. Besides being more procedurally complicated, quasi-experiments are also lower in internal validity. Thus, we also explore ways in which certain factors may adversely affect the internal validity of experimental research. In summary, this chapter tackles these three more advanced types of designs, as well as strategies for analyzing these designs. First, though, we describe several concepts that are important to understanding the designs in this chapter.

BASIC CONCEPTS

Recall from Chapter 5 that a *factor* is an independent variable controlled by the researcher. A complex design will have more than one factor and each factor will have two or more *levels*. For example, a simple experiment that has a treatment group and a control group has one factor with two levels. In a complex design in which one independent variable is amount of caffeine (200 mg, 100 mg, placebo) and the other independent variable is sleep deprivation (no sleep, 4 hours, 8 hours), we would say the experiment has two factors, each with three levels. The generally accepted terminology is that this is a *3 × 3 complex design*.

Main Effects

Because a complex design has two or more independent variables/factors, there are more potential effects that could be statistically significant. There are two kinds of effects that can be produced in a complex design. The first is a **main effect**. A main effect is a test of whether an independent variable is statistically significant *across all of the levels* of the other independent variable(s). To understand a main effect, consider the simplest of complex designs: an experiment with two independent variables with two levels for each independent variable (a 2 × 2 design). The results of a complex design of the experiment can be displayed in a table. For example, an experiment by Epley and Kruger (2005) had two independent variables—*expectancy* and *type of communication*—each with two levels. Specifically, participants were led to believe that they would interact with either an intelligent or an unintelligent person and that this communication would take place either on the telephone or via email. Table 6.1 shows the results of this experiment. In an experiment with two independent variables, there are two main effects to be tested. In this experiment, the main effects are *expectancy* (expecting the person to be intelligent vs. unintelligent) and *type of communication* (voice vs. email). The researchers found a statistically significant main effect for expectancy. That is, participants who were led to believe that they were interacting with an intelligent person rated that person as more intelligent that those who were led to believe that they were interacting with an unintelligent person. Looking at Table 6.1, then, we find that the rating of 3.0 for the intelligent expectancy is significantly different from the rating of 1.4 for the unintelligent expectancy. The main effect for type of communication was not statistically significant. In other words, there was no *overall* difference between the perceived intelligence of those who communicated via voice versus those who communicated via email. Looking at Table 6.1, then, 2.8 from the voice condition is not significantly different from 1.6 of the email condition. (It is true that 2.8 might *seem* different from 1.6, but the difference is not statistically significant. This illustrates the importance of conducting statistical tests instead of relying on simple "eyeballing" of the data. We show you how to conduct these statistical tests at the end of this chapter.) So, in this experiment, there is one main effect that is statistically significant and one main effect that is not statistically significant.

Interactions

Main effects measure whether the levels of one independent variable are significantly different when *combined* across the levels of all the other independent variables. An **interaction** is the effect of one independent variable at a *particular level* of another independent variable in the same study. Imagine mean scores from the hypothetical 2 × 2 complex design shown in Table 6.2.

TABLE 6.1 **Results of a Complex Design with Two Independent Variables**

Expectation	Type of Interaction		
	Email	Voice	Total
Intelligent	3.2	2.9	3.0
Unintelligent	0.1	2.8	1.4
Total	1.6	2.8	

TABLE 6.2 **Interaction Effects in a 2 × 2 Complex Design**

Independent Variable 2	Independent Variable 1		
	Level 1	Level 2	Main Effect of IV2
Level 1	3.0	7.0	5.0
Level 2	7.0	3.0	5.0
Main Effect of IV1	5.0	5.0	

The bottom row and the far right column of the table show the means for the main effects. As can be seen, the main effects for the two independent variables are not statistically significant. For purposes of this hypothetical illustration, we are designating all identical scores as not statistically significant and all nonidentical scores as statistically significant. So, the main effect means for Independent Variable 1 are 5.0 for the first level and 5.0 for the second level. The main effect means for Independent Variable 2 are also 5.0 for both levels. However, inspecting the four-cell means in the interior of the table reveals statistical differences. These are interaction effects because the effect of one independent variable varies as a function of different levels of the other independent variable.

In the Epley and Kruger experiment, there is a large effect for expectancy (intelligent vs. unintelligent) for the email condition, but no effect for expectancy in the voice condition (Table 6.1). This is an interaction, because the effect of one independent variable (expectancy) differs as a function of the level of the other independent variable. Specifically, the rating in the email condition is 3.2 for the intelligent expectancy and only 0.1 for the unintelligent expectancy (a significant effect). However, in the voice condition the ratings are 2.9 and 2.8 for the intelligent and unintelligent expectancy conditions, respectively (a nonsignificant effect). Because an independent variable has different effects based on the level of the other independent variable, we say an interaction is present.

If an interaction is present, interpreting the main effects is less important. In the Epley and Kruger experiment, the main effect for expectancy is statistically significant, but what is really interesting about this study is that the effect for expectancy is very large for the email condition (3.2 vs. 0.1) and nonexistent for the voice condition (2.9 vs. 2.8). So, looking at the main effect does not tell the whole story. Instead, when an interaction is significant, it is most helpful to examine simple main effects. A **simple main effect** is the analysis of one independent variable at a particular level of the other independent variable. In a two-variable study, there are four possible simple main effects to examine. As a researcher, you must choose which simple main effects to analyze based on how well each analysis helps explain your theory. In the Epley and Kruger study, the four possible simple main effects to be analyzed are:

1. Intelligent versus unintelligent expectancy for the voice condition (2.9 vs. 2.8)

2. Intelligent versus unintelligent expectancy for the email condition (3.2 vs. 0.1)

3. Voice versus email communication for the intelligent condition (3.2 vs. 2.9)

4. Voice versus email communication for the unintelligent condition (2.8 vs. 0.1)

Epley and Kruger chose to report the first two—the simple main effect of expectancy (intelligent vs. unintelligent) for the email condition and for the voice condition. These analyses showed a statistically significant expectancy simple main effect in the email condition (3.2 statistically different from 0.1) and no significant simple main effect in the voice condition (2.9 not statistically different from 2.8).

Analyzing interactions and the subsequent simple main effects provides a great deal of theoretical power to social science research. If researchers theorize that there is an expectancy effect for intelligence, such that people would perceive those they believed to be intelligent as *more* intelligent than those they believe to be unintelligent, then this complex design helps clarify that hypothesis. In fact, Epley and Kruger found that the expectancy condition was present only in the email condition. This provides future researchers with theoretical clarification about the conditions under which expectancy effects will occur. The Your Turn box gives you the opportunity to identify main effects and interactions. Next, we turn to three types of more advanced designs that are often used in experimental research.

YOUR TURN

Main Effects and Interactions

Here is a 2 × 2 table of a natural-groups design. The dependent variable is college students' answers to the question from the National Survey of Student Engagement: "If you could start over, would you attend the same institution you are now attending?" The scores range from 1.0 (definitely no) to 4.0 (definitely yes). The independent variables are gender and whether the student was a member of a fraternity/sorority. (For the purposes of this exercise, assume that a difference of 0.1 or less is not statistically significant and that a difference of 0.2 or more is statistically significant.)

Identify the two main effects. _____

Identify the four possible simple main effects that could be analyzed.
_____

_____

Which main effects and simple main effects are significant?

_____

_____

How would you interpret these findings? _____

_____

Member of a Fraternity/Sorority

Gender	No	Yes	Total
Male	3.4	3.2	3.3
Female	3.4	3.4	3.4
Total	3.4	3.3	

REPEATED-MEASURES DESIGNS

Up to this point, in both Chapter 5 and this chapter, we have described between-groups designs. In Chapter 5 we covered between-groups designs with one factor/independent variable and in the previous section we described between-groups designs with two factors/independent variables. In this section we describe repeated-measures designs. These are designs in which participants are exposed to more than one level of the independent variable. Another way to think about repeated-measures designs is that the dependent variable is measured more than once.

A straightforward example of a repeated-measures design is a study in which participants are asked to complete a questionnaire or performance task on two different occasions. This usually occurs at the beginning and end of an event, such as a semester in college. In this case, the independent variable is *time* and it has two levels, pretest and posttest. In Chapter 5 we explained that analyzing data from an independent variable with two levels involves a *t* test. The same principle applies in this case as well, and we describe this technique in the "Data Analysis" section of this chapter. For now, it is sufficient to know that a repeated-measures design with two levels of the independent variable is the basic model. This basic model can be extended to more than two levels, just as the between-groups example was extended to more than two levels in Chapter 5. For example, a researcher interested in measuring students' attitudes over their four years in college could use a repeated-measures design. If researchers collected data during all four years, the independent variable would again be *time* and in this instance it would have four levels. Notice that this study could be performed as a between-groups design, in which case researchers would take different samples of first-years, sophomores, juniors, and seniors. This design might be preferable, given that a repeated-measures design would take four years to complete (you would have to collect data from the same people for four years!).

Other studies are more amenable to a repeated-measures design. For example, an educational psychologist who is interested in recall memory and recognition memory of grade-school children could give children tasks that involved both recall and recognition. (*Recognition memory* is the ability to correctly identify a concept that has been learned and *recall memory* is the ability to generate a concept that has been learned.) In such a study, children would be exposed to more than one level of the independent variable (that is, *memory type*), so this would be a repeated-measures design with two levels.

Why would researchers choose a repeated-measures design over a between-groups design? One advantage is economy. Repeated-measures designs do not use as many participants. For example, in an experiment with three levels of the independent variable, you would need three participants for one *replication*. The term replication is used in a slightly different way here. In Chapter 1, replication referred to being able to demonstrate the findings of a study in a different context, location, or with a different sample. In this context, **replication** refers to a set of completed data for all the levels of the independent variable(s). In a repeated-measures design, you would need only one participant, who would experience all three levels of the independent variable.

A second advantage of the repeated-measures design is reduced error variance. **Error variance** is the variation in the scores of the dependent variable that cannot be accounted for by the independent variable. Error variance has two components. First, **within-group**

error variance is error variance due to random fluctuations in the performance of *one group* of people due to characteristics of the people in the study. For example, changes in attention span, mood, and tiredness would produce within-group error variance. Second, **between-group error variance** is error variance due to differences *between the groups* in the experiment. Although we randomly assign people to conditions to eliminate this kind of variance, we can never eliminate it completely, so there will always be some between-group error variance in an experiment with more than one group. In other words, even with random assignment, the people receiving one level of an independent variable will be slightly different from people receiving another level of an independent variable. This difference is between-group error variance.

In a repeated-measures design, because the same group of people is being tested, researchers have to contend only with within-group error variance. Because there are no between-groups comparisons, there can be no between-group error variance. Thus, it makes sense that a design with only within-group error variance will have less error variance than a design that has both types of error variance.

So, you may ask, why does all of this matter? The concept is bit obscure and hard to follow, but it has a concrete implication. Error variance is used to compute the test statistics we have learned, such as the ts in t tests and the Fs in ANOVA. As a rule, the *smaller* the error variance, the *larger* the t or the F. Thus, with repeated-measures designs, researchers are more likely to get significant results. Although there is statistical power in repeated-measures designs, there are other concerns to be addressed, and it is to those concerns that we now turn.

Practice Effects

The main disadvantage of a repeated-measures design is what researchers call practice effects. **Practice effects** occur when participants' performance in an experiment changes simply because they have done the experimental task multiple times, rather than because of the experimental manipulation. Imagine an experiment examining memory for word lists as a function of using different memory strategies: (1) rote memorization, (2) using the word in a sentence, or (3) creating a rich visual image for the word. This experiment has one factor, *memory strategy*, with three levels. If this study were conducted using a repeated-measures design, participants would experience practice effects because they are doing the same task three times. If they improved in memory for words, it may be because of practice. If their performance decreased, it may be because they became fatigued (think of *fatigue effects* as the flip side of practice effects). Either way, changes in scores on the dependent variable might be unrelated to the independent variable, but due rather to practice or fatigue effects.

Counterbalancing

Researchers address the problem of practice effects by using one of three methods of counterbalancing. **Counterbalancing** is a method of alternating the order of delivery of the independent variable to reduce practice effects. First, researchers can use what is called an **ABBA design**. This is when one order of the levels of the independent variable is presented for one participant, then for the next participant the opposite order is used. This technique works well for repeated-measures variables with only two levels.

For example, if the independent variable is looking at a black computer background versus looking at a bright yellow computer background, half of the participants could receive the black-yellow order and half could receive the yellow-black order. The ABBA design will also work for more than two levels, but it is not as effective. With three levels of the independent variable, like the memory experiment described earlier, the two orders of an ABBA counterbalancing might be rote-sentence-image and image-sentence-rote. However, because "sentence" is always the middle trial, order effects could still be possible.

If the practice effects you are anticipating are strictly linear (that is, participants get either progressively better or worse on the task over time), then ABBA will work well. However, if you believe that the practice effects will change abruptly and will not be gradual, then ABBA will not be an optimal strategy. For example, in the memory experiment, because the *sentence* condition is always in the middle using the ABBA approach, the researchers cannot examine the effect of other memory strategies in the middle position. Depending on your hypothesis, you may find it important to view all the memory strategies in all of the positions.

A second approach to counterbalancing, called a Latin Square design, solves this problem. In a **Latin Square design**, each level of the repeated-measures independent variable appears in each position. So, in our memory experiment, each of the memory strategies will appear in the first, second, and third position as the independent variable is delivered to the participant. A problem with the ABBA design is that (with three levels) one of the levels stays in the same order during the whole experiment. A Latin Square solves that problem by having each level of the independent variable appear in each order. Table 6.3a shows an example of a Latin Square for three levels and Table 6.3b shows an example of a Latin Square for four levels (in this example, we added a fourth level of the independent variable and called it *no learning*).

A third possible way to counterbalance in a repeated-measures design is called **all-possible-orders counterbalancing**. In this type of counterbalancing, each level of the independent variable appears in each position and each level precedes and follows every other level equally often. So, an independent variable with *n* levels will require *n*! ("n factorial") orders. Table 6.4 shows the six possible orders of the memory experiment described earlier. The philosophy underlying this technique is that any practice effects will balance out over time.

TABLE 6.3a   Example of a Latin Square Design with Three Levels of the Repeated-Measures Variable

Trial 1	Trial 2	Trial 3
Rote	Sentence	Image
Sentence	Image	Rote
Image	Rote	Sentence

TABLE 6.3b Example of a Latin Square Design with Four Levels of the Repeated Measures Variable

Trial 1	Trial 2	Trial 3	Trial 4
Rote	Sentence	Image	No learning
Sentence	Image	No learning	Rote
Image	No learning	Rote	Sentence
No learning	Rote	Sentence	Image

TABLE 6.4 Example of All-Possible-Orders Counterbalancing

Trial 1	Trial 2	Trial 3
Rote	Sentence	Image
Rote	Image	Sentence
Sentence	Rote	Image
Sentence	Image	Rote
Image	Rote	Sentence
Image	Sentence	Rote

With many levels of a repeated-measures variable, it will take many participants to achieve all-possible-orders counterbalancing. Specifically, if there are n levels of the independent variable, it will take $n!$ participants to complete all the orders—and even then you will have only one complete replication of all of the orders. So: Is it worth it to employ a repeated-measures design rather than a between-groups design? The answer to this question varies based on the researchers' needs and available resources. The best general advice we can give is that although the elegance, statistical power, and economy of participant hours is attractive, if you anticipate (or find through pilot testing) that practice effects are common and noticeable, we recommend employing a between-groups design.

This discussion of counterbalancing may seem tedious and somewhat complicated. However, remember that you can always look up the specifics of a particular counterbalancing technique in this book or another research book. What is more important to remember is the philosophy of counterbalancing: namely, counterbalancing of order of presentation in a repeated-measures design is meant to average out practice effects over time, so that any changes practice might make in the dependent variable will be roughly the same for all levels of the repeated-measures variable. The Your Turn box gives you the opportunity to try the three counterbalancing techniques.

YOUR TURN

Counterbalancing

Researchers were interested in assessing students' beliefs about learning and knowledge in different academic disciplines. Researchers constructed a 20-item questionnaire to measure what students believe about these different academic disciplines. (For example, one question reads: "In this field, most questions have only one right answer.") Students responded on a five-point scale, with "1" being *strongly disagree* and "5" being *strongly agree.* Students were asked about three different academic disciplines: biology, psychology, and mathematics. Design counterbalancing plans using the following techniques: ABBA, Latin Square, and all-possible-orders.

ABBA	Trial 1	Trial 2	Trial 3
1.			
2.			
Latin Square			
1.			
2.			
3.			
All-Possible-Orders			
1.			
2.			
3.			
4.			
5.			
6.			

COMPLEX DESIGNS

As stated at the beginning of this chapter, a *complex design* is an experiment with more than one independent variable. In this section we describe two types of complex designs: designs that have two between-groups factors and designs that have one between-groups factor and one repeated-measures factor.

Complex Designs with Between-Groups Factors

In a complex design with two between-groups factors, each participant in the experiment receives only one level of each of the independent variables. The Epley and Kruger (2005) experiment described at the beginning of this chapter is an example of a 2 × 2 between-groups design. Each participant in the experiment received an expectation that he or she would interact *either* with an intelligent or an unintelligent person. Each participant communicated with this person *either* via voice or email. If the experiment had 40 participants, the researchers would place 10 participants in the intelligent/voice condition, 10 in the unintelligent/voice condition, 10 in the intelligent/email condition, and 10 in the unintelligent/email condition. Such a design, in which all the levels of one independent variable are paired with all the levels of the other independent variable, is called a **completely-crossed design**.

Between-groups factorials can be extended to any number of independent variables and any number of levels of those independent variables. For instance, the Epley and Kruger study could have been extended beyond expectancy and communication to include race/ethnicity (with four levels: black, white, Latino, Asian), and type of interaction that the participant had with the target person (with three levels: positive, negative, and neutral). This would have made a 2 × 2 × 4 × 3 design! As you can probably imagine, such designs get very complicated very quickly. They also become very expensive in terms of research participants. Just one replication of this hypothetical experiment would have required 48 participants (do you see why 48?). Complex designs with several factors also become very complicated statistically. We spoke of interactions earlier in this chapter, and will explore how to analyze them at the end of this chapter, but with three independent variables there exists the possibility of one three-way interaction (and its accompanying simple main effects), three two-way interactions (and their accompanying main effects), and three main effects (and their post-hoc tests). A detailed discussion of such analyses is beyond the scope of this book, but we alert you to it to make you aware of both the potential power and the potential complexities of multifactor designs. The Your Turn box is a demonstration of the random-assignment techniques learned in Chapter 5 applied to an experiment with two independent variables.

Mixed Designs

A **mixed design** is a complex experimental design that contains at least one between-groups factor and at least one repeated-measures factor. An experiment by Moshe Naveh-Benjamin and colleagues (Naveh-Benjamin, Craik, Guez, & Kreuger, 2005) provides an excellent example of this type of design. They studied word-recall memory as a function of four factors: aging, attention, word relatedness, and memory

YOUR TURN

Complex Designs

Here is a list of 40 participant names. The experiment is a test of the effects of memory strategy (imagery vs. no imagery) and cognitive load (a word presented every 6 seconds vs. a word presented every 10 seconds) on memory performance. Using what you have learned about random assignment, assign each participant to a strategy and cognitive-load condition.

Name	Strategy Condition 1 = imagery, 2 = no imagery)	Cognitive Load (1 = 6 seconds, 2 = 10 seconds)
Anderson		
Antonini		
Baltmanis		
Buckley		
Bulkeley		
Burton		
Eisenbrandt		
Farrell		
C. Gerig		
J. Gerig		
Geuder		
Hahnfeld		
Heller		
Kouchnerkavich		
Krolik		
Lewis		
Maharg		
Mack		
McEvoy		
Molter		
Muelenberg		
Muellner		
Oosterheert		
Otterness		
Price		
Rayberg		
Reynolds		
Roefer		
Ryczek		

Sato
Seymour
Skaistis
D. Smith
J. Smith
Swanezy
VanAssen
VanDordt
VanderLind
VanderPloeg
Wicklund

strategy. Specifically, they tested whether the following factors affected how well people could recall words: age (younger adult vs. older adult), memory strategy (given tips on how to improve memory vs. no training), distraction (participants gave sole attention to memory task vs. participants were distracted by a second task), and word relatedness (word pairs were related vs. unrelated). In all, then, this was a 2 (age) $\times$ 2 (strategy) $\times$ 2 (distraction) $\times$ 2 (relatedness) mixed design. Age and strategy were between-groups factors and distraction and relatedness were repeated-measures factors. In other words, participants studied words in both the distracted condition and the not-distracted condition. Also, participants studied some word pairs that were related and some that were unrelated.

To simplify matters, we will focus on the part of the experiment that involves age (young vs. old) and relatedness (related words vs. unrelated words). This portion of the experiment is a 2 $\times$ 2 mixed design, with age as a between-groups factor and relatedness as a repeated-measures factor. The percentage of recall of each of the four conditions is shown in Table 6.5. The researchers found a significant age-by-relatedness interaction. Analysis of the simple main effects showed that the older adults showed greater improvement when the words were related than the younger adults did. The younger adult showed greater improvement with related words, but not as great an improvement as the older adults showed.

Implementing a mixed design involves combining the strategies for between-group experiments from Chapter 5 with the strategies for repeated-measures experiments from this chapter. For the between-groups factor, participants are randomly assigned to the different levels of that factor. For example, the Naveh-Benjamin et al. (2005) study had a between-groups condition called *strategy* with two levels: giving participants memory tips versus not giving them memory tips. Just like any between-groups design, half of the participants should be randomly assigned to use a memory strategy and half *not* to use a memory strategy.

TABLE 6.5 **Interaction Effects in a Mixed Design**

	Participant Age		
Type of Word Pairs	**Young**	**Old**	**Ages Combined**
Related Pairs	.74	.57	.65
Unrelated Pairs	.60	.26	.43
Word Pairs Combined	.67	.41	.54

Note: Data show the proportion of words correctly recalled, from Naveh-Benjamin, Craik, Guez, and Kreuger (2005), Experiment 1.

After randomly assigning the between-groups factor, you should assign the levels of the repeated-measures factor *within each level* of the between-groups factor. In the Naveh-Benjamin study, the repeated-measures factor was related versus unrelated words. Taking first the participants assigned to the strategy condition, participants get assigned the two different types of words. The same occurs for the no-strategy condition. For both groups, make sure you implement the proper counterbalancing techniques to eliminate practice effects. The Your Turn box provides an opportunity for you to design this experiment.

One additional point is worth making: Sometimes the between-groups factor is a natural-groups variable. This was the case in the Naveh-Benjamin et al. study, in which the between-groups variable was age. As noted in Chapter 5, natural-groups variables cannot be randomly assigned. In this case you should divide your participants into the natural groups (for example, young vs. old) and then counterbalance the repeated-measures factor for each natural group separately. This will achieve the same result as randomly assigning participants to different between-groups factors.

YOUR TURN

Mixed Design

Here is a list of 40 participant names. The experiment tests the effects of a memory strategy (strategy vs. no strategy) and word relatedness (related vs. unrelated pairs) on recall performance. Using what you have learned about random assignment for between-groups factors and counterbalancing for repeated-measures factors, assign each participant to a strategy (between-groups) and related (repeated-measures) condition. The first is provided to get you started.

Name	Strategy Condition (1 = imagery, 2 = no imagery)	Relatedness Condition (indicate counterbalancing order; R = related pair, U = unrelated pair)
Anderson	1	R-U
Antonini		
Baltmanis		
Buckley		
Bulkeley		
Burton		
Eisenbrandt		
Farrell		
C. Gerig		
J. Gerig		
Geuder		
Hahnfeld		
Heller		
Kouchnerkavich		
Krolik		
Lewis		
Maharg		
Mack		
McEvoy		
Molter		
Muelenberg		
Muellner		
Oosterheert		
Otterness		
Price		
Rayberg		
Reynolds		
Roefer		
Ryczek		
Sato		
Seymour		
Skaistis		
D. Smith		
J. Smith		
Swanezy		
VanAssen		
VanDordt		
VanderLind		
VanderPloeg		
Wicklund		

Solomon Four-Group Design   The **Solomon four-group design** is a special case of the mixed design, used when the presence of a pretest might create a practice effect. It is considered a quasi-experimental design, so it provides an excellent transition into the discussion of the next section of the chapter. The design involves four groups and appears as follows:

Group 1:	Pretest	Treatment	Posttest
Group 2:	No Pretest	Treatment	Posttest
Group 3:	Pretest	Placebo	Posttest
Group 4:	No Pretest	Placebo	Posttest

The major benefit of this design applies to studies in which researchers believe that the presence of a pretest could in some way affect scores on the dependent variable at the posttest. For example, if a data-collection instrument asks about particularly sensitive matters, which may in turn cause a change in a person's behavior or attitude in the future, a Solomon four-group design may be appropriate. For example, Hunt and Hunt (2004) examined the effects of an intervention designed to raise awareness of the problems people with disabilities face in the workplace. They developed an intervention to teach workers about these dilemmas and administered the Attitudes Toward Disabled Persons Scale (ATDPS) according to the four-group design shown here:

Group 1: ATDPS pretest with intervention

Group 2: No ATDPS pretest with intervention

Group 3: ATDPS pretest with no intervention

Group 4: No ATDPS pretest with no intervention

A Solomon four-group design is appropriate if there is something about the ATDPS instrument itself that could change attitudes or behaviors. This design allows the researchers to separate out the effects of the intervention from the effects of simply filling out the ATDPS. We next turn to a discussion of quasi-experiments and the challenges faced by researchers who conduct investigations in real-life settings.

QUASI-EXPERIMENTAL DESIGNS

As we begin our discussion of quasi-experimental designs, it will be helpful to review the characteristics of high-quality experiments discussed in Chapter 3. According to Shaughnessy, Zechmeister, and Zechmeister (2006), a "true" experiment has three qualities: (1) introduction of an independent variable by the researcher, (2) control of the experimental setting, and (3) presence of the proper comparisons (for example, a control group). It is possible to achieve these criteria in an experimental setting. However, in quasi-experimental settings, it is more difficult. In this section we describe what a quasi-experiment is and challenges faced by researchers who conduct quasi-experiments.

What Is a Quasi-Experiment?

A *quasi-experiment* (defined in Chapter 2) is a study that takes place in a real-life setting as opposed to a laboratory. For example, Padgett and Reid (2002) examined the effects of a student diversity program at a university in the western United States. In this quasi-experiment, they compared students who participated in the diversity program to students who did not participate. Their dependent variables were, among other things, GPA and graduation rate. They found no significance difference between the two groups on GPA, but found that those who took the diversity program had higher graduation rates than those who did not participate in the program. Sounds great, right? The conclusion from the data seems straightforward: providing students with diversity training increases graduation rates. Unfortunately, with quasi-experimental designs, such conclusions are not so easily drawn.

Difficulties with Experiments in Real-Life Settings

The difficulties with experiments in real-life settings correspond to the three characteristics of true experiments just discussed. Specifically, in a true experiment the independent variable is introduced by the researcher. In quasi-experiments, this is not always the case. Sometimes the researchers introduce an independent variable in a real-life setting. For example, state education officials could introduce a new mathematics curriculum to some districts but not others. However, it could also be the case that an intervention was created and implemented by someone else and then studied by researchers.

Also, in true experiments researchers have control over the experimental setting. This is not so in quasi-experiments. The influence of possible external factors cannot be estimated or controlled. For example, if a major racial incident broke out on campus during the Padgett and Reid diversity study, this would likely affect the outcome of the study, thus creating an extraneous variable. In other words, researchers who conduct quasi-experiments never achieve the degree of control that laboratory researchers obtain.

Finally, true experiments have proper comparisons. Quasi-experiments usually have a comparison group, such as in the study by Padgett and Reid: They had some who took the diversity training and some who did not. However, if the two groups are not randomly assigned to conditions, the comparison has less internal validity than a true experiment. Such non-random assignment to conditions constitutes what researchers call a **non-equivalent control group**: a comparison group that is created by some method other than traditional randomization (see Cook & Campbell, 1979).

Some quasi-experiments will, to some extent, look like true experiments on these three dimensions of control over the independent variable, control over assigning participants to conditions, and control over the setting. In the next section we expand on these three characteristics by looking at ways in which the internal validity of experiments is called into question. Given the lack of control of quasi-experiments, it is not surprising that these threats to internal validity occur more frequently in quasi-experimental designs.

Threats to Internal Validity

In this section we consider factors that can threaten the internal validity of an experiment, or the ability to interpret the relationship between cause and effect. The reason we discuss these threats to internal validity in the quasi-experiment section is that quasi-experiments are particularly susceptible to these problems. Although laboratory research can be plagued by them as well, for the most part there are specific techniques available to counteract these threats in a lab setting (for example, counterbalancing, random assignment, matching). However, in quasi-experimental research, researchers may need to live with some ambiguity about their conclusions. Thus, it is important to become knowledgeable about these issues and how they can limit your findings.

Why, you might ask, would you even bother to conduct an experiment that might be limited by threats to internal validity? The answer is that, although the internal validity of quasi-experiments is not as high as that of laboratory experiments, quasi-experiments bring with them added external validity, because they take place in real-life settings with participants who regularly inhabit that setting. In short, researchers who conduct quasi-experiments trade the added external validity for a possible decrease in internal validity.

History One possible threat to internal validity is history. **History** is when participants in a study experience some common social or cultural event, not related to the independent variable, that could affect the outcome of the study. Because laboratory experiments do not usually last for very long (one or two hours), the chance of history affecting the results is minimal. However, in a quasi-experiment conducted over a long period of time, history does indeed pose a threat. Major cultural events are most noteworthy historical threats. Conducting an intervention on school bullying in the midst of a school shooting would be a tragic example of history. Another example of history would be conducting an intervention on religious tolerance in the midst of violence perpetrated by an extremist religious group. Historical threats are impossible to control, although it is essential to be aware of them.

Maturation **Maturation** is when the participants change during the course of the experiment. Examples include changes in ability, physical strength, vision, and intellectual growth or decline. Like history, maturation becomes more likely the longer the experimental intervention takes place. Author VanderStoep once worked with a cardiologist who designed an educational intervention for patients who had congestive heart failure. Even though the program was successful, the physician and the researcher were always working against time and the poor health conditions of his patients.

You can think of practice effects as a type of maturation. Earlier we discussed practice effects in terms of repeated-measures experiments. Those practice effects are solved by counterbalancing the order of presentation of the dependent variable. However, in quasi-experimental designs you do not have that luxury. Over time, if people's scores get better or worse as a function of completing the dependent variable often, you have a potential practice effect. Imagine an intervention to improve factory productivity. If productivity is continuously measured while the intervention is going on, it would be difficult to determine if any improvement is due to the intervention or simply because people are getting better at their jobs.

Perhaps (we hope!) you are thinking that the way to solve this problem is with the presence of a control group. If so, you are thinking like a researcher. However, the researchers' interest in a control group conflicts with the practical constraint that a control group might not be available. If you are a factory owner, you probably own only one factory, and therefore finding a control group would involve assigning half of your employees to the intervention and half to a control group. If all the employees work at the same site and talk to each other, implementing such a control group is problematic. Therefore, a control group is desirable from the researchers' perspective but undesirable from the practitioners' perspective.

Instrumentation **Instrumentation** effects occur when the scale, survey, or performance measure used to measure the dependent variable changes over time. This could happen if researchers change instruments in the middle of a study. For example, if a school district is studying the effects of a new mathematics curriculum on achievement, and the state mandates a change in the state assessment instrument, the study would be a victim of instrumentation threat. Another instrumentation threat occurs if researchers change their criteria or judgments (unknowingly) during the course of a study.

Yet another instrumentation threat arises if all the participants score at the highest level on the dependent measure. This is known as a **ceiling effect**. For example, if all or almost all of the participants rated something a "5" on a five-point attitude scale, there would be no way to detect any differences. As another example, suppose that on a pretest of an educational intervention all of the students are already performing at or near 100% correct; in this case there will be no way to judge the effectiveness of the intervention. This problem is best solved by *pilot testing* (testing the instrument on a different sample before beginning the actual research project) the instrument to make sure there is no ceiling effect.

Regression to the Mean To understand this threat to internal validity, you need to know that any score on any social science scale, test, or survey is a measure of two things: true score and measurement error. The *true score* is what the participant would score if researchers had perfect measurement ability and people never varied from setting to setting. The *measurement error* is the part of a score (say, on a test) that is not due to actual ability, such as fatigue, motivation, or blind luck. Imagine an intelligence test. Sometimes the measurement error works in participants' favor (in a good mood, guessed correctly), giving them scores *above* their true scores. At other times, the measurement error works against participants (in a bad mood, guessed incorrectly), giving them scores *below* their true scores. With that as background, we can now define **regression to the mean** as a fundamental law of statistics stating that scores that are way above or way below the mean will, on a subsequent measure, return or regress back toward the true mean. If the out-of-the-ordinary score is way above average, the next time the score is likely to be lower; if the score is way below average, the next time the score is likely to be higher.

Why is regression to the mean a threat to internal validity? Because if changes in mean scores are a result of regression to the mean rather than the independent variable, then the cause-effect relationship cannot be determined. As an example, imagine that a school principal selects students with standardized test scores below the 25th percentile. The next school year, the principal offers a great deal of enrichment for these students, including after-school study opportunities, one-on-one tutoring in the classroom, and parent-education courses on how to help children achieve in school. At the end of the subsequent school year, she finds tremendous improvement in these students' test scores. Putting aside our belief that this is a wonderful effort by the principal, it may be the case that changes in test scores are a result of regression to the mean rather than her great interventions. Why? Some of those students with low scores were in fact scoring near their "true" mean, but some of those students may simply have had measurement error frowning on them on that test day. Thus, because regression to the mean tells us that measurement error will statistically correct itself, those students are going to score higher the next time regardless of the intervention.

Attrition We discussed attrition in Chapter 2 when we covered sampling. It is when participants drop out of a study. On its face, such a fact would not be a source of concern. However, when the dropout occurs more often in the treatment group or more often among one group of people, then attrition is a problem. For example, consider a voluntary program to encourage teenagers to abstain from cigarette smoking. If participation in the program is voluntary, and those initially predisposed to smoke find the program preachy and boring, then dropout among this group will be greater. Consequently, those left in the program are going to be more motivated than those who dropped out. Therefore, if the researchers find that smoking rates are down as a result of the program, it could be because of the program, but it could also be because of attrition: those who were inclined to smoke dropped out and those who were motivated not to smoke stayed with it, thus creating an artificially high nonsmoking rate among those in the treatment group.

The challenges to quasi-experimental designs discussed in this section should not discourage people from conducting such studies. Indeed, some of the best findings in the different fields of social science have come from quasi-experimental designs. The purpose of this section is to alert researchers to the extra care needed to implement a quasi-experimental design.

DATA ANALYSIS

Now that we have described how to successfully conduct an experiment or quasi-experiment, it is time to analyze the data. In this section, we describe analysis techniques for repeated-measures and complex designs. In Chapter 5 we showed you that a t test is used to analyze a between-groups design with two groups, and that an F test (ANOVA) is used to analyze a between-groups design with more than two groups. The same techniques are used for repeated-measures designs: a t test for the two-group case and an F test (ANOVA) for more than three groups. We show you how to perform these repeated-measures tests in this section.

For complex designs, the proper technique is again an ANOVA, but in this case it is called a *two-way ANOVA*. As mentioned earlier, for complex designs, the first step is to test whether the interaction is statistically significant. If the interaction is *not* significant, you next analyze the main effects separately. If the interaction *is* significant, you analyze the simple main effects. We describe the analyses for repeated-measures, between-groups, and mixed designs, and then in each section provide a Your Turn box to practice analyzing complex designs.

Repeated-Measures ANOVA

Recall that in repeated-measures designs participants receive more than one level of the independent variable. (Another way to say it is that the dependent variable is measured on more than one occasion.) The most basic form of this type of design involves two levels, such as a pretest-posttest design. In Chapter 5 we showed how a between-groups design with two levels is analyzed with an independent-samples *t* test. In a repeated-measures design with two levels, the statistical test that is used is called a paired *t* test. The **paired *t* test** tests whether two means in a repeated-measures study are statistically different. Although the computation of the two tests is slightly different, SPSS handles this part for you. The Your Turn box gives you the opportunity to conduct a paired *t* test.

YOUR TURN

Paired Samples *t* Test

Enter the following data into an SPSS dataset. The dataset contains pretest and posttest measures of a science-achievement test. The test was a 10-item test of material covered in the course. The pretest scores were collected before students took a course entitled "Science and Technology for Everyday Life." The posttest scores were collected from students at the end of the semester.

Pretest	Posttest
3	9
3	9
6	6
4	9
3	8
5	7
1	8
2	9
4	7
5	9
5	9
2	8
3	8

5	8
4	9
3	8
0	8
2	8
4	9
2	8
2	8
4	9
2	9
4	7
5	9
4	7
3	8
3	7
5	8
0	8
4	7
3	8
3	7
4	8
6	6
5	9

To perform the paired *t* test, pull down the Analysis menu. Select Compare Means, then Paired-Samples *t* test. Click the variable that is the pretest, then click on the variable that is the posttest. Both variable names will turn black. Click the arrow to move them to the right side of the dialog box. Click OK.

What are the pretest and posttest means? _____

What is the value of the *t* test and its accompanying *p* value?_____

How would you interpret these findings? _____

If the independent variable in a repeated-measures design has more than two levels, the procedure to test significant differences is called a **repeated-measures ANOVA**. Recall that in Chapter 5 we demonstrated an ANOVA for a between-groups design with three or more levels. The same principle applies in the repeated-measures case (although through a slightly different computation, which is handled in SPSS). If the F statistic from the ANOVA is significant, just as with the between-groups case we must conduct post-hoc tests. In the repeated-measures case, this simply amounts to conducting paired t tests for the pairs of means you would like to compare. For example, if a university assessment director wants to study students' changes in attitudes over four years in college, she would need to conduct a repeated-measures ANOVA. The Your Turn box illustrates how to conduct this ANOVA and the subsequent post-hoc tests.

YOUR TURN

Repeated-Measures ANOVA

Enter the following (hypothetical) data into SPSS:

Fresh	Soph	Junior	Senior
1	2	3	3
2	1	2	3
2	2	1	3
3	3	3	1
3	1	1	3
1	2	4	2
1	2	2	2
2	2	2	2
2	3	2	3
3	2	3	3
4	2	3	4
1	2	3	4
1	3	2	3
2	2	3	3
2	2	3	2
3	2	2	3
2	2	4	1
2	1	2	2
2	2	3	3

These hypothetical data measure students' responses to the following question from the National Survey of Student Engagement: "Please indicate the extent to which you had serious conversations with students of a different race or ethnicity than your own." Students responded on a four-point scale with "1" being *never,* "2" being *sometimes,* "3" being *often,* and "4" being *very often.* The same group of students was asked this question in each of their four years of college. (This is what makes this a repeated-measures design. If students from different graduating classes had been asked the same question, it would have been a between-groups design.) To conduct a repeated-measures ANOVA:

1. Select *Analyze/General Linear Model/Repeated Measures.*
2. Type a name in the Within Subjects Factor box. It will say "factor1" as a default, and you can leave that if you want. But you could change it, to "year," for example.
3. Type the number of levels of the repeated-measures factor (in this case, 4).
4. Click *Add.* The independent variable you just named will appear in the large box below.
5. Click *Define.* A box will appear for you to enter the levels of your repeated-measures independent variable. Enter the variables *Fresh, Soph, Junior,* and *Senior* one at a time. They will move from the left to the right side of the screen.
6. Click *Options* at the bottom. Move the independent variable you just created from the left box to the right box. Select *Descriptive Statistics* from the bottom. This will display the mean values for each level of the independent variable as shown below.
7. Click *OK.*

The results you get should produce mean scores for the four years. If you got 2.05, 2.00, 2.53, and 2.63 for the freshmen, sophomore, junior, and senior means, respectively, you did this correctly. The F statistic for this data set is 4.203. It shows up several times under *Multivariate Tests(b).* The explanation for the other statistics you see in this portion of the output is beyond the scope of this book. What is important is to focus on the F value and its p value. This indicates if there is any statistically significant difference between the four levels of the independent variable. When the overall effect is significant, you must conduct follow-up tests to determine where those differences exist (just as with between-groups ANOVA). Unlike the between-groups design, which employs a test such as the Tukey HSD test, follow-up tests in a repeated-measures design are simply paired t tests (see above) of the different pairs of means you would like to compare. In this case, for example, it seems clear that freshmen and sophomores do not differ significantly, nor is it likely that juniors and seniors differ. It would be interesting, though, to compare sophomores to juniors (see the previous Your Turn box for information on conducting paired t tests). What do the results of this study show? _____

_____

_____

ANOVA for Complex Designs

When Interaction Is Not Significant We first describe the case when the interaction is not significant. When this occurs, we move immediately to the main effects. If a main effect is significant and has only two levels, we treat it just like we treated a *t* test in Chapter 5—with only two levels of an independent variable, simply inspecting the means tells us which group is significantly higher. However, if the significant main effect has three or more levels, we must conduct post-hoc tests, just as in Chapter 5. A common post-hoc test is the Tukey HSD. For example, consider the output in Figure 6.1. The main effect for the first variable (INDVAR1) is significant, $F = 90.947, p < .001$. Because IND-VAR1 has three levels, we need to request the Tukey HSD procedure to determine which of the means differ from one another. In this case, the output at the bottom of Figure 6.1 (under *Multiple Comparisons*) shows that all three post-hoc comparisons are significant: level 1 (mean = 4.875) is significantly different from level 2 (mean = 7.875), level 2 is significantly different from level 3 (mean = 1.875), and level 1 is significantly different from level 3.

When Interaction Is Significant If the interaction *is* significant, we must analyze simple main effects. Conducting these analyses in SPSS is beyond the scope of this book (Green & Salkind, 2005, is an advanced data analysis text with an excellent explanation of these techniques). However, the Your Turn box gives you an opportunity to look at a graphical representation of a complex design with a significant interaction, and asks you to interpret the graph in terms of simple main effects.

Mixed-Design ANOVA Recall that a mixed design has one between-groups factor and one repeated-measures factor. Interpreting a mixed-design ANOVA is the same as interpreting a complex-design ANOVA with two between-groups factors. The first step is to check whether the interaction is statistically significant. If the interaction is *not* significant, main effects are analyzed. If a significant main effect has only two levels, then we examine the means in the SPSS output to determine which level of the independent variable produced a higher score on the dependent variable. If the significant main effect has more than two levels, we handle it the same way as we would in an ANOVA with one factor: by conducting post-hoc tests. Specifically, if the repeated-measures variable is the significant effect, the post-hoc test to be used is paired *t* tests (see earlier in this chapter). If the between-groups factor is the significant main effect, the post-hoc test to be used is the Tukey HSD (see Chapter 5).

If the interaction is statistically significant, simple main effects must be analyzed just as with complex designs involving two between-groups factors. As with other interaction effects discussed earlier in this chapter, conducting tests on simple main effects of a mixed design is beyond the scope of this book. However, the Your Turn box gives you an opportunity to interpret a graph of a 2×4 mixed design.

Tests of Between-Subjects Effects

Dependent Variable: DEPVAR

Source	Type III Sum of Squares	df	Mean Square	F	Sig.
Corrected Model	144.375[a]	5	28.875	36.474	.000
Intercept	570.375	1	570.375	720.474	.000
INDVAR1	144.000	2	72.000	90.947	.000
INDVAR2	.375	1	.375	.474	.500
INDVAR1 * INDVAR2	.000	2	.000	.000	1.000
Error	14.250	18	.792		
Total	729.000	24			
Corrected Total	158.625	23			

[a]R Squared = .910 (Adjusted R Squared = .885)

1. INDVAR1

Dependent Variable: DEPVAR

INDVAR1	Mean	Std. Error	95% Confidence Interval Lower Bound	Upper Bound
1.00	4.875	.315	4.214	5.536
2.00	7.875	.315	7.214	8.536
3.00	1.875	.315	1.214	2.536

Post-Hoc Tests: Multiple Comparisons

Dependent Variable: DEPVAR
Tukey HSD

(I) INDVAR1	(J) IND-VAR1	Mean Difference (I-J)	Std. Error	Sig.	95% Confidence Interval Lower Bound	Upper Bound
1.00	2.00	−3.0000*	.44488	.000	−4.1354	−1.8646
	3.00	3.0000*	.44488	.000	1.8646	4.1354
2.00	1.00	3.0000*	.44488	.000	1.8646	4.1354
	3.00	6.0000*	.44488	.000	4.8646	7.1354
3.00	1.00	−3.0000*	.44488	.000	−4.1354	−1.8646
	2.00	−6.0000*	.44488	.000	−7.1354	−4.8646

Based on observed means.
*The mean difference is significant at the .05 level.

FIGURE 6.1. *Selected statistical output from a two-way ANOVA*

YOUR TURN

ANOVA for Complex Designs

Enter the following data into SPSS:

Instruct	Probtype	Depvar
1	1	70
1	2	50
1	1	72
1	2	63
1	1	72
1	2	62
2	1	80
2	2	70
2	1	82
2	2	72
2	1	83
2	2	74
3	1	90
3	2	92
3	1	92
3	2	94
3	1	94
3	2	90

The variable *Instruct* describes one of three types of teaching mathematical problem-solving: standard/control (1), emphasis on computation (2), or emphasis on real-life applications (3). The variable *Probtype* refers to the type of mathematics problems students were asked to solve, either easy (1) or hard (2). This is the way to set up the data if both independent variables are between-groups factors. (We show you how to set up the data from repeated-measures designs in the next Your Turn box.) *Depvar* refers to the percentage of problems students correctly solved after the instructional intervention. To conduct a two-way analysis of variance, take the following steps:

1. Pull down the *Analyze* menu and select *General Linear Model/Univariate.*
2. Place *Depvar* in the *Dependent Variable* box and *Instruct* and *Probtype* in the *Fixed Factor(s)* box.

3. Select the *Options* tab. Move the two main effects and the interaction (Instruct*Probtype) from the left side to the right side (labeled *Display Means for*). Below that, select the Descriptive Statistics box.
4. Select the *Plots* tab. Place I*nstruct* in the *Horizontal Axis box* and *Probtype* in the *Separate Lines* box.
5. Click *OK.*

Is the interaction significant? If so, the simple main effects must be analyzed. Although we will not analyze simple main effects using SPSS, inspecting the following graph will give you an indication of the nature of the simple main effects. If you have done the analysis correctly, you should get a graph that looks like Figure 6.2.

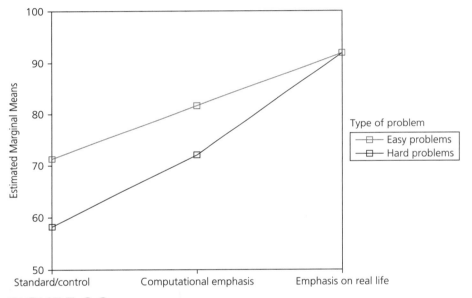

FIGURE 6.2.   *Two-way ANOVA with significant interaction*

Based on the graph, how would you describe in words the nature of this interaction and simple main effects?_____
_____
_____

YOUR TURN

Your Turn: Mixed Design ANOVA

Enter the following data into SPSS:

Gender	Fresh	Soph	Junior	Senior
1	1	0	0	0
1	0	0	2	3
1	2	2	1	0
1	3	2	0	1
1	0	0	1	0
1	1	1	0	2
1	1	1	2	2
1	2	2	0	2
1	0	0	2	0
2	0	2	4	4
2	1	0	2	4
2	1	0	2	1
2	0	0	3	2
2	3	2	2	2
2	3	3	2	3
2	2	4	3	4
2	0	3	1	4
2	1	4	3	3
2	1	3	2	4

These are the (hypothetical) data on students' reading behavior over time in college. The first variable is gender. Using the *Values* column in *Variable View,* code it as 1 = male and 2 = female. The next four columns are the responses, for each of four years of college, to the question: "How many books have you read on your own that were not part of course assignments?"

1. Select *Analyze/General Linear Model/Repeated Measures.*
2. Type a name in the Within Subjects Factor box. It will say "factor1" as a default, and you can leave that if you want (or you can rename it something like "year").
3. Type the number of levels of the repeated-measures factor (in this case, 4).
4. Click *Add.* The independent variable you just named will appear in the large box below.

5. Click *Define*. A box will appear for you to enter the levels of the repeated-measures independent variable. Enter the variables *Fresh, Soph, Junior,* and *Senior* one at a time. They will move from the left to the right side of the screen.
6. Click the variable *Gender* and enter it in the box that says *Between-Groups Factor(s).*
7. Click *Options* at the bottom. Move the between-groups factor, the repeated-measures factor, and the interaction from the left-hand side to the right-hand side. Select *Descriptive Statistics* from the bottom of this box. This will display the mean values for each level for the two main effects and the interaction.
8. Click *OK*.

We show some of the results here. The ANOVA for a mixed design will be covered in a more advanced course. Still, we do present the mean scores and the graph (see Figure 6.3). As can be seen from the results, the men and women in this sample do not appear to differ in the number of books that they read in the first year of college. However, over the course of their college journey, women read more than men. In this case the interaction is not statistically significant ($p = .056$), although the graph clearly shows a trend. If the interaction had been significant, it would have required the analysis of simple main effects. In this study, there are five possible simple main effects to be analyzed. Can you identify what they are?

_____

_____

_____

_____

Descriptive Statistics

	GENDER	Mean	Std. Deviation	N
First Year	male	1.1111	1.05409	9
	female	1.2000	1.13529	10
	Total	1.1579	1.06787	19
Second Year	male	.8889	.92796	9
	female	2.1000	1.59513	10
	Total	1.5263	1.42861	19
Third Year	male	.8889	.92796	9
	female	2.4000	.84327	10
	Total	1.6842	1.15723	19
Fourth Year	male	1.1111	1.16667	9
	female	3.1000	1.10050	10
	Total	2.1579	1.50049	19

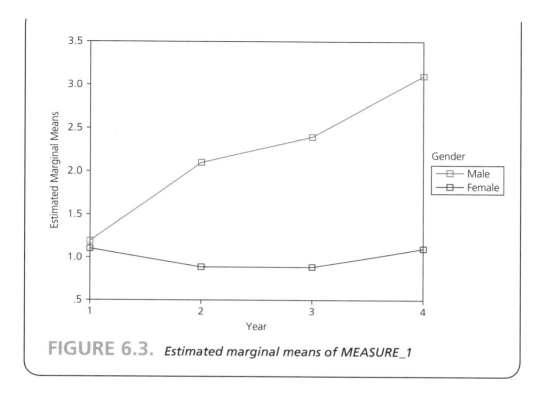

FIGURE 6.3. *Estimated marginal means of MEASURE_1*

SUMMARY

This chapter provided strategies for conducting and analyzing advanced experimental designs. Conducting repeated-measures designs involves taking into consideration practice effects and attempting to balance those effects equally over the different levels of the independent variable. This will ensure that any difference observed in the dependent is a result of the independent variable and not simply improvement or decline due to experience or fatigue. Conducting complex designs with between-groups factors involves the same procedures as described for one-variable experiments in Chapter 5 (for example, random assignment, matching). Conducting mixed-design studies with one between-groups variable and one repeated-measures variable involves combining the strategies for conducting between-groups and repeated-measures designs in the same experiment.

Quasi-experimental designs are experiments whose purpose is to measure the effect of an independent variable on a dependent variable that occurs in a real-life setting. Researchers who conduct quasi-experiments gain important insight into people's performance in settings where those people actually live, work, and learn. However, quasi-experimental designs are hampered by threats to internal validity, which make statements about causality less certain.

Finally, analysis of data from complex designs involves first checking for a statistically significant interaction between the two variables. If the interaction is significant, the next step is to analyze simple main effects. If the interaction is not significant, the next step is to analyze main effects, which is similar to treating each independent variable as a separate experiment.

KEY TERMS

ABBA design
all-possible-orders counterbalancing
between-group error variance
between-groups design
ceiling effect
completely-crossed design
complex designs
counterbalancing
error variance
history
instrumentation
interaction
Latin Square design

main effect
maturation
mixed design
non-equivalent control group
paired *t* test
practice effects
regression to the mean
repeated-measures ANOVA
repeated-measures design
replication
simple main effect
Solomon four-group design
within-group error variance

CHAPTER

7

WHAT IS QUALITATIVE RESEARCH?

LEARNING OBJECTIVES

- Explore the narrative, storytelling qualities underlying qualitative research.
- Identify the differences in qualitative and quantitative research assumptions regarding purpose, focus, method, and criteria for truth.
- Describe how qualitative research emerged out of a critique of certain aspects of quantitative research.

In this chapter we explore what it means to take a qualitative research perspective. We not only discuss what is unique about qualitative research, but also seek to understand the qualitative perspective by contrasting it with what you have already learned about the quantitative perspective. When a researcher assumes a qualitative perspective, the type of questions asked and the type of answers found are different. The decision to use a qualitative or quantitative research method should depend on your research questions.

TELLING A STORY . . . QUALITATIVELY

Sometimes when you read the report of a quantitative study, the findings leave you asking for more. Questions zip through your mind. You want to know the *story* behind the statistics. You want to know about the *individuals* who make up the averages, and especially those who constitute the **outliers**—the few cases in quantitative studies that are far above or below the averages.

This happens when I (author Johnston) read OSHA statistics. The Occupational Safety and Health Administration publishes quantitative data each year on work-related injuries, including an analysis of accidents by occupation. As a qualitative researcher who grew up in rural Iowa, I know that there is a **grand narrative**—a story—underlying the OSHA statistics regarding farm-implement accidents. By analyzing a story according to the characteristics of a grand narrative, we gain insight into the meanings and functions of events.

A grand narrative is characterized by a **prescribed sequence**, **required elements**, **identifiable functions**, and a **script**. The grand narrative of a murder mystery novel, for example, follows a genre-specific plot sequence and required elements, including: murder, discovery of body, investigation by a likeable detective with some inherent personal weakness, and the apprehension of a murderer who has been corrupted by greed, lust, or some other sin. A grand narrative also serves identifiable functions or purposes. Common functions of grand narratives include helping a community make sense of some phenomenon or providing a moral lesson.

The people of a community or culture who share a grand narrative also know how to assume a particular role to participate in the construction of the narrative script. You know, for example, how to construct a birth narrative by asking all the right questions when someone reports the birth of a baby: Is it a girl or a boy? How big was it? How long was the labor?

People in rural Iowa know how to participate in the farm-accident narrative. Growing up in Iowa, I observed and participated in this narrative many times. As a qualitative researcher reflecting on these memories, I was struck by the consistent format of this narrative.

> *Troy lost his thumb! Got his sleeve caught in the thresher!*
> *(Listener interjects: Was he able to find it [the thumb]?)*
> *He was clear in the southwest pasture.*
> *[How he got his sleeve caught might interest OSHA, but is not a very important story element for the grand narrative. Indeed, to ask how he got his sleeve caught might raise questions as to Troy's competence, so this part of the story is generally skipped over quite quickly and the focus goes immediately to the journey of the appendage.]*
> *Ripped his thumb right off. He couldn't find it at first …*
> *[increase drama]*
> *but crawled around under the thresher*
> *[insertion of scary image for listener—did he turn the thresher off first?]*
> *and finally found it about 15 feet away!*
> *Had to walk two miles back to the house to get his truck.*
> *(Listener might interject at this point because important story element, the "vessel," is missing: "But what did he carry it in?")*
> *He put it in the lid to his thermos and walked about two miles to the truck.*
> *He drove the 10 miles into town and they got it reattached.*
> *[almost anticlimactic after the hero's journey.]*

The teller of the narrative goes immediately to the punch line of the story: "Troy lost his thumb!" Shortly after the "Oh my!," the listener should ask, "Were they able to find it [the thumb]?" This prompts the teller to initiate the plot sequence: description of the location of Troy's accident; description of the severing of the appendage; Troy's search to recover the appendage; Troy's search for a vessel in which to carry the appendage; Troy's journey to the nearest phone, vehicle, or person; and (it is hoped) the doctor's miraculous reattachment of the severed appendage. If any part of the sequence is skipped, the listener prods the teller back to the grand narrative sequence by asking, for example: "How far was he from the house?"

Note the required elements of this story that are very important to the grand narrative in the rural community in which I grew up: finding the appendage, transporting the appendage, getting to the hospital. An outsider to the community would not recognize the importance and necessity of these elements for the narrative. Finding the appendage speaks to the hero's presence of mind in an emergency situation and also acts as an instructional tale to teach the community the importance of this step for recovery.

The vessel is also an important narrative element. Sometimes the injured in these stories spend an inordinate amount of time looking for the vessel to carry the appendage. This story element speaks to the presence of mind of the injured hero, who not only recovers the appendage but also finds an appropriate vessel for transporting it. It is also important to note that the hero invariably drives himself or herself to the hospital in these narratives.

So what does an analysis of farm-accident grand narratives tell us that the OSHA statistics do not? Qualitative research is more likely to explore *processes* (for example, how the community makes sense of the accident) than *outcomes* (the frequency of farm accidents). Qualitative research focuses on the *meanings* of experiences by exploring how people define, describe, and metaphorically make sense of these experiences. The grand narrative has identifiable functions for the community, in that it instructs its members in emergency procedures and models the presence of mind required in such an emergency.

In terms of OSHA's goal to improve worker safety, it might be important to know that the injured farmer is cast in a hero-quest narrative, and if successful in this quest becomes a community legend. The farmer in the author Johnston's hometown, who severed part of his arm, recovered the arm, opened the cattle gate, walked back to the house, and drove himself (one-armed and bleeding profusely) to the hospital, is legendary. The story of the hero's journey has been retold for decades, across generations of family and friends. Stories that vary from the grand narrative (e.g., the injured who lose their presence of mind, never recover the severed appendage in a sacred vessel, are close to the house or phone at the time of injury, or who rely on others to drive them to the hospital) are not quite as legendary. Thus, to be effective, any OSHA safety program would have to develop the image of the safe worker as hero to counter the grand narrative of the injured hero. The injured farmer is an epic warrior whose battle wounds are testimony to his character.

TWO WORLDVIEWS ON RESEARCH: REALITY AND KNOWLEDGE

The study of knowledge is called **epistemology**, and the epistemological assumptions of qualitative and quantitative approaches to research are radically different. A quantitative research perspective assumes that knowledge is "out there" to be discovered; there is a physical, knowable reality that can be observed by a trained researcher. Moreover, this reality can be dismantled and its parts extensively examined. The lab scientist examining subatomic particles is making epistemological assumptions similar to those of the social scientist who is developing a written test to assess reading competencies. The physical scientist studies the different components of atoms or molecules and the social scientist studies the different components of reading comprehension (e.g., decoding, comprehension strategies).

Contrast this view of knowledge with a qualitative research perspective. A qualitative perspective assumes that knowledge is constructed through communication and interaction; as such, knowledge is not "out there" but within the perceptions and interpretations of the individual. In short, knowledge is constructed or created by people. A qualitative perspective assumes that you cannot analyze and understand an entity by analysis of its parts; rather, you must examine the larger context in which people and knowledge function. This concept is called the **social construction of reality**.

Let's look at an example. Qualitative research focuses on the social and cultural construction of meaning. You probably believe that weather changes are a result of changes in barometric pressure. Someone else—let's call him Wayon—from another culture, geography, or worldview, knows (with the same sense of certainty) that weather reflects the moods of the gods. Assuming a socially constructed view of reality, you cannot say that Wayon is wrong and you are right. Wayon simply has a different view of reality, which is just as real and valid for him as yours is for you. You call it barometric pressure, he calls it gods.

How does the social construction of reality influence research? Let's explore rock climbing as an example. Quantitative research could tell us the number of people who participate in rock climbing, the ranking of rock climbing as a sport in various countries, and even some personality predictors of interest in rock climbing. Qualitative research could tell us what rock climbers think about the process of rock climbing. Reid describes how "mountain climbers positively relish the almost perfect vigor of their discipline's cardinal directive: Go to the edge and perform flawlessly, and you will survive (probably) to go to the edge again" (1991, p. 8). Lyng (1990) analyzes the function of "edgework"— the making of life-and-death decisions under extreme stress—as a response to a lack of power and control in one's life. Building on this research, Kiewa (2001) analyzed the stories of rock climbers and found that self-determination (control over the structure of the activity) and control over self (one's competence to achieve a flawless performance) explained both motivation to engage in the activity and satisfaction with the experience. The qualitative data inform our understanding of what the sport of rock climbing means to those who engage in it.

COMPARISON OF QUANTITATIVE AND QUALITATIVE RESEARCH

Qualitative research taps into people's interpretations of their experiences. One way to understand what this interpretive focus means is to contrast the qualitative perspective with what you have already learned about quantitative research. Remember, though, that this comparison does not suggest that one approach is better than the other; the nature of your research question should dictate whether you pursue a qualitative or a quantitative approach. Qualitative and quantitative approaches do, however, represent different ways of asking research questions. Specifically, qualitative and quantitative approaches differ in purpose, focus, method, and criteria for truth (Table 7.1).

Purpose: Description

The purpose of qualitative research is more *descriptive* than *predictive*. The goal is to understand, in depth, the viewpoint of a research participant. Realizing that all understanding is constructed, different research participants are going to have different interpretations of their own experience and the social systems within which they interact. Moreover, the researcher is going to impose his or her cultural, social, and personal identity on any interpretation of the research participants' experience. For these reasons, the qualitative approach is typically less concerned with *aggregate generalizations*. Much of qualitative research does not claim to be generalizable. Rather, it claims only to represent the people studied.

The quantitative perspective in you must, at this point, be screaming, "Aaaaaaaack! Confounding variables! Messy, messy, messy!" And this is true. However, description is essential for understanding. Description explicates the *process* of variable relationships.

Using quantitative data, we might find a statistically significant relationship between an independent variable and a dependent variable, and we might even have some ground to speculate about causality between these two variables. This can be done with little or no understanding of the process whereby these two variables are related. For example, communication studies literature has innumerable articles on the effects of gender or biological sex on communication. We can predict, for example, that women are more likely to add tag questions onto the end of a statement: "It's a nice day out today, isn't it?" We can predict that men will speak four times more often than women in a public forum discussion. Yet, what this research does not tell us is *why*.

TABLE 7.1 Comparison of Qualitative and Quantitative Approaches to Research

	Qualitative	Quantitative
Purpose	Description	Prediction
Focus	Generalize to large population	Give voice to silenced people and groups
Methods	Inductive analysis of "texts"	Deductive analysis of units (individual, corporations, etc.)
Criteria for Truth	"Aha" criterion; adequate and realistic	Statistics, replication, and cumulative findings

Deborah Tannen's (2001) more qualitative research on gender differences in communication led to her discovery that communication means different things to men and women. Tannen contends that for men, communication is a means to assert hierarchical status. For women, communication is a means to achieve connection and relationship. This theory explains a great deal about men's and women's behavior: men are reluctant to ask for directions when lost because it puts them in a one-down position of helplessness in relation to the direction-giver; women, in contrast, have an insatiable need to talk about "the relationship" to continually affirm connection to the relational other. Tannen's research seeks to describe *why* there are gender differences in communication.

Focus: Voice of the Marginalized

The focus of qualitative research is to give *voice* to people at the margins of a culture. Thus, qualitative research has become the favored methodology for those scholars doing Marxist, feminist, gay and lesbian, and cultural studies. Qualitative research highlights those people who—by sheer number—are outside the standard deviation, and are not represented in reports of quantitative averages. According to qualitative research, every case is valid and potentially worthy of study. Every case is representative of a specific person's life experiences and interpretations of those experiences; as such it represents truth and reality for that person. In contrast, the focus of quantitative research is to find the typical, the average, the trend that can be generalized to large populations. Qualitative researchers would contend that there are a lot of people who are not accurately represented by the typical case, average, or trend. Rather, we can at best achieve an approximate understanding of how an individual interprets his or her experience. The focus of qualitative research is to describe the meaning of participants' experiences even if the participant or experience is not typical of the majority experience.

Methods: Inductive

The key distinguishing feature between qualitative and quantitative methods is that quantitative methods are deductive and qualitative methods are inductive. A **deductive approach** is a process of reasoning that flows from a theory/hypothesis to systematic empirical observation to conclusion. An **inductive approach** is a process of reasoning that follows a reverse path—observation precedes theory, hypothesis, and interpretation. Qualitative researchers let the data "speak" to them and try to avoid going into a study with a preconceived idea of what they will find.

Let's imagine that you want to know whether an intimate relationship will endure. Taking a quantitative, deductive approach, you might construct a survey that measures the effects of commitment, relational satisfaction, number of arguments, sexual attraction, and intimacy (independent variables) on length of relationship (dependent variable). Indeed, a number of researchers have measured these very variables and determined that similarity of values and attitudes is the best predictor of relational longevity (Myers, 2002).

Though your survey may tell you a great deal about the relative importance of these variables on relational longevity, you might feel that you are missing the "guts" or "drama" of what occurs in relationships as couples negotiate commitment, fights, sexual attraction, and intimacy. Taking a qualitative approach, you might interview couples, individually and together, about their relationships. You might hear couples talk with some consistency about their "first big fight." Upon further probing in your interviews, you might determine that the first big fight is somehow important to the continuation of a relationship, but, taking an inductive approach, you hesitate to speculate how. Now your interviews focus almost exclusively on the first big fight. You ask participants to tell you stories about this fight: what was it about, what happened, how was it resolved? After the interviews, you analyze these stories and look for patterns. You may well find, as Siegert and Stamp (1994) did, that the first big fight marks a clarification of the meaning of a relationship, represents a negotiation of the extent of each person's commitment to the relationship, and decreases uncertainty about the future of the relationship. In addition to the finding of quantitative researchers that similarity in attitude is predictive of relational longevity, Siegert and Stamp found that communication—specifically, willingness to negotiate differences through communication—predicted which couples would survive the first big fight. These findings add to our understanding by showing how similarity in values and attitudes may well be an outcome of the willingness to negotiate similarities and differences.

Methods in qualitative research are varied and extensive, and we address these methods in depth in Chapters 8 through 10. For now, suffice it to say that qualitative methods employ **observations**, **interviews**, and/or the analysis of some type of **text**. The term *text* is broadly defined in qualitative research to include spoken word (people's stories, conversations, or speeches), visual representations (photos, films, video, visual art), written texts (historical documents, books, newspaper articles, reports, prose or poetry), artifacts of a culture (monuments, buildings, roads, malls), or a cultural group (homeless people, gangs, residents in AIDS communities).

Observations, interviews, and texts are analyzed for meanings and themes. Consider some examples. For Deborah Tannen, the text analyzed was the Thanksgiving Day conversation of a group of friends. She discovered subtle regional differences in the conversation style of East and West Coast people. East Coast people were more likely to employ intense, "machine-gun" questions and to interrupt more, which to some degree put off their West Coast friends (Tannen, 1984). For Janice Rushing, the text analyzed was the blockbuster film, *Titanic*. She compared the film to classical myths and concluded that the film exploits the tension between the masculine excesses of technology and the feminine ideal of romantic love (Rushing & Frentz, 2000).

Criteria for Truth: Phenomenological Validity

The key to any type of research is a community standard among researchers of what constitutes proof. In quantitative research, that proof is statistics. If the p value is less than .05 (conventional level of significance for social researchers), we conclude that the outcome observed is probably due to the independent variable and not to measurement error or sheer chance. In quantitative research, we also describe our methods in great detail so that other researchers can replicate our studies; if several different researchers get the same results, we have confidence that we have discovered a truth. (See Chapter 3.) If Deirdre Johnston does a study and Scott VanderStoep builds on her results by using her variables or measurements, but finds that those variables do not work, this line of inquiry falls like a house of cards, and other, more productive lines of inquiry are developed. In other words, quantitative research that cannot be replicated will likely not be robust enough to stand the test of time.

Qualitative research does not use statistics or replication as standards of proof. Qualitative research does not translate variables into numbers, so there can be no statistical analyses. Furthermore, qualitative research assumes that the analysis of a text is idiosyncratic to the researcher doing the analysis, and to the time, culture, and situation in which the analysis is conducted. Thus, true replication is impossible.

The sign of a good qualitative research study is that the analysis provides a new and compelling interpretation of a text. By *new*, we mean novel, unique, and engaging. By *compelling*, we mean logical and supported by rich descriptive examples that persuade the reader to adopt the researcher's interpretation of the text.

Arnold (2000) conducted a study to explore college students' constructions of the concept "feminism." Based on 123 qualitative responses, Arnold found that although college students' descriptions of feminism were generally positive, their descriptions of feminists were less positive, and that despite their positive descriptions of the ideals of feminism, many of the students were reluctant to self-identify as feminists.

My students in gender communication attest to the validity of the perceptions of feminism voiced by the students in Arnold's study. They further concur with Arnold's conclusions that, as college students, they believe in the ideals of feminism (e.g., rights and equality), but do not claim to be feminists themselves because they perceive feminists as "making an issue out of sex and gender differences."

Students who have read this particular study report an "Aha!" phenomenon: "That happened to me!" "That sounds just like my roommate!" "I know what she's talking about!" We can therefore conclude that Arnold tapped into a true and accurate approximation of the experience of some students. The more formal name for the "Aha!" criterion is **phenomenological validity**. When we achieve phenomenological validity, the interpretation of the data speaks to the lived experience of the research participants and others who identify with them.

YOUR TURN

Telling the Story . . . Qualitatively

Think about the statistical summary on global changes shown here. How would you explore each of these stories qualitatively? Discuss how your qualitative description would meet the following criteria:

- purpose of description
- focus on marginalized voices
- inductive method
- phenomenological validity

1. Your generation will change jobs 10 to 14 times by age 38.

2. One in eight couples married in the United States in 2007 met online.

3. If MySpace were a country, it would be the 11th largest in the world.

4. The number of text messages sent each day exceeds the population of the planet.

5. The average teenager spends 6.5 hours per day engaged with media (Internet, television, phone, or radio) outside of school time.

6. Information is increasing so rapidly that what a college student learns in his or her first year of college will be outdated by his or her third year.

7. There are 2.7 billion searches on Google each month.

Source: "Shift Happens: Globalization and the Information Age" (utube.com: http://www. youtube.com/watch?v=pMcfrLYDm2U), developed by Karl Fisch and updated by Howie DiBlasi.

CRITIQUE OF QUANTITATIVE RESEARCH

The increased popularity and acceptance of qualitative methods in the social sciences in the past 25 years is to some extent the result of a reaction against quantitative research assumptions. Though it is no longer necessary to pit these research perspectives against each other, it is instructive to know the historical arguments that shape qualitative research assumptions. Quantitative methods were historically associated with a worldview called **positivism**. A positivist approach embraces certain assumptions about truth and reality. Qualitative research methodology is the phoenix that has arisen from the ashes of positivist assumptions. People now say we live in a post-positivist, postmodern world. It is important to remember that quantitative social scientists have questioned and now abandoned some of the assumptions of positivism. However, a comparison with positivist assumptions helps us to understand the rationale for qualitative ways of knowing. In this section we compare the assumptions of positivist research (traditional quantitative social science methods) with those of **post-positivist** research (qualitative and more contemporary quantitative methods).

Objectivity vs. Subjectivity

First, positivists assume that there is **objectivity** in the world, and that the researcher is an objective observer and reporter of data. Systematic social science methods, such as sample selection procedures, measurement of variables, and statistical analysis, presume that the researcher is unbiased and may well find that a beloved hypothesis is not supported by the data. Post-positivists (postmodernists) believe it is impossible for a researcher to be objective. Researchers are **subjective**: A researcher has a gender, race, ethnicity, culture, nationality, religion, family, personality, and attitude that filter his or her observation of the data. All perception is biased by who we are and who we claim to be. Note the introduction to an art exhibit by French artist Sophie Calle at the Venice Biennale, Venice, Italy, July 2007 (Figure 7.1). Calle gave a break-up email she received from her lover to 107 women with different occupational identities. Each woman analyzed and performed the letter from her occupational perspective as a writer, a psychologist, a criminologist, a comedian, a dancer, and so on. The exhibit presents these varied interpretations of the break-up letter: the writer corrects the ex-lover's grammar in red ink, the forensic psychologist speculates about his antisocial personality traits and labels him a "twisted manipulator." The markswoman shoots up the letter, and the dancer mocks the sentiments in music and dance. The result was 100 sometimes poignant, sometimes comical interpretations of the same letter.

One person's perception is neither right nor wrong, just different. Now, let's extrapolate this concept to research. The field of medical research in the 20th century was male-dominated. Male researchers understandably saw the world through male-gendered eyes, and therefore, it appears, were at a loss to explain female-gendered behavior. "Hysteria," as it was called in the first half of the 20th century, was considered a female psychiatric disorder, but we now know that panic attacks have a biological origin and afflict males and females equally. Valium, fondly known as "mother's little helper," was widely prescribed for women in the 1960s, rather than addressing the underlying psychosocial issues that cause depression and anxiety.

Another example from medicine is the former paucity of medical research on the causes of miscarriage. Thirty percent of pregnancies are believed to end in miscarriage and no one thought this was worthy of study and prevention? Women were told, "You'll have another baby." It is understandable that male researchers would be more interested in male risks and male diseases—understandable, but not justifiable.

Post-positivists contend that *the researcher influences the behavior of those studied*. In the natural sciences, this is called the **Heisenberg uncertainty principle**. The act of observation causes a change in the actions of what or who is studied. It is easy to understand how this could happen with studies of people. One of my favorite examples is a friend in graduate school who was studying loneliness in the elderly by conducting

> I received an email telling me it was over.
> I didn't know how to respond.
> It was almost as if it hadn't been meant for me.
> It ended with the words, "Take care of yourself."
> And so I did.
> I asked 107 women, chosen for their profession or skills, to interpret this letter.
> To analyze it, comment on it, dance it, sing it.
> Exhaust it. Understand it for me. Answer for me.
> It was a way of taking the time to break up.
> A way of taking care of myself.

FIGURE 7.1. *Sophie Calle's exhibition at the Venice Biennale, Venice, Italy, July 2007*

in-depth interviews in nursing homes. Lo and behold, her research participants got less lonely as the study progressed, because an intelligent, gregarious woman was taking an interest in the details of their experience and was visiting them on a regular basis to conduct personal interviews! What is truly fascinating is that natural scientists in a field called quantum physics are coming to the same conclusion: subatomic particles inexplicably change to be consistent with the type of particle the researcher is seeking to observe. It is beyond the scope of this book to address new findings in quantum physics, but you should check out some books on this phenomenon (for example, Talbot, 1992) and think about how this might affect our understanding of social science methods.

Research Subjects vs. Participants

A second assumption of positivists is that research participants are *subjects* to be manipulated, controlled, and randomly assorted into groups in an experiment. It was not until the 1990s that researchers changed their terminology from "subjects" to **research participants**. This reflects a response to the well-founded criticism that researchers were treating those in research studies at a third-person distance that could imply or breed apathy. Post-positivists believe that to construct a person as a "subject" is to risk objectifying that person. This means that we treat the person as though he or she is an object, not a person. Whenever people are reduced to aggregate data (frequencies, means, etc.), there is a risk of **objectification**. According to a positivist assumption, the researcher takes the position of expert and the research participant is constructed as an unknowing other. As a result, the researcher has power and knowledge, whereas the research participant is sometimes purposely left in the dark.

Post-positivists further argue that much research carried out in the positivist tradition was complicit with **colonialism/imperialism**. This means that the researcher assumed a superior position to the people or culture studied. Implied superiority infected much of early qualitative ethnographic research as well. Rosaldo (1989) describes the "Lone Ethnographer" who tramped into the jungle to find the strange and alien natives and returned with pictures, artifacts, and a colonialist view of the "primitive other" to entertain the educated elite of American society. Geertz (1988), in his analysis of the traditional assumptions of early ethnographic research, excerpted the field notes of one researcher's experiences in New Guinea and the Trobriand Islands, 1914–1918:

> On the whole, the village struck me rather unfavorably. There is a certain disorganization . . . the rowdiness and persistence of the people who laugh and stare and lie discourage me somewhat. . . . Went to the village hoping to photograph a few stages of the bara dance. I handed out a few sticks of tobacco, then watched a few dances, then took pictures—but the results were poor . . . they would not pose long enough for time exposures. At moments I was furious with them, particularly after I gave them their portions of tobacco and they all went away . . . (pp. 73–74).

Recent research raising similar issues has questioned the "tourist gaze" of contemporary postcards, in which tourists seek out depictions of ethnic group members in indigenous dress and settings to "exoticize" the Other (Thurlow, Jaworski, & Ylanne-McEwan, 2005).

Research participant, as opposed to *subject*, constructs the people from whom data is collected as collaborators in the research project and fully voiced contributors to the research process. This challenge to positivist assumptions has led researchers to use informed consent (see Chapter 1) to ensure that participants are fully informed of the procedures and aware of their right to withdraw from the study at any time. Quantitative researchers now avoid using the most blatant and dangerous forms of deception and coercion that characterized much social research of the l950s and 1960s. The work of social psychologist Stanley Milgram (1974), for example, led subjects to believe they were administering dangerous electric shocks to other college students; Phillip Zimbardo (1971) created a prison role-play experiment in which college-student "guards" physically, verbally, and psychologically abused college students playing the role of prisoners.

Qualitative researchers take the research participant concept even further, holding that only the research participant can authentically describe her interpretation of her experience. The role of the researcher is merely to report the research participants' interpretations. Any analysis of the data is clearly identified as the researcher's interpretation, and has no lesser or greater weight than anyone else's interpretation.

Isolation vs. Social Embeddedness

A third assumption of positivists is that subjects can be isolated and observed, much like we isolate a bacterial strain in a Petri dish for observation under a microscope. Postpositivists contend that people are embedded in a social world and entwined in social relationships. As such, they cannot be isolated for study or sorted into groups on the basis of similar criteria. This is because for every way in which two people might be similar on some distinguishing feature, they are dissimilar on dozens of others.

All qualitative methods are concerned with how people make sense of their experiences by creating meaning. Meaning, however, is not equated with truth.

> *[The multiple perspectives offered by ethnographic research] complicate and enrich social analysis, but they do not represent the one and only authentic truth. Human beings always act under conditions they do not fully know and with consequences they neither fully intend nor can fully foresee.... [Our] objects of analysis are also analyzing subjects whose best perceptions, not unlike our own, are shaped by distinctive cultures, histories and relations of inequality. Neither ethnographers nor their subjects hold a monopoly on truth (Rosaldo, 1989, p. xviii).*

A colleague and author Johnston were presenting some research at an academic conference recently and were reminded of the **social embeddedness** of research when it came to question-and-answer time. We were feeling pretty confident about our conclusions regarding differences in the mothering practices and ideals of at-home and employed mothers. A woman in the audience raised her hand and asked what the differences were between white mothers and mothers of color. We acknowledged that, alas, our sample was predominantly white mothers and that the 10 mothers of color in our sample, representing different races and ethnicities, constituted too small and diverse a group to draw any conclusions. We turned quickly to the next questioner, who asked, "What about mothers living below the poverty line?" We acknowledged that, alas, our sample was predominantly middle-class. Another hand shot into the air and a woman asked, "What are your results regarding lesbian mothers?" By this time we were far less confident about our conclusions, and we looked longingly for a hole in the stage with a tunnel leading directly to the airport!

The post-positivist researcher recognizes that generalizations are seldom accurate; if they can be made, they are quite specific. I (author Johnston) can tell you a great deal about the mothering practices and ideals of the mothers interviewed, but I must be careful not to generalize these conclusions to other mothers. Post-positivists would argue that I cannot even generalize to other white, middle-class mothers of preschool children, because other mothers have any number of characteristics that differentiate them from or within this group: marital status (married/divorced/single), age (teenage/20s–30s/40s–50s), family-of-origin modeling (own mom stayed home/employed/returned to work later), family and friend support for career or staying home, and so forth. When we fully explore the possible combinations of social groups within which any given person is embedded, the experience of any given individual becomes quite idiosyncratic. Post-positivists say that this is fine: We can learn a lot from Reagan's experience of motherhood, even as we recognize that Reagan's experience is unique to her and is neither fully shared nor fully understood by anyone else.

Stasis vs. Change

In our efforts to force social science methods to conform to natural science expectations, we also forget that *people change*. The Petri dish is sterile and maintains a consistent environment for bacterial growth. When we study people, though, we get a one-minute, one-hour, one-day slice of their experience. We often err in assuming that this slice of life is unchanging and stable over time. Sociologists have found that immigrant groups often cling to traditions and rituals of the "old country" that characterized the culture at the time they left. Immigrants are often surprised to find, decades later, that their cherished rituals and traditions are quite foreign to people living in the old country. Holland, Michigan, holds a Tulip Festival each spring, and 1,200 townspeople dress up in clothing from the 19th-century rural Dutch countryside (complete with wooden shoes) to perform the *Klompen* dance for tourists. A few years ago a university dance professor videotaped the *Klompen* dancing and showed the tape at an academic dance conference in the Netherlands. She reported that there was an "audible gasp" from the audience at the sight of their distant American cousins performing a cherished Dutch tradition that was completely unfamiliar to them. Although neither quantitative nor qualitative researchers are completely ignorant of the confounding nature of time in research, qualitative researchers often criticize quantitative researchers for generalizing across time, and not acknowledging that any conclusions drawn apply to the past—at the moment of the study—and not to the present or future.

Power vs. Action

The fourth positivist assumption is that the ends justify the means. In other words, the ethical implications of making predictions and generalizations are justified based on the benefit that will come from doing so. Indeed, positivists believe that *knowledge is power*, and that this power and control will improve the human condition. This makes some sense: Research on earthquake prediction, flood control, crop rotation, vaccinations, and nutritional knowledge has improved the human condition. In general, knowing the effects of one variable on another has enabled us to improve health care, education, and social services.

Nevertheless, prediction, explanation, and understanding of the aggregate, or the majority population, perpetuates the power of dominant cultural groups. The experience of White teachers in Native American classrooms, for example, reveals the influence of culture on learning style. The White teachers' style, dominated by verbal instruction, is often ineffective. Further experience in the classroom has revealed that Native American students have, from a very young age, been taught visually, not verbally. The children are taught to observe their elders, and only after adequate observation do they attempt to replicate a task. Teachers coming from a different cultural background found that the Native American children were reluctant to answer their questions or to complete an assignment without first being assured of some understanding and competency. Some teachers may have wrongly concluded that these children were not intelligent or capable, further perpetuating the educational privilege of the dominant culture group.

Many post-positivist researchers are proponents of an ethical standard called **action research**. Rather than conducting research for the purpose of writing an esoteric academic journal article enjoyed by professors and graduate students and used primarily to torture undergraduates, the goal of action research is to problem-solve a situation for the betterment of the community participating in the study. All pretenses of objectivity are abandoned. The researcher in action research is fully enmeshed in the social system under study. Moreover, the researcher is an agent of change for the social system. We discuss action research in more detail in Chapter 8.

YOUR TURN

Evaluating Positivist Assumptions

Compare the following three studies for positivist or post-positivist assumptions. Each of the studies addresses the question of whether sexual double standards for men and women still exist. Sexual double standards are beliefs that sexual behavior by boys and men is expected and accepted, whereas the same sexual behavior by girls or women is condemned.

You will be reading summaries of each study excerpted from Crawford and Popp (2003), "Sexual Double Standards: A Review and Methodological Critique of Two Decades of Research."

Which of the three studies is most positivist? Which is most post-positivist? Discuss each of the following in your answers:

- objectivity vs. subjectivity
- subject vs. research participant
- isolation vs. social embeddedness
- stasis vs. change
- power vs. action

A. Eder, D., Evans, C., & Parker, S. (1995). Gender and adolescent culture. New Brunswick, NJ: Rutgers University Press.

Eder et al. "observed lunchtime activity, attended extracurricular activities, conducted individual and small group interviews, and recorded audio and video tapes of students' spontaneous conversations with peers. Within the middle school peer culture, girls (but never boys) sometimes were negatively labeled simply because they showed interest or assertiveness in respect to sexuality. Girls who initiated any kind of sexual overture (e.g., "making a pass") were labeled "bitches," "sluts," and "whores." The sanction against female sexual agency extended to wearing attractive clothing and makeup, which also could earn the label of whore. The routine uses of sexual insults aimed at girls by boys, and to a lesser extent by girls, suggested that middle school students "do not believe that girls should be sexually active or have a variety of boyfriends, while such behaviors are viewed as normal and acceptable for boys" (p. 131, cited in Crawford & Popp, 2003, p. 22).

B. Sprecher, S., & Hatfield, E. (1996). Premarital sexual double standards among U.S. college students: Comparison of Russian and Japanese students. Archives of Sexual Behavior, 25, 261–288.

Sprecher and Hatfield (1996) found that men endorsed a double standard for women and men who were dating casually (defined as dating less than one month) but not for women and men who were dating seriously (defined as almost one year) or who were pre-engaged (had seriously discussed the possibility of getting married). In the US, 389 male and 654 female undergraduates (77% White) completed a premarital sexual permissiveness scale for themselves, a "male," and a "female." The permissiveness scale asked the participants to rate the acceptability of sexual intercourse at each of five dating stages (first date, casually dating, seriously dating, pre-engaged, engaged). Male participants held significantly more permissive attitudes for a male (the total score for items referring to a male) than for a female. Men's endorsement of a double standard was strongest at the first date but also existed for intermediate dating stages. Overall, U.S. men reported greater endorsement of double standards than did U.S. women (Crawford & Popp, 2006, p. 17).

C. Moffat, M. (1989). Coming of age in New Jersey. New Brunswick, NJ: Rutgers University Press.

Moffat studied peer culture on a university campus, focusing on sexual beliefs and attitudes and using a variety of methods. He conducted participant observation while "passing" as a student living in a men's dormitory, and he analyzed sexual autobiographies written by students in his sexuality classes. He reported that the majority of students believed in heterosexual double standards and classified women into dichotomous categories of "good" women or sluts. Moffat characterized the attitudes of male students he studied as follows: "Men have the right to experiment sexually for a few years. There are a lot of female sluts out there with whom to experiment. And once I have gotten this out of my system, I will then look for a good woman for a long-term relationship (or for a wife)" (p. 204, cited in Crawford & Popp, 2006, p. 23).

CRISIS OF REPRESENTATION

In conclusion, the rise of qualitative methods is partly a response to criticism of quantitative methods. Denzin and Lincoln (1994) refer to this as the **crisis of representation**. Social scientists, both qualitative and quantitative, must answer the following challenges:

- Whose experiences are being presented as normative?

- Whose interpretations of these experiences are valid—the research participant's or the researcher's?

- Do the researcher's interpretations have more or less authority than those of the research participants?

- To what extent is the researcher creating new knowledge that perpetuates the power of dominant groups in the culture (e.g., the agenda of patriarchal, heterosexual, wealthy, European-American groups)?

The crisis of representation is the challenge of every qualitative researcher to represent the research participants, their lived experience, their community, and their culture. The researcher makes decisions about what to ask, how to ask it, how to record the data, how to analyze and categorize the data, and what is written about it. These decisions inherently threaten the representation of the voice and experience of the participants. Krieger contends: "When we discuss others, we are always talking about ourselves. Our images of 'them' are images of 'us'" (1991, p. 5). Qualitative researchers must strive, in their research designs, to let research participants talk for themselves. To the extent that the researcher "allows" others to speak, selects who can speak, speaks for the participants, or translates and synthesizes the voices of the participants, the research participants are still silenced (Denzin, 1990).

How research is evaluated depends on the perspective of the researcher. There are **quantitative purists** who attempt to evaluate qualitative research using the standards of quantitative research: sample, variable, measurement, statistics, and the like. In the minds of these scholars, it is no surprise that qualitative research appears inadequate. There are also **qualitative purists** who apply post-positivist criticism to quantitative research. In the minds of these scholars, quantitative research is perceived as an oversimplified reduction of a complex psychosocial system, confounded by researcher bias. Qualitative purists argue that qualitative research is completely incompatible with the idea of establishing criteria for evaluating its outcomes (Hammersley, 1992). According to this perspective, if there is no single interpretative truth, and if any form of reporting and disseminating research findings privileges certain perspectives, any claims of validity, reliability, or correctness by any other evaluative standard are pure folly.

Somewhere in the middle reside the **reformed quantitative researchers**. These social scientists embrace the richness of qualitative approaches but attempt to make the qualitative research live up to positivist expectations in terms of theory, design, sample, and analysis. Also somewhere in the middle are **reformed qualitative researchers** who accept the value of aggregate data, such as averages and frequencies, to inform their analyses.

Researchers are bridging the gap between qualitative and quantitative methods in numerous ways. A qualitative report might acknowledge a small sample size but attempt to prove that the sample is representative of similar people within the population from which it was drawn. Similarly, you will see studies that employ a **triangulation** of methods (i.e., using more than one methodology to address the same question) to establish the validity and reliability of the data: for example, a quantitative survey combined with qualitative interviews, or a quantitative experiment combined with a qualitative focus group. Moreover, you will see qualitative studies that use both quantitative and qualitative analyses of data, such as the reporting of descriptive statistics for particular themes or patterns discovered in narrative data.

Thankfully, new scholars, like yourselves, are being trained in both qualitative and quantitative methods. Despite the political minefield of scholarly argument over which approach is more rigorous and worthy, the best approach is to learn the procedures and processes of both quantitative and qualitative approaches. It makes sense that a mix of methodologies, maximizing the benefits of both approaches, will provide the richest and most complete understanding of the phenomenon under study. It also makes sense that the research question should dictate the mode of inquiry. Some questions lend themselves to quantitative approaches, other questions lend themselves to qualitative approaches, and some questions call for an integration of both qualitative and quantitative methods.

SUMMARY

Qualitative research focuses on the constructed reality of the research participants. It differs from quantitative research in its purpose, focus, methods, and criteria for truth. It rejects many of the quantitative assumptions about research that are based on objective, positivist beliefs about the world, and instead sees reality as constructed in the mind of the knower and situated in cultural and historical contexts. Quantitative purists reject the claims of qualitative researchers as anecdotal and idiosyncratic. Qualitative purists reject claims of quantitative researchers as (1) reflecting the bias of the researcher's analysis and interpretation, and (2) ignoring the minority voices that are not reflected in aggregate summary data. We urge students to adopt a mixed methodology that embraces the best of both qualitative and quantitative approaches. The future of social science research rests on the integration of approaches that provide both breadth and depth in our understanding and knowledge of social behavior.

KEY TERMS

action research

colonialism/imperialism

crisis of representation

deductive approach

epistemology

grand narrative

Heisenberg uncertainty principle

identifiable functions

inductive approach

interviews

objectification

objectivity

observations

outliers

phenomenological validity

positivism

post-positivist

prescribed sequence

qualitative purists

quantitative purists

reformed qualitative researchers

reformed quantitative researchers

required elements

research participants

script

social construction of reality

social embeddedness

subjective

text

triangulation

CHAPTER

8

PLANNING YOUR QUALITATIVE STUDY: DESIGN, SAMPLING, AND DATA ANALYSIS

LEARNING OBJECTIVES

■ Learn the steps for designing a qualitative study.

■ Identify and evaluate the focus of inquiry for a qualitative study.

■ Develop a method for qualitative study by defining the sampling and data collection procedures.

■ Understand the basics of theme identification used in the coding of qualitative data.

■ Identify and apply the criteria used to evaluate qualitative studies.

My elementary school-age daughters are creative and love art. Most art projects conducted at preschool camps or art classes have a set of prescribed sequential procedures: the teacher stands before the group of students, holds up a part of the project—one or two pieces at a time—and instructs the students in the step-by-step assembly of the project. Any student who picks up the wrong piece of the colorful, enticing objects spread out before them, at the wrong time, is considered uncooperative. The children leave the camp, the art class, or the classroom and run to their parents with identical art objects that are (nearly) perfect in design. The parents can immediately identify the "uncooperative" child, for he or she carries a reindeer holiday ornament that looks more like a bald turkey with its red wattle hanging off its tail. The parents and the children quickly learn to be disappointed if the end product does not look like everyone else's. I myself prefer the unseasonal bald turkey that looks like it has been in a blender accident to the red-nosed reindeer ornament. Perhaps that is why I enjoy qualitative research!

Quantitative research projects—like elementary art instruction in the United States—follow a set of prescribed sequential procedures: identifying a research question, exploring theoretical foundations of the question, identifying independent and dependent variables, developing hypotheses, selecting or creating measurement procedures for each variable, selecting a sample, developing assessment instruments, collecting data, coding data, and analyzing data. The end product, an academic research report, should follow the preset order and include the required sections, such as abstract, literature review, method, and so on. To continue the art-project analogy, the end product should look like the picture on the box. As many graduate students working on dissertations have learned, there is little tolerance for deviation. Woe to the researcher who develops an instrument before she conceptually defines the variable, or to the researcher who collects data without first having his theory in place.

Qualitative research provides a home for those adults who as uncooperative kids liked to color outside the lines, grab all the supplies, and slather on some paste to see what emerged. Qualitative researchers essentially break all the design rules. This is risky: sometimes the end result looks like blender turkey art. More often, there is eloquence in the design and insights that *emerge* from this less constrained creative process. Lincoln and Guba, in their classic work on naturalistic inquiry, explain the nature of **emergence** in the design of qualitative research:

> [T]he design of a naturalistic inquiry (whether research, evaluation or policy analysis) cannot be given in advance; it must emerge, develop, unfold . . . . The call for an **emergent design** by naturalists is not simply an effort on their part to get around "hard thinking" that is supposed to precede inquiry; the desire to permit events to unfold is not merely a way of rationalizing what is at bottom "sloppy inquiry." The design specifications of the conventional paradigm form a procrustean bed of such a nature as to make it impossible for the naturalist to lie in it—not only uncomfortably, but at all (1985, p. 225, boldfacing added).

Qualitative research must address many of the same design issues as quantitative design—sample, variables, measurement, analysis—but these issues cannot be determined in advance of data collection. These processes may well change, as the data collected dictate the questions and the design. Qualitative research employs a **circular** research design.

Kristin Wright (2003) designed a study to explore how terminally ill people and their families make sense of death and dying. Wright did not begin her research with a research question or hypothesis. Rather, in her work as a family therapist, Wright began keeping notes on people's experiences with death and dying. Wright then spent several years as a participant observer working with hospice patients. Disturbed by the detrimental effects of misinterpretations or oversimplifications of Kübler-Ross's (1973) stage theory of dying, Wright decided to conduct in-depth interviews of people living with terminal illness. Her interview method was not prescribed: She conducted from one to ten interviews with each participant; some interviews were done with family members present, some were not. As Wright attempted to analyze the hundreds of pages of interview transcripts, she became frustrated that her categories did not adequately reflect the depth of participants' experiences. So, she changed approaches. She (re)conceptualized her category system and began looking for "relationships with death." Using this metaphor to guide her thinking, six relationships with death emerged: imprisoned by death (hopeless and angry; focus on death despite presence of life); carpe diem (death is a reminder of the preciousness of life); carpe mortem (death is a process of living, and living is a process of dying; death and life are a journey); life and death transformed (meaning of death is reframed in religious terms or fantasy role-plays); silenced by death (keep death at bay by not mentioning it); and waiting for death (sensing death, experiencing death visually, impatience for the inevitable). As you can see, Wright's design was not linear and unchanging, but *circular* and continually adaptive. After data collection and extensive analysis, the research question emerged: How do terminally ill people and their families construct life and living in the face of impending death?

DESIGNING QUALITATIVE RESEARCH

There are guidelines for designing a qualitative study. Although we follow the same sequence as you have learned in this textbook for designing a quantitative study, it is important to note that the following guidelines are not necessarily addressed in the listed order, or checked off the list in an exhaustive or linear fashion. Rather, there is a constant backtracking circularity, such that your progression through the research process might look like unlucky rolls of the dice in a board game: step #1: focus; go to step #2: analyze fit with qualitative approach; modify step #1 (focus) given qualitative assumptions; skip to step #4: find participants; continue to step #5 (develop method) through step #7 (data collection); given initial data collection, go back to step #4 and redefine subsequent participant selection; return to step #7 (data collection). Go back to start again (#1), because, given your first eight interviews, your focus was completely unfounded! This chapter guides you through a series of questions for designing a qualitative study.

In this chapter you will see how the principles and theoretical assumptions underlying qualitative research (Chapter 7) are tied to the decisions made in the design of a qualitative research project. So, let's assume that you have a general question in mind. How do you take this research question and develop it into a qualitative study?

Guiding Question #1: What Is the Focus of the Inquiry?

Lincoln and Guba (1985) identify two purposes of focus in naturalistic designs. Much like the focus needed for a research paper, focus in naturalistic inquiry establishes boundaries for the investigation. It is easy to get lost in qualitative research without some guiding compass directing your inquiry toward what you want to know. As with any research project, jumping into the project without a clear focus will likely lead to a great deal of wasted effort and frustration.

The second purpose of focus in naturalistic inquiry is to filter data. In naturalistic inquiry you are likely to have a great deal of information available. It is necessary to have a clear focus in mind to determine what should be included and what should be excluded from analysis. An example of a research study with a broad, but still sufficient, focus is the motherhood study conducted by Johnston and Swanson (2006). The interviews of at-home, part-time employed, and full-time employed mothers addressed: (1) benefits and stresses associated with work decisions for both mother and children; (2) how work decisions were made; (3) social support received from spouse, family, friends, and culture for those work decisions; (4) the construction of the ideal "good mother" and "good father" in American culture; and (5) perceptions of support for mothers from specific social institutions. As you can see, these interviews covered a lot of ground. However, the overall focus of the study—how at-home, part-time employed, and full-time employed mothers define what it means to be a "good mother"—was maintained. Moreover, the use of structured interviews ensured that all mothers responded to all of these probes. A less structured interview might result in mothers telling stories in one area and not addressing the other areas, thus leaving the researcher with little complete data for comparisons across the three groups of mothers.

Example of a Focused Inquiry of Meaning: A Study of Sexual Victimization Sherry Hamby and Mary Koss (2003) had a very precise focus for their qualitative study of terms used to measure sexual victimization. Hamby and Koss wanted to know how the wording in sexual victimization surveys affected the accurate reporting of sexual victimization. They conducted five focus groups with the clearly defined purpose of exploring the meaning of *sexual coercion*. They found a wide range of meanings as to what constitutes *coercion* in sexual activity, ranging from peer pressure to lose one's virginity, to partner pressure to demonstrate relational commitment through sexual intimacy, to partner rape. Not only do the words to convey sexual coercion, such as *unwanted*, *nonvoluntary*, and *forced*, have different meanings, but perceptions of coercion also varied depending on the sex of the perpetrator and the physical size differences between the perpetrator and the victim. These findings are important because they suggest that the wording used on surveys of sexual victimization may lead to inaccurate reporting. However, it is easy to imagine that a focus group on sexual victimization could easily get off track and delve into any number of topics if the group moderators did not have a clear sense of focus.

Guiding Question #2: Does the Focus Lend Itself to Qualitative Inquiry?

The decision to pursue a qualitative study should be made on the basis of the research question, not on the basis of a researcher's skill or interest in doing a qualitative study. A vivid analogy is author Johnston's fix-it household efforts: I have the bad habit of using all sorts of tools for the wrong purposes because I am too lazy to go fetch the appropriate tool. I will attempt to use the pliers as a hammer and the wrench as a screwdriver. This sloppy work approach yields an outcome of stripped screws and mangled nails. Students make similar errors in researching material for papers: They pick the most accessible research tool (e.g., the Internet) instead of choosing a tool that serves the function of their research topic (e.g., newspaper archives, or in-depth scholarly books in the library).

Some research questions are best answered with quantitative designs and some are best addressed with qualitative designs. You *should not* choose a qualitative design if:

- you want to assess causality

- you want to generalize your results beyond your sample population

- you want to report the occurrence of an objective, measurable social behavior (e.g., IQ, performance of a skill, presence of a trait, incidence of a behavior)

You *should* consider a qualitative design if:

- multiple social realities surround the issue you want to study and you want to understand the construction of these multiple realities

- values and perceptions of values play a role in your question

- validity is dependent upon observation in a naturalistic setting

- social desirability bias may lead respondents to misrepresent themselves on conventional quantitative instruments

A final consideration in choosing a qualitative or quantitative design is to think about the role of theory in your inquiry. We have talked about how, in qualitative research, theory often emerges from the data. Qualitative researchers use the expression "the data speak to me" to describe the emergence of theory as a result of data analysis. Theory may be developed after the data are analyzed. This is called **grounded theory**. Not all qualitative research studies use a grounded theory approach; some qualitative studies are theory-driven. However, it is safe to assume that when grounded theory is presented, it is likely the product of qualitative inquiry.

A Call for Qualitative Inquiry: Powwows and Faux Powwows Kathleen Glenister Roberts (2003) sought to analyze the Native-American-style powwow produced by and for White Americans. Roberts found that this "pseudo cultural" event differed greatly from the powwows produced by and for Native Americans.

Roberts explored how the "pseudo" powwows emphasize individual identity in a way that Native American powwows do not. Clearly, there are multiple social realities involved in this issue: the reality and meaning of the Native American tradition for Native Americans, and the reality and meaning of the powwow for White Americans who have transformed the experience into a commodity. There are cultural values at stake: Native American sacred symbols and rituals, and White Americans' co-optation of these symbols into their own individualistic cultural value system. Naturalistic setting and observation are essential to validity, as one cannot arrange an authentic powwow performance—the meaning of the performance is tied to the context and environment in which it is performed. Finally, when a study seeks to understand how cultural identities are co-opted and made into commodities by the dominant culture, self-reported quantitative data are likely to be biased by social desirability effects. Native Americans and White Americans alike may be motivated to minimize issues to avoid jeopardizing economic gain from tourist powwows.

YOUR TURN

To Quantify or Qualify—That Is the Question

Using the criteria discussed earlier in this section, ascertain whether each of the following studies is best pursued using a qualitative method or a quantitative method, based on the information provided in the title alone. What characteristics of a qualitative or quantitative inquiry are revealed in the following titles? Share your conclusions and criteria with a classmate. If you have reached a different conclusion or applied different criteria, discuss this. Are there some studies that could be explored with either quantitative or qualitative methods? If so, what are the benefits of each approach for the topic of research as defined in the article title?

Title of Work	Quantitative or Qualitative?	Criteria Used to Make Your Decision
Park, C., & Sacks, O. (2001). *Exiting nirvana: A daughter's life with autism.*		
Parameswaran, R. (2001). *Feminist media . . . in India: Exploring power, gender and culture in the field.*		
Gilgun, J. (1999). *Fingernails painted red: A feminist semiotic [meaning] analysis of a "hot" text.*		
Coles, R. (1990). *The spiritual life of children.*		
Barling, J. (1996). *Prediction, experience, and consequences of violence.*		

Title of Work	Quantitative or Qualitative?	Criteria Used to Make Your Decision
Kuther, T., & Higgins-D'Alessandro, A. (2000). *Bridging the gap between moral reasoning and adolescent engagement in risky behavior.*		
Suitor, J., & Carter, R. (1999). *Jocks, nerds, babes and thugs: A research note on regional differences in adolescent gender norms.*		
Waiters, E., Treno, A., & Grube, J. (2001). *Alcohol advertising and youth: An analysis of what young people find appealing in alcohol advertising.*		
Thakker, D., & Solomon, P. (1999). *Factors influencing managers' adherence to the Americans with Disabilities Act.*		

Guiding Question #3: What Sampling Procedure Will Be Used?

Qualitative researchers want to understand under what conditions a particular behavior occurs, not whether the behavior is representative. As previously discussed, the goal of quantitative research is to achieve a random sample that is representative of a population so that you can generalize your results to the population. Qualitative researchers view such sampling as privileging the voices of the majority. Qualitative researchers are skeptical that any conclusions can be broadly generalized to a large population, because any effort to generalize extrapolates the characteristics of a sampling unit beyond the context that gives it meaning.

Prioritizing the description of human behavior in a particular social context over concerns of generalizing to a broader population prompts qualitative researchers to employ non-random sampling techniques. As you learned in Chapter 2, non-random techniques include **convenience** and **snowball samples**. Qualitative researchers also use **purposeful samples**. Purposeful samples are comprised of people based on a particular attribute, and are often designed to arbitrarily include equal representation of groups that may not be equally represented in society. For example, a purposeful sample could be designed to represent one-third Latinos, one-third African Americans, and one-third Asian Americans, despite the fact that these groups are not represented in equal numbers in United States demographics.

YOUR TURN

Reviewing Non-Random Sampling Techniques

What type of sample is employed in each of the following example studies?

a. Professors frequently use students enrolled in their classes as their research participants, and therapists use clients as their research participants.

b. Erin Sahlstein (2004) studied long-distance intimate relationships. Participants were recruited from undergraduate communication courses, adults within the community, and personal contacts with the researcher. There were two criteria for participation: (1) unmarried but currently in a romantic long-distance relationship, and (2) opportunity to interact face-to-face within the timeframe of the study.

c. Jack Glaser et al. (Glaser, Dixit, & Green, 2002) conducted interviews with 38 participants in White racist Internet chatrooms.

d. James Beggan wanted to know what sort of man reads *Playboy* and how *Playboy* influences readers' self-reported constructions of masculinity. How does one find a sample of *Playboy* readers? Beggan and Allison (2003) ran a letter soliciting participation in his study in the "Forum Reader Response" section of *Playboy* magazine. Twenty-two people responded, ranging in age from 26 to 76, and representing a variety of occupations, including dentists, professors, artists, and lawyers.

Qualitative research studies typically have much smaller samples than quantitative research studies; 20 to 35 participants is not unusual. The size of a qualitative sample is considered sufficient when the criterion of **redundancy** is met. The goal of qualitative research is to present a range of perspectives or information on a topic. The redundancy criterion is met when the inclusion or recruitment of an additional respondent does not significantly add new information and understanding.

Guiding Question #4: What Instrument Is Used to Collect Data?

Lincoln and Guba strongly advocate that the best instrument for qualitative naturalistic inquiry is the human. Moreover, according to Lincoln and Guba (1981), humans should work in **research teams**. Team members, if properly chosen, can serve multiple functions. They can:

■ offer diverse values

■ represent multiple disciplinary perspectives

- assume varying roles in the research process (e.g., data collection, data analysis)

- contribute specialized skills

- provide mutual internal checks on validity and reliability

- provide support to fellow team members

Lincoln and Guba warn that nonhuman instruments can only tap into the dimensions built into the instrument. In contrast, human instruments are shaped by experience and can respond and adapt to the research encounter. "[Nonhuman] instruments cannot reflect the constructions of the respondents, but only those of the instrument maker" (1981, p. 239).

An Example of Development of a Qualitative Instrument An interesting study that demonstrates the development of a qualitative instrument was conducted by John Robertson et al. (Robertson, Johnson, Benton, Janey, Cabral, & Woodford, 2002). In an effort to define gender constructs (e.g., "women are more _____," or "men are more _____"), Robertson showed respondents six drawings and asked respondents to describe the person who made each drawing and guess whether the artist was male or female. Robertson employed a team approach to data analysis. Using a Consensual Qualitative Research (CQR) system, team members were assigned to three- or four-person groups for data analysis. Working individually, each team member assessed similarities in meaning across the written responses and placed these sentences, words, or phrases into categories. Next, the individual proposed his or her categories to the team, and the team worked to develop consensus on the title and content of each category. The categories were then reviewed by auditors from another group. Only when the auditors and the original group reached consensus were the categories considered to be fully defined. The final step was reaching consensus among all coders to develop a final list of categories and their defining features. Redundancy in categories across the coding groups had to be eliminated. This process created a list of central ideas reflecting how people in the sample construct what "feminine" and "masculine" mean. The results? The three top constructs for females were: low self-esteem, emotionally distressed, and restricted/oppressed. The top constructs for males were more positive: successful/accomplished, adventuresome/risk-taker, strong/determined, and problem solver. The one negative construct associated with males was emotionally distressed.

Guiding Question #5: How Will Data Be Collected?

At this point it is important to understand the range of available data-collection techniques. Qualitative studies use **interviewing** (face-to-face question-and-answer process), **ethnographic observation** (observing people enacting culture), analysis of **documents and material culture** (written texts or cultural artifacts), and **visual analysis** (e.g., interpretation of mediated communication texts such as films or television programs).

Two questions should guide the data-collection process, according to Lincoln and Guba (1981). First, what is the degree of **fidelity** in the reproduction of the data? *Fidelity* refers to the purity of the recorded data in comparison to the actual lived experience being assessed. Consider, for example, the difference in fidelity between field notes describing a dance versus a videotape of the performance.

The second question guiding data collection is the degree of **structure** in the data-collection methods. *Structure* refers to the degree of flexibility in adapting methods during the course of data collection. Low structure is preferable in qualitative research. For example, in evaluating data-collection procedures, you should ask if the methods provide opportunities to change questions, to record insights as data is collected, and to go back to previous data to determine the direction of subsequent data collection.

Challenging the Fidelity and Structure of Data Collection Doctor-patient communication has long interested communication studies researchers, and findings from this research are now being introduced into medical training. Patients often feel that doctors do not understand or empathize with them. It's like the old joke: *Patient:* "Doctor, doctor! It hurts when I raise my arm." *Doctor:* "Then don't raise your arm." Mishler studied doctor-patient interaction and concluded that patients invoked the voice of the lifeworld—that is, discussion of symptoms contextually grounded in their life situation, experiences, and problems. In contrast, doctors invoked the voice of medicine—that is, the scientific voice that decontextualizes symptoms by making them more abstract and removed from personal and social situations. Mishler concluded that the divergent communication focus of patient and doctor resulted in misunderstanding and ineffective treatment.

Consider a comparison of the studies of Mishler (1984) with that of Christine Barry et al. (Barry, Stevenson, Britten, Barber, & Bradley, 2001). Barry et al. challenged Mishler's findings on grounds of fidelity and structure, suggesting that the data-collection procedures prevented the researcher from recognizing more complex interactions. In regard to fidelity, Barry et al. challenged Mishler for relying solely on conversations between patients and white male doctors. To remedy this, Barry et al.'s sample of doctors was comprised of 50% women. In addition, Barry criticized Mishler for using only written translations of doctor-patient interactions. To address this, Barry et al. collected data on patients' nonverbal communication and lifestyles to provide rich context cues for analyzing the voice of the "lifeworld" in the verbal data.

In regard to structure, Barry et al. challenged Mishler for relying solely on transcripts of doctor-patient consultations. The Barry et al. study remedied this by adding patient interviews before and after the doctor visit and doctor interviews. Barry compared the patients' pre-visit communication goals and post-visit communication satisfaction with the content of the actual doctor-patient conversation. Mishler, on the basis of only one doctor-patient interview employing the voice of the lifeworld, condemned the voice of medicine as "inhumane." In contrast, Barry et al. found evidence of several different doctor-patient interaction patterns. Barry et al. found that for single straightforward problems, when both doctor and patient invoked the voice of medicine, communication was effective. Communication was also effective when both doctor and patient engaged the voice of lifeworld; patients were recognized as unique psychological entities as well as physical beings. Ineffective communication resulted when patients' attempt to use the voice of lifeworld was ignored or blocked by the doctors' use of the voice of medicine.

Guiding Question #6: How Will Data Be Analyzed?

Whereas data analysis neatly follows data collection in quantitative research, we have already noted that the process of qualitative research is cyclical. Data analysis should occur after the first data are collected, and the initial analysis should determine the focus and strategies used in subsequent data collection. In this manner, errors in data collection can be identified and addressed early in the research process. Moreover, instruments, questions, and even methods can be changed, adapted, and refined throughout the data-collection process. In this manner, the results drive the methods.

YOUR TURN

Qualitative Data Analysis of First Impressions

Deciphering the themes that emerge in qualitative data is not an easy and obvious task. Work with a partner to collect six to eight interview responses to the following question: "Describe your first impression of our college/university when you arrived for a campus visit." You can collect your data in person or via email. Work with your partner to identify themes in the responses.

1. Try to organize these themes into meaningful categories. List the themes that emerge as you read your responses:

   _____

   _____

   _____

2. Now try to organize your themes into two or three categories:

   _____

   _____

   _____

3. Can you provide some interpretation of how these categories are alike or different, and what characteristics underlie category membership?

   _____

   _____

   _____

4. Work to develop a one-sentence "insight" or "finding" regarding students' first impressions of your college/university.

   _____

   _____

   _____

If I Don't Know What I'm Looking for, How Do I Know When I've Found It? There are three steps or phases of inquiry in qualitative research: (1) determine what is happening; (2) find out about it; and (3) verify that what *you* think is happening is really what *the research participants* perceive is happening. You should begin with **exploratory questions** designed to find out what is salient or important in the culture, group, experience, or text you are analyzing. Once you have a grasp of what is going on (or think you do), it is time to go back and ask the research participants if your interpretations are accurate. This is called **reflexive validity.**

To demonstrate the three phases of inquiry, let's explore a study of teenage girls' perceptions of physical education. In the United Kingdom, some teenage girls hold negative attitudes about physical education classes. Cockburn and Clarke (2002) conducted a qualitative study using **reflexive inquiry** procedures. First they conducted interviews (phase one); then they conducted focused follow-up interviews (phase two); and finally, to assess validity, they went back to the interview respondents and verified their analyses (phase three). Cockburn found a relationship between sports images and heterosexual desirability. UK female teens (in 2002!) perceived a "femininity deficit" from engaging in P.E. activities, which jeopardized their attractiveness to the opposite sex.

The **grounded theory approach** (Glaser & Strauss, 1967) is a process of discovering a theory through data exploration and analysis. The first step in data analysis is to look for **themes.** We may not know *a priori* (that is, before we begin) what these themes are, but they may become evident during the analysis of data. One way in which you recognize a theme is when you begin to see the same idea repeated within a case and/or repeated across cases. You want to look for words, phrases, or behaviors that meet the criteria of **frequency across cases**, **dominance in emphasis**, and **repetition within cases.** Once a theme or themes are identified, you can start to develop a hypothesis or theory about the pattern or theme that is emerging. Next, you can take that hypothesis or theory and seek verification in the rest of the data. In this way, the hypothesis or theory is qualified, refined, and developed so that it becomes more specific. Further analysis seeks to specify *what* is occurring, *when* it is occurring, under what conditions it occurs (*where*), *how* certain processes relate to or yield its occurrence, *who* is the agent and/or recipient of this occurrence, and *why* this phenomenon is occurring (that is, what function does it serve for the people involved?). Following the identification of "**thematic units**" (Krippendorf, 1980) or "**core categories**" (Strauss & Corbin, 1990), the data are coded to determine category members. This process involves a cyclical process of redefining category labels and definitions to best reflect the nature of the data.

Identification of Themes: Gangs, Family, and Love In his ethnographic study of Chicago street gangs, Dwight Conquergood (1994) began to notice certain phrases and words in his conversations with gang members. He identified a theme. Many words in the gang members' discourse symbolized love and family: *brothers, homeboys, homeys, homz, bloods, bro.* One gang member explained, "Kings is not only a gang, it's a family. Everybody cares about one another. You can never leave one behind" (p. 363). The common greeting of the Latin Kings is "*Amor,*" the Spanish word for love. Places within gang territory are called "cribs" or "cradles." These thematic units led Conquergood to the development of a theory of gangs as communities. It follows from Conquergood's theory that if gangs serve a family function for their members, efforts to deter gang membership by scaring or shaming youth are unlikely to be effective. Rather, this theory would suggest that to deter youth from joining gangs, an alternative structure for fulfilling family relational needs must be provided. This is a good example of inductive or grounded theory development.

This cyclical process of **theme identification** and organization of themes into **categories** eventually leads the researcher to more complex analyses. The researcher explores how categories are alike and different. One way to analyze categories is to look for underlying **metaphors**. Buzzanell and Burrell (1997), for example, explain individual differences in interpersonal conflict styles by demonstrating how people's descriptions of their conflict communication included metaphors. The researchers analyzed reported conflict scenarios for consistent patterns of metaphor usage (themes) and organized these into meaningful clusters (categories). The researchers found three metaphorical conflict schema: conflict is impotence (victimizing process), conflict is war (battle with personal costs), and conflict is a rational process (collaborative experience).

Guiding Question #7: What Final Procedures Ensure Proper Care and Respect for Researchers and Participants?

The logistics of a qualitative study are similar to those of a quantitative study in terms of designing the study, preparing data-collection instruments and procedures, getting approval from a Human Subjects Review Board, training researchers in data collection, setting up schedules, and managing a budget. There are, however, a few additional logistical considerations for a qualitative study.

As previously discussed, data-collection procedures must be continually monitored and revised according to initial data analysis. As part of this review of data-collection procedures, research teams need to arrange for periodic **debriefings** with each other. Due to the intensive, immersion experience of conducting face-to-face interviews, or participating in or observing a culture, researchers risk becoming overly enmeshed in the people and problems they are researching. For example, a student researcher had to seek treatment for depression after conducting interviews with people who were recently bereaved for a study assessing what type of social support messages were most and least comforting.

When planning a qualitative study, one should also incorporate special **exit procedures** into the research design. Typically, validity is ascertained by taking the write-up of the results back to the research participants for review. If the research participants take issue with the researcher's interpretation of their lived experience, validity is in question— whose experience is it, anyway? This procedure provides participants with additional voice and perspective in the framing of conclusions and interpretations. Qualitative researchers often set up review committees comprised of a subset of the sample to handle this procedure. Exit procedures also include plans for disseminating the results of the study to the research participants and helping participants access relevant decisionmakers to pursue any recommendations for change that are generated by the research process.

Guiding Question #8: Discussing Conclusions—How Are Qualitative Studies Evaluated?

Studies published in qualitative research journals employ evaluation criteria that are specific to the objectives of qualitative analysis. Criteria for evaluating qualitative research include authenticity, situated knowledge, emotionality and caring, and action.

Authenticity questions how authentic the data are in reflecting the lived experiences of the participants. Words, many qualitative scholars argue, are poor representations of experience. Therefore, to meet the criterion of authenticity, the qualitative researcher must also account for *tacit knowledge* that is revealed through nonverbal means and inferred from what is not spoken. Authenticity is associated with the concepts of **phenomenological validity** and reflexive validity that we discussed earlier. If participants do not agree with the researcher's interpretations and representations of their own lived experience, there is a problem with authenticity. Another threat to authenticity is if the *recording of the data* does not accurately reflect the experience of the participants, or if the *method of data collection* somehow interferes with the experience of the participants. For example, field notes cannot reflect the subtleties of linguistic patterns and nonverbal expressions, and these meanings could compromise the authenticity of the research because this information is lost to the researcher.

YOUR TURN

Exploring the Criteria Used to Evaluate Qualitative Research Design

There is a *Far Side* cartoon by Gary Larson that shows the Lone Ranger, after retirement, sitting in a chair reading an "Indian Dictionary." The Lone Ranger muses, "Oh, here it is . . . 'Kemosabe: Apache expression for a horse's rear end' . . . what the hey?"

How does the Lone Ranger's discovery relate to authenticity and phenomenological validity? What are other examples in which research characterizing a culture or group of people does not accurately reflect the participants' perception of their lived experience?

In general, it helps to think about authenticity in terms of voice. The personal voice is the most authentic, and any movement away from personal experience is a move away from authenticity. Another consideration is, whose voice or point of view is presented: the researcher's or the participant's? The qualitative research tradition has long challenged the voice of science, arguing that the presumed legitimacy of the voice of science encourages its use for social control. In qualitative research, the voice of the researcher and the voice of science are not privileged over the voice of the participant. Denzin (1989) promotes an approach to research that he calls **interpretive interactionalism.** Interpretive interactionalism is research based on the experience of the writer—it is the only truly authentic research because it is biographical, personal, and focused on self.

Another criterion for evaluation of qualitative studies is the acknowledgment of **situated knowledge.** Does the researcher fully explore how he or she interacts with the history, setting, context, culture, and participants? Or how the research methods affect the context, culture, and participants? Heider (1988) noted that the characteristics of the researcher—such as personality, gender, culture/ethnicity, values, or theoretical orientation—influence what the researcher chooses to study, what the researcher sees, what the researcher reports, and what ultimate interpretation the researcher creates.

The culture, language, gender, ideology, and interpretive frameworks of the researchers and participants are prisms through which all information and understanding are filtered. In this sense, the qualitative researcher's most important research tool is himself or herself. As a researcher, you should attempt to fully explore how your individual characteristics influence the information you seek and the information you select as important enough to record. There are, inevitably, multiple interpretive truths situated in the culture, ideology, language, and gender of all people involved in the research process. The qualitative researcher must not only acknowledge these multiple truths, but ensure that no single truth is privileged over another. Denzin and Lincoln describe the research process itself as a "social act" (1998, p. 298); research processes are affected by the interpretations of researchers, participants, and contexts and the interactive effects that researchers, participants, and contexts have on each other.

Qualitative researchers have generated important and challenging new criteria for evaluation that include **emotionality and caring.** A good qualitative study should provoke deep emotional understanding and empathy in the reader. Denzin and Lincoln describe how "readers are able to live their way into an experience that has been described and interpreted" (1998, p. 325). Qualitative researchers are encouraged to put themselves into the text they are creating. The ethic of caring sets expectations for a long-term personal relationship between researcher and participants. Research communities cannot be viewed as means to accomplish research goals, but rather must become mutual partners in a caring relationship.

Many scholars believe that qualitative research should also be evaluated according to the criterion of **action.** This means that research is not an end in and of itself; rather, research should be a means toward social change, policy change, problem solving, or program development or evaluation. The area of **critical studies** in particular sets an expectation that research should identify oppression in society and the outcomes should give voice to the disenfranchised, empower the silenced, and ultimately bring about social change.

YOUR TURN

Evaluation of First-Impression Data

What conclusions did you reach regarding students' first impressions of your college/university (see the previous Your Turn exercise)? Using the criteria of authenticity, situated knowledge, emotionality and caring, and action, what is your evaluation of your first-impression data?

1. Are there threats to authenticity in your procedure, data, or analysis? What might those threats be? _____

   _____

2. How does situated knowledge influence your data and analysis? _____

   _____

3. Do your data meet the criteria of emotionality and caring, or of action? YES NO

4. Given this evaluation, how might you improve your procedure, data, or analysis? _____

Denzin and Lincoln (1998) suggest that qualitative research has faced a crisis of **legitimization.** *Legitimization* refers to the criteria we have been discussing: how do qualitative researchers make claims of reality and truth? If reality and truth are constructed and there are multiple realities and truths situated in cultures, contexts, and individual interpretations, how can research be evaluated? If methods emerge from data analysis, how can the rigor of qualitative research be assessed? The criteria of authenticity, situated knowledge, emotionality and caring, and action go a long way toward creating standards for assessing the legitimacy of qualitative research. Qualitative researchers recognize, however, that the legitimacy of research can always be challenged and questioned, as the researcher is inevitably part of the process being studied.

SUMMARY

This chapter provides a step-by-step guide for designing your qualitative study. This "checklist" of guiding questions takes you sequentially through a process of decision-making for conducting a qualitative research project. This chapter introduces the concepts of focused inquiry, sampling, data collection, data analysis, and evaluation in qualitative research. Now that you have an overview of research design, you are ready to proceed to Chapter 9, which explains how to use and conduct specific qualitative research methods, such as interviewing, focus groups, and case studies.

KEY TERMS

action

authenticity

categories

circular

convenience sample

core categories

critical studies

debriefings

documents and material culture

dominance in emphasis

emergence

emergent design

emotionality and caring

ethnographic observation

exit procedures

exploratory questions

fidelity

frequency across cases

grounded theory

grounded theory approach

interpretive interactionalism

interviewing

legitimization

metaphors

phenomenological validity

purposeful sample

redundancy

reflexive inquiry

reflexive validity

repetition within cases

representative

research teams

situated knowledge

snowball sample

structure

thematic units

theme identification

themes

visual analysis

CHAPTER

9

QUALITATIVE RESEARCH METHODS: ETHNOGRAPHY, PHENOMENOLOGY, CASE STUDY, TEXTUAL ANALYSIS, AND APPLIED RESEARCH

LEARNING OBJECTIVES

- Compare and contrast five different qualitative research methodologies.
- Learn the characteristics of ethnography, phenomenology, case study, textual analysis, and applied research.
- Identify the method and its assumptions when reading qualitative research.

John Creswell, a professor of educational psychology who specializes in research methods, asks fellow scholars what type of qualitative research they are doing. More often than not, he reports, he is met with a blank stare (Creswell, 1998, p. 3). He continues by noting that until a few years ago, there was a tendency for scholars across the social sciences to ignorantly label all qualitative research "ethnography." The rapid increase in popularity of qualitative methods in the past 20 years has resulted in the use of qualitative methodology in ways that make the theoretical purists shudder. Some of the theoretical criteria that differentiate qualitative methods are glossed over when methods are adopted by scholars who received their training in quantitative analysis. In addition, there are scholars who are seduced by qualitative tools—such as interviewing and participant observation—and are less invested in learning the theoretical foundation of the method.

When discussing qualitative research, we will make a clear distinction between tools and methods. **Tools** are the data-collection techniques, such as interviews, focus groups, and oral histories (Chapter 10), and can be used across a number of different methods. **Methods** define the focus of the study.

Qualitative methodologies differ in five ways:

1. *Focus:* Where do we look for meaning? Is meaning reflected in behavior? Cognition? Systems and practices of a culture?

2. *Role of Researcher:* Whose meaning is reported? Is it the meaning of the research participants? The interpretation of the researcher? Some combination of both?

3. *Meaning:* What meanings are being explored? The meaning of a cultural practice? The meaning of everyday experiences? The meaning of a film or speech?

4. *Location:* Where is the research conducted? Does one go into the field? Hole up in a library?

5. *End Product*: Is the outcome of the research a description, a recommendation, an interpretation, or an evaluation of a program?

The method you choose to employ in a qualitative study is determined by how you answer these five questions. This chapter explores five different types of qualitative methods: ethnography, phenomenology, case study, textual analysis, and applied research (see Table 9.1). For each of these qualitative methods, we explore the following questions:

1. What is the *focus?*

2. What is the *role of the researcher?*

3. How does the method focus on *meaning?*

4. *Where* do you conduct research?

5. *How* do you do the research, and what *form* does it take when it is done?

ETHNOGRAPHY

What Is the Focus of the Investigation in Ethnography?

It is easy to distinguish the ethnographic method from other qualitative methods by its focus on culture. Meaning, according to this method, resides in cultural practices.

TABLE 9.1 **A Comparison of Qualitative Characteristics of Research**

	Where Do We Look for Meaning?	Whose Interpretation?	What Is the Unit of Analysis?	What Is Outcome Goal?
Ethnography	Culture	Balance of researcher and participant	Community	Cultural map
Phenomenology	Experience of phenomenon	Co-researchers	Individuals and groups	Essence of phenomenon
Case Study	Characteristics of bounded system	Researcher	Organization, group, individual, or critical incident	Describe and interpret case
Textual Analysis	Language and symbols	Researcher	Texts or conversation	Interpretation
Applied Research	Constructed experience with program	Collaboration of participants and researcher	Individual, group, or organization	Evaluation/ problem solving

Therefore, ethnography involves the observation and recording of conversations, rituals, performances, ceremonies, artifacts, jokes, and stories.

The ethnographic perspective has been described as a unique "way of seeing" (Wolcott, 1999). The ethnographer sees the cultural practices and performances observed as serving greater functions—other than the obvious—and having symbolic meanings. These functions and meanings are the very threads that create, reflect, and sustain the culture. The ethnographer sees the practices of a culture as reflections of the *cultural past*, performances of the *cultural present*, and directions for cultural *change and growth*. The cultural practice of hip-hop music, for example, has roots in African American spirituals, blues, and jazz. Hip-hop, like earlier African American music traditions, was originally an expression of opposition to the dominant culture that exploits and oppresses African American people. Several researchers have explored the functions and meanings of hip-hop cultural identity, cultural change, and growth. Yousman (2003), for example, argued that White youths' consumption of rap music and hip-hop culture is interrelated with aspects of racism; the appropriation of rap by the dominant culture dilutes the oppositional power of the genre. Watkins (2001) explored how the popularization of rap music was the result of social, economic, and technological change, and how the original meaning of rap, as a reflection of cultural past and present, was lost.

YOUR TURN

What Function Does a Cultural Practice Serve?

Richard Lee (1979) studied the Dobe !Kung culture of the Kalahari. The !Kung women are typically the gatherers and the !Kung men are the hunters. The !Kung live communally and share the food they have gathered and killed. There is little concept of private property or ownership in their culture.

Trenholm and Jenson described the ritual of the hunt:

> Strict norms govern the way a hunter announces his results when he returns from a successful hunt. He must sit in silence until someone asks him how the hunt went. He must then say that he found nothing of any worth. On the following day, when his companions go out with him to collect the kill, they are expected to do so with a minimum of enthusiasm, complaining loudly about the distance and wretchedness of the game. Instead of being offended, the hunter agrees, apologizing for his lack of skill (2004, p. 17).

What function does this ritualized practice serve for this culture? Discuss your answers in a group and then compare your answers to the findings of Lee in the Your Turn box at the end of the chapter.

What Is the Role of the Researcher in Ethnography?

A central tenet of the ethnographic method is that you must try to understand a culture from the perspective of the members of that culture, not by comparing the culture to your own culture or imposing your own interpretation on cultural behaviors. Figuring out how to accurately reflect and represent a culture is a difficult task.

Ethnographic research conducted in the early part of the 20th century has been criticized for a lack of sensitivity and respect for the people and cultures observed. More recent ethnographic research has been criticized for overenmeshment of the researcher in the culture studied. "If classic ethnography's vice was the slippage from the ideal of detachment to actual indifference, that of present-day reflexivity is the tendency for the self-absorbed Self to lose sight altogether of the culturally different other" (Rosaldo, 1989, p. 7). There is an elusive balance between involvement, sensitivity, empathy, and perspective-taking, on the one hand, and analytic distance, on the other. The ethnographic researcher must continually negotiate this tension.

How Does Ethnography Focus on Meaning?

The challenge of ethnography is to "see" meaning from the perspective of the culture studied. Rosaldo, for example, explored the meaning of headhunting. He begins his book *Culture and Truth*: "If you ask an Older Ilongot man of northern Luzon, Philippines, why he cuts off human heads, his answer is brief, and one on which no anthropologist can readily elaborate: He says that rage, born of grief, impels him to kill his fellow human beings" (1989, p. 1). Rosaldo later describes how appalling the Ilongot headhunters find war. Only if you understand headhunting as a cleansing of grief, rather than as an act of aggression, is it possible to understand this paradox. Rosaldo explains that it was only after his wife, fellow ethnographer Michelle Rosaldo, fell to her death from a cliff in the Philippines where they were conducting fieldwork that he began to understand. Only then did he fully experience the rage, born of grief, of which the Ilongot headhunters spoke.

Herdt (1987) studied the meaning of masculinity among the Sambian people. He explained a practice whereby young boys ingest the semen of their elders, but he did so through the eyes of the Sambian culture. They believed that masculinity could be transmitted from adult males to youths. This cultural practice was founded in beliefs that semen was a life-giving force and a form of sustenance (like breast milk) that would make boys strong. You can imagine the meaning attributed to this practice by Western audiences: Americans interpreted the practice in terms of child abuse, pedophilia, and homosexuality. Decades ago, Herdt appeared on the *Tonight Show* and the host, horrified, abruptly cut to a commercial when Herdt began to detail his observations of Sambian culture. The ethnographic research of Herdt and Rosaldo reminds us how very difficult it is to understand the meanings and functions of the cultural practices of a culture different from our own.

YOUR TURN

An Ethnography of College-Student Culture

How would you conduct an ethnography of college-student culture? Brainstorm a list of cultural practices and performances you would analyze. Check your list to ensure that it is a comprehensive representation of most practices reflecting a typical college student's lived experiences. How do the practices you have identified *reflect the cultural past, perform the cultural present,* and *direct culture change and growth*?

Now go through your list one more time and discuss the underlying functions and meanings of the cultural practices you identified. Try to go beyond superficial meanings to explore new and profound interpretations that you may not have thought about before.

Where Do You Do Ethnography?

Traditional ethnography involved going far away to do fieldwork in some exotic cultural locale. Twenty-first century ethnography, however, invites the researcher to do ethnographic research in local communities. Ethnography is conducted where people are, and the researcher does fieldwork to observe people engaging in routine behaviors within their natural environment.

A central part of embarking on an ethnographic study is the task of defining the place where the everyday living will be observed. Lull (1990), for example, researched families viewing television. Researchers hung out in participants' homes and participated in the daily life of the family: eating with them, doing chores, playing, and watching television. From these observations, Lull concluded that people use television not only as a passive form of entertainment, but also as a means to interpersonal interaction that served an important function for the maintenance of interpersonal relationships.

How Do You Do Ethnography, and What Form Does It Take When It Is Done?

Ethnography is a process of creating a cultural map of human social behavior. An ethnography may include descriptions of cultural ceremonies, rituals, rites of passage, and daily events and behaviors. The ethnography tells a story about the experiences of others, as interpreted by the researcher. It is a written representation of a culture that not only describes the practices of the culture but also analyzes the functions and purposes of those events, describes the conditions under which particular behaviors or practices occur, and suggests some greater significance and deeper understanding of the culture.

Ethnographies are variously described as **cultural "maps" of human social behavior, written representations of culture, stories of culture**, or **cultural performances.** Whereas traditional ethnography is defined as the written representation of a culture,

YOUR TURN

Ethnographic Analysis of the Family

Think about how you might conduct an ethnographic study of your family. How might you "see" your family as an ethnographer? Answer the following questions to get you thinking about your family in new ways:

1. Identify the members of your family by name and role. Consider, for example, who plays the role of peacemaker, communication switchboard operator, clown, challenger, victim, persecutor, troublemaker, attention-getter, enabler, bully, controller, caregiver, or instigator. Create your own role labels as well.

2. How do the behaviors of individual family members affect each other and the family as a whole? Draw diagrams of subgroups or alliances within the family system. For example, are Brittany and Kyle aligned together against Mom and Dad (see Figure 9.1)? Or are Mom and Brittany aligned with each other vis-à-vis Kyle and Dad (see Figure 9.2)?

FIGURE 9.1.

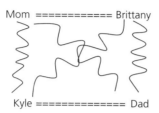

FIGURE 9.2.

3. What daily events, rituals, or celebrations define the family culture?

Now that you have engaged in "seeing" your family ethnographically, what research questions emerge that could guide an ethnographic study of your family?

more recent work in documentary film has also been labeled as ethnographic research. This does not mean, however, that just any film or documentary qualifies as an ethnography. The unique construction of meaning within a given culture must be the focus of the work to make it an ethnography.

YOUR TURN

Video Ethnography

View one of the following videos and report back to your class your analysis of the extent to which the video meets the criteria of an ethnography:

1. The focus of the investigation.

2. How the method focuses on meaning.

3. Where the ethnography was conducted.

4. How the major findings were presented.

Nanook of the North (1922)

All Under Heaven: Life in a Chinese Village (1987). Produced by Robert Gordon, NY: New Day Films

Barbie Nation: An Unauthorized Video (1988). Produced by Susan Stern, NY: New Day Films

Beyond the Veil (1997). Produced by Andrew Gregg, Princeton, NJ: Films for the Humanities and Sciences

Coming to Say Goodbye: Stories of AIDS in Africa (2002). Produced by John Ankele and Anne Macksoud, MaryKnoll, NY: MaryKnoll World Productions

Fires in the Mirror: Crown Heights, Brooklyn and Other Identities (1993). Produced by Anna Deavere Smith, Alexandria, VA: PBS Video

Girls Like Us: Four Years in the Lives of Four Girls (1997). Produced by Jane C. Wagner and Tina DiFeliciantonio, NY: Women Make Movies

Selling Anthropology: Cultural Anthropology through Film (1997). Produced by Karl Heider, Boston, MA: Allyn & Bacon

PHENOMENOLOGY

What Is the Focus of the Investigation in Phenomenology?

Phenomenology is based on the philosophical work of Edmund Husserl. An assumption underlying this philosophy is that there exists in every experience a true essence or structure. "Phenomenology asks for the very nature of a phenomenon, for that which makes a some-thing what it is—and without which it could not be what it is" (Van Manen, 1990, p. 10). Phenomenology focuses on *how people experience a particular phenomenon*; that is, the *sine qua non* of an experience. Phenomenologists explore how individuals construct their meanings of the experience, and how these individual meanings shape group or cultural meanings. How, a phenomenologist asks, is experience translated into consciousness? A phenomenon for study might be the experiential reality of college students' casual sexual hookups (Paul & Hayes, 2002), or what it is like to be an African American first-generation college student in the 21st century (Orbe, 2003). A phenomenologist would ask, "What is the true essence of grief? What does it feel like? What thoughts are associated with it? How is it remembered? How is it talked about and shared with others? What meanings are created to make sense of it?" Van Manen noted that phenomenology always involves retrospective reflection on an experience. "A person cannot reflect on lived experience while living through the experience. For example, if one tries to reflect on one's anger while being angry, one finds that the anger has already changed or dissipated" (1990, p. 90).

A Phenomenological Study of Giving Birth: "Who's Having This Baby?" Drawing from 130 birth narratives, Sterk, Ratcliffe, Hay, Kehoe, and VandeVusse (2002) sought to understand the lived experience of giving birth. The authors, assuming five different academic perspectives, analyze the lack of power experienced by many women in their own birthing experience. The rhetorician researcher analyzed the power relationships revealed in the communication of the participants. The historian explored how women's bodies and the birthing process have been constructed as an assembly production line, rather than as a profoundly personal, relational, and emotive experience. A literary scholar argued that women's silencing has led to a lack of understanding of the phenomenon of birthing. Each scholar brought a different interpretive framework to the analysis of the birthing narratives.

What Is the Role of the Researcher in Phenomenology?

A unique feature of phenomenology is the demand on the researcher to suspend all judgments about what is real. Phenomenologists maintain that human experience makes sense to those who live it. Phenomenologists talk about the "**reality of consciousness**," a phrase which suggests that reality resides in the interpretation or consciousness of an experience. Your experience as a college student, therefore, is not in the going to classes and studying for exams. The reality of your experience is your interpretation of going to classes and taking exams. If you place a "happily challenged" interpretation on your experience of studying research methods, that is your reality. In a sense, your experience becomes real only to the extent that you construct meanings and summaries that inform you what your experience is or has been. The goal and role of the researcher is to get into the experience of the participants and see it as they see it. In this sense, the researcher and the research participants are co-researchers. It is useful to think of the researcher as a sort of medium or facilitator in this process (Gluck & Patai, 1991). The medium/researcher relays the voices with minimal reinterpretation or reshaping.

How Does Phenomenology Focus on Meaning?

Phenomenologists study the *meaning of everyday life*. Orbe (1998), for example, developed a phenomenological study of the communication experiences of nonmajority groups within the dominant American culture, such as women, people of color, gays/lesbians/bisexuals, people with disabilities, and persons of lower socioeconomic status. Orbe wanted to understand the experience of communicating with a dominant culture that had communication norms different from one's own. For example, European Americans, who enjoy the dominant power structure in the United States, frequently denigrate ethnic and minority groups for being "too angry" or "out of control" in their articulation of oppression and discrimination. This silences the nonmajority cultural groups by denigrating the style of communication and ignoring the substance of the message.

Orbe's research demonstrates why a phenomenological method is absolutely necessary given the nature of the research question. Orbe had to understand the phenomenon as experienced by nondominant groups. Look at the potential circularity here: Any other methodological perspective might have forced respondents to frame their experience according to the expectations of the dominant culture, thereby muting the very experiences Orbe sought to understand.

Where Do You Do Phenomenology?

One of the challenges of phenomenological research is reaching a number of participants who have experienced the same phenomenon. The death of a loved one, giving birth, and the experience of cancer are not confined to specific locales, so the researcher goes to where people with experience of a particular phenomenon can be found.

The creation of **virtual communities** on the Internet has made the selection of participants for phenomenological research much easier. Because these virtual communities are open to anyone, it is quite common for the researcher to analyze people's written interpretations of their experience on blogs (online diaries) and support-group websites. Anderson (2006), for example, is interested in the phenomenon of caring communication. She is analyzing the online support messages for a dying young man at caringbridge. org. The website provides unique access to the experience of caring and loss by family members, friends, and strangers who have experienced similar losses. The website allows comparison of messages to the family, messages addressed to the dying man before his death, and even messages to the man up to two years after his death.

How Do You Do Phenomenology, and What Form Does It Take When It Is Done?

The phenomenological researcher begins with narrative data, reduces the stories and descriptions to their essential themes, and engages in a systematic analysis of the words and concepts used to describe the phenomenon. The researchers and participants are co-researchers in this endeavor, and the ultimate goal of the researcher is to create a better understanding of a specific phenomenon by highlighting the interpretations of those who actually experience it. The final outcome of a phenomenological study is a description of the essence or essential common structure of an experience (Husserl, 1967). This report should, as closely and clearly as possible, reflect the reality described by the participants.

YOUR TURN

The Phenomenological Analysis of Falling in Love

In a group of three to four people, share your narratives of the meaning—the essence—of falling in love. You might begin by exploring what it feels like, what it sounds like, what it looks like, what it tastes like, what it smells like, and how this phenomenon affects your mind, spirit, and body. What themes emerge from these narratives? What can you conclude about the phenomenology of love? What does a phenomenological focus on this question offer that other qualitative foci might not?

CASE STUDY

What Is the Focus of the Investigation in a Case Study?

A case study differs from an ethnography (focus on culture) and phenomenological study (focus on a phenomenon). Stake describes a case as a "specific, complex, functioning thing," that is, a bounded system. "The case is an integrated system. The parts do not have to be working well, the purposes may be irrational, but it is a system. Thus people and programs clearly are prospective cases. Events and processes fit the definition less well" (Stake, 1995, p. 2). Examples of systems include an organization, a corporation, an ongoing support group, or a group of college students. A system may be bounded by space (e.g., a particular college), time (e.g., class of 2010), or purpose (e.g., education majors). A system is characterized by wholeness, interdependence of its parts, nonsummativity (a sense that the overall case or system is greater than the sum of its parts), and a tendency toward equilibrium. A family, for example, demonstrates the characteristics of a system. It is defined by (1) wholeness—it is an entity unto itself and distinct from other families; (2) interdependence—the actions of one member have a reverberating influence on other family members; (3) nonsummativity—the family is greater than the sum of its individual members because its rituals, traditions, intimacy, and history are greater than any individual member; and (4) equilibrium—the family creates habitual patterns of behavior that, whether functional or dysfunctional, are difficult to change. An organization, an event, a program, and a political or social group are just a few examples of systems.

There are several types of case studies. A researcher may choose to conduct a single-case study or a collective case study. A collective case study involves a comparison of several related cases, such as a comparison of several corporate organizations. A case study can also be focused on one person, and called a biographical case study, or focused on one event, and called a critical incident study.

A Case Study of Criminal Rehabilitation Andrews and Andrews (2003) conducted a longitudinal observation of a secure criminal rehabilitation unit in Great Britain. Specifically, the researchers were interested in the role of sports as a method for rehabilitation. They discovered that sports activities that did not focus on regulations and were not highly competitive, but did include positive feedback, did show evidence of rehabilitation benefits. They cautioned, on the basis of their one case, that the introduction of sports that did not have these three characteristics might have detrimental effects.

What Is the Role of the Researcher in a Case Study?

The role of the researcher is less specifically defined in a case study than in other qualitative methods. The researcher's voice and perspective are typically more prevalent than the voice and perspective of the informants.

How Does a Case Study Focus on Meaning?

The purpose of a case study is to understand the characteristics that define a particular bounded system, and perhaps to describe an event or process occurring within that system.

YOUR TURN

Case Study of Corporate Advertising

Search the Internet for data regarding the controversial advertising campaigns of one particular corporation (e.g., Abercrombie & Fitch, United Colors of Benetton, Dolce & Gabbana, New Mexico Alien Tourism ad). Write a brief case-study report describing the context of the case, the major themes that emerge from the investigation, and your interpretations of the case. Remember to note the limitations of your case study given the secondary data that you are gleaning from Internet sources. A good case study based on primary research would include interviews with company sources and other relevant parties.

Where Do You Do a Case Study?

Case studies are sometimes conducted on site, and sometimes conducted from historical documents. The researcher does, however, need to define a **sampling rationale** for the case or cases selected for analysis. The sampling rationale varies according to the nature of the research question. Sometimes a researcher will select cases that are similar; at other times, he or she will select cases on the criterion of difference. Sometimes the researcher will select cases based on typicality and sometimes on the criterion of uniqueness.

How Do You Do a Case Study, and What Form Does It Take When It Is Done?

The outcome of a case study is a description and interpretation of the case. Of particular focus is the description of the **context of the case**, which is the social, economic, cultural, geographical, or historical setting. In addition to description, the researcher presents an analysis of the major themes or issues that emerge from the investigation, and may also provide interpretations or recommendations (Stake, 1995; Stake, 1994). As you can see, the researcher's voice is much more apparent in a case study than in an ethnography or phenomenological study.

TEXTUAL ANALYSIS

What Is the Focus of the Investigation in Textual Analysis?

Textual analysis involves the identification and interpretation of a set of **verbal or non-verbal signs**. Everything that you encounter, from clothing to books to food to architecture, is a sign. A *sign*, according to philosopher Charles Sanders Peirce, compels you to think about something other than itself (Peirce, 1998).

A Textual Analysis of the Vietnam War Memorial Carole Blair et al.'s (Blair, Jeppeson, & Pucci, Jr., 1991) analysis of the Vietnam War Memorial in Washington, D.C., reveals things about our culture, history, and values that you may not have thought about. The study attracts one's attention first because it argues that a war memorial is a text: a collection of signs to which we attribute meaning. In her analysis, Blair notes that the Vietnam War Memorial is different: (1) the VMW is black, other war memorials are white; (2) the VMW is built into the side of a hill, other war memorials are tall and soaring; (3) the VMW has a polished granite surface that reflects the image of the visitor, other war memorials have dull rock finishes; (4) the VMW attracts the donation of personal items like teddy bears and clothing, other war memorials are decorated with flowers; and (5) the VMW presents the individual names of all the Vietnam War dead, other war memorials more often present an anonymous recognition of the soldiers lost. In her analysis, Blair argues that the VWM focuses on the human losses of war, not the glories of war. The VWM personalizes the dead in a way that other war memorials do not. Moreover, the visitor to the VWM becomes a part of the memorial. When the visitor sees his or her face superimposed on the names of the dead, he or she can no longer be anonymous or unaccountable. The visitor is not allowed the luxury of maintaining a safe distance from the very personal representation of the dead.

What Is the Role of the Researcher in Textual Analysis?

The researcher is the interpreter of the selected text or texts. According to the assumptions of textual analysis, there are an infinite number of possible interpretations of any given text and each interpretation is equally valid to the extent that it reflects the meanings attributed to the text by the interpreter. The researcher's interpretation is, therefore, only one of many possible valid interpretations of a given text. In textual analysis, the researcher seldom seeks the interpretations of others; the researcher's own interpretation is salient.

How Does Textual Analysis Focus on Meaning?

Meaning is at the heart of textual analysis. Meaning can be analyzed from the perspective of the speaker's intent, the audience's reaction, the historical or cultural context in which the text was created, or the contemporary historical and cultural context in which the text is experienced today. Thus, each perspective on meaning will likely yield a different interpretation of a text.

There are three broad types of textual analysis, each of which takes a slightly different perspective on meaning: the rhetorical perspective, the critical studies perspective, and the discourse analysis perspective. The **rhetorical perspective** focuses on persuasion and influence. An assumption underlying the rhetorical perspective is that texts have meanings and meanings influence people. Researchers engaged in textual analysis believe that pornography, violent films, advertising, and gender and racial stereotypes *do* influence people's beliefs, attitudes, and behaviors. Not all researchers agree as to the specific type or degree of this effect, but textual analysis research assumes that meanings do have an effect. From a rhetorical perspective, we *experience culture through texts*. We can come to understand our tradition, our values, and our identity only through the interpretation of cultural texts.

YOUR TURN

Reading Cultural Texts

Think about your experiences with a new and unfamiliar culture. If you have traveled outside your country, or even outside your region of the country, you have encountered a new culture. If you have entered a new school or joined a new social or religious group, you have experienced a cultural change. Try to remember how you made sense of this new culture. We experience culture through *texts*—signs to which you attribute specific meanings and interpretations. Did you observe people? What signs did you study? What meanings did you attribute to this new experience? Were there some signs you interpreted incorrectly? If so, how did you learn you were wrong?

When Barack Obama was campaigning for president, he was criticized for not wearing a flag label pin. The text—the presence or absence of a lapel pin—had different meanings for different people (a lack of patriotism; support for troops, but not for the Iraq War, for instance). and influenced voters attitudes about his candidacy.

The **critical studies perspective** sees texts as sites of power struggle. Embedded in popular culture texts (e.g., films, television, music, etc.) are messages about who has power and who does not. Critical studies scholars examine texts for evidence of overt and latent oppression, stereotyping, and discrimination. Texts often present one viewpoint, and that viewpoint often constructs and reinforces the power of a particular group. An example of this is Martha Soloman's analysis of the Tuskegee medical reports. In the 1930s in Tuskegee, Alabama, the U.S. Public Health Service conducted a medical experiment to study the natural progression of syphilis in an African American male population. The 399 males recruited for the study were deceived: they were told that they were receiving treatment for the disease when in fact they received no treatment. Moreover, they were denied penicillin when it became available as an effective treatment. The purpose of the study was to document the slow and devastating progression of the disease over time—in essence, to watch the participants die. Reports of this study were published in medical journals between 1936 and 1973. There was no outcry from the medical community regarding the ethics of this experiment even though the effects of untreated syphilis were well known.

Martha Soloman (1994) conducted a textual analysis of the medical reports of the Tuskegee experiments. She concluded that the language used in the published medical reports served to dehumanize the men in the study. She noted, for example, that the men in the study were referred to as "hosts" of the disease and "syphilitics." As a result, the men in the study *became* the disease and lost their identity as suffering individuals and humans. Solomon's critical study highlights the racism that allowed this study to continue, unquestioned, for nearly 40 years.

The **discourse analytic perspective** maintains that the window to understanding a particular culture, a particular social group, or a phenomenon is through the detailed analysis of conversations and stories. The underlying assumption of discourse analysis is that it is through *communication* that meanings are created and sustained. Two specific kinds of discourse analysis are conversation analysis and narrative analysis.

Conversation analysis is the interpretation of a naturally occurring conversation. The words and the nonverbal communications and behaviors (collectively referred to as *nonverbals*) are analyzed to explore how the conversation is structured and what functions the specific utterances serve. Frankel and Beckman (1989) conducted a conversational analysis of doctor-patient interaction. They found that doctors structured the interaction as an interview, but that patients were more likely to structure the interaction as a conversation. An interview is comprised of direct questions with the expectation of very specific answers. In contrast, a conversation starts with generalities and pleasantries before progressing to the primary purpose of the interaction. Frankel and Beckman found that patients employing a conversational structure were still waiting to discuss the primary purpose of their visit when the doctor had already left to see the patient in the next room.

Narrative analysis is the analysis of naturally occurring storytelling. Researchers are interested in how the story is structured and also what functions the story serves, such as building community, maintaining relationships, or establishing group identity and values. Webster (2002), for example, studied the life story reminiscence of the elderly and identified four functions that this public storytelling serves: death preparation, intimacy maintenance, teaching, and connection.

Where Do You Do Textual Analysis?

Textual analysis is conducted wherever you find a text. Any object or verbal or visual text that carries symbolic meaning is a source for textual analysis. A roommate's clothing choice compels you to think about his or her personality; the books on your bookshelf reflect your interests and identity; the building materials and shape of the building you are sitting in say things about the culture, values, economics, and functions of the space anticipated by the building's creators. In this sense, a film, a speech, an advertisement, a magazine, a book, a television show, a statue or memorial, a landscape, or a music video are all texts that carry interpretive meaning and can therefore be analyzed.

How Do You Do Textual Analysis, and What Form Does It Take When It Is Done?

Textual analysis may be based on existing written documents or transcriptions of oral data. When you are working with a document or preexisting text (e.g., a film, speech, news report, or music video), a number of analytic techniques are available. To give you just a few examples, **Marxist criticism** looks for signs of disparity in wealth and power; **feminist criticism** looks for gender inequalities; **culture-centered criticism** explores the interpretation of a text from different cultural perspectives of meaning.

When working with conversation analysis, the research questions are focused more on the functions of each utterance, the sequencing of utterances, and how the utterances serve to construct particular realities and meanings. The process of transcribing interviews and conversations is tedious and time-consuming. Not only must you type the words, but you must also record or note the physical nonverbals (e.g., leans forward) and the paralinguistic cues (e.g., stutters, rising intonation, loudness, etc.). Exhibit 9.1 shows an example.

The final research report does not include a transcription of the entire document or conversation analyzed. It is common for the researcher to present one interpretation of the text and provide specific examples or excerpts from the text to support this interpretation.

EXHIBIT 9.1 An Example of a Transcript for a Conversation Analysis

You will notice from the conversation transcript reproduced here that real conversations do not read like playscripts. Real conversations start and stop, go off topic, and include overlaps and interruptions. Tannen (1984, p. 91) provided the following transcript of a Thanksgiving dinner: "Following is an extended segment of the dinner conversation in which Steve, Peter, and I all simultaneously persist in talking about our own topics, with little or no response from anyone. This segment occurs while we are eating."

(1)   Deborah: I wonder how our ...⌐grandparents and parents felt

(2)   Peter: /?/   ⌊cranberry sauce. ⌋

       Deborah: About Thanksgiving.

(3)   Peter: Cranberry sauce.

(4)   Deborah: It wasn't their holiday.

(5)   Peter: It's a wonderful holiday.

                        ...

(6)   Peter: Is that the cranberry sauce?

             P, acc

(7)   Deborah: I wonder if they did it⌐

(8)   Chad: ⌊One holiday a year for stuff

                    ⌐for stuffing yourself ?

(9)   Peter:⌊Y'know what we should really have?

(10)   Steve: Could we get this off the table? ⌐

(11) Deborah: ⌊ / ?   / ⌊→

                  Y' know if they used to do it for the kids, or whether →

(12)   Peter: ⌊I'd like it off →

       Deborah: they really felt it.

       Peter: the table.⌐

(13)   Steve: It keeps coming back on the table. It must have a will of its own. →

                   ⌐That's all I can say. [*clipped tone throughout*]

(14)   Peter: ⌊We should have more napkins

Excerpted from Tannen, D. (1984). *Conversational style*. Norwood, NJ: Ablex.

YOUR TURN

Advertising Analysis

Can you see opportunities for Marxist, feminist, or culture-centered criticism in advertisements? Search magazines for print advertisements that lend themselves to textual analysis using Marxist, feminist, or culture-centered themes. Pick one type of criticism per ad and provide two to three sentences of textual analysis for each.

It is also necessary, in the report of a textual analysis, to provide a detailed description of the historical and cultural context of the text. It may be necessary to describe the historical and cultural context at the time the text was created, as well as the contemporary historical and cultural context in which the text is being analyzed. Is it possible, for example, to analyze an ancient Hebrew text (the Bible) for its interpretation in a contemporary American society? A. J. Jacobs, in his book, *The Year of Living Biblically* (2007), encountered some challenges eating locusts, stoning adulterers, and sacrificing animals in contemporary America when he attempted to live explicitly by the literal rules of the Old Testament for one year.

APPLIED RESEARCH METHODS: ACTION AND EVALUATION RESEARCH

What Is the Focus of the Investigation in Applied Research?

Traditional research methods have been criticized for being too abstract, too scientific, too theoretical, too laden with jargon, and too focused on data for the sake of data. You probably felt a bit of this frustration when you first tried to read academic journal articles reporting primary research studies.

The goal of **action research** is to demystify research methods and research results. Action research is an ethical and moral calling to use research findings to better our lives as individuals and communities. As such, action research is more applied than theoretical, and more oriented toward problem solving than toward increasing knowledge for its own sake. Indeed, some action researchers would say the only justifiable goal of asking people to participate in a research study is that the results be used directly to improve the lives of those studied.

Action Research Examining Community Building in a Residence for Persons with AIDS Mara Adelman and Larry Frey conducted a research project with the Benedictine House community, a residence for people with AIDS. Over the course of several years, they worked with the residents to study the process of community building. There are clearly certain challenges to community building in a group with a high attrition rate due to death, and a consequent high turnover in group membership. Most communities have more common denominators for constituting a group (e.g., occupation, belief/value system, socioeconomic class, education, age, etc.) than the single random denominator of being infected by the same disease. Adelman and Frey did more than observe and report on the community-building activities of the group: They became participants in the group and helped to solve issues that affected the "sense of community" experienced by the members (Adelman & Frey, 1997). For a sense of the quality and richness that interviewing brings to the understanding of a group, watch Adelman's and Shultz's video documenting this project: *The Pilgrim Must Embark* (1994).

Adelman and Frey (1997) interviewed the residents and the administrators of this community with a personal touch. Rather than focusing exclusively on questions about chores and distribution of duties, the researchers also engaged the residents in a discussion of their hobbies, their interests, and their identities. The very act of participating in the research process likely helped residents to reclaim their individual identities at a time when their AIDS identity and communal identity were dominant. In addition, the researchers participated in residents' meetings, support sessions, and board meetings as researcher-collaborators seeking positive changes to improve the communal experience of the residents.

Evaluation research focuses on assessing the effectiveness of a particular program or course of action in solving a particular problem. Evaluation research is used extensively in education, where researchers compare the effectiveness of various teaching models. Evaluation research is less common in other social sciences, but is receiving increased attention as an applied research method. Bart and O'Brien (1985), for example, interviewed 84 women who had been victims of sexual assault to evaluate the efficacy of different behaviors in preventing rape.

What Is the Role of the Researcher in Applied Research?

The role of the researcher in action and evaluation research is to work collaboratively with research participants to solve problems. With these particular methods, the intended audience for the research results is the participants themselves.

In action research, the people studied are actually participants in the research process, making decisions about data collection, interpretation, and analysis. The researcher and participants have an egalitarian relationship. Ideally, according to Reinharz, "the distinction between the researcher(s) and those on whom the research is done disappears" (1992, p. 181). There is also an assumption in action research that participation in the research process will empower those studied to implement the findings and make significant changes.

Evaluation research is often more politicized. Typically, numerous stakeholders are affected by the evaluation results. Jobs, funding, and program continuation may actually be at stake, or may at least be perceived by the participants to be at risk. Participants and researchers may not have an egalitarian relationship, and though participants may be asked for input in the research design, participants may not have a voice in the final decision regarding research procedures.

How Does Applied Research Focus on Meaning?

Compared to the other qualitative research methods we have discussed, there is more focus on outcome—that is, solving a problem or evaluating a program—than meaning in applied research. Though not the primary focus of action research, understanding the construction of meaning by the research participants is still an integral part of the research process.

A part of program evaluation research is often an exploration of how people construct their experiences with the program. Denzin and Lincoln identified four typical questions addressed in program evaluation research. Two of these questions focus on perception and meaning: (1) "How is the program experienced by various stakeholders?" and (2) "In what ways are the premises, goals, or activities of the program serving to maintain power and resource inequities in the society?" The other two questions are less clearly tied to construction of meaning and might therefore be explored by either quantitative or qualitative methods: (3) "Are desired outcomes attained and attributable to the program?" and (4) "Which parts of the program work well [and] how effective is the program with respect to the organization's goals?" (1998, p. 376).

Where Do You Do Action Research?

Action research is conducted in the local community or organization that is the focus of study. Researchers interact with participants in the field and are as involved as possible in the processes and experiences of the participants.

How Do You Do Applied Research, and What Form Does It Take When It Is Done?

An essential part of action research is the *collaboration* with research participants on each stage of the research project, including identifying research questions, developing data-collection procedures, analyzing the information, and sharing the results. Action research also implies a long-term commitment to working with the research participants. The idea of diving into a community or group, collecting data, and then leaving is not consistent with the ideals of action research.

YOUR TURN

Action Research Exercise—Class Management

Working in a small group, address Denzin's and Lincoln's four evaluation research questions in relation to your research methods class. What recommendation would you propose for improving the class? Make sure you have as many recommendations regarding the student's responsibility for outcomes as you do for the professor's responsibilities.

YOUR TURN

Research Findings for Study Presented in Analysis of the !Kung

Why do the !Kung insult the meat? "Lee tells us that the heavy joking and derision are directed toward one goal: the leveling of potentially arrogant behavior in a successful hunter." Lee believes that "insulting the meat" is a way of maintaining a sense of equality. Because the !Kung depend on sharing for survival, generosity is something that should not be praised but simply expected. Praise might lead to pride and arrogance, potential threats to the !Kung way of life. As Tomazho, one of the !Kung, expressed it:

> When a young man kills much meat, he comes to think of himself as a chief or a big man, and he thinks of us as his servants or inferiors. We can't accept this. We refuse one who boasts, for someday his pride will make him kill somebody. So we always speak of his meat as worthless. In this way we cool his heart and make him gentle (2004, p.17).

Source: Trenholm, S., & Jenson, A. (2004). *Interpersonal communication*, p. 17. New York: Oxford University Press.

Evaluation research begins with a case study that describes the background and context of the program. After an understanding of the situation is achieved, the next step is to create the criteria for evaluation. The researchers will be making value judgments about the merits of the program, so stakeholders therefore have strong feelings about what criteria for evaluation are employed. Based on the data, the researchers then assess the strengths and weaknesses of the program.

Action and evaluation research result in proposals that include *recommendations* for change or improvement. Again, it is important to emphasize that ideally these recommendations do not come from the researcher per se, but rather from the collaborative efforts of all involved. In this way, all the stakeholders in the process feel that they have some ownership of the recommendations and proposals for change.

SUMMARY

This chapter reviewed five different qualitative methods. These methods differ in focus, the role of the researcher, and what meanings are explored. These methods also differ in where and how research is conducted and the form of the final research report. The commonality among all these methods is the assumption that verbal and nonverbal symbols are imbued with meaning and that meaning is subject to the interpretation of the receiver. In the next chapter, we explore specific qualitative research tools that can be used in ethnography, phenomenology, case study, textual analysis, and applied research methods.

KEY TERMS

action research
applied research
biographical case study
case study
collective case study
context of the case
conversation analysis
critical incident study
critical studies perspective
cultural "maps" of human social behavior
cultural performances
culture-centered criticism
discourse analytic perspective
ethnography
evaluation research

feminist criticism
Marxist criticism
methods
narrative analysis
phenomenology
reality of consciousness
rhetorical perspective
sampling rationale
single-case study
stories of culture
textual analysis
tools
verbal or nonverbal signs
virtual communities
written representations of culture

CHAPTER

10

QUALITATIVE RESEARCH TOOLS: INTERVIEWING, FOCUS GROUPS, AND OBSERVATION

LEARNING OBJECTIVES

- Identify the difference between research methods and research tools.
- Compare and contrast three different research tools.
- Learn the steps to conducting effective interviews, focus groups, and observations.

Documentary filmmaker Alan Berliner set out to make a film about his family's history as Russian-Jewish immigrants to the United States. What he envisioned was a warm, informative interview with his father about his father's life as a first-generation American and his grandfather's immigration. What he encountered was an obstreperous respondent (his father) who gave yes-or-no answers, dismissed the significance of the project, and repeatedly insulted him: "[This film is going to be a] guaranteed FLOP!" "You want me to make up stories? . . . My life is nothing! You're trying to make something out of nothing!" "Alan, you have one bad habit and you'd best get over it . . . [just because you think something is important, you think everyone thinks it's important]." What began as a study of a particular family's immigration evolved into an enlightening analysis of the binding and confounding aspects of complex relationships. The resulting documentary, *Nobody's*

Business, is a study of the conflict and connections that define family and father-son relationships.

This chapter explores the nuts and bolts of doing qualitative research. What kind of information do you need? What options are there for obtaining this information? How do you compile and analyze this information into a cohesive and compelling qualitative research report? Berliner's *Nobody's Business* provides a succinct illustration of this process.

THE FIRST TOOL: DEFINING THE CONTEXT

No matter what type of qualitative research you are conducting, the following checklist will be useful as you consider what type of information is needed. Some of the following areas may be explored in more depth than others, depending on the nature of your project and research question, but you should at least consider the implications of each of the following areas as you develop your data-collection plan.

Situational Analysis

The **situational analysis** is a rich description and interpretation of the situation, context, or problem. Who are the key players? What are the key issues? What are different perspectives and interpretations of the current or historical situation?

In *Nobody's Business,* for example, Berliner explored his father's career, family life, and childhood as a way to flesh out the context in which his family was created. The exploration of his father's life led him to explore the lives of his grandfather and great-grandfather. He traveled to Poland to record the towns, streets, and cemeteries where his ancestors lived and died. Berliner recognizes that any situation is viewed differently by different people, and he offers a rich analysis of the different perspectives and interpretations of the current and historical situations by contrasting his own enthusiasm for his findings with his father's dismissal of them. Berliner asked his father to respond to a picture of his grandfather: "Looks like an old Jew . . . I have no emotional response!" Trying to elicit some connection, Berliner showed a picture of his father's grandmother: "What do you want me to tell you? 'Oh I love them, I love them'? I don't give a @#$% about them!" Berliner also interviewed his adult cousins as to their perceptions of his grandfather and their knowledge and understanding of their family origins. Though they were more affirming than his father, Berliner found that his cousins had never bothered to ask about their grandfather's origins. The family's lack of insight into who they are and where they came from provides a background for the father-son relational issues played out in the course of the interview.

Historical Analysis

Insight into current situations can often be gained by analyzing the people, problems, policies, and responses that have defined the past; this is called **historical analysis.** Berliner traveled to the Family History Library in Salt Lake City, Utah, to find Social Security, census, immigration, marriage, and birth records. He found old maps and video footage of the people and places defining the context of Russia and Poland at the turn of the century. He used this footage to imagine his grandfather's childhood (going to yeshiva, living in poverty), and to imagine his great-grandfather's aspirations for his son as the son immigrated to America. Berliner even uncovered a document suggesting that his father is two years older than he thinks he is. The themes that emerge from the historical analysis further illuminate the context for understanding the generational progression of father-son relationships.

Relational Analysis

The interpersonal connections among people and an exploration of what these relationships really mean to the people involved can imbue a qualitative study with feeling, intimacy, and emotion. **Relational analysis** focuses on relationships and the interpretations and feelings associated with those relationships. Berliner uncovered a letter written by his great-grandfather in Poland to his son as he departed for America. The great-grandfather's letter is brimming with the kind of relational emotional disclosure Berliner yearned for from his own father: "the tears of my wounded heart overflow [and I cannot speak all the things I want to say to you as you leave for America] . . . You, son of mine, have been destined to be a great rabbi. . . ." The great-grandfather's words stand in stark contrast to Berliner's father's harsh response: "This is not the first time or the last time a son disappointed a father." Berliner's grandfather became, not a rabbi, but a tailor. From this small excerpt, you can begin to see the pattern of woundedness in father-son relationships that emerges from Berliner's analysis.

Psychological Analysis

The exploration of people's attitudes, feelings, beliefs, motives, values, and goals characterizes the kind of **psychological analysis** that adds richness and depth to a qualitative study. Berliner, for example, interviewed each of his cousins about their perceptions of their grandfather. The descriptors are revealing: he was a loner, he was domineering, he was a very cold man. The stories reveal even more: He never said, "I love you." Berliner's father's refusal to talk about his own father is perhaps more revealing than any story he could have told: "I don't want to talk about him [my father]. Go on to the next question *[threatening]*. This interview is going to be over soon and. . .!" From the interview excerpts, we begin to replace the image of Berliner's father as a cold-hearted, obnoxious, and angry man with the image of a man who is trying desperately to hide his wounds and vulnerability.

Event Analysis

In the development of a qualitative study, certain events and activities may emerge as pivotal and therefore warrant in-depth analysis. **Event analysis** explores the meaning and interpretation of these critical events. In Berliner's study, two life events help shape our understanding of his father: the war and home movies. Berliner's father talks about his war service as the best years of his life and discloses how he cares more about his Army buddies than his own grandparents. This is contrasted with his reluctance to talk about his marriage and divorce. When asked whether he loved his wife when he got married, he responds: "How the hell do I know?" When asked why he recorded hours and hours of 8mm home movies of the family in the early years, he claims that his hearing aid isn't working and he doesn't hear the question—which is repeated several times. Juxtaposed against the happy family movies of a young father and mother playing with their baby son, we grasp the shattered dreams of Berliner's father, grandfather, and great-grandfather.

Outcome Analysis

The **outcome analysis** reveals a deeper meaning underlying the surface-level content of the data. Sometimes the outcome analysis focuses on the functions that certain rituals or meanings serve for a community or culture, and sometimes the outcome analysis yields an evaluation of a program or an action plan for change. The quality of the outcome analysis depends on the analytical and problem-solving skills of the researcher. Berliner's documentary is a good example of how the initial research objective—to explore the family's origins—yielded a much deeper understanding of the intimacy and pain of relationships, and the intergenerational influence of family patterns.

QUALITATIVE RESEARCH TOOLS: HOW TO COLLECT DATA

As you now know, a qualitative study involves the analysis of language and nonverbals in observations and interviews, the analysis of current and historical documents, and even the analysis of oneself. This chapter explores several qualitative research tools, such as interview, focus groups, observation, and autoethnography. It is important to remember that these tools can be used across the various research methods discussed in Chapter 9. An ethnography, for example, might employ interviews, a focus group, and observations.

Interviews

One of the most popular qualitative research tools is interviewing. Beginning researchers typically recognize the need to learn the skills of experimental design or content analysis, but many erroneously presume that interviewing is like chatting. After all, if you can talk, you can interview, right? In reality, interviewing requires a great deal of knowledge, experience, skill, and finesse.

Types of Interviews There are basically three types of interviews: informal, guided, and structured. An **informal interview** allows the researcher to go with the flow and create impromptu questions as the interview progresses. Although there is no preset list of questions, an informal interview, as with every type of data collection, requires preparation and focus to be effective. The researchers need to have objectives clearly in mind as to what they hope to accomplish. Moreover, the interviewer must have the preparation and skill to direct the interview in fruitful directions depending on the response of the participant. The advantage of the informal interview is that the researcher's *a priori* theories are less likely to bias the data collection. The generation of a list of questions in a structured interview necessarily directs the interview in preplanned ways toward specific researcher goals; the direction of the informal interview is much more dependent on the responses of the interviewee. Informal interviews, therefore, are more likely to yield serendipitous (unexpected) discoveries. The disadvantages of an informal interview are that interviews with different people are not comparable and the data are not generalizable. In addition, informal interviews, because of their lack of structure, typically take more time to conduct and more time to analyze. Because the data gleaned may vary greatly from one interview to the next, it is a challenge to identify consistent themes and form interpretations or draw conclusions.

A **structured interview** follows a set of prescribed questions. The structured interview is written with probes, transitions, and follow-up questions. This takes some of the pressure off the researcher, who in an informal interview has to think of probes and follow-ups on the spot. In this sense, the structured interview provides more data-collection control than the informal interview, and it is less dependent on the intuition and skill of the interviewer. Because the questions in a structured interview are the same for each and every interview, the data from one interview to another are comparable. It is therefore more likely that themes and patterns that emerge across a number of respondents may be generalizable to others. Compared to informal interviews, the data are also easier to synthesize and analyze. In addition, the structured interview is typically more time-efficient than the informal interview, because the interviewer and respondent are kept on track by the prepared questions.

The primary limitation of the structured interview is, as you might guess, the diminished opportunity to pursue serendipitous discoveries that emerge from unexpected and interesting responses. Given the emergent discovery process inherent to qualitative research, there is also the risk that the researcher's agenda will unduly shape the data collection when using a structured interview. The questions asked, and consequently the topics discussed in the interview, may be more reflective of the salient features of the researcher's interpretation of the situation than of the respondent's. The structured interview also carries the researcher's agenda into the data-collection process.

A compromise technique that has some of the benefits of both informal and structured interviews is called the **guided interview.** The guided interview follows an outline of questions, but not all of the prescribed probes, transitions, and follow-ups are established prior to the interview. The interviewer is given freedom to deviate from the interview questions as needed to pursue serendipitous findings and fruitful directions.

Interview Format and Types of Questions Once you have decided whether to prepare an informal, guided, or structured interview, you should consider the *format* of the interview. It typically makes sense to begin with background information to establish the context. **Background information** includes such personal information as demographics (e.g., age, marital status, education level, socioeconomic status), pertinent personal history with the group or program under study, and factual information questions that will help you to understand the operations of the culture, group, or program under study. **Demographic and factual questions** are typically easy to answer, and beginning with this type of question can help to put the respondent at ease.

The second part of the interview should address the respondent's *experience* with the group, culture, or program under study. In this part of the interview, **description**

questions are used: "What is your job description?" "You've just walked in the door of your office. Describe what you do first. What do you do next, and next?" "You said you prepare for the morning conference. How do you prepare for the conference meeting?" **Sensory questions** are a specific type of description question. Sensory questions ask respondents what they see, hear, smell, touch, and taste as part of the experience under study. The researcher must play the naïve observer in this part of the interview. Sometimes the most obvious of questions regarding the experience or description of a setting can yield rich understandings.

The third part of the interview should explore the respondent's *meanings, interpretations,* and *associations* in regard to the experiences described. To get at these underlying constructions of meaning, it is sometimes helpful to ask **comparison questions.** To understand the meaning and experiences of skater culture, one might ask, "How is a set [series of moves] that is 'smooth' different from a set that is 'diamonds'? How is a set that is 'sick' better or worse than a set that is 'smooth'?" To ascertain meanings, interpretations, and associations, it is also helpful to ask **feeling questions** ("How do you feel about . . ."), **opinion questions** ("What do you think or believe about . . ."), and **value questions** ("To what extent is this good/moral or bad/immoral?").

Seidman (1991) recommends using a three-interview format, with each interview dedicated to one of the three foci: background, experience, and meaning. This allows the researcher to use the background information to develop questions about the experience and to use the understanding of the experience to develop questions about the meanings and associations of key concepts.

In checking your format, you should be attentive to **past, present, and future perspectives** on background, experience, and meaning. Imagine the education researcher who assesses a student's present performance and misses the significant dip in performance revealed by a comparison to previous test scores. Imagine the clinical psychologist who is comforted by a client's lack of past self-injurious behavior but fails to assess current suicidal ideation. Imagine the forensic psychologist who fails to assess homicidal intent. While it is said that past behavior is the best predictor of future behavior, it would be folly to ignore the impact of vision, goals, and ideation on future behavior.

Sequencing

Each interview requires a setup, the building of rapport, and a closing. Each of these components serves important functions for the interviewer-respondent relationship.

The **setup** informs the participant of the roles and expectations for the interviewer and interviewee. The purpose of the interview, the estimated length of the interview, and the type of questions to be explored should be previewed. This communication of expectations helps the respondent know how to act, reduces apprehension, and helps to establish rapport with the respondent. The level of disclosure in an interview increases as the interviewer moves from descriptive questions to meanings, interpretations, and associations.

Affirmation and feedback are particularly important to build **rapport.** As the respondent reveals more personal information, the nonverbals of the interviewer must communicate interest, respect, appreciation, empathy, and acceptance. Head-nodding, a forward lean, and nonfluencies such as "uh-huh" are useful feedback techniques when used subtly and in moderation. Verbal feedback may, in certain situations, be appropriate, but should be used with caution. Too much verbal response from the interviewer can shift the focus of the interview away from the respondent. Interviewer responses can also have the effect of being evaluative or judgmental. Either a shift in focus or perceived evaluation can effectively shut down respondent disclosure.

The **closing** of the interview should bring the respondent back to the present environment. This means that you cannot leave a respondent in the depths of interpretation and disclosure. The skillful interviewer gradually decreases the intensity of the questions in the closing process. Author Johnston recently witnessed an interview that neglected the closing technique by following the respondent's intimate disclosure of the tragic death of her daughter with an abrupt, "Well! That's all the questions I have. Thanks."

The closing offers the opportunity to affirm the respondent's contribution to the research. This can be done through a direct statement and also by employing a closing question. The use of a **closing question** is consistent with the values of qualitative research. When an interview is structured, the researcher's agenda takes precedence over the respondent's agenda. An open-ended closing question such as "Is there anything else that you'd like to add?" or "Is there anything that I haven't covered in the interview that you'd like to talk about?" gives the respondent an opportunity to address, redirect, and/or correct the research agenda.

The closing of an interview should also clarify the future relationship between the interviewer and respondent. This might include future interviews or meetings, but should at the least involve a commitment to provide research results to the respondent. If the interview marks the closure of a long-term field involvement, the conclusion of this relationship should be fully discussed and acknowledged. If the interview brought up particularly personal or sensitive disclosures, the interviewer should provide information on and/or arrange for appropriate referrals for counseling, employee support, or legal or governmental intervention.

Rapport

Martin Buber (1965) distinguished between communication that assumes an "I-It" relationship and communication that assumes an "I-Thou" relationship. Buber characterized **I-It** communication by its positioning of the other person as a means to the goals. In I-It interview communication, the respondent becomes an object, an ID number in a computer file. The interviewer engages the person to elicit the most information possible, but has little empathic concern for the respondent as an individual. In contrast, in an **I-Thou** interview, the respondent is revered as an individual, not as a representative of some group. The respondent's story is received with consideration for the human dignity of the person and his or her experience.

The interviewer should strive to create a communication environment conducive to disclosure. This requires relational liking and trust. People are unlikely to disclose to an interviewer whom they dislike or distrust. To a greater or lesser extent, depending on the personalities involved, the interviewer-respondent relationship may be mutually disclosive, interactive, conversational, intimate, and empathic.

Importantly, however, the interviewer must also be continually conscious of **boundaries** between self and other. This process is often difficult, and many qualitative researchers dissolve relational boundaries with participants to such a degree that it is detrimental to themselves, the participants, and the research process. The outdated but descriptive anthropology expression was that the researcher had "gone native" or become one with the persons and culture studied. The dissolution of relational boundaries between interviewer and participants may result in researcher burnout or a level of researcher emotional involvement that makes it difficult for the researcher to pull back from the situation to accurately report the results. The dissolution of boundaries can also be detrimental to participants, who may come to depend on the intimate relationship established in trust with the researcher. The needs of the participants may exceed what the researcher is able to provide. One example of this is when interviewer and participant fall into a therapeutic relationship. If the researcher is not trained as a clinical therapist, it is not only unethical but also dangerous to assume that role. Ultimately, the dissolution of boundaries is detrimental to the research process because the research may never be completed, reported, and disseminated for the benefit of the participants and others.

The key is to develop an *empathic, but separate,* relationship with research participants. The interviewer's mantra should be: "I will listen. I will affirm your experience. I will care. I cannot fix all the problems I see. Indeed, it may not be in my role or capacity to fix anything at all."

Wording of Interview Questions

Bad questions yield bad data. Many researchers have sad tales to tell about their first attempts at developing interview protocols and the unexpected response (or lack of response) by participants. The one good thing about an interview disaster is that you learn a great deal about what *not* to do the next time. *Freakanomics* authors Levitt and Dubner (2005) told the story of a University of Chicago graduate student sent into the Southside Chicago projects to ask respondents, "What's it like to be black and poor?" There are several problems with this situation, not the least of which is the wording of the question!

The wording of interview questions is critical. Subtle variations in the wording of questions can lead to reticent responses (curt yes-or-no answers) or to elaborately detailed responses, uncontrolled crying or a rich description of feelings, and omissions of important information or disclosure of details previously unknown to the researcher. My spouse, a psychiatrist, had to conduct an interview under observation as part of his medical board exam. He asked the patient all the typical questions, including demographics, medical history, and criminal history, and inquired about current presenting medical symptoms or problems. He was about to wrap up the interview when it occurred to him to ask about the patient's mother. The patient said, "Oh, she died when I burned her house down." Well, that might be important to the psychiatric evaluation!

Three basic rules will guide you as you develop interview questions. Interview questions should be open-ended, single-issue, and should avoid "why?" **Open-ended questions** require more than a dichotomous yes-or-no or one-word response. Consider the comparison of closed- and open-ended questions in Table 10.1. Look at how the subtle change in wording elicits a more descriptive response. Even the most reticent interviewee will find it

TABLE 10.1   Closed- vs. Open-Ended Questions

Closed-Ended	Open-Ended
Do you drink alcohol?	What's your opinion of underage drinking? How would you describe your own weekly alcohol intake?
Do your friends drink alcohol?	Tell me about a situation or party where you observed friends drinking . . .
Do you drink and drive?	What sort of choices do you and your friends/people you know make regarding drinking and driving?
Do you/your peers engage in binge drinking?	Tell me about drinking games . . . Have you ever seen anyone really drunk? Tell me about that . . .

difficult to give short answers to truly open-ended questions. When I was graduating from university, I interviewed for jobs at a number of large advertising agencies in New York City and Chicago. In one interview, I walked into a boardroom where 12 people sat around the table, was gestured to the chair at the end of the table, and was given the ultimate open-ended interview question/directive: "You have 30 minutes. Tell us about yourself." That was the last thing said by any of the interviewers for the next painful 30 minutes. As a 21-year-old college student, ignorant of the ways of the boardroom, I bombed the question. As a 40-something college professor, I wish I had another chance. What I did not appreciate at the time was the eloquence of this question. Advertising executives give sales presentations. I was asked to give an impromptu yet mesmerizing presentation for a product I should know something about: myself. My response should have been an advertisement for hiring me.

Interview questions, like survey questions, should also be **single-issue** formats. Consider the examples in Table 10.2 of multiple- and single-issue questions. Multiple-issue questions confound the respondent with thoughts of: *What do you really want to know? Which question should I answer? I would answer each of those questions differently, what should I do?* Particularly in an informal interview, when the questions are not carefully framed in advance, it is easy to slip more than one issue into a question.

The final consideration when developing interview questions is to *avoid "why" questions.* Patton (2002) maintains that "why" questions are difficult to answer. A person's motivation for behavior or attitudes is complex and typically involves a multitude of reasons, some of which are conscious and some of which are unconscious. Consider the examples of "why" questions in Exhibit 10.1 and the possible reactions of an interview respondent. Although the purpose of your interview may be to discover people's motivations and justifications for their behavior or attitudes, there are better ways to ascertain

TABLE 10.2 Multiple- vs. Single-Issue Questions

Multiple-Issue	Single-Issue
Do you diet and exercise excessively?	Are you on a diet? Do you exercise daily?
Are you an involved college student?	[Implies multiple types of involvement] Are you involved in extracurricular activities? Are you actively engaged in your coursework? Do you play sports or intramurals? Do you hold a job? Are you involved in volunteer work?

this information than to ask "Why?" One way to tap into motivations and justifications is to break them into smaller categories. To ascertain *why* teenagers smoke, you could break this issue down into parts: school satisfaction questions, family support questions, beliefs about the health effects of smoking, sex/gender role questions, and own-parent modeling questions. It is then possible to ask follow-up questions specific to each participant's responses to compare the importance of these factors in their decision: "Which was more important to your decision to start smoking, tension at home or problems at school?"

EXHIBIT 10.1 Avoid "Why?" Questions

Examples from an assessment of grade-school children's reading:

1. Why don't you like to read? [Child would have difficulty identifying eyesight problems, tracking problems, comprehension problems.]
2. Why don't you want to learn to read? [Places responsibility for problem on child and constructs problem as something the child can both define and control.]

Examples from a study of Internet use:

1. Why do you spend so much time on the Internet? [Better to explore what specific uses and gratifications user realizes from Internet usage.]
2. Why does your Internet usage interfere with your personal relationships? [Better to explore "how" usage affects relationships.]

A final consideration in framing interview questions is to strive for **clarity.** Editing questions to eliminate unnecessary words typically makes the interview questions more direct and succinct. It is important to pretest interview questions for understandability.

It is possible that you are using words or phrasing that are not readily understood by your participants. Pretesting uncovers questions that are open to several interpretations, some of which may not be your intended interpretations.

YOUR TURN

Interviewing

Choose one of the following topics or develop your own research topic and create a structured interview of about 10 questions, using the guidelines in this chapter.

Possible Interview Topics:

1. Worst Date Experiences
2. Greatest Accomplishment in Sports, Academics, Extracurriculars, or Volunteer Activities
3. Most Embarrassing College Experience

When you think your interview is complete, evaluate the interview according to the following checklist:

____ Are questions open-ended?
____ Are questions single-issue?
____ Have you avoided "why" questions?
____ Do your transitions and questions facilitate your rapport with the respondent?

After you have revised your interview script, conduct your interview with a member of the class. Ask your respondent to evaluate your interview script on the same criteria.

Interview Respondent's Evaluation:

____ Were questions open-ended?
____ Were questions single-issue?
____ Did the interview avoid "why" questions?
____ Did transitions and questions facilitate rapport with the interviewer?

Based on your experience conducting the interview, and on your respondent's evaluation, what revisions in your interview script are necessary?

Interview Question Techniques

The amount of disclosure and the veracity of information volunteered by an interview participant can depend on how questions are structured. An interviewer, according to Patton (2002), strives to develop rapport—an empathic relationship—with participants, but must also remain neutral in regard to the *content* of what is being said. The interviewer must convey to participants that the behaviors or attitudes they are describing are not being judged. When the salad-maker you are interviewing discloses that he never washes his hands because of a nasty skin condition, it is best *not* to say, "Oh my gosh, that's disgusting!" Better to respond with a rapport-building statement, "The skin condition must be very difficult for you," and follow-up questions to get more information for your Health and Human Services report: "What is the name of the skin condition?" and "Is the skin condition contagious?" Patton (2002) outlines six types of questions that can elicit disclosure and also help the interviewer develop rapport while maintaining **neutrality.**

Example questions pose an example in the question to give the respondent a sense of the type of response and level of response solicited. "I'm going to ask you some questions about a recent verbal conflict you've had with someone important to you. Try to think of a specific conflict or argument you've had recently. Some people, for example, talk about arguments with their boyfriend/girlfriend, and some people recall arguments with their mom or dad or sibling." The examples used in this question clarify the question by defining the personal relationship that is implied by "someone important to you." The examples also spur a respondent's memories of recent conflicts. You must be careful, however, that in using an example you do not pose a **leading question:** "I have heard all sorts of stories from students and faculty about problems with this teacher. What problems have you had?"

Another question technique is **role-playing.** The role-playing question can transport the respondents out of an uncomfortable and artificial situation (the interview) as they imagine themselves in the situation or context that you wish to understand. Role-playing questions are often used in communication research because researchers cannot always be on the spot to observe and record a naturally occurring message. When conducting a study on bereavement messages, I knew that I could not crash funerals and visitations to record support messages given to the bereaved. I could, however, describe a context that would be realistic to the experience of a college student to elicit what college students *thought* they would say in such a situation: "One of your friends has just returned to school following the sudden death of a sibling. You are approaching your friend and thinking about what you will say. Your friend turns to acknowledge you, and you have an opportunity to talk together. What do you say?"

Role-playing questions are not without limitations. You need to think about whether the people you will be asking to assume a role are of the right age and personality, and even in the appropriate context to do so. When my physician spouse was interviewing for medical residency programs, a physician at a top medical school who interviewed him engaged in a role-playing scenario. The interviewer asked Jim who knew him best, and he said me, his spouse. The interviewer then told Jim I was at the door and that he should get up and let me into the office. When my imaginary self was seated, Jim was asked to take my role and talk about what type of person he was. At the end of this role-play Jim was asked to escort the imaginary me to the door. This role-play was so contrived that Jim left resolute in the decision to *not* do his medical residency with this program.

Presupposition questions can be quite effective when addressing sensitive subjects. Presupposition questions use grammatical structure to make an assumption. Rather than asking if someone drinks alcohol, a presupposition question assumes that everyone drinks and instead focuses on how much. For example, "How much alcohol do you drink each week?" rather than, "Do you drink alcohol?" Presupposition questions are used extensively in collecting medical histories. Rather than asking whether a person has engaged in same-sex behavior, a presupposition question asks: "How many same-sex partners have you had?" Rather than asking whether a person has had unprotected sex, a presupposition question asks: "When was the last time you had unprotected sex?" If the interviewer assumes that behaviors that could be viewed as embarrassing already occur—in a sense making them normative—it is less likely that the respondent will feel the need to deny such behavior.

One of the most apparent differences between experienced and inexperienced interviewers is the use of **follow-up questions** or **probes.** Probe questions, which are typically impromptu responses to something the participant has said, ask for more details and explanation. Sometimes a probe is obvious, such as: "When did this happen?" or "Where did this happen?" Sometimes a probe is less obvious because it deals less with the details of what happened and more with the participant's interpretation of or response to what happened: "How did you feel when that happened?" The interviewer, through experience and sheer intuition, needs to be able to pick up on the verbal and nonverbal cues of the respondent to know when there is more information underlying the surface response.

Silence is also an important interview technique. The interviewer must give sufficient time for the respondent to think about the question, organize a response, and articulate a response. The interviewer, often anxious that the interview keep moving, is prone to jump in with the next question or follow-up questions before the respondent has fully answered the first question. I recently observed a professor in a classroom leading a discussion with college students. The teacher would raise a provocative question, then panic at the lack of immediate response from the students and jump in with a series of four or five additional questions. The students were stunned, confused: Which question should they answer? What was that thought they had had about the first question? What was that first question, anyway? American communication culture has little tolerance for silence. We drum our fingers on the table, or cough, or jump in with a comment to cover any lingering silence. In an interview, prolonged silence—as long as your respondent is cooperative and engaged—can be very productive.

Transitions are comments that help the interview progress smoothly from topic to topic. Transitions help respondents to put a context or organizational label on what has been covered and what will be coming up. When respondents have a sense of how the interview is progressing, why you have asked the questions you have asked, and what types of topics will be addressed next, respondents are more at ease. A transition might sound like this: "Thank you, Jeremy. You're doing a great job. Your answers will help us understand how you read. The next part of our conversation will be about how you play with kids at school. You'll have a chance to tell me about what you like to do, and what things you don't like to do."

Patton (2002) describes a particular type of transition, which he calls an **"attention-getting preface"** that can make the interview more interesting. Attention-getting prefaces include: "The next question is a bit awkward to ask . . ." or "The next question is very important to our evaluation of this program . . ." or "The next question is very personal . . ." or "We really want to understand your perspective. The next questions ask about your feelings and opinions regarding. . . ." Transitions are important to the flow of an interview. A good interview is an aesthetic experience that moves eloquently from disclosure of feelings to surface description, from past to present, from personal to social/global.

YOUR TURN

Developing Different Types of Interview Questions

Work with one classmate to develop interview questions that would be relevant for another classmate (e.g., a recent conflict).

Demonstrate as many of the six special question techniques as possible:

- example questions
- role-playing
- presupposition questions
- follow-up questions/probes
- silence
- transitions

Team up with another pair and practice your interviews on each other.

What techniques did you use?

_____

Which worked well?

_____

Which were awkward?

_____

What could you change to make the technique more effective?

_____

_____

_____

Focus Groups

When there is only a one-shot opportunity for data collection, focus groups may be a reasonable alternative to conducting a number of individual interviews. Focus groups bring together a group of six to ten people who, under the guidance of a moderator, engage in a group question-and-answer discussion.

Sampling

Selecting members of a focus group is never random, so intentional decisions must be made to achieve the best group composition in light of the research question. There are times, for example, when the research question calls for a focus group homogeneous on particular characteristics; at other times, the research question may call for a focus group composition designed to reflect heterogeneity on variables of interest. When the issue is complex, Krueger (1994) recommends that you have no more than seven participants in a focus group.

There are some situations in which focus groups have advantages over interviews. The primary advantage of focus groups is the opportunity for group interaction. The "**synergistic group effect**" (Stewart & Shandasani, 1990) provides information that individual interviews cannot. People's behaviors and attitudes are not made individually in isolation, but in a social context. A focus group can be invaluable for observing and analyzing **social influence.** For this reason, focus groups are frequently used to study purchasing decisions, advertising effectiveness, and voting behavior. Like interviews, focus groups vary from informal (general prompts) to structured (preset questions). One advantage of an informal focus group is the opportunity to *reduce the influence and role of the researcher*. The group can take charge of the discussion and the researcher can observe (Morgan, 1997).

A number of research studies reveal limitations of focus groups. The **group communication effect** in focus groups can be detrimental. Sussman et al. (Sussman, Burton, Dent, Stacy, & Flay, 1991) report that focus-group responses were more extreme than survey responses. This can create compounding problems if an extreme attitude is presented by a particularly outspoken and dynamic person and the whole direction of the focus group diverts toward extremism. I commissioned a focus group with residents of a suburban community to create ideas for a marketing campaign for the struggling downtown business area. The moderator of the focus group asked for descriptions and metaphors that described the downtown area. One outspoken gentleman yelled out "Road kill!" and I watched through a one-way observation glass in horror as the remainder of the focus group discussion digressed to a highly animated competition for the most creative negative description of road kill and associated metaphors for the downtown area.

Another tradeoff of choosing focus groups over interviews is *less depth and breadth in information*. In general, compared to one-on-one interviews, individual response time is limited, and fewer questions can be adequately covered. In addition to the time factor, there is something about being in a group that can influence the depth and breadth of information. Fern (1982) found that focus groups generated only 70% of the ideas generated in interviews. Kaplowitz (2000) discovered that people are 18 times more likely to disclose personal information in an interview than in a focus group, and Krueger (1994) suggested that focus groups are more likely to uncover major themes than subtle differences.

It is also possible that the articulation of strong opinions by outspoken people will silence those who hold contrary views. Noelle-Neumann (1984), a media scholar, calls this the **spiral of silence theory**. According to Noelle-Neumann, people may perceive that they hold a minority opinion even when, in reality, there are others who would agree with them. However, based on their perception that their opinion is contrary to the powerful articulated opinions surrounding them, they remain silent, thereby perpetuating a spiral of silence. In her theory Noelle-Neumann is specifically describing the effects of the mass media, but we can use this theory to understand how group dynamics might influence what opinions emerge as salient in a focus group. The use of computer-mediated focus groups is becoming more frequent, and there is some suggestion that computer-mediated interaction can reduce respondent anxiety and facilitate participation.

Structure of Focus Group

Conducting a focus group, like an interview, requires verbal and nonverbal skills, the ability to communicate empathy, and the insight to pursue particular responses with fruitful follow-up questions.

YOUR TURN

Focus Group or Interview? Choosing Which Is Best

Identify three research questions that might be best explored using a focus group.

1. _____

2. _____

3. _____

List two benefits of using a focus group over interviews for each of the research questions you just listed.

1. _____   _____

2. _____   _____

3. _____   _____

There are numerous techniques for moderating a focus group, but in essence, a focus group should include the following:

■   *Introduction:* The purpose of the focus group should be clearly presented. At this stage, group members should be introduced and their respective roles defined. The moderator should create a comfortable climate for interaction. Setting the focus-group climate includes establishing rapport with the participants, alleviating respondent apprehension, and helping the group to get acquainted.

■ *Preview:* The moderator should establish the communication culture of the group by previewing the format or type of the questions that will be presented, and establishing the communication expectations for participant interaction. Specific guidelines for respecting differences of opinion, maintaining politeness, directing order of talk, managing disagreement, and honoring self-disclosures should be addressed. Expectations regarding anonymity and confidentiality should be created. The moderator should at this point also disclose any recording devices being used, and the subsequent use of the information gathered.

■ *Discussion:* Once the climate for interaction is created, the communication guidelines established, and the purpose, procedure, and dissemination of the focus-group data presented, it is time to engage the discussion. The keys to a successful focus-group discussion are focus and follow-up. It is better to focus on one or at most a few issues than to try to cover a number of different issues in a focus-group context. This will allow the moderator to develop impromptu lines of questioning to follow up on participants' responses. Focus and follow-up yield more in-depth information. When developing focus-group questions, you can begin with the same guidelines as for interview questions. In a focus group, however, the moderator must also facilitate group communication. The best discussions occur when participants talk to each other, rather than directing their responses directly to the moderator. The best discussions are also characterized by spontaneous response reflecting the eruption of an idea or opinion, rather than a prescribed format of going around the group and talking in turn. Though going around the group is sometimes necessary, it should not be used consistently throughout the focus group. The best discussions emerge when the moderator varies the question and response styles.

■ *Activities:* In addition to using discussion questions, focus groups sometimes employ activities, such as role-plays, group interaction games, drawing, paper-and-pencil surveys or scales, observation of participants' experience, or response to a video, written text, or visual. You can imagine, for example, how each of these might be used in a focus group for product marketing. One might ask participants to role-play telling a friend about the new product, or to engage in a game putting product pieces together or matching product characteristics to brands. Attitudinal surveys or personality assessments might be useful for marketing purposes, as would observations of participants using and interacting with the product. Advertising is often pretested in focus groups by asking participants to respond to various jingles, slogans, visuals, or themes.

■ *Moderating:* The role of the moderator is to facilitate group participation, monitor the time and progression of the focus group through the discussion questions, and to bring the focus group to a close. The moderator of a focus group often has to manage difficult respondents who either are reluctant to engage in the process or are hyperstimulated to dominate the process. A few techniques that are helpful when managing group discussions are to recognize the reluctant or dominant participant by name. After recognizing the dominant participant by name, acknowledge the feeling she or he has identified, affirm the person's contribution to the process, and then move the discussion on by acknowledging others who need to speak or by acknowledging time constraints. Alternatively, after calling the reluctant participant by name, acknowledge his or her nonverbals and ask if your interpretation of the nonverbals is correct; then affirm the person's contribution to the process and ask for his or her response.

YOUR TURN

Designing Innovative Focus-Group Activities

You have been hired by your college/university admissions office to conduct a focus group of prospective students that will help refine the recruiting materials produced by your college/university.

1. Define your focus group. Who will you select to participate? What will be the composition of the group? What is your rationale for this group?
2. What is the goal of this focus group? What do you want to know?
3. Propose an innovative activity to assess the desired information from this particular group. Describe this innovative activity.

Observation

Another common qualitative research technique is direct observation. The ultimate trade-off between interview and observation techniques is reliance on participants' perceptions or reliance on the researcher's perceptions. Sometimes, such as when researching socially undesirable, traumatic, or highly ego-involved behavior, people are not accurate reporters of their own experience, and their reports are subject to selective perception and filtering. In such a situation the researcher might opt for direct observation. It is necessary to remember, however, that observation, in turn, is subject to the bias of the researcher's perception, interpretation, and analysis.

Observation is, of course, dependent upon access to the group you wish to study. The role of the researcher may vary a great deal depending on the nature of the group being studied. If the researcher has natural membership in the group, this is called **full immersion.** If the researcher interacts with the group as a researcher, this is called **artificial immersion.** With full immersion, the advantage is connection and rapport. Conversely, with artificial immersion, the advantage is some degree of objective separation or distance. The risk of full immersion is overenmeshment with the group that prevents awareness of some processes that are occurring. Conversely, the risk of artificial immersion is that the researcher can never fully be a group participant; the perspective of the researcher is forever that of an outsider looking in. "The ideal in evaluation is to design and negotiate that degree of participation that will yield the most meaningful data about the program given the characteristics of the participants, the nature of the staff-participant interactions, the socio-political context of the program, and the information needs of intended evaluation users" (Patton, 2002, p. 267).

The researcher role can vary from **complete participant,** to **primary participant and secondary observer,** to **primary observer and secondary participant,** to **complete observer** (Gold, 1958). Some of the richest data are ascertained from participant observation whereby the researcher assumes the role of a group member. One example of participant observation research is recounted in Barbara Ehrenreich's (2001) best-selling book, *Nickel and Dimed: On (Not) Getting By in America,* in which she assumes the role of a minimum-wage worker for a year in order to be able to write a firsthand experience of the working poor in America. An example of a researcher transitioning through observer and participant roles is recounted in David Covington's (1995) book *Salvation on Sand Mountain,* in which he entered a snake-handling religious community in the Appalachian mountains as a newspaper reporter, but began to identify with the goals and values of the group to the extent that he stayed there as a member of the community for more than a year.

Once group access is attained and the researcher's role is determined, the **process of observation** begins. First, the researcher simply observes, attending to the details of the setting, people, and activities. Next, the researcher strives to describe the setting, people, and activities of the group. The third step is to attempt to understand the meaning of these activities for individual participants and/or the group identity. Throughout these three stages the researcher is taking copious **field notes,** which are characterized by "**thick description.**" Efforts are made to record participants' own voices as closely as possible. For this reason, video camera recording is increasingly being used to document observation research. Even with the availability of audio and video recording, many qualitative researchers also incorporate handwritten field notes. The benefits of field notes are that they can be less intrusive than recording equipment and thereby encourage participants to actually talk to the researcher, not the camera or recorder. Field notes also provide the opportunity for reflection, interpretation, and analysis as these thoughts occur to the researcher.

There are three ethical considerations unique to observation research. First, is the observation **overt** or **covert**? In other words, do the people being observed know that they are being observed? This is particularly problematic when recording equipment is being used. Second, is it ethical to pretend to share the values and goals of a particular group in order to infiltrate the group? Third, if you are to some degree a participant of the group, does leaving the group raise ethical questions?

Observation research is a cyclical process whereby the researcher swings from a **sociocultural perspective** to a **self perspective** in relation to what is being observed. In this cyclical process, the researcher repeatedly moves from the social and cultural analysis of what is being observed to an active reflection of the impact of what is being observed (self-analysis). The researcher's self-knowledge and self-identity affect the perception and interpretation of what is observed. Qualitative researchers recognize that the impact of observation and participation on the researcher enriches the data.

YOUR TURN

Observation

Work with a partner to identify an area on campus where you can observe cell phone behavior. Establish a mutually convenient time when both you and your partner can be in the area to observe students for a half-hour period. The focus of your inquiry will be college students' cell phone behavior. Pick a couple of specific questions to guide your inquiry. For example, when do college students use their cell phones in public places? How does cell phone usage affect interactions with others who share this space? How do cell phone conversations affect interactions with friends who are present with the cell phone user? What do college students talk about on their cell phones?

Take field notes of your observations. What are three major insights or questions that emerged from your initial observation?

1. _____
2. _____
3. _____

What three insights or questions emerged from your partner's observations?

1. _____
2. _____
3. _____

Were your insights similar or radically different?

_____

What are three things you learned about conducting observations?

1. _____
2. _____
3. _____

Autoethnography

A variation of observation research in which the researcher reports his or her own personal experience is called **autoethnography.** Ellis and Bochner (2000) report 36 different names for this research technique, including "new ethnography," "performative study," "personal narrative," and "postmodern ethnography." Autoethnographies frequently take the form of stories; sometimes these stories are based on personal experience and sometimes they are fictional. Van Maanen (1988) identifies three types of autoethnographies: **confessional tales** that help the author-researcher make sense of a real experience; **impressionist tales** that challenge conventional thinking about an issue by presenting the nonconventional perspective from the perspective of a character in a story; and **critical tales** that present the voice of a marginalized person. An example of an autoethnography is Goodall's (1991) analysis of the rock-and-roll band "Whitedog" from the participant perspective of being the band's rhythm guitarist. Yielding much more depth than a simple account of a "day in the life" of a rock-and-roll band, Goodall's analysis reaches into the dialogue of the band members to analyze how white, middle-class men bond through stylized aggression. Goodall described the stylized aggression in male bonding communication as verbal conflict with verbal reference to physical or violent resolution of conflict, characterized by sexual innuendo and profanity.

Critics of autoethnography claim that the technique is completely subjective, anecdotal, and provides only one person's perspective. Critics further condemn autoethnography for blurring the boundaries between scholarship and literary fiction—is it "scholarship" to report a fictional account of an experience, or to report only one's own experience?

Autoethnographers respond by challenging empirical research on the same grounds: Don't quantitative and qualitative researchers rely on subjective reports also? Don't you rely on people's stories and anecdotes? Don't you arbitrarily select certain persons whose perspective you will represent and report? Who says there is a boundary between scholarship and literary fiction? It's only a difference of writing genres.

Autoethnographic reports take a variety of forms, from poetry to story to script. Some even take the form of visuals. Autoethnographers "sometimes struggle against conventions of writing and print" (Lindlof & Taylor, 2002, p. 289), and certainly struggle with the prescribed format of traditional research reports. In this sense autoethnographers are like contemporary artists who feel constrained by the one-dimensional canvas. Contemporary artists want to convey more than historical or religious scenes and still lifes; they want to convey emotions like loneliness and concepts like loss of identity, chaos, and violence. The canvas is not expansive enough to convey these existential experiences, so the contemporary artist shapes three-dimensional objects jutting off the canvas, plugs in video recordings, or creates three-dimensional objects that sit on the floor in the center of the gallery.

Autoethnography, like other research techniques, must meet standards of validity and reliability. Autoethnographers evaluate research on the following criteria: Does the autoethnography promote understanding of the experience described? Does it promote self-awareness for the researcher/reporter? Does it speak to the experience of the reader? Is its presentation eloquent, such that it has an aesthetic or literary quality? Autoethnography, like art, is evaluated both for its conceptual impact and for its aesthetic quality. Also like art, it is difficult to evaluate. Several years ago, an article published in an academic journal elicited quite a controversy among communication professors. The article, entitled "SexText" and published in *Text and Performance Quarterly* (Corey & Nakayama, 1997), consisted of a fictionalized description of acting in gay pornography. The article contains some explicit descriptions of homosexual acts, shaving cream, razors, and sensitive body parts. Scholarship? Some said, "No. It's fiction. It reads like a play script. It only got published due to its titillating topic matter, and it has nothing of relevance to say about communication." Others said, "Yes. This playscript is the most powerful way to convey that the human body is a text—the body, like a book, is a set of symbols with interpretive meaning."

SUMMARY

It is important to remember that the best pursuit of your question may require the use of multiple tools. We have spent much of this chapter discussing interviewing techniques because interviewing is used so extensively in qualitative research. We have also explored the research tools of focus groups, observation, and autoethnography. We call the employment of multiple tools **triangulation** (as discussed in Chapter 7). Thinking about three-dimensional space will help you remember the concept of triangulation. If you were to visually display the process of viewing something from multiple perspectives or vantage points—not just from vertical or horizontal planes, but from a third spatial perspective—you would have a triangulated perspective. In research, using multiple researchers to explore multiple interpretive perspectives, or using multiple tools or methods to explore a phenomenon, are all examples of triangulation.

KEY TERMS

artificial immersion

attention-getting preface

autoethnography

background information

boundaries

clarity

closing

closing question

comparison questions

complete observer

complete participant

confessional tales

covert

critical tales

demographic and factual questions

description questions

event analysis

example questions

feeling questions

field notes

follow-up questions

full immersion

group communication effect

guided interview

historical analysis

I-It

impressionist tales

informal interview

I-Thou

leading question

neutrality
open-ended questions
opinion questions
outcome analysis
overt
past, present, and future perspectives
presupposition questions
primary observer and secondary
    participant
primary participant and secondary observer
probes
process of observation
psychological analysis
rapport
relational analysis
role-playing

self perspective
sensory questions
setup
silence
single-issue
situational analysis
social influence
sociocultural perspective
spiral of silence theory
standards of validity and reliability
structured interview
synergistic group effect
thick description
transitions
triangulation
value questions

CHAPTER

PRESENTING YOUR RESEARCH FINDINGS

LEARNING OBJECTIVES

- Learn the characteristics and purposes of the three most common ways of presenting results of your research.
- Apply the guidelines for presenting effective research posters, oral presentations, and written research reports.
- Identify and apply the guidelines for writing about persons with respect to race, ethnicity, sexual orientation, and disabilities.

This chapter concludes our journey through the research process. Our final stop is several options for presenting your results, depending on the nature of the research and the audience to which you would like to present it. Some research reports are visual, such as a poster at a symposium, conference, or workshop. Some research reports are oral presentations, where you speak to an audience about your findings, usually with the help of visual or video media. Finally, some research reports are written, such as a program evaluation, a journal article, or a book.

Your goal as the research expert will be to communicate your findings to people who might not have your degree of expertise. If you work in some type of applied setting, such as being an evaluation coordinator at a social service agency or a data analyst at a market research firm, you will be writing up the results of your findings for your supervisor or your client on a very regular basis. Perhaps your career will take you into college or university teaching, in which case you will be making poster presentations and oral presentations, as well as preparing manuscripts for publication in journals or books. Along with teaching, these activities will be the lifeblood of your work.

Different careers will bring different research and communication expectations, but all careers (not just research) in the social and human sciences will require effective communication of data and complex ideas. In this chapter we outline what we believe are the essential components for effective visual, oral, and written communication of research methods and results.

This chapter has four main sections. In the first section, we describe how to present your research in a poster. In the second section, we present guidelines for effective oral presentation of research, and in the third section we present guidelines for how to write up your research for a research paper or journal article. In the final section, we address specific guidelines for how to write about persons in regard to their gender, race, ethnicity, sexual orientation, and disabilities.

PRESENTING YOUR RESEARCH WITH A POSTER

Research projects are often presented in a poster format. This seems strange to many students who are just beginning to learn about social science research, but it is a fairly common outlet for disseminating information in the social and natural sciences. Most often, a number of posters are presented together in a large room. This is referred to as a "poster session." It may be a bit difficult to imagine a complex research project presented on a poster. It may also be difficult to imagine a large poster session with spectators walking from poster to poster reading about various research studies.

There are, however, at least three advantages to this forum. First, if displayed properly, the poster will have an effective summary of the research findings in large, colorful text with visually appealing graphics to accompany the text. Second, "readers" of the poster can browse at their own pace, stop for longer times at posters in which they are interested, and move quickly past those in which they are not interested. Finally, with the poster authors standing near the poster, they can engage in dialog with anyone who wants to explore the research ideas further or in more depth.

Poster sessions often take place at professional meetings. In fact, as this chapter is being edited, author VanderStoep is attending the American Psychological Association conference, where hundreds of posters will be presented. In addition, poster sessions also occur at colleges and universities. Many schools have "research celebrations" in which students present posters of their research. At a more micro-level, some professors hold poster sessions in their classes. The process of putting together a poster helps students learn to synthesize complex research and boil it down to its basic elements. Moreover, the experience of a poster session stimulates discussion as students explain their research to each other.

The key to building an effective poster is readability and visual appeal. A poster must be pleasing to the eyes or no one will stop and look at it. The following information was adapted from an American Political Science Association compilation for preparing eye-pleasing and informative posters.

Content

■ For empirical studies, divide your poster into five sections: abstract, method, data, results, and conclusions. (We describe these components later in this chapter when describing how to write quantitative studies.)

■ For theoretical or philosophical papers, prepare your poster as you would a set of PowerPoint slides.

Visual Appeal

■ Use visuals and text to grab readers' attention and stimulate their curiosity. Make the poster engaging to potential visitors and prepare it so that they will want to ask questions and discuss the content of the poster.

■ Make text easy to read. Use a font size of no less than 16 point, and a larger size for titles and author names. Visitors should be able to read most of the text standing at a distance of three to four feet.

■ Use lots of visual and graphic information. Pay attention to the visual impact and aesthetics of your poster. Posters with too much text are not as visually appealing to visitors and are more likely to cause your potential audience to pass by.

Remember that poster-session attendees will be visiting dozens of posters. With that in mind, you should have two goals. First, you want those who visit your poster to leave remembering one important finding from your study. Second, you want those who have advanced interest in the topic to engage the poster at a higher level. Use your poster as a springboard for one-on-one discussion about your project. There must be enough information on the poster to prompt an informed and interested person to continue discussion of the research beyond the poster session. This continued conversation can take any number of forms. A reader may ask for a draft of the written report, ask follow-up questions, or correspond with you about your findings after the conference. To that end, you should have your contact information readily available on a business card and you should have a written draft of your research report that you can pass out to people who request additional information. Your contact information should be on the cover page of the written research report.

PRESENTING YOUR RESEARCH IN AN ORAL PRESENTATION

Another modality for presenting your work is an oral presentation. These sessions often take place at professional and academic conferences. Most people find that presenting before an audience is both more nerve-wracking and more exciting than a poster session, especially the first time you present. An advantage of making an oral presentation is that you can go into more depth than with a poster. You can provide more explanations and examples to support your research. Another advantage is that you have a captive audience. Of course you cannot make people listen to you, but the audience is waiting—and hoping—to be captivated! You set the agenda, you decide the topics. The stage is yours.

Another advantage to an oral presentation is that your audience is more likely to remember what you present because of their undivided attention, the elimination of noise that poster sessions tend to create, and the increased comprehension that comes from hearing about a project rather than passively reading about it from a distance.

The following guidelines will help you prepare and present your material in a professional, useful, and engaging manner.

Know Your Audience

It is unlikely that anyone in the audience will know the material you are presenting better than you do. This should be a source of relief to you, especially if you are new to presenting research. Given the fact that others will not know as much as you do, it is important to gauge the background knowledge of your audience. What may seem like a review to you may not be a review for the audience. Do not be afraid to review what you consider to be basic findings or to give introductory descriptions of the previous literature.

Similarly, a presentation to undergraduate students will be different from a presentation to graduate students or practitioners working in the field. Audience members will have different levels of background knowledge about the topic. Regardless of the background of the audience members, your goal should be to give audience members one or two main points to remember. Remember that those who attend research presentations will be hearing several presentations like yours, so it is unlikely that they will remember extensive detail. If you can get audience members to remember one or two main points, they will be able to take that information back to their home college or organization to assist them in their professional activity.

Organize and Focus Your Presentation

The content of your presentation should follow the general outline that is used for all reporting of research: introduction (literature review), method, results, and conclusion. You must provide enough background information about the introduction and methods that the audience can understand the purpose of your study. In a speech format, however, you should make the results and conclusions the main focus of your presentation. This is the new information that your audience is waiting to hear.

Stay within Your Time Limits

Adhering to your time limits demonstrates professionalism, respect for other presenters, and preparation. Know how much time you have and *stay within your limits*. If the organizer of your paper session does not communicate with you prior to the session, you should contact the organizer prior to the presentation to confirm time limits. Audiences will forgive pauses, lost trains of thoughts, and other speaking mishaps, but they are exceptionally unforgiving if you exceed your time limit. Rambling or rushed presentations reflect lack of preparation, and overly lengthy presentations cheat other presenters out of their full presentation time. In the calculation of time, make sure you allow one or two minutes for questions at the end, unless the format of the program specifies otherwise. At the risk of sounding preachy or uptight, we believe this to be a very valuable part of professional presentations. Be clear, be brief, and be done.

Use Visuals Effectively

Visual aids are nearly mandatory, and have accompanied 99.9% of the presentations we have ever attended. As with a poster session, large font sizes on your visual aids are essential. Testing them on the projection screen is the best way to determine their readability. In the past five years, most professional conferences have moved to having a computer and a projector available in all meeting rooms. You can produce your visuals in PowerPoint or other presentation software and copy the slideshow to a CD or flash drive (see Exhibit 11.1). Confirming that a computer projector is available at the conference is, of course, essential, and some of our more neurotic colleagues still bring plastic overhead transparencies as a backup in case of computer failure.

EXHIBIT 11.1   **Guidelines for PowerPoint Presentations**

- Visuals do not, in and of themselves, make an effective presentation. Each visual should be evaluated for its contribution to the points you want to make. Photos and cartoons flashing on the screen for the sole purpose of having something to look at can distract attention from your presentation.

- There should be a logical organization and progression to your visuals. When used correctly, PowerPoint can help presenters organize their outlines and stay on point during their presentations.

- Refer to the visuals as they appear on the screen. You should read the text on your PowerPoint slides. If you are saying one thing and your audience is forced to read something else, the audience is processing what they are reading and not what you are saying. Also, no matter how good your formatting is, some audience members may not be able to see the screen clearly.

- Use effects in moderation. It is important not to overdo a good thing with PowerPoint presentations. Too much color, too many flying bullet points, and too many sound effects become exceedingly irritating to an audience.

- Limit the amount of text on your slides. Use text to highlight a main point on which you will elaborate verbally. Do not read your entire presentation from the text on a PowerPoint slide! There are two reasons why this is important to an effective presentation. First, reading extensive text from a screen is fatiguing for an audience. (This is why you fall asleep in the lectures of professors who overuse PowerPoint.) Second, most of your audience can probably read much faster than you can speak aloud. Repetition of what one has already read is extremely irritating. Third, if all of your information is on your slides, why is it necessary to attend and hear your presentation? If all you have to say is on your slides, you might as well just hand out your PowerPoint printout and send everyone home. (This is why you get frustrated with classes in which the lectures add little or nothing to the content of the lecture slides that are available online.)

Practice Your Delivery

There is no substitution for practice. You should go through your presentation, from start to finish, verbatim and timed, a minimum of three times prior to your actual performance. It is also a good idea to practice in front of a mirror. Here are a few standard delivery techniques to keep in mind:

- Maintain eye contact. You can look down at your notes, but you also need to look up and into the eyes of your audience on a regular basis. Make sure that you look to people sitting on both sides of the room, and people sitting toward the back as well as those in front. Eye contact engages the attention and participation of your audience. You should also look in the direction that you want your audience to look. If you are referring to something on a visual, look toward that visual. This will keep the audience members' eye focus moving back and forth from you to your visuals. You want the audience to focus their attention on you, the speaker, and not only on your visuals.

- Use a strong speaking voice. Your speaking voice should be louder and slightly deeper than your conversational voice. If you are speaking without a microphone, make sure you project your voice to the back of the room. There is nothing more deadly than sitting through a presentation that you cannot hear.

- Rely on notes in moderation. Some people prefer to write out their entire presentation verbatim. Others prefer to speak from an outline or note cards. Either approach is fine; it is simply a matter of what makes you most comfortable. A few professional speakers can successfully abandon notes altogether, but this is more often a sign of lack of preparation. In any event, it is always a good idea to have parts of your talk memorized. This allows you to look up from your notes, maintain good eye contact, and even move around the stage or podium as you speak.

- Integrate professional and conversational styles. Too professional and your presentation seems stuffy; too conversational and your presentation seems unprofessional. On the one hand, you do not want to read your notes or paper to your audience (too stuffy and boring!), but on the other hand you do not want to pepper your speech with "yah," "y'know," "like," and "ummmm" as you might in casual conversation. A good presenter varies the presentation style from professional to conversational at different points in the speech. A safe approach for the beginner speaker is to start professional and lighten up a bit at some point toward the end of the presentation with a more humorous, informal, or conversational comment or insert. Balance and moderation are key.

PRESENTING YOUR RESEARCH IN A PAPER

There are two general categories of written research papers: academic journal articles and research reports for a client or organization. The primary difference between the two is audience. With academic journal articles, you are writing for professors and students who are interested in theory development. With research reports for client organizations, you are writing for an organization's board or leadership, the members of which may have varied background in research methods. The primary purpose of the research report for a client organization is typically to help the organization in strategic planning. In this section we first introduce the characteristics of social science research writing, and then explore how to write up a quantitative research study and a qualitative research study.

Characteristics of Social Scientific Writing

The Dartmouth Writing Program website (http://www.dartmouth.edu/~writing/materials/student/soc_sciences/write.shtml) describes the process and characteristics involved in writing social science papers. People who have experience writing papers in English or history classes may find the style in social science to be relatively dry and abrupt, but this style allows social scientists to bring precision and efficiency to their research writing. This style conveys a great deal of information in a formulaic organization; as such, it makes it easy for readers to find essential information. This style demands consistency. Certain information must be provided in a social science research report. This criterion for effective research reporting makes it possible to replicate studies and to compare studies that yield contradictory results. The strict format for presenting research results helps to maintain the validity and reliability of social science research.

The first characteristic of social science papers is that they have shorter paragraphs than humanities papers. Second, sentences seem, to use the Dartmouth program's word, "unremarkable" in their tone and content. Third, social scientists employ passive voice (for example, "passive voice is used by social scientists" rather than "social scientists employ passive voice") to a greater extent than other disciplines. The passive voice puts the emphasis on the behavior or the observation, rather than on the subjective observer. Of course, this attempt to keep the observer out of the narrative is not always appropriate; for example, in Chapters 7–10 we discussed the influence the observer can have on the observed. Historically, though, in social science, use of the passive voice has allowed the writer to emphasize the evidence over the person gathering the evidence. Making a persuasive argument in social science involves constructing evidence from data to support your claim. In other disciplines you have more license to support your claim with rhetorical power—that is, persuasive strategies, emotional arguments, opinions, and various interpretations of evidence.

Different social science disciplines (such as education, political science, kinesiology, sociology, communication, and psychology) have different standards for writing format and style. Most quantitative social science disciplines adopt the standards of the American Psychological Association (referred to as APA style). Specifically, the *Publication Manual of the American Psychological Association* (2001), currently in its fifth edition, contains valuable information about how to construct a research manuscript. In this section we summarize important elements of content and form that you should know when preparing a written report of your research. The ultimate goal of the APA *Publication Manual* is to prepare authors for submitting research manuscripts to academic journals. For this reason, some of the information (particularly with respect to formatting) is meant to make communication between the author and an editor uniform. Even though most of you will not be submitting manuscripts for publication (at least not right away), these guidelines will still be helpful as you begin your research-writing career. You will find that many professors require papers to be written in a particular style (APA, Chicago, MLA, American Sociology Association, etc.). These requirements may seem repressive, but as with the communication between writers and editors of a journal, a common style ensures a shared language and conformity in conveying a great amount of complex information in an efficient way.

Six Sections of a Research Paper

There are six sections of a research report: abstract, introduction, method, results, discussion, and references. This is the typical structure for all written research reports and should be used as a template for presenting your research in a written format. There is a little variation in these sections when presenting a qualitative study, and there is more leeway for deviation from strict adherence to this format when presenting a research report for a client organization. However, this structure for a written research report is always a good place to start. In this section we discuss what goes into each of these required sections of a research report. We also discuss how to deal with tables, figures, and statistical data in your report, and how to format your paper.

Abstract The **abstract** is a summary of the research project. The abstract appears first because it allows readers to decide whether the topic is of enough interest to continue reading more of the paper. Different publication outlets will specify different lengths for the abstract. In general, abstracts are limited to 150 words. Some researchers think this is the hardest part of the paper to write. Many find it easier to write the abstract last, because writing the whole paper gives you an idea of what ideas are important enough to be included in the abstract. The abstract should contain one-sentence summaries of the main sections of the paper: introduction, method, results, and discussion.

Introduction The **introduction** sets the stage for the research. If you are writing an article that you would like other professional researchers or practitioners to read, the introduction should contain a review of the research literature that is relevant to the current investigation. Social science research is cumulative and builds upon prior research.

Research advisors' preferences as to the **literature review** vary: some would like a full (near-exhaustive) review of the literature, whereas others want the introduction to look more like it is ready to go out for journal publication. For a conference presentation or a journal manuscript, the literature review should not be exhaustive; rather, it should set the stage for the upcoming study. Some journals suggest about seven manuscript pages for the literature review. For an undergraduate honor's or master's thesis, the literature review will be much longer, perhaps 15 to 20 pages.

In addition to reviewing the literature (that is, existing published research studies upon which your research is building), the purpose of this section is to introduce the area being studied and make the case for why we should care about research in this area. Specifically, the APA *Publication Manual* suggests that writers: (1) state why the problem is important, (2) link the research method to be used to the area of inquiry, and (3) describe the theoretical implications of the proposed investigation. The *Publication Manual* recommends that these questions be answered in one or two paragraphs.

At the end of the introduction, the hypotheses of a quantitative study should be stated. We believe that the best introductions are those that describe the literature so that the study to be presented seems very intuitive to the reader and springs forth very naturally from reading the introduction and summary of prior research. We are always impressed with researchers who have digested the literature and framed the problem in such an obvious way that, when the hypotheses are stated at the end of the introduction, we say to ourselves, "Of course! Why didn't I think of doing that study?" Such a skill is indeed impressive and will not develop overnight. However, having a firm grasp of the studies that preceded yours and asking questions about what is left unanswered by the previous studies will take you a long way toward acquiring this skill.

Method This is the *how-to* section. The **method section** is the recipe for the study, and all the ingredients of the study and instructions regarding how these ingredients were combined and processed must be included. We described previously the emphasis on precision and accuracy in social scientific writing, and it is perhaps nowhere more important than in the method section. Precision is crucial because it allows prior researchers to compare their methods to yours and will allow future researchers to use your study as a basis for planning their own studies.

In most cases, the method portion of a paper has subsections. The first subsection is usually labeled *Participants*. Other researchers will want to know the sample used in your study, both for comparison with past research and for formulating future studies. Selection procedures (e.g., random selection) are usually mentioned, as well as sample size and demographic characteristics such as age, sex, race/ethnicity, and in what line of work or education the participants are currently engaged.

The second subsection is often labeled *Materials* or *Apparatus*. A *Materials* subsection would most likely be used in an observational, survey, or correlational study. This section would include a description of the surveys, questionnaires, or other instruments you administered to the participants. Surveys, questionnaires, and other instruments are often included in their entirety in an appendix section. An *Apparatus* subsection would most likely be used in a report of experimental research, particularly if it involved instrumentation. For example, this section describes the timing devices, advanced computer programs, or technical equipment used (e.g., "physiological data were collected using the EMG100C Electromyogram Amplifier from Biopac Systems, Inc.").

The final subsection is usually called *Procedure*. This truly is the "how-to" section. It describes the step-by-step sequence of actions that the researchers performed and the events that the participants experienced. In a descriptive or correlational design, it is important to identify the specific methods of observation and any survey instruments used. In an experimental study, it is important to describe the design in terms of random assignment, counterbalancing, and the tasks in which participants engaged.

Results This is the fun part! Did the findings support your predictions? In the **results section**, you get to answer these questions. The results that you report should be direct tests of the hypotheses that you stated earlier. The hypotheses will be tested by employing the appropriate statistical test (see Chapters 4–6). For example, if you hypothesized that increased caffeine intake results in increased reaction time, you would make mean comparisons (*t* test or ANOVA) between the different levels of caffeine you gave your participants. Specifically, you might say something like, "Consistent with the study's hypothesis, those in the 100-mg condition had a faster reaction time ($M = 452$ ms) than those in the placebo condition ($M = 751$ ms). This effect is statistically significant, $t(38) = 4.52$, $p < .001$)." (The APA *Publication Manual* identifies several symbols for **statistical designations**, one of which is *M*, which stands for mean. See Table 11.1 for a summary of common statistical designations. Also note the very specific uses of upper and lower case for these designations.)

Because the research has already occurred when the manuscript is written, the method and the results sections are written in the past tense. Also, if you have any figures (such as graphs) or statistical tables (such as mean scores), you would place them at the end of the paper but describe and refer to them in the results section. Tables should be used to convey a large quantity of information in a concise format. When it is manageable to do so, it is preferable to present statistical results written out in the text of the paper.

Discussion Of the four components of a social science paper described thus far, the **discussion section** is the one that allows the writer the most freedom and flexibility in writing style and content. In this section, the researchers are allowed to be more speculative about the nature of the findings and their interpretations of the findings.

TABLE 11.1 Statistical Designations for Reporting Analyses in Tables and Results Sections

Statistical Designation	Interpretation
SD	standard deviation
p	significance level
t	t-value
F	F-value
χ^2	chi-square (the chi is produced by typing a lowercase "c" in Symbol font)
n, N	number of valid cases included in the analysis; lowercase "n" usually refers to a portion of the sample and uppercase "N" refers to the entire sample
M	mean

The discussion usually begins with a brief narrative summary of the support (or lack of support) for the hypotheses. The discussion then turns to how the findings relate to previous research. If there are equivocal findings (meaning that the findings of your study are different from other researchers' findings), you should speculate as to why this is so. Was there a difference in sample, measurement, or procedure? Was there a flaw in the previous research, which you redressed?

The discussion section is also where you acknowledge the limitations of your study. Was your sample too small? Was your sample biased in some way? Was your measurement flawed? Is it problematic to generalize beyond the experimental condition? It is essential that you, the author, acknowledge any problems with the validity and reliability of the study. No research project is perfect, and in retrospect there will always be things we wish we had done differently. It is better for you to admit these limitations up front than to have a reviewer or reader challenge the eloquence of your research design, the veracity of your findings, or the overall integrity of your study.

Another component of the discussion section is the suggestion of avenues for future research. No one study will answer every question, so as the author of the current study you can take the liberty of suggesting to future researchers what's next (or what should be next). This can be done in a paragraph or two and should not be extremely detailed. Instead, you should speak in more general terms about possible future studies. For example, as discussed in Chapter 5, a study by Thomas Gross (1990) found a negative correlation between scores on a test anxiety scale and performance on exams. Suggestions for future research might include expanding the concept of anxiety to behavioral rather than simply self-report measures. Similarly, future research could move from a self-report index of anxiety to a qualitative interview of anxiety. Furthermore, the concept of academic achievement could be expanded to include broader measures than just exam scores, and even beyond achievement scores to include narratives about participants' school experiences. In general, as the author you should try to plant seeds so that future research will be generated by your own research. If a research study generates more research, it is said to have **heuristic value**.

Perhaps the most important section of the discussion is the exploration of the implications of your research findings. VanderStoep believes this portion of the discussion section is easy for the author and entertaining for the audience—"and it's fun, too!" Johnston contends that this is the most difficult section to write. Consider a person who has devoted an entire semester or academic year to a research project (or in the case of a graduate student, several years). This person is deeply invested in the project and therefore knows many or all aspects of the topic. Channeling these reflections into the discussion section to share these thoughts with the audience speaks to the significance of your research endeavor. It is essential to answer the "so what?" questions; that is, why is your research important? Why are your results compelling? How will this affect others, our lives, and our society? Are research implications fun or challenging to write? You decide.

Sonja Trent-Brown (1995) asked participants to identify whether the voice on an audiotape was a White or African American person. She found that people could accurately detect the voice as an African American male 90% of the time when participants listened to a full paragraph (saying the Pledge of Allegiance), 83% of the time when participants listened to one sentence from the Pledge, and only 72% of the time when presented with a single word. This research has important implications for a variety of life domains. For example, people seeking information on rental properties may be treated differently based on how they sound on the telephone. In fact, an undergraduate project by Jacob Kain and Randall Owen (2005) tested this hypothesis by having undergraduates make phone calls inquiring about an advertised rental unit. The names given by the student researchers sounded stereotypically European American, Latino, or African American. The undergraduate researchers found that landlords reported that their apartment was available 64% of the time for those presumed to be White respondents, 58% of the time for those presumed to be African American respondents, and only 38% of the time for those presumed to be Latino respondents. The discussion section should be the place where creative and forward-looking thinking takes place in order to inspire future research.

References Every research paper includes a **reference section** or bibliography that provides complete and accurate citations of all sources mentioned in the paper. Sources read but not directly referred to in the text of the paper should not be included in the reference list. In APA style, citations are listed in alphabetical order by author in a section entitled "References" at the end of the paper. The reference section is double-spaced and the second and subsequent lines of a citation are indented five spaces. Exhibit 11.2 presents a sample reference section with citations for a book, journal article, and chapter in an edited book. For complete style guidelines, please refer to the *Publication Manual of the American Psychological Association,* 5th ed. (2001).

Inclusion of Tables and Figures The *Publication Manual* recommends that you use tables for communicating specific information, such as exact mean values, and that you use figures for displaying complex relationships. Displaying a statistically significant interaction in a complex design is an example of a good use of a figure. The specific format for tables and figures in manuscripts prepared using the *Publication Manual of the American Psychological Association* (2001) is quite detailed. For further details, we refer you

EXHIBIT 11.2 Citation Format for APA Style

References

Frankel, R., & Beckman, H. (1989). Conversation and compliance with treatment recommendations: An application of microinteractional analysis in medicine. In Brenda Dervin et al. (Eds.), *Rethinking communication* (pp. 60–74). Newbury Park, CA: Sage.

Jacobs, A. J. (2007). The year of living biblically: One man's humble quest to follow the Bible as literally as possible. New York: Simon & Schuster.

Sussman, S., Burton, D., Dent C. W., Stacy, A. W., & Flay, B. R. (1991). Use of focus groups in developing an adolescent tobacco use cessation program: Collective norm effects. *Journal of Applied Social Psychology, 21,* 1772–1782.

to that manual or to the sample paper in Appendix A. All of the text in a manuscript will be formatted by a publisher and turned into pages that will appear in a journal or book chapter. However, figures should be prepared as *camera-ready*. This means that an image of the figure will be captured electronically and appear just as you have prepared it. For that reason, the figure caption should be on a separate page. It will be added as text right below the figure. We again refer you to the APA *Publication Manual* for specific details.

Formatting the Manuscript The *Publication Manual* contains dozens, if not hundreds, of pages related to how to format manuscripts. Many of these guidelines are important for translating the paper or file you produced on a computer into the form the editors and publishers will need to publish it in a journal. Many professors ask for an APA-formatted paper in research methods courses. In addition, it is a good idea to know how to prepare a paper for publication. Many undergraduate students submit research to undergraduate research conferences and are asked to prepare their papers for publication in a "Proceedings" of the conference. In addition, you may find that you are preparing research reports for publication in your future career. Regardless of the final destination of your paper, it is helpful to review a few of the more commonplace formatting guidelines suggested by the *Manual*:

- Double-space the entire manuscript.
- Prepare the title page according to specifications:
    - Type the title about one-third of the way down the page. Double-space and put your name and any co-authors' names on the next line. Double-space again and type your affiliation (e.g., school or employer) on the third line. All three of these lines should be center-justified.
    - Create a *running head.* Two-thirds of the way down the title page, type the words "Running Head" followed by a colon. After the colon, type a three- or four-word title that summarizes the research. This is the title that would go at the top of journal or book pages if the manuscript were published.
    - Create a *short title.* Print the first three or four words of your title in the upper right-hand corner of each page (including the title page). This is called the *short title.* Type the page number right below it. This is best done in the "header" function of your word-processing program.
- Insert the abstract on page 2, double-spaced in block paragraph form.
- Center-justify the top-level headings of your paper—specifically Method, Results, and Discussion. Do not make Introduction its own label. Rather, type the title of the paper on the top of page 3 (first manuscript page) and then begin the introduction.
- After the text portion of the paper is completed, place material in the following order: references, appendices, tables, figure captions, and figures.
- Examples of these formatting requirements are shown in the sample papers in Appendixes A and B. Of course, other information beyond the scope of this chapter

is found in the *Publication Manual* itself. (Also, many journals make their specific submission, style, and formatting requirements available to authors through their websites. Many social science journals basically follow APA style, but each tends to have its own little quirks and variations. This may be true of individual professors as well; if you are given specific instructions in these areas, it is best to heed them!)

Presenting Your Qualitative Research in a Written Report

The form and content of a qualitative study will differ somewhat from the report of a quantitative study. In general, it is best to start with the general sections of a standard research report (abstract, introduction, method, results, and discussion) to ensure that you have included all the necessary information to convey your research study. In a qualitative study, though, these sections are sometimes labeled a little differently. Just as with the discussion of writing quantitative reports, we will not be able to cover all aspects of writing a qualitative report; rather, we provide the basic framework for constructing a written report of a qualitative study. For more in-depth coverage of this topic, we recommend Pyrczak and Bruce (2005) or Patton (2002).

Abstract The abstract serves the same functions and includes the same essential information in the write-up of both qualitative and quantitative research studies.

Introduction The introduction of a qualitative project should include a review of the relevant literature, similar to the introduction of a quantitative study. You as the author should also, however, discuss why you selected a qualitative methodological approach. This can be done in the introduction or in the method section, but it is often particularly helpful to include this in the introduction, especially if the potential audience is familiar with and expecting a quantitative study (Pyrczak & Bruce, 2005).

Method Identify and describe the qualitative methodology and techniques used in your study. For example, the methodology might be ethnography and the technique might be observation. Be specific about the content of interview questions or what behaviors were being observed. You should also identify the sample and how it was selected; for example, whether it was a convenience sample, and the basis for including and recruiting participants in the sample.

Data Analysis and Interpretation The results of a qualitative study are presented in a section labeled "Data Analysis and Interpretation" or some variation on that theme. Qualitative researchers do not usually think of their findings in terms of objective "results," but in terms of "analysis," "interpretations," and "themes."

The specific techniques used to analyze the qualitative data should be reported here. The sequential procedures for analysis should be detailed. There are specific procedures for data analysis (see Chapter 9), and the process of identifying themes and coding data elements must be fully described and documented. The reader of your research must be able to understand how you found the themes in the data, and trust your procedures enough to agree that the themes you claim to have found really are there. You will need to present actual examples of the themes and categories that you claim emerged from the data. A major challenge for qualitative researchers is deciding how many examples of actual data to include. Patton recommends using enough data to "allow the reader to enter into the situation and thoughts of the people" (2002, p. 503). Once that has been done, it may not be wise to include large amounts of description or long quotations. You might have to boil down hundreds of pages of interview transcripts to a handful of key examples for your research report.

In the data analysis and interpretation section of a qualitative study, it may still be appropriate to include quantitative data. Percentages, frequencies, or other quantitative descriptions are often appropriate and helpful for understanding the range and scope of the themes identified in the data (recall the discussion in Chapter 7 regarding researchers who employ both methodologies).

Besides describing the data coding and analysis, the other major component of this section is the interpretation of the data. One goal for the author is to help the reader understand the significance of the different parts of the findings. Quantitative researchers can use means, correlations, and statistical tests to make claims about the importance of particular findings. Qualitative researchers instead use their interpretive skills. The authors must make decisions about the strength of their findings. In qualitative data, researchers look for repetition, dominance, and frequency of particular themes. Qualitative researchers also rely on the assumption that an event is as significant as the person who is living it claims it to be.

Conclusion The final section of a qualitative report may be labeled "Discussion," "Conclusion," "Implications," "Recommendations," or "Applications," depending on the nature of the research, the audience for the report, and the purpose the research report will ultimately serve. In any event, this section should—like the conclusion of a quantitative study—address limitations, implications, and directions for future research.

REDUCING BIAS IN RESEARCH REPORTING

The APA *Publication Manual* devotes a section to discussing ways in which our language may be biased, and recommendations for reducing that bias. Although as a writer, the choice of words is ultimately yours, it is also the case that with word choice comes responsibility. For example, you must commit to being accurate, being clear, and using the generally accepted grammatical conventions constructed by language experts. So too, as an author, you have a responsibility to avoid hurtful language, or language that denigrates a particular group of people. Often the use of particular words is not intended to be offensive, but is still objectionable to some readers. Direct knowledge and experience are the best aids to developing a more sensitive voice. It is in this vein of responsibility that the APA asks authors to pay attention to these matters.

Race and Ethnicity

Appropriate terms designating groups of people by race or ethnicity change over time. If you are studying a particular racial or ethnic group, it may be helpful to ask members of the group what descriptive term they prefer. In the absence of that knowledge, it is generally accepted to use *White* and *Black* as racial designations; however, *European American* and *African American* are also appropriate and are even more common in some contexts than White and Black.

With regard to ethnicity, it is helpful to be as specific as possible. It is also advisable to consult with the group being studied to determine what descriptive term they prefer. The term *Hispanic* is appropriate, but *Latino* is currently more common in some contexts. If possible, more specific terms are preferred, such as *Cuban, Cuban American, Central American,* or *Mexican American.* Likewise, with indigenous peoples of North America, the preferred term is *Native American* or *American Indian,* but specific reference to tribal affiliation (e.g., Navajo, Hopi) is preferable if that information is available.

Gender

The term *gender* is preferable to *sex* in most cases. If you are referring to differences based on biological aspects of maleness and femaleness, using the word *sex* is appropriate. (For example, "we determined the sex of the rats before we assigned them to conditions" would be accurate.) In social science research, however, we are often interested in *gender differences*—that it, differences that are due to the social and culture influences on how we define what it *means* to be male or female. *Gender* is technically the arbitrary sociological and cultural construction of differences based on biological sex (for example, arbitrary distinctions we have learned from our culture are that boys are strong and girls are weak or that boys are tough and girls are emotional). Be careful to use the terms *sex* and *gender* accurately. They are not interchangeable.

Use *male* and *female* as adjectives; for example, "male and female participants were interviewed in separate rooms." Refer to humans aged 18 and over as *women* and *men* (not *ladies* and *gentlemen*). The terms *girls* and *boys* are appropriate for those under the age of 18, but you could also use the phrase *young men and women* if you felt it appropriately described your sample. You should use the term *older adult* rather than *elderly,* and needless to say *little old lady* (which was actually used in some older published medical reports) can no longer be used.

Sexual Orientation

Sexual orientation refers to a person's enduring sexual attraction. To describe someone with a homosexual orientation, the terms *lesbian* for women and *gay* for men are preferred to the more general term *homosexual.* Sexual *orientation* refers to a person's disposition. Sexual *behavior* consistent with one's orientation usually follows, but it is possible that those with a same-sex orientation could engage in opposite-sex sexual behavior and vice versa. *Bisexual* most commonly refers to sexual behavior with both men and women. *Transsexual* technically refers to a person who has changed his or her biological sex, and *transgendered* refers to a person who has a gender identity that is different from his or her biological sex. It is important to make a clear distinction in your writing between behavior and orientation, and not to assume that they are the same.

Disability

You should use the term *disability* in reference to people who have certain conditions that would be limiting. Use the term *handicap* to describe the nature of the limitation rather than the person. An acceptable phrase is *persons with disabilities.* This phraseology emphasizes the person first, rather than the limitation or condition, and avoids the labeling and dehumanizing effects of terms such as *the blind, the handicapped,* and so on. This is not merely political correctness; rather, it reflects the very nature of social science research and its view of research participants.

SUMMARY

The burden of communication is always on the communicator. The keys to writing effective social science manuscripts are precision, clarity, and brevity. There are certain guidelines to follow, and learning the form and format of your particular discipline is vital. We have given you an overview of one formatting option, which is the industry standard for many of the social sciences. However, it takes much time and practice to master any form, and we (with a combined 28 years of experience) still refer to manuals and consult our colleagues for writing and citation advice. It is important to learn the proper way to refer to certain persons and groups, so that you demonstrate sensitivity and care for the people who so graciously agreed to participate in your research study.

KEY TERMS

abstract
discussion section
heuristic value
introduction
literature review

method section
reference section
results section
statistical designations

REFERENCES

Adelman, M. B., & Frey, L. (1997). *The fragile community: Living together with AIDS*. Mahwah, NJ: Lawrence Erlbaum Associates.

Adelman, M. B., & Schultz, P. (1994). *The pilgrim must embark* [documentary film]. Mahwah, NJ: Lawrence Erlbaum Associates.

American Psychological Association. (2001). *Publication manual* (5th ed.). Washington, DC: Author.

Anderson, I. K. (2006). The development of communication norms in an online support group. In K. Galvin & P. Cooper (Eds.), *Making connections* (4th ed.) (pp. 363–371). Los Angeles, CA: Roxbury.

Andrews, J., & Andrews, G. (2003). Life in a secure unit: The rehabilitation of young people through the use of sport. *Social Science Medicine, 56,* 531–550.

Arnold, L. B. (2000). "What is a feminist?" Students' descriptions. *Women and Language, 23,* 8–18.

Atkyns, R. L., & Hanneman, G. J. (1974). Illicit drug distribution and dealer communication behavior. *Journal of Health and Social Behavior, 15,* 36–43.

Balmer, P., Siler, B., & Sorenson, M. (2004). *Vocation: Career and calling.* Paper presented at conference of the Midwestern Psychological Association, Chicago, IL.

Barry, C., Stevenson, F., Britten, N., Barber, N., & Bradley, C. (2001). Giving voice to the lifeworld: More humane, more effective medical care? A qualitative study of doctor-patient communication in general practice. *Social Science & Medicine, 53,* 487–505.

Bart, P., & O'Brien, P. (1985). *Stopping rape: Successful survival strategies.* New York: Pergamon Press.

Baumeister, R. F., Twenge, J. M., & Nuss, C. K. (2002). Effects of social exclusion on cognitive processes: Anticipated aloneness reduces intelligent thought. *Journal of Personality and Social Psychology, 83,* 817–827.

Baumrind, D., Larzelere, R. E., & Cowan, P. A. (2002). Ordinary physical punishment: Is it harmful? Comment on Gershoff (2002). *Psychological Bulletin, 128,* 580–589.

Beck, A. T., Ward, C. H., Mendelson, M., Mock, J., & Erbaugh, J. (1961). An inventory for measuring depression. *Archives of General Psychiatry, 4,* 561–571.

Beggan, J., & Allison, S. (2003). What sort of man reads *Playboy*? The self-reported influence of *Playboy* on the construction of masculinity. *Journal of Men's Studies, 11,* 189–206.

Blair, C., Jeppeson, M. S., & Pucci, E., Jr. (1991, August). Public memorializing in postmodernity: The Vietnam Veterans Memorial as prototype. *Quarterly Journal of Speech, 77,* 263–288.

Blanck, P. D., Bellack, A. S., Rosnow, R. L., Rotheram-Borus, M. J., & Schooler, N. R. (1992). Scientific rewards and conflict of ethical choices in human subjects research. *American Psychologist, 47,* 959–965.

Bolt, M. L. (2001). *Instructor's resources to accompany Myers' Psychology* (6th ed.). New York: Worth.

Buber, M. (1965). *Between man and man.* New York: Macmillan.

Burton, A. M., Wilson, S., Cowan, M., & Bruce, V. (1999). Face recognition in poor-quality video: Evidence from security surveillance. *Psychological Science, 10,* 243–248.

Buzzanell, P. M., & Burrell, N. A. (1997). Family and workplace conflict: Examining across context and sex. *Human Communication Research, 24,* 109–146.

Cockburn, C., & Clarke, G. (2002). "Everybody's looking at you!": Girls negotiating the "femininity deficit" they incur in physical education. *Women's Studies International Forum, 25,* 651–665.

Conquergood, D. (1994). Homeboys and hoods: Gang communication and cultural space. In Lawrence R. Frey (Ed.), *Group communication in context: Studies of natural groups* (pp. 23–55). Mahwah, NJ: Lawrence Erlbaum.

Cook, T., & Campbell, D. (1979). *Quasi-experimentation: Design & analysis issues for field settings.* Chicago: Rand McNally.

Coplan, R. J., & Rubin, K. H. (1998). Exploring and assessing nonsocial play in the preschool: The development and validation of the Preschool Play Behavior Scale. *Social Development, 7,* 72–91.

Corey, F. C., & Nakayama, T. K. (1997). SexText. *Text & Performance Quarterly, 17,* 58–68.

Covington, D. (1995). *Salvation on Sand Mountain: Snake handling and redemption in Southern Appalachia.* New York: Penguin.

Crawford, M., & Popp, D. (2003). Sexual double standards: A review and methodological critique of two decades of research. *Journal of Sex Research, 40,* 13–26.

Creswell, J. W. (1998). *Qualitative inquiry and research design: Choosing among five traditions*. Thousand Oaks, CA: Sage.

Denzin, N. (1990). *Studies in symbolic interaction: A research annual*. Vol. 11. Greenwich, CT: JAI Press.

Denzin, N. (1989). *Interpretive interactionism*. Newbury Park, CA: Sage.

Denzin, N., & Lincoln, Y. (1994). *Handbook of qualitative research*. Thousand Oaks, CA: Sage.

Denzin, N., & Lincoln, Y. (Eds.). (1998). *Collecting and interpreting qualitative materials*. Thousand Oaks, CA: Sage.

Dinger, M. K., Oman, F., Taylor, E. L., Vesely, S. K., & Able, J. (2004). Stability and convergent validity of the Physical Activity Scale for the Elderly (PASE). *Journal of Sports Medicine & Physical Fitness, 44*, 186–192.

Donaldson, A., Hill, T., Finch, C. F., & Forero, R. (2003). The development of a tool to audit the safety policies and practices of community sports clubs. *Journal of Science & Medicine in Sport, 6*, 226–230.

Eder, D., Evans, C., & Parker, S. (1995). *Gender and adolescent culture*. New Brunswick, NJ: Rutgers University Press.

Ehrenreich, B. (2001). *Nickel and dimed: On (not) getting by in America*. New York: Metropolitan Books.

Ellis, C., & Bochner, A. P. (2000). Autoethnography, personal narrative, reflexivity: Researcher as subject. In N. K. Denzin & Y. S. Lincoln (Eds.), *Handbook of qualitative research* (2nd ed.) (pp. 733–768). Thousand Oaks, CA: Sage.

Epley, N., & Kruger, J. (2005). When what you type isn't what they read: The perseverance of stereotypes and expectancies over e-mail. *Journal of Experimental Social Psychology, 41*, 414–422.

Fern, E. F. (1982). The use of focus groups for idea generation: The effects of group size, acquaintanceship, and moderator on response quantity and quality. *Journal of Marketing Research, 19*, 1–13.

Festinger, L. (1957). *A theory of cognitive dissonance*. Stanford, CA: Stanford University Press.

Frankel, R., & Beckman, H. (1989). Conversation and compliance with treatment recommendations: An application of microinteractional analysis in medicine. In Brenda Dervin et al. (Eds.), *Rethinking communication* (pp. 60–74). Newbury Park, CA: Sage.

Gamst, G., Dana, R. H., Der-Kerebetian, A., Aragon, M., Arellano, L., Morrow, G., et al. (2004). Cultural competency revised: The California Brief Multicultural Competence Scale. *Measurement and Evaluation in Counseling & Development, 37*, 163–183.

Geertz, C. (1988). *Works and lives: The anthropologist as author*. Stanford, CA: Stanford University Press.

Gershoff, E. T. (2002). Corporal punishment by parents and associated child behaviors and experiences: A meta-analytic and theoretical review. *Psychological Bulletin, 128*, 539–579.

Glaser, B. G., & Strauss, A. L. (1967). *Discovery of grounded theory: Strategies for qualitative research*. Chicago: Aldine.

Glaser, J., Dixit, J., & Green, D. (2002). Studying hate crimes with the Internet: What makes racists advocate racial violence? *Journal of Social Issues, 58*(1), 177–193.

Gluck, S. B., & Patai, D. (Eds.). (1991). *Women's words: The feminist practice of oral history*. New York: Routledge.

Gold, R. L. (1958). Roles in sociological field observations. *Social Forces, 36*, 217–223.

Good, C., Aronson, J., & Inzlicht, M. (2003). Improving adolescents' standardized test performance: An intervention to reduce the effects of stereotype threat. *Journal of Applied Developmental Psychology, 24*, 645–662.

Goodall, H. L., Jr. (1991). *Living in the rock-n-roll mystery. Reading context, self and others as clues*. Carbondale: Southern Illinois University Press.

Green, S. B., & Salkind, N. J. (2005). *Using SPSS for Windows and Macintosh: Analyzing and understanding data* (4th ed.). Upper Saddle River, NJ: Prentice Hall.

Gross, T. F. (1990). General test and state anxiety in real examinations: State is not test anxiety. *Educational Research Quarterly, 14*, 11–20.

Guralnick, M. J., Hammond, M. A., & Connor, R. T. (2003). Subtypes of nonsocial play: Comparisons between young children with and without developmental delays. *American Journal on Mental Retardation, 108*, 347–362.

Hamby, S., & Koss, M. (2003). Shades of gray: A qualitative study of terms used in the measurement of sexual victimization. *Psychology of Women Quarterly, 27*, 243–255.

Hammersley, M. (1992).*What's wrong with ethnography? Methodological explorations*. London: Routledge.

Harter, S. (1978). Effectance motivation reconsidered: Toward a developmental model. *Human Development, 21*, 34–64.

Hawkins, D., Pepler, D. J., & Craig, W. M. (2001). Naturalistic observations of peer interventions in bullying. *Social Development, 10*, 512–527.

Heider, K. G. (1988). The Rashomon effect: When ethnographers disagree. *American Anthropologist, 90,* 73–81.

Herdt, G. (1987). Transitional objects in Sambia initiation. *Ethos, 15,* 40–57.

Hofer, B. (1994, August). *Epistemological beliefs and first-year college students: Motivation and cognition in different instructional contexts.* Paper presented at the meeting of the American Psychological Association, Los Angeles.

Hofer, B., VanderStoep, S. W., & Pintrich, P. R. (1996, August). *Disciplinary differences in epistemological beliefs.* Paper presented at the American Psychological Association, New York.

Hunt, C. S., & Hunt, B. (2004). Changing attitudes toward people with disabilities: Experimenting with an educational intervention. *Journal of Managerial Issues, 16,* 266–280.

Husserl, E. (1967). The thesis of the natural standpoint and its suspension. In J. J. Kockelman (Ed.), *Phenomenology* (pp. 68–79). Garden City, NY: Doubleday.

Inman, M. L., McDonald, N., & Ruch, A. (2004). Boasting and firsthand and secondhand impressions: A new explanation for the positive teller-listener extremity effects. *Basic & Applied Social Psychology, 26,* 59–76.

Inman, M. L., VanderStoep, S. W., & Lynman, N. R. (2003). *Effectiveness of manual trunk release handles.* Paper presented at the Society of Automotive Engineers International, Warrendale, PA.

Jacobs, A. J. (2007). The year of living biblically: One man's humble quest to follow the Bible as literally as possible. New York: Simon & Schuster.

Jarvis, L. H., Merriman, W. E., Barnett, M., Hanba, J., & VanHaitsma, K. S. (2004). Input that contradicts young children's strategy for mapping novel words affects their phonological and semantic interpretation of other novel words. *Journal of Speech, Language & Hearing Research, 47,* 392–406.

Johnston, D., & Swanson, D. (2006). Defining mothers: The social construction of motherhood by work status. *Sex Roles: A Journal of Research, 54,* 509–519.

Johnston, D., & Swanson, D. (2004). Moms hating moms: The internalization of mother-war rhetoric. *Sex Roles: A Journal of Research, 51,* 497–509.

Kain, J. I., & Owen, R. J. (2005). *Differential treatment in the lakeshore rental housing market.* Unpublished manuscript, Holland, MI.

Kaminer, Y., Burleson, J., & Goldberger, R. (2002). Psychotherapies for adolescent substance abusers: Short- and long-term outcomes. *Journal of Nervous & Mental Disease, 190,* 737–745.

Kaplowitz, M. D. (2000). Statistical analysis of sensitive topics in group and individual interviews. *Quality & Quantity, 34,* 419–431.

Kaplowitz, M. D., Hadlock, T. D., & Levine, R. (2004). A comparison of Web and mail survey response rates. *Public Opinion Quarterly, 68,* 94–101.

Karabenick, S. K., & Moosa, S. (2005). Culture and personal epistemology: Middle Eastern students' beliefs about scientific knowledge and knowing. *Social Psychology of Education, 8,* 375–393.

Kiewa, J. (2001). Control over self and space in rockclimbing. *Journal of Leisure Research, 33,* 363–382.

Krieger, S. (1991). Social science and the self: Personal essays as an art form. New Brunswick, NJ: Rutgers University Press.

Krippendorf, K. (1980). *Content analysis: An introduction to its methodology.* Beverly Hills, CA: Sage, 1980.

Krueger, R. A. (1994). *Focus groups. A practical guide for applied research* (2nd ed.). London: Sage.

Kübler-Ross, E. (1973). *On death and dying.* London: Routledge.

Lahaut, Y. M. H. C. J., Jansen, H. A. M., van de Mheen, D., & Garretsen, H. F. L. (2002). Non-response bias in a sample survey on alcohol consumption. *Alcohol & Alcoholism, 37,* 256–260.

Laughlin, P. R., VanderStoep, S. W., & Hollingshead, A. (1991). Collective versus individual induction: Recognition of truth, rejection of error, and collective information processing. *Journal of Personality & Social Psychology, 61,* 50–67.

Lee, R. (1979). *The !Kung San: Men, women, and work in a foraging society.* Cambridge, MA: Harvard University Press.

Lepper, M. R., Greene, D., & Nisbett, R. E. (1973). Undermining children's intrinsic interest with extrinsic reward: A test of the "overjustification" hypothesis. *Journal of Personality & Social Psychology, 28,* 129–137.

Levitt, S., & Dubner, S. (2005). *Freakanomics: A rogue economist explores the hidden side of everything.* New York: HarperCollins.

Lincoln, Y., & Guba, E. (1985). *Naturalistic inquiry.* Beverly Hills, CA: Sage.

Lincoln, Y., & Guba, E. (1981). *Effective evaluation.* San Francisco, CA: Jossey-Bass.

Lindlof, T., & Taylor, B. (2002). *Qualitative communication research methods* (2nd ed.). Thousand Oaks, CA: Sage.

Lull, J. (1990). *Inside family viewing: Ethnographic research on television's audiences.* New York: Routledge.

Lyng, S. (1990). Edgework: A social psychological analysis of voluntary risk taking. *American Journal of Sociology, 95*, 851–886.

Madson, L. (2005). Demonstrating the importance of question wording on surveys. *Teaching of Psychology, 43*, 40–43.

Milgram, S. (1974). *Obedience to authority.* New York: Harper & Row.

Mills, G. E. (2003). *Action research: A guide for teacher researchers* (2nd ed.). Upper Saddle River, NJ: Merrill-Prentice Hall.

Mishler, E. (1984). *The discourse of medicine.* Norwood, NJ: Ablex.

Moffat, M. (1989). *Coming of age in New Jersey.* New Brunswick, NJ: Rutgers University Press.

Morgan, D. L. (1997). *The focus group guidebook. The focus group kit* (Vol. 1). Thousand Oaks, CA: Sage.

Myers, D. G. (2008). *Social psychology* (9th ed.). Boston: McGraw-Hill.

Myers, D. G. (1996). *The pursuit of happiness.* New York: HarperCollins.

Myers, S. A. (2002). Perceived aggressive instructor communication and student state motivation, learning, and satisfaction. *Communication Reports. 15*, 113–121.

Naveh-Benjamin, M., Craik, F. I. M., Guez, J., & Kreuger, S. (2005). Divided attention in younger and older adults: Effects of strategy and relatedness on memory performance and secondary task costs. *Journal of Experimental Psychology: Learning, Memory, & Cognition, 31*, 520–537.

Ng, C. F. (2000). Effects of building construction noise on residents: A quasi-experiment. *Journal of Environmental Psychology, 20*, 375–385.

Noelle-Neumann, E. (1984). *The spiral of silence.* Chicago: University of Chicago.

Orbe, M. (2003). African-American first-generation college student communicative experiences. *Electronic Journal of Communication, 13*, 2–3. Retrieved July 1, 2008, from http://7979-shadow.cios.org.lib.hope.edu/journals/EJC/013/2/01322.html

Orbe, M. (1998). *Constructing co-cultural theory: An explication of culture, power, and communication.* Thousand Oaks, CA: Sage.

Padgett, V. R., & Reid, J. F. (2002). Five year evaluation of the student diversity program: A retrospective quasi-experiment. *Journal of College Student Retention, 4*, 135–142.

Patton, M. Q. (2002). *Qualitative research and evaluation methods* (3d ed.). Thousand Oaks, CA: Sage.

Paul, E., & Hayes, K. (2002). The casualties of casual sex: A qualitative exploration of the phenomenology of college students' hookups. *Journal of Social & Personal Relationships, 19*, 639–661.

Peirce, C. S. (1998). *The essential Peirce: Selected philosophical writings* (Vol. 2, 1893–1913). Peirce Edition Project, eds. Bloomington & Indianapolis, IN: Indiana University Press.

Perry, M., VanderStoep, S. W., & Yu, S. L. (1993). Asking questions in first-grade mathematics classes: Precursors to mathematical thought. *Journal of Educational Psychology, 85*, 31–40.

Pyrczak, F., & Bruce, R. R. (2005). *Writing empirical research reports* (5th ed.). Glendale, CA: Pyrczak Publishing.

Rasmussen, C., & Bisanz, J. (2005). Representation and working memory in early arithmetic. *Journal of Experimental Child Psychology, 91*, 137–157.

Reid, R. (1991). *Mountains of the great blue dream.* New York: HarperPerennial.

Reinharz, S. (1992). *Feminist methods in social research.* New York: Oxford University Press.

Roberts, K. G. (2003). Emotivism and pseudocultural identities. *Howard Journal of Communications, 14*, 195–208.

Robertson, J., Johnson, A., Benton, S., Janey, B., Cabral, J., & Woodford, J. (2002). What's in a picture? Comparing gender constructs of younger and older adults. *Journal of Men's Studies, 11*, 1–27.

Rosaldo, R. (1989). *Culture and truth: The remaking of social analysis.* Boston: Beacon Press.

Rosenhan, D. L. (1973). On being sane in insane places. *Science, 179*, 250–258.

Rubin, K. H., Coplan, R. J., Fox, N. A., & Calkins, S. D. (1995). Emotionality, emotional regulation, and preschoolers' social adaptation. *Development & Psychopathology, 7*, 49–62.

Rushing, J., & Frentz, T. (2000). Singing over the bones: James Cameron's *Titanic. Critical Studies in Media Communication 17*, 1–27.

Sahlstein, E. M. (2004). Relating at a distance: Negotiating being together and being apart in long-distance relationships. *Journal of Social & Personal Relationships, 21*, 689–710.

Sales, B. D., & Folkman, S. (Eds.). (2000). *Ethics in research with human participants* (1st ed.). Washington, DC: American Psychological Association.

Schwab-Stone, M. E., Shaffer, D., Dulcan, M. K., Jensen, P. S., Fisher, P., Bird, H. R., et al. (1996). Criterion validity of the NIMH Diagnostic Interview Schedule for Children Version 2.3 (DISC-2.3). *Journal of American Academy of Child & Adolescent Psychiatry, 35*, 878–888.

Seidman, I. E. (1991). *Interviewing as qualitative research*. New York: Columbia University Teachers College.

Share, D. L. (2004). Orthographic learning at a glance: On the time course and developmental onset of self-teaching. *Journal of Experimental Child Psychology, 87*, 267–298.

Shaughnessy, J. J., Zechmeister, E. B., & Zechmeister, J. S. (2006). *Research methods in psychology* (7th ed.). New York: McGraw Hill.

Siegert, J. R., & Stamp, G. H. (1994). "Our first big fight" as a milestone in the development of close relationships. *Communication Monographs, 61*, 345–360.

Skinner, B. F. (1997 [1957 original]). *Schedules of reinforcement*. Acton, MI: Copley.

Smith, C. A., & Frieze, I. H. (2003). Examining rape empathy from the perspective of the victim and the assailant. *Journal of Applied Social Psychology, 33*, 476–498.

Soloman, M. (1994). The rhetoric of dehumanization: An analysis of medical reports of the Tuskegee Syphilis Project. In W. L. Nothstine, C. Blair, & G. A. Copeland, Eds., *Critical questions: Invention, creativity, and the criticism of discourse and media* (pp. 307–322). New York: St. Martin's Press, 1994.

Sprecher, S., & Hatfield, E. (1996). Premarital sexual double standards among U.S. college students: Comparison of Russian and Japanese students. *Archives of Sexual Behavior, 25*, 261–288.

Stake, R. E. (1995). *The art of case study research*. Thousand Oaks, CA: Sage.

Stake, R. E. (1994). The fleeting discernment of quality. In L. Mabry (Ed.), *Evaluation and the post-modern dilemma: Advances in program evaluation* (Vol. 3) (pp. 41–60). Greenwich, CT: JAI.

Steinberg, L. D. & Dornbusch, S. (1991). Negative correlates of part-time employment during adolescence: Replication and elaboration. *Developmental Psychology, 27*, 304–313.

Sterk, H., Ratcliffe, K., Hay, C., Kehoe, A., & VandeVusse, L.(2002). *Who's having this baby? Perspectives on birthing*. Lansing: Michigan State University Press.

Stewart, D. W., & Shandasani, P. N. (1990). *Focus groups: Theory and practice*. Newbury Park, CA: Sage.

Strauss, A., & Corbin, J. (1990). *Basics of qualitative research: Grounded theory procedures and techniques*. Newbury Park, CA: Sage.

Sussman, S., Burton, D., Dent, C. W., Stacy, A. W., & Flay, B. R. (1991). Use of focus groups in developing adolescent tobacco use cessation program: Collective norm effects. *Journal of Applied Social Psychology, 21*, 1772–1782.

Talbot, M. (1992). *The holographic universe*. New York: HarperCollins.

Tannen, D. (2001). *You just don't understand: Women and men in conversation*. New York: Quill.

Tannen, D. (1984). *Conversational style: Analyzing talk among friends*. Norwood, NJ: Ablex.

Thurlow, C., Jaworski, A., & Ylanne-McEwan, V. (2005). "Half-hearted tokens of transparent love": "Ethnic" post-cards and the visual mediation of host-tourist communication. *Tourism, Culture & Communication, 5*(2), 1–12.

Trenholm, S., & Jenson, A. (2004). *Interpersonal communication*. New York: Oxford University Press.

Trent-Brown, S. (1995). Voice quality: Listener identification of African-American vs. Caucasian speakers. *Journal of the Acoustical Society of America, 98*, 2936.

Van Maanen, J. (1988). *Tales of the field: On writing ethnography*. Chicago: University of Chicago Press.

Van Manen, M. (1990). *Researching lived experience: Human science for an action sensitive pedagogy*. New York: State University of New York.

VanderStoep, S. W., Fagerlin, A., & Feenstra, J. (2000). What do students remember from introductory psychology? *Teaching of Psychology, 27*, 89–92.

VanderStoep, S. W., & Norris, B. P. (2005). Religious beliefs and their relationship to cognition, motivation, and behavior. In M. L. Maehr & S. K. Karabenick (Eds.), *Advances in motivation and achievement* (pp. 187–218). Greenwich, CT: JAI Press.

VanderStoep, S. W., & Pintrich, P. R. (2008). *Learning to learn: The skill and will of college success* (2nd ed.). Upper Saddle River, NJ: Prentice Hall.

Watkins, S. C. (2001). A nation of millions: Hip-hop culture and the legacy of Black nationalism. *Communication Review, 4*, 373–398.

Webster, J. (2002). Reminiscence functions in adulthood: Age, race and family dynamic correlates. In J. Webster & B. Haight, (Eds.), *Critical advances in reminiscence work: From theory to application* (pp. 140–152). New York: Springer.

Williams, M. A. (2004). Now and later: The role of personality and cognition in considering the future. *Psi Chi Journal of Undergraduate Research, 9*, 82–88.

Witvliet, C. V. O., Ludwig, T. E., & VanderLaan, K. (2001). Granting forgiveness and harboring grudges: Implications for emotions, physiology, and health. *Psychological Science, 12*, 117–123.

Witvliet, C. V. O., Worthington, E. L., Root, L. M., Sato, A. F., Ludwig, T. E., & Exline, J. J. (2008). Retributive justice, restorative justice, and forgiveness: An experimental psychophysiology analysis. *Journal of Experimental Social Psychology*, *44*, 10–25.

Wolcott, H. F. (1999). *Ethnography: A way of seeing.* Walnut Creek, CA: AltaMira.

Wright, K. (2003). Relationships with death: The terminally ill talk about dying. *Journal of Marital & Family Therapy*, *29*, 439–453.

Xu, L., Siegrist, J., Cao, W., Li, L., Tomlinson, B., & Chan, J. (2004). Measuring job stress and family stress in Chinese working women: A validition study focusing on blood pressure and psychosomatic symptoms. *Women & Health*, *39*, 31–46.

Yousman, B. (2003). Blackophilia and blackophobia: White youth and the consumption of rap music, and White supremacy. *Communication Theory*, *13*, 366–391.

Zimbardo, P. (1971). *Stanford prison experiment.* Stanford, CA. Zimbardo.

APPENDIX

A SAMPLE MANUSCRIPT FROM A QUANTITATIVE STUDY

Using a Non-Majors Course to Improve Students'
Motivation for Science

Place Authors' Names Here
Place University's or Organization's Name Here

Running Head: IMPROVING STUDENT MOTIVATION

ABSTRACT

We evaluated the efficacy of a non-majors science course to improve students' motivation for science, beliefs about science, and course content achievement. A total of 139 students participated in the course over three semesters. Three findings were clear and robust. First, students' motivation for science changed from the beginning to the end of the semester. Students showed positive increases from the beginning to the end of the semester in intrinsic motivation for science, task value of science, control beliefs for learning science, self-efficacy for science learning, and effort regulation. Students also showed a decrease in test anxiety from the beginning to the end of the semester. Second, students' beliefs about science showed positive changes from the beginning to the end of the semester. On a self-report instrument, students indicated (at posttest) that they recognized more real-life applications of science in everyday life, that they would use science more often when they graduated from college, and that they had more confidence in studying science at the end of the semester than at the beginning of the semester. Third, students showed increased achievement in a course-specific content test. Average class achievement at the beginning of the semester ranged from 34% to 54% at pretest and from 69% to 83% at the end of the semester.

USING A NON-MAJORS COURSE TO IMPROVE STUDENTS' MOTIVATION FOR SCIENCE

Despite our modern dependence on technology, the United States is "woefully lacking in technological literacy" (Wulf, 2002). There is an increasing recognition of the need for scientific and technological literacy for all Americans. The National Research Council places particular emphasis on the need for K-12 teachers to be technologically and scientifically literate (Person & Young, 2002). The goal of the present study was to determine if a course entitled "Science and Technology for Everyday Life" made improvements in students' motivation for learning science and perceptions of the value of science.

PREVIOUS LITERATURE

Several researchers have attempted to develop materials for non-science majors, especially undergraduates pursuing teacher certification. Robinson and Fadali (1998) proposed a capstone course with an emphasis on design projects to train pre- and in-service teachers in engineering principles. Genalo, Gallagher, and Golden (2001) used Lego Mind Storms and simple machines to expose K-12 teachers to engineering. Steele (2001) hosted a summer workshop that included discussions, experiments, and field trips about engineering. Two classroom activities developed by high school teachers have been described by Sharp, Chandler, and Peterson (2001). Titcomb (2001) has created a concise design guide for high school teachers. Jones and Wang (2001) have utilized the design problem of protecting a falling egg in a science education course. Four-day summer workshops of mini-lectures and demonstrations of the design-and-build process have been conducted by deGrazia (2001). The present study develops a course that covers a wide spectrum of technological topics, includes projects involving the construction of familiar technological devices, and requires writing on technological subjects.

Much research in educational psychology has determined that there are several psychological predictors of achievement. Students who show high intrinsic motivation, high task value, and sophisticated learning strategies show higher achievement. This has been shown to be particularly true in college science and social science courses (VanderStoep, Pintrich, & Fagerlin, 1996).

COURSE DESCRIPTION

The "Science and Technology of Everyday Life" course is intended for students from non-science majors. The objective of the course is to develop a familiarity with how various technological devices work and an understanding of the basic scientific principles underlying their operation. The course focuses on the wide variety of technology used in everyday life to help in engaging the students' interest. The single biggest constituency for the class is pre-service teachers (26%).

The course format is three hours of lecture and three hours of laboratory per week over a fifteen-week semester. Laboratories involve activities such as disassembling a car engine and building a simple electronic music keyboard. The lecture portion of the course is taught in a single section. Each laboratory section is run by one faculty member assisted by undergraduate teaching assistants. The text is David Macaulay's *The New Way Things Work*.

COURSE TOPICS

The course topics were selected to represent the technologies most frequently encountered in everyday life and were based partly on the results of surveys of student interests. Topics covered include the automobile, radio, television, computer, and medical-imaging equipment.

The first topic discussed was the automobile. The automobile was described as a group of interconnected systems, each performing a particular function. The systems studied were the engine, fuel and air, exhaust, cooling, lubrication, power train, brakes, steering, suspension, and electrical. The components associated with each system and their interrelations were described. Common problems were discussed. In this portion of the course, emphasis was placed upon helping students with little technical background to become accustomed to the process of thinking through cause-and-effect relationships. Such a facility is essential to understanding any technological system. In the laboratory, students disassembled and reassembled four-cylinder automobile engines. This activity brings non-science students into a degree of contact with technology that they are unlikely to have experienced previously.

The next segment of the course discussed technological devices that are based on applications of electricity and magnetism. Topics covered include the photocopier, batteries, the electric motor, electric power plants, and house wiring. The principles of science addressed were electrostatics; the concepts of current, voltage, and resistance; basic electrical circuits; joule heating; and electromagnetic induction. The course next focused on light and electromagnetic waves. Devices studied include incandescent and fluorescent lighting, lasers, lenses and eyeglasses, and photographic film and processing. We described the electromagnetic frequency spectrum along with the fundamentals of wave propagation.

METHOD

Participants

Participants were undergraduates enrolled in "Science and Technology for Everyday Life" at a private Midwestern college. A total of 139 students participated during the 2003–2004 academic year: 47 students in the Fall 2003 semester, 54 in the Spring 2004 semester, and 38 in the May Term (four-week summer session) 2004. We present the results separately for each term.

Motivated Strategies for Learning Questionnaire

Students completed several scales of the Motivated Strategies for Learning Question-naire (MSLQ) (Pintrich, Smith, Garcia, & McKeachie, 1991). Specifically, we collected data using the following scales:

Intrinsic Motivation. Intrinsic motivation measures the extent to which students are inspired to learn because of the challenge of learning new things, curiosity about the topic, or the joy that comes from understanding complex material. Many students come to this course with science "phobia" or a dislike for science and technology. This aversion to science learning could be due to several factors, and is likely related to previous unsat-isfying experiences with scientific and technical learning.

Extrinsic Motivation. Extrinsic motivation measures the extent to which students are inspired to learn because of rewards such as praise, grades, money, or competition.

Task Value. Task value measures the extent to which students feel that what they are learning is relevant, useful, and personally meaningful. This measure is particularly important for this project, as one of the goals of this project is to demonstrate to students all of the benefits that will accrue to those who study engineering. Anecdotally, a com-mon complaint of college students seems to be that they will "never use" what they are learning in college after they graduate. It is hoped that students will see increased task value for science learning as a result of taking this course.

Self-Efficacy. Self-efficacy measures students' beliefs about their ability to achieve on school-learning tasks. If students feel competent and empowered to succeed in school, they will have high scores on self-efficacy. This measure also is particularly important for this project, as one of the goals is to increase students' belief that science learning and problem-solving are tasks that they can complete. This will be particularly important to students in this class, as so many of them will go on to be elementary school teachers. If the students from this class can develop a sense of scientific self-efficacy, they can communicate that positive belief to their future students that they, too, can achieve in science.

Control Beliefs. Related to self-efficacy, the Control Beliefs subscale measures the extent to which students believe that hard work in school will result in positive outcomes. If students feel as though effort will result in accomplishment, they will score high on this scale.

Critical Thinking. A five-item scale measuring the extent to which students analyze and critique arguments and assertions.

Metacognition. This scale measures students' planning behavior, goal-setting, and monitoring of learning progress.

These scales have been used on hundreds of campuses and translated into several languages. The psychometric properties are reliable and predict achievement, particularly in science and social science courses (VanderStoep, Pintrich, & Fagerlin, 1996). The items are also course-specific, so the beliefs measured on these scales are measuring beliefs about this specific science course. Students also completed a 10-item Beliefs about Science questionnaire created for this project. Students completed these measures at both the beginning of the semester (pretest) and the end of the semester (posttest).

We also constructed a 10-item questionnaire designed to measure students' beliefs about science. This questionnaire was intended to capture the extent to which students believed that science was useful, easy to learn, and accessible to lay people as opposed to not useful, difficult to learn, and esoteric.

Finally, we constructed a 10-item achievement test. We gave students this test on the first day of class and then again during the last week of the semester. We constructed only one form of this achievement, rather than creating two forms and counterbalancing their order of presentation. We felt that a whole semester was a sufficient amount of time to erase any practice or memory effects that might otherwise occur as a result of multiple administrations of an instrument.

Procedure

Students in the course completed the MSLQ and the achievement test at the beginning of the semester and the end of the semester. The instructor for the course administered the pretest during class time in the first week of class and administered the posttest during the week before final-exam week. Students were asked to place their names on the instrument so that the data could be matched to compare change scores.

RESULTS

Changes Scores on MSLQ Scales

We conducted paired *t* tests to determine if changes occurred from the beginning of the semester to the end of the semester on any of the dependent measures. Table 1 shows the results from 40 students who took the course during the Fall 2003 semester. Most of the findings were consistent across all three semesters of study, suggesting the robust nature of most of the findings. For the MSLQ scores in the Fall semester, students showed increases (from the beginning to the end of the semester) on intrinsic motivation, $t(39) = 2.26$, $p = .03$, task value, $t(39) = 2.54$, $p = .015$, self-efficacy, $t(39) = 2.54$, $p < .001$, and a decrease in test anxiety, $t(39) = 2.60$, $p = .013$.

Change Scores on Beliefs about Science Questionnaire

The 10-item Beliefs about Science questionnaire did not demonstrate good psychometric scale properties (i.e., low Cronbach alpha), so instead of comparing pretest to posttest scale means, we analyzed each item separately. Table 2 shows the significant results from 40 students who took the course during the Fall 2003 semester. We found that 4 of the 10 items showed increases from pretest to posttest. The items showing such increases from pretest to posttest in two of the semesters were: (1) "I can think of real-life uses for science in my own life," $t(39) = 4.75$, $p < .001$; (2) "I will use science a lot when I graduate from college," $t(39) = 2.11$, $p = .041$; (3) "I study more for science courses than for others," $t(39) = 2.31$, $p = .033$; and (4) "I have confidence when I study science," $t(39) = 3.37$, $p = .002$.

Change Scores in Course Content Knowledge

Students completed a content achievement exam at the beginning and end of the semester. The topics covered and the items used on the exam are shown in Appendixes A and B (exam was modified after Fall semester to better reflect the course content objectives, and to increase the difficulty to create more variance in student scores). Results clearly showed that students entered the course knowing very little about technology upon entering the course and that they had learned a great deal by the time they completed the course. This was true for all three semesters we offered the course. Table 8 shows the percentage increases for all three semesters.

DISCUSSION

The current study uses findings from the educational psychology literature in a science education context. We were able to construct a non-science course for non-science majors that demonstrated increased motivation, increased task value, and improved adaptive beliefs about science. We also demonstrated learning through content achievement test scores that improved from the beginning to the end of the semester. Given that many of the students enrolled in this course were pre-service elementary teachers who will be teaching science in their classrooms, we find it very important to lower anxiety, increase perceived value, and increase motivation for science learning. This course accomplished those objectives.

We are encouraged about these findings. Future research will explore modifying the existing structure of the course slightly to make it serve as an introductory engineering course to determine if similar findings can be obtained from a different sample. Ultimately, it may be possible to use this approach to improve engineering education by making it more attractive and available to undergraduates at the beginning of their college careers.

REFERENCES

deGrazia, J. L. (2001, October). *Engineering workshops for K-12 teachers.* Presented at the 31st ASEE/IEEE Frontiers in Education Conference, Reno, NV.

Genalo, L. J., Gallagher, M., & Golden, J. (2001, June). *An engineering linkage to K-12 teachers.* Presented at the 2001 ASEE Annual Conference, Albuquerque, NM.

Jones, R. K., & Wang, E. (2001, October). *Experiences with an engineering technology course for education majors.* Presented at the 31st ASEE/IEEE Frontiers in Education Conference, Reno, NV.

Person, G., & Young, A. T. (Eds.). (2002). *Technically speaking: Why all Americans need to know more about technology.* Washington, DC: National Academy Press.

Pintrich, P. R., Smith, D., Garcia, T., & McKeachie, W. (1991). *A manual for the use of the Motivated Strategies for Learning Questionnaire* (Technical Report No. 91B-004). National Center for the Improvement of Postsecondary Teaching and Learning, University of Michigan.

Robinson, M., & Fadali, M. S. (1998, November). *A model to promote the study of engineering through a capstone course for preservice secondary science and math teachers.* Presented at the 28th ASEE/IEEE Frontiers in Education Conference, Tempe, AZ.

Sharp, J. M., Chandler, T. L., & Peterson, T. A. (2000, June). *Teaching teachers to apply engineering: A tale of two classrooms.* Presented at the 2000 ASEE Annual Conference, St. Louis, MO.

Steele, J. P. H. (2001, June). *A NEAT (New Engineering and Applied Technology) workshop for secondary teachers.* Presented at the 2001 ASEE Annual Conference, Albuquerque, NM.

Titcomb, S. L. (2001, October). *An engineering design guide for high school teachers.* Presented at the 31st ASEE/IEEE Frontiers in Education Conference, Reno, NV.

VanderStoep, S. W., Pintrich, P. R., & Fagerlin, A. (1996). Disciplinary differences in self-regulated learning in college students. *Contemporary Educational Psychology, 21*, 345–362.

Wulf, W. A. (2002). The case for technological literacy. National Academy of Engineering, National Academies Op-Ed Service Archive. Retrieved [date] from http://www4.nationalacademies.org/onpi/oped.nsf/0/BAAEBA228 E66163B85256 C3A006D8393?OpenDocument

Appendix A

Content Achievement Quiz, Fall 2003

Please answer to the best of your ability but your score will not count toward your course grade.

1) The microwave oven operates primarily through application of which principle of physics? (Circle one)

   Joule heating   Electromagnetic waves   Induction

2) In electronic devices, weak currents are increased in strength through the action of which component? (Circle one)

   Diode   Circuit breaker   Transistor   Solenoid

3) In an automobile, what is a function of the "cam"? (Circle one)

   Ignite fuel   Maintain wheel alignment   Open valves   Circulate coolant

4) If a car fails to start, which of these components are NOT likely to be part of the problem? (<u>Circle all that apply</u>)

   Battery   Torque converter   Alternator   ABS   Shock absorber

5) The speaker in a radio, stereo system, or pair of headphones produces sound using which principle of physics? (Circle one)

   Electromagnetism   Joule heating   Electromagnetic induction   Refraction

6) True or False: A magnet has two poles called a positive pole and a negative pole.

7) True or False: Voltage is the electrical pressure or "push" that causes the flow of current.

8) A LASER can NOT be which color? (Circle one)

   Blue   Green   Red   White

9) True or False: The ASCII controls the rate at which the computer executes instructions.

10) True or False: All other things the same, a computer with a 400 MHz clock is faster than a 2 GHz computer.

Appendix B

Content Achievement Exam, Spring 2004 and May Term 2004

Please answer to the best of your ability but your score will not count toward your course grade. <u>Circle one answer.</u>

1) The underlying principle behind how a microwave works (creates heat) is closest to which of these other devices found in the kitchen?

   Cordless phone   Conventional   Coffeemaker   Refrigerator   Radio
                      stove or oven

2) In electronic devices such as a television, weak signals are increased in strength through the action of which component?

   Diode   Capacitor   Transistor   Coil   Resistor

3) In an automobile, what is a function of the "cam"?

   Ignite fuel   Maintain wheel   Open valves   Circulate   Recharge
                   alignment   coolant   battery

4) Which of the following is least essential to the operation of a car? Which could break or stop functioning with the least impact on the ability of the car to continue running?

   Exhaust   Timing belt   Intake valve   Crankshaft   Catalytic
   manifold   converter

5) If a car fails to start, which of these components is MOST likely to be part of the problem? (Pick one)

Differential   Torque converter   ABS   Alternator   Shock absorber

6) The speaker in a radio, stereo system, or pair of headphones produces sound using which principle of physics?

Electromagnetism   Joule heating   Electromagnetic   Refraction   Radio waves
                                     induction

7) Energy of motion can be transformed into electrical energy using which of the following principles?

Electromagnetism   Electromagnetic   Joule heating   Refraction   Radio waves
                    induction

8) A LASER can NOT be which color? (Circle one)

Blue   Green   Red   White   Yellow

9) In computers, the term "ASCII" refers to:

a) A component that controls the rate at which the computer executes instructions.

b) A method to convert the letters and characters on the keyboard into sequences of the binary digits 0 and 1.

c) The part of the computer that performs calculations and executes instructions.

d) The procedure used to connect most of the computer's integrated circuit chips.

e) The name of a manufacturer of computer components.

10) An MRI machine operates using primarily which one of the following phenomena?

Heat   Light   Sound   Radio waves   X-rays

Table 1

MSLQ Change Scores as a Function of Taking the "Science and Technology for Everyday Life" Course, Fall 2003

MSLQ Scale	Pre Mean	Post Mean	*t*	*p*
Intrinsic Motivation	4.72	5.02	2.26	.030
Extrinsic Motivation	4.56	4.48	<1	ns
Task Value	5.03	5.41	2.54	.015
Control Beliefs	5.43	5.68	1.606	ns
Self-Efficacy	5.39	6.05	5.137	<.001
Test Anxiety	3.59	3.10	2.596	.013
Organization	4.40	4.04	1.556	ns
Critical Thinking	3.95	3.70	1.581	ns
Self-Regulation	4.31	4.18	1.324	ns
Effort Regulation	5.14	5.13	<1	ns

Table 2

Beliefs-about-Science Change Scores as a Function of Taking the "Science and Technology for Everyday Life" Course, Fall 2003

Item	Pretest Mean	Posttest Mean	t	p
I can think of real-life uses of science in my own life.	5.51	6.36	4.75	<.001
I will use science a lot when I graduate from college.	4.00	4.56	2.11	.041
I study more for science courses than for others.	4.25	3.75	2.21	.033
I have confidence when I study science.	4.05	4.58	3.37	.002

Table 3

Change Scores in Course Content Knowledge from "Science and Technology for Everyday Life"

Semester	Percent Correct		t	p
	Pretest Score	Posttest Score		
Fall 2003 (N = 47)	55.7	83.2	12.8	<.001
Spring 2004 (N = 48)	42.5	69.2	10.6	<.001
May Term 2004 (N = 36)	34.2	80.3	14.9	<.001

Note: Includes only those students who took the content knowledge test at both the beginning and end of the semester.

APPENDIX

A SAMPLE MANUSCRIPT FROM A QUALITATIVE STUDY

Defining Mother:
The Experience of Mothering Ideologies by Work Status[*]

Place Authors' Names Here
Place University's or Organization's Name Here

RUNNING HEAD: MOTHERING IDEOLOGIES

[*] A later version of this paper was published: Johnston, D. D., & Swanson, D. H. (2006). Defining mothers: The social construction of motherhood by work status. *Sex Roles: A Journal of Research, 54,* 509–519.

ABSTRACT

The purpose of this study was to explore how mothers construct their worker-parent identity within a cultural context of competing mothering ideologies. We used narrative data from interviews with 95 married mothers with at least one child under the age of 5 to compare the construction of intensive mothering expectations by middle-class full-time employed mothers, part-time employed mothers, and at-home mothers. Whereas previous research has shown that mothers alter work status to live up to intensive mothering expectations, our results show that mothers also alter their construction of intensive mothering expectations to reconcile these demands with their work status choices. The results also suggest that mothers with different employment decisions differ in their construction of Elvin-Nowak and Thomsson's (2001) three discursive positions—accessibility, happy mother/happy child, and separation of work and home.

Keywords: motherhood, work and family, ideology and identity

DEFINING MOTHER: THE EXPERIENCE OF MOTHERHOOD IDEOLOGIES BY WORK STATUS

We live in an era of contested motherhood ideologies. However culturally and historically aberrant (Coontz, 1992; Degler, 1980; Shorter, 1975) and individually restrictive (Mauschart, 1999; Rich, 1976) the dominant motherhood ideology of the last century may have been, motherhood expectations were clearly defined. The traditional mother ideology defined a "good mother" as full-time, at-home, White, middle-class, and entirely fulfilled through domestic aspirations (Boris, 1994). Scholars have challenged the patriarchal assumptions of the traditional motherhood ideology as restricting mothers' identities and selfhood (Glenn, 1994), perpetuating the economic dependence of mothers (Chang, 1994), and excluding mothers who are adolescents (Bailey, Brown, Letherby & Wilson, 2002), older, single, lesbian (Lewin, 1994), or women of color (Collins, 1994; Dill, 1988; Glenn, 1994). As a result we now experience an era in which a number of mothering ideologies compete for ascendancy (Buxton, 1998; Collins, 1994; Darnton, 1990; Golden, 2001; Hays, 1996; Thurer, 1995). The purpose of the present study was to assess how contemporary American mothers construct their mothering identity in a cultural context of competing mothering ideologies.

Efforts to define mothering ideology inevitably return to Hays's (1996) definitive work on intensive mothering as the dominant mothering ideology of our culture. *Ideologies* are patterns of beliefs, ideas, opinions, and values that are used to create meaning (Freeden, 2003). Ideologies define *what exists*, *what is good*, and *what is possible* (Therborn, 1980). As such, ideologies do not reflect an objective reality, but rather promote a particular construction of reality. Freeden (2003) further noted that ideologies are at times hidden to the groups that are most affected by them and are sometimes hidden even to the very groups that produced them.

Intensive mothering, according to Hays (1996), is a child-centered, expert-guided, emotionally absorbing, labor-intensive, financially expensive ideology in which mothers are primarily responsible for the nurture and development of the sacred child and in which children's needs take precedence over the individual needs of their mothers (p. 46). The pervasiveness of the intensive mothering ideology in our culture is supported by a number of studies (cf. Garey, 1999; Hattery, 2001; Ranson, 1999; Wall, 2001). Thurer (1995), for example, explored celebrity mother-bashing and the pop-psychology preoccupation with "mother blame" (p. 293). Thurer argued that the effect of this cultural focus was to keep mothers entrenched in intensive mothering expectations. Hays (2003) further suggested that the intensive mothering ideology has become more culturally salient as more mothers enter the workforce. This can be explained, in part, by Foucault's theory (Foucault, 1978) that the cultural hegemony perpetuates itself by setting up for failure those who attempt to counter hegemonic ideals. In other words, mothers entering the work force are a threat to the cultural power structure and intensive mothering expectations are a way to create expectations for "good mothering" that are mutually exclusive with working outside the home. Hays (1996) described how the logic of the marketplace (e.g., profit, success, personal achievement) is inherently at odds with the logic of intensive mothering (e.g., child-centered mothering requires omnipresent accessibility). As a result, it is difficult for mothers to negotiate a position that fulfills the expectations of both public and private sphere ideology. Hochschild (1989) reiterated this theme when she suggested that the work culture's labor expectations are more consistent with the breadwinner-father and stay-home-mother reality of the 1950s and 1960s than with the parent-workers of today struggling to enact both roles simultaneously.

Both at-home and employed mothers have internalized this ideology (Hays, 1996), but they find a variety of ways to position themselves within these ideological contradictions (Garey, 1995, 1999). Garey (1995) studied nurses who chose to work the night shift and found that they choose shift work to maintain the image of full-time domestic motherhood during the day. Hattery (2001) similarly identified "innovators" in her study who identified with at-home mothering and therefore managed their full- or part-time employment without paid childcare. Macdonald (1998) found that employed mothers use nannies and au pairs to create a mystique of intensive mothering for their children. Zavella (1987) and Segura (1994) found that employed mothers attempt to justify their employment for financial reasons in order to avoid criticism of being selfish by putting their careers ahead of their children's intensive needs.

The results of these studies suggest a great deal of cognitive rationalization to reconcile employment with intensive mothering expectations. Where are the full-time employed mothers who work for the sake of their career identity, require paid childcare, yet still strongly identify with the mother role? The dismissal of this group even by researchers as "reluctant mothers" (Garey, 1995) or "non-conformists" (Hattery, 2001) only serves to perpetuate the mystique of intensive mothering and its myth of the incompatibility of employment and "good" mothering.

Elvin-Nowak and Thomsson (2001) identified three discursive positions that reflect contemporary mothering values of employed mothers in Sweden. The focus of the first position is that the accessibility of the mother is necessary for children's psychological development and well-being. The second position is that the happiness of the mother is a necessary condition for the happiness of the child. The third position separates women's roles, such that work and motherhood are valued as separate identity spheres.

Elvin-Nowak and Thomsson found that employed women in Sweden construct these mothering expectations in order to meet their own needs both as mothers and as independent women. The options for resolving dialectics—that is, opposing tensions that simultaneously pull a person toward multiple polemically contradictory behaviors—are selection, segmentation, cyclic alteration, or reframing (Baxter, 1988; Baxter & Montgomery, 1996). A mother, for example, might select to stay home and abandon her work-identity, or select a career that results in the rejection of intensive mothering expectations. Alternatively, a mother might compromise both career aspirations and intensive mothering expectations (IME) in an effort to sustain both. A third option is to segment her work and mother identities in separate contexts, or cyclically alternate between work and mother identity at different times.

The most sophisticated response, according to Baxter and Montgomery (1996), is reframing. A mother might reframe her construction of IME and/or career expectations in such a way that tension no longer exists. For example, a mother might reframe intensive mothering as highly involved interactive parenting without continual accessibility. Or, as in Uttal's (1996) study, employed mothers might reframe intensive mothering as intensive parenting, such that intensive functions can be jointly accomplished by mothers, fathers, and other caregivers. Reframing is also evident in the integration of work and mothering by working third shift, such as Garey's (1999) nurses, or out of the home, such as Hattery's (2001) innovators.

The present study extends previous research that has shown that mothers change situational factors (e.g., shift schedules or working out of the home) to meet intensive mothering expectations (Hattery, 2001; Garey, 1999). We explored whether mothers may also change the construction of intensive mothering expectations to meet the constraints of their work status (Elvin-Nowak & Thomsson, 2001; Uttal, 1996). Modeling the discursive analysis of Elvin-Nowak and Thomsson (2001), this question will be explored by identifying the discursive positions upon which mothers construct their ideals of what makes a "good mother." We extended the work of Elvin-Nowak and Thomsson (2001) by exploring the construction of intensive mothering by United States at-home, part-time employed, and full-time employed mothers.

RQ: Do mothers construct intensive mothering expectations (IME) differently based on full-time employed, part-time employed, or at-home work status?

METHOD

We conducted interviews with 95 married mothers. A modified network sampling technique (Biernacki & Waldorf, 1981) was used to generate an initial list of 75 women based on community referrals (schools, churches, clubs, neighborhoods) of mothers who had at least one pre-school age child. Fifty-four women agreed to participate and were the source of 41 additional referrals. We used an average of 1.8 referrals from any one woman to avoid over-enmeshment of the sample with like-minded groups.

The mothers ranged in age from 22 to 51 years. Although all participants had at least one pre-school child, 70 percent of the women had more than one child (sample average = 2.16 children), and their children ranged in age from 8 weeks to 23 years. We interviewed women who self-defined as employed full-time ($n = 30, 32\%$), employed part-time ($n = 26$, 27%), and staying home full-time with their children ($n = 39$, 41%). The majority of the women who comprised the sample were White, married, and middle-class, and all had an education of high school or above.

The interviews were semi-structured and open-ended, averaged 2 hours in length, and were usually conducted in the woman's home. The narrative data were first coded thematically (Glaser & Strauss, 1967; Strauss & Corbin, 1990). Themes were analyzed by work status using NUDIST qualitative data analysis software and interpreted for frequency, repetition, and dominance of discursive interpretations (Burr, 1995; Wetherell & Potter, 1988). The validity of the themes was assessed by analyzing the frequency of the themes by mothers' work status.

We embrace the phenomenological ideal of presenting the results in participants' own voices. Participants' own words are used to make the points in the Data Analysis section, rather than a discourse analytic procedure whereby the researchers interpret the meaning of the narrative. Pseudonyms are used to protect the confidentiality of the interviewees.

To explore cultural and personal mothering expectations, participants were asked: "How would you define the ideal 'good mother'?", "How are you a 'good mother'?", "How could you be a better mother?" To explore work-family tensions, participants were asked: "How did you make your decision to be an employed mother or stay-at-home mother?", "How difficult was this decision to make?", "How happy are you now with your decisions?", "What are the benefits/stresses of your decision on you/your child?" To explore how mothers constructed worker/parent identity participants were asked: "Do you feel a competing tension between your desires to be a good mother and making contributions outside of the home?", "To what extent do you integrate your child responsibilities and your household or employment responsibilities?", "To what extent do you separate these responsibilities in your life?", "How do you integrate or separate your child responsibilities and your household or employment responsibilities?"

DATA ANALYSIS AND INTERPRETATION

Three discursive themes emerged in participants' constructions of the ideal mother. Accessibility, mother-child happiness, and separation of spheres emerged as central to how the women defined themselves in regard to their identity as mothers. These three themes are consistent with those identified by Elvin-Nowak and Thomsson (2001); however, the results of our study suggest that women alter the construction of these themes, depending on their own maternal work status.

Accessibility as a Discursive Position

At-home mothers. When asked what makes a "good mother," by far the most frequent, dominant, and repeated theme in the responses of *at-home mothers* was "being there." A "bad mother" is one who is "not there" or who "works" and consequently is not always available to her child. Although "being there" reflects a rather passive mother role, it discursively constructs the mother as central, essential, and irreplaceable for the child's development: "Time. It's not quality. It's quantity. Because you never know the moment of quality, when it will happen" (Ann).

The level of incessant accessibility described by at-home mothers creates stress. When asked how they could be better mothers, at-home mothers consistently voiced a desire for more patience and an ability to monitor their tempers in interactions with their children. At-home mothers told stories about "yelling" and "completely losing it" with their children that were quantitatively more frequent and qualitatively more intense than the experiences of either part-time or full-time employed mothers. "I can get angry. Sometimes quickly. It can be an explosive anger" (Brenda). "I told her three times to get off the stool. And then I just lost it, and I screamed at her, and she started crying . . . When you lose your temper you wonder if they'd be better off with someone else" (Melissa). "I feel like I'm constantly screaming at my kids . . . I think, oh my God, I hope the neighbors don't hear that. I'm like, who IS this woman? She's out of control" (Sharon). "Oh, patience. Patience, patience. I pray for patience every day. Patience. I pray for patience. Yep. Patience is key" (Judy).

To examine further what "accessibility" means to at-home mothers, we searched for images, descriptors, and metaphors—the presence or emphasis of which were unique to at-home mothers. At-home mothers talked about child discipline more than part- or full-time employed mothers did. The meaning of accessibility was tied to a belief that the presence of the mother keeps the child on the path of moral rectitude and that the child's behavior is a reflection of the mother. "If people tell you your child is polite and well behaved I think that does reflect on me as a parent" (Melissa). "I think in my consistency with him I'm a good mother—setting rules, letting him know that there are limits" (Jane). "I am kind of a tyrant . . . I have rules, and I have expectations, and some people might think my expectations are high on my kids, but everywhere we go I have people comment, 'Your kids are so good,' and 'Don't your kids ever get ornery?' or 'Don't they ever throw fits?' . . . Sometimes I think, 'Oh, I'm being too hard on them,' but the more I read Dobson, I think I'm doing okay" (Judy). (This is a reference to conservative evangelical writer James Dobson and his books on disciplining children.)

At-home mothers also anchored their construction of accessibility to self-sacrifice. "I feel selfish when I say, 'Wait a minute, it's time for me.' I tend to wait until my breaking point to say I need some time" (Samantha). "Just because of my personality I tend to take care of others before I take care of myself. I'll uuh you know go run errands or go to the grocery store or do something for a neighbor before I'll take a shower . . . I'm the last to be taken care of" (Cynthia). "I never get to take care of myself. If I take care of myself it's completely at the expense of everyone else" (Rhonda). "I'm good at putting my kids first. I'm good at hiding my frustration and stress level. I don't like put my needs in front of theirs . . . That makes me . . . a good mom" (Christine).

Part-time employed mothers. Part-time employed mothers constructed accessibility not as constant physical accessibility, but as periodic quality interaction. "It's okay for me to be out a bit. My children will survive without me for 10 to 20 hours a week" (Hope). Good mothering is constructed in terms of the number of one-on-one activities and the quality of communication between mother and child. "We have a lot of fun together as a family. We play a lot. We go hiking. We have family night every Friday night, almost every Friday night without fail. And swim together. And I feel like I've created in my home an environment where my children can be creative . . . they color, they paint . . ." (Lindsay). "I mean like, reading books to her all the time and doing flash cards and stuff like that is really going to help her. So that's really important to me and I feel like that's why I'm a good mom" (Mindy). "I plan a family night each week. I do stuff that the kids enjoy. We have a meal together every night. We have devotional time together every day. I try to make sure that I have individual time [with each child] throughout the week" (Susan). "I find myself at the end of the day looking back to say, 'Did I have some neat one-on-one time with each of my kids?'" (Vicky).

DEFINING MOTHER

The discourse of part-time employed mothers differed most from other mothers in the focus on communication with children. Accessibility was constructed as emotional openness and connection. "They don't walk away from us not having an answer to their question" (Kathy). "He needs some time when we can just sit and listen to him come up with these interesting things" (Vicky). "I'm constantly talking to him . . . I'm there for him" (Nancy). "We sit so much and just talk and play" (Nina). "They're willing to tell me what's going on. I will encourage them and help them if needed and if appropriate" (Amy).

Consistent with emotional accessibility is the need for patience. Almost all of the part-time employed mothers noted that they were good mothers because of their patience, or said they could be better mothers if they were more patient and had less temper. "Patience. I have a very bad temper and I find myself taking a deep breath and walking away and giving myself a time out" (Kathy). "Patience is a big thing . . . I can be really strong-willed, and sometimes it's more of a battle of wills, where I need to just say okay you know, let it go" (Sue).

Full-time employed mothers. Full-time employed mothers are not always able to be physically accessible to their children. Therefore, it is not surprising that they primarily constructed good mothering in terms of psychological and emotional accessibility. Three themes emerged in the good mothering narratives of full-time employed mothers: empowerment of children, affection and play, and focused attention and problem solving.

The descriptors, metaphors, and images that were unique to the narratives of full-time employed mothers included: teaching kids to keep in touch with their feelings, building their self-esteem, getting to know the child as an individual, and promoting independence and boundaries. Full-time employed mothers constructed their mother role as empowering children. "I think I'm very good with allowing the kids to be who they are. And just letting that be, while providing guidance in areas that we think are absolutely essential. Discipline or guidance to shape them into socially responsible beings, but to have very few restrictions on, for instance, expression of feelings, things like that" (Leanne). "She really is her own person . . . I'm trying to be a good mother now by just [recognizing that] . . . She likes frilly clothes . . . She likes things that I never did and that's okay" (Jennifer). "When I look at my son I know one thing that I pray that I can give him is self-esteem, self confidence" (Kris). "I try to promote . . . self-esteem in her by showing her different ways we're proud of her and we love her" (Annie).

Full-time employed mothers also emphasized nurturance, love and affection, and laughing/having fun/playing with their children more than did other mothers. "I try to meet them where they are; get down with them and get silly, have fun and play with them" (Wendy). "We have a lot of fun together . . . we enjoy each other" (Mandy). "I'm fun. I make things really fun for my children. Very upbeat. Very encouraging" (Sara).

Mother accessibility is not omnipresent, nor is it passive. Accessibility is available as needed, and it is psychologically and emotionally focused and responsive. "When there are problems or when they're going through something I'm willing to drop whatever it is I'm doing" (Pat). "I think a good mother is attentive and responsive to her child . . . I am responsive to my son when he has his concerns" (Pam). "Focusing on them and getting them what they need. I think that is what defines a good mother" (Stacey). "I do try to make them the priority when I am with them, that they get my undivided attention . . . I try real hard to give them each individual time with me" (Mandy).

Full–time employed mothers said that they could be better mothers if they had more time to spend with their children; they said that they wanted to be more physically accessible to their children. They reported feeling rushed, busy, and tired, and having difficulty balancing the needs of their workplace with the needs of their children. "It broke my heart the other day. We bought my oldest son some computer games, and he told my mom that, 'Mommy hasn't had time to show me all of those yet.' It killed me" (Heather). "I would love to be able to sit on the floor and play Legos with my kids and trucks with my little one . . . [but] the laundry's got to be done, the dishes have got to be clean, and I can't sit still. I try very hard, but it's really hard" (Donna). "I'd be a better mom if I weren't feeling so fragmented between work and home. In particular, the two jobs, because I do find that my patience gets shorter and shorter as I feel like I'm meeting fewer and fewer of people's expectations or my own expectations and just being tired all the time" (Mandy).

One trade-off full-time employed mothers make to be accessible to their children is to sacrifice housework. "I'm not the one who has the meals planned every night, and I'm not the one that has the laundry done, and I'm not the one who has a sparkling clean house . . . my priority is being with my kids, and that's how I think I'm best at being a mom. I really try to spend my time with them" (Heather). "I feel that [I'm a good mother] for spending time with her, spending family time together, you know, at night not cleaning, not doing dishes . . . it's time for her until she goes to bed" (Heidi).

Work Status Decision and Construction of Happiness

At-home mothers. At first, it appeared that most at-home mothers, having made their decision, were not conflicted about the decision. Many participants constructed the decision to stay home not because a happy mother makes a happy child, but rather because a happy child is the raison d'etre of a good mother. "I'm happy he's happy" (Natalie).

DEFINING MOTHER

"There's a lot of things I'd like to do . . . but I've sort of settled my mind that I'm not going to do that until I've seen my children get through their lives" (Ellie).

Others constructed the decision to stay home as self-fulfillment. "I worked 2 days a week, which was totally against my heart . . . I knew in my heart that I wanted to stay home and I didn't . . . I was very tangled up inside about that" (Ann). "It's what I always wanted. I love my children. I love being there doing the day to day" (Sharon).

Yet, beneath this happy projection, other realities are lurking. It is difficult for mothers to admit to any emotional state short of absolute bliss. "98% of the time I am glad that I am home . . . you know, except for those stressful days when they reduce me to tears" (Deb). "I really have to draw on my inner resources . . . There are people that I run into, like when I talk to you [employed interviewer]. You don't have to pretend that your life is great and that you have all the answers and that your house is always immaculate and you're out there making Martha Stewart wreaths" (Rhonda). "I thought I'd sit and play with him all the time. But then you also feel those pressures of having dishes done and wash counters and floors clean . . . You end up doing house stuff and bills" (Natalie).

At-home mothers reported being lonely and missing adult interaction. "My brain just kind of turns to mush because I'm with kids all day" (Deb). "[At] a party or social gathering . . . once they realize you're a stay-at-home mom, 'Let's not go any further with this conversation . . . she doesn't have much to contribute'" (Lori). "When I'm around people that work . . . they know different things that are going on that I don't know only because I'm at home with kids . . . I guess knowledge is what it is" (Emily). At-home mothers talked about isolation and loss of identity. "It's kind of isolating, and you might not be growing and developing as a person . . . I think there's a tendency to have your whole identity wrapped up in your children" (Melissa).

Part-time employed mothers. Part-time employed mothers embraced the happy mother-happy child discourse more wholeheartedly than did the other two groups: "It makes me a better mom because my kids have a break from me, I have a break from my kids" (Kathy). "If we've had a couple of days where they're like ornery and tired and grumpy, and mom's ornery, tired, and grumpy—not a good combination. If I can get away just even for a couple of hours and come back I'm much more able to handle the stresses of small children" (Sue). "Definitely I'm more patient because I get to go work" (Jan). Part-time employed mothers claimed to be better mothers because they worked and asserted that to be only a mother is not good for either the mother or the child.

All of the part-time employed mothers reported being happy or very happy (i.e., "90 to 100 percent" happy). Their happiness is associated with experiencing a sense of balance. "Part-time is working out really well. It's a good sense of balance" (Jamie). "I like having a break. I'm happy with being able to have a little bit of disposable income of my own. I like being able to mingle with people. I feel a sense of balance right now" (Nina). "I just love what I do because I work and I'm at home" (Mindy). Part-time employed mothers did not counter their happiness with acknowledgement of negatives or stresses.

Full-time employed mothers. Full-time working mothers were less happy than part-time employed mothers. The degree to which full-time employed mothers were unhappy is not associated with their job satisfaction or their desire to parent, but with their inability to spend as much time as they would like with their children. "I guess ideally we get home at a quarter to six every night, and bedtime is 8:30. That's not a whole lot of time, and I feel like . . . I'm shortchanging her, and she's being raised by the daycare provider instead of me or her father" (Annie). "I feel guilty that I haven't seen her hardly all day" (Heidi). "On the drive home or sometimes at night when I go you know I don't even have time to teach my kids how to tie their own shoes" (Pat).

Employed mothers embraced the happy mother-happy child position to the extent that they believe mothers should have an identity outside of motherhood. Yet, time away from children due to full-time employment creates cognitive dissonance. To resolve this dissonance, full-time employed mothers made rationalizations to justify their time away. "I know that I'm going to miss x, y, or z, but that's ok. I also know that even though I realize they do this—[child care providers are taught not to say anything when a child does a 'first' and let the parents discover it]—it still works" (Megan). "I miss being the one to teach them everything, but I tend to be an overachiever so it's probably a good thing that I'm not the one trying to teach them" (Pat). A full-time employed mother who changed her work status to part-time explained: "Our first babysitter . . . was as good a parent as I was, and my kids were learning . . . better values from her than they were from me. I never felt like they were missing me, but I got to a certain point where I realized I was the one missing out" (Beth).

Worker-Parent Identity and the Construction of Separate Spheres

At-home mothers. At-home mothers resolved work-home tension by selecting one sphere: the home. At-home mothers did not construct motherhood in a way that allows for any other alternative. If a good mother is ever-present in the home sphere, employed mothers are excluded from good motherhood. "I made the commitment to give up my career to be at home and that comes first. Any leftover of me you're welcome to have!" (Sharon).

"I made this decision to *be with* [my son] that's where my priority needs to be" (Samantha). "I just feel like I'm not contributing to the family just because of the fact that I used to bring home a paycheck . . . [my husband] has to constantly reassure me that 'you're at home with the kids all day long, you're raising our children, you're keeping them out of daycare, you're giving them a great environment to grow up in, you're giving them lots of love,' and then I think well, you know, *I am*" (Cynthia).

Part-time employed mothers. Part-time employed mothers used two strategies to resolve tension between home and employment. They separated home and work spheres and compromised their careers for their families. Some part-time employed mothers separated work and home and reported little tension between the two. "I feel like it's totally separate. I'm a good mom. My contribution outside the home is a job" (Nancy). "I spend 9 hours a day with him, from the time I wake up until the time I go to work . . . I have a lot of time that I spend with him, when I'm not with him, he's sleeping so I feel like I get most of his day"(Nancy).

Most part-time employed mothers reported tension between home and work spheres, but resolved the tension by compromising career for family. "I used to be on a lot of committees . . . my committee is motherhood right now" (Lindsay). "I feel if I worked more I'd feel better about me, but at what cost to the kids?" (Kathy). "I've sacrificed more of the job for the mom part . . . That first year I thought I was really going to make a go of it. I cried all the time because I wasn't giving 100 percent anywhere . . . I've put things in perspective and I've made my choices" (Nina).

Part-time employed mothers prided themselves in their ability to participate in both spheres and to be accepted by both at-home and full-time employed mothers. "I can talk the talk of stay-home moms and I can talk the talk of working moms. Depending on who I'm with, I can fit in with either camp" (Theresa).

Full-time employed mothers. Full-time employed mothers found it difficult to maintain separate work and home spheres. Children impinge on workplace and time, and work impinges on family space and time. In their narratives, full-time employed mothers talked about how child responsibilities overflow into the work sphere. "I drop my kids at daycare, and I have to express my milk before I go to class, and I run over to daycare to nurse at noontime, and then before I know it it's time to express milk again mid-afternoon" (Megan). "There are times during the week where it's really stressful. She gets sick. We have to decide who's staying home this time" (Jennifer). "Being a teacher, you also have to take classes. That's starting to creep up on me, and I've been trying to throw that into the equation also. I just don't know how I can be a student, a teacher, a mom, and a wife at the same time" (Anne).

In parallel fashion, work responsibilities spill into the home sphere. "That night is stressful because as soon as I cover city council meetings I have to come home and write two to three stories by midnight. So I'm on the laptop, and she's wanting something and [he's] wanting something. Sometimes I'll scream at her . . . It's the only time we clash is when I'm on deadline and she's wanting something" (Wendy). "When you're at work you think you should be home, and when you're at home [you're thinking about work]. I do work part of the time at home and part of the time in my office" (Sherry). "The family supersedes work . . . If the kids get sick it'd be very easy for me to cancel everything I have—unless it's a visit to a dying person or a funeral or worship" (Leanne).

The mental separation and transition between home and work is difficult. "When I'm at work it's hard for me to concentrate and settle in and feel good about what I'm doing at times . . . And when I'm at home with them I think, 'Oh this client needed that paper . . . sent to them' . . . being either place makes a tension" (Martha). The sheer stress of work also impacts the home sphere. "The [special event] that's coming up I just absolutely hate it because I'm gone for basically two and a half days. Where I don't see the kids at all except to come and be so tired you can't hardly think. I can't hardly cook or do anything because I'm so exhausted" (Sherry).

The discourse of full-time employed mothers reflects ambivalence between wanting to do it all and realizing that doing it all, all of the time, is impossible. Full-time employed mothers alternatively focus and excel in one sphere and then in the other. "I want to be the best professor that I can be. I want to be the best psychologist and researcher that I can be, and, clearly, the best mom that I can be. That doesn't work. Something has to give. At times I will be a good teacher, at times I won't be as good, but I'll be a better mom" (Susanna). "Guilt. If you're doing your best at work you feel guilty about what you're not doing at home. And if you're doing your best at home . . . you feel guilty about what you're not contributing at work . . . [It's] an omnipresent feeling" (Marcy). "If I just had all of my time to myself I could have a lot more publications and a lot more completion of projects, but I'm old enough and far along enough in motherhood and marriage to realize that I wouldn't want to be that person" (Lucy).

The experiences of full-time employed mothers reflect cyclic alteration. Motherhood and employment remain in tension. True reframing would transcend the tension. Attempts to integrate career and motherhood are itself a source of stress. For full-time employed mothers, work and family is constructed as give and take; priorities of family and work are areas under a swinging pendulum, which, although periodically out of balance, are perceived to achieve equilibrium over time.

DISCUSSION

The results of the present study suggest that mothers construct the meaning of accessibility, maternal happiness, and separate spheres differently based on employment status. At-home mothers' construction of good mothering as "always being there" effectively excludes full-time working mothers from good mother status. The construction of the happy mother-happy child position by part-time employed and full-time employed mothers effectively excludes at-home mothers if they do not have an identity outside of motherhood. The self-sacrificing mother-happy child position maintained by at-home mothers effectively excludes full-time employed mothers who are perceived as putting their own needs ahead of those of their children. In light of Therborn's (1980) definition of ideology—*what exists, what is, and what is possible*—we found that mothers are ironically constructing their mothering identity in ways that *constrain* their range of choices.

By modifying mothering expectations to reinforce their work decision, all mothers can claim that their personal work status decision benefits their children. At-home mothers are accessible, part-time mothers emphasize quality communication with children, and full-time employed mothers focus on empowering their children and building their children's self-esteem. Yet, all three constructions have limitations: full-time employed mothers reported not having enough time with their children, and at-home mothers reported losing their patience with their children. Part-time mothers reported no obvious detrimental effects on their children, but they did note career sacrifices in terms of power, credibility, and full participation in the public sphere.

The findings of the present study should be considered in light of two limitations: the differentiation of mothers by work status, and the homogeneity of the sample. Clearly, there are many subtle differences within groups of mothers defined by work status decision. A number of scholars have defined work identity (cf. Duncan & Edwards, 1999; Golden, 2001; Perry-Jenkins & Crouter, 1990) and the factors that influence it (Golden, 2001; Potuchek, 1992). The weighing and integration of mothering ideology and worker identity (e.g., perceived financial need to work and career/job fulfillment) need to be explored in future research.

Another limitation of our study is the homogeneity of the sample. The results say little about the identity construction of women of color, less-educated, less financially privileged, single mothers, or lesbian mothers. This study does, however, provide a large sample upon which identity patterns are based. Hattery's (2001) analysis was based on 28 interviews, and her nonconformist category relied on the narratives of only three mothers.

Hays's (1996) study was based on 38 mothers and Gerson's (1985) on 30 mothers. Elvin-Nowak and Thomsson's (2001) and Garey's (1999) studies included only employed mothers.

Cyclical Nature of Ideology and Maternal Employment Decisions

The findings of the present study raise questions of causality. Do mothers choose a work status based on their mothering ideology, or does a mothering ideology emerge to fit the conditions of their work status experience? The majority of at-home mothers reported making their work status decision primarily based upon their ideological convictions. In contrast, part-time and full-time employed mothers talked about how employment decision shaped their mothering ideology and how their mothering ideology was reinforced by their employment decision. There was no evidence in the narrative data of part-time and full-time employed mothers that their mothering ideology drove them to seek employment. Thus, the construction of mothering ideology most likely reflects both processes: mothers choose a work status based partly on their mothering ideology, and their mothering ideology emerges in part to fit their lived experience with a particular employment decision. As predicted by consistency theories, the data suggest that mothers must find cognitive ways to reconcile their employment decision and their mothering ideology. It therefore makes sense that the ideological constructions revealed in the narratives vary by work status. The achievement of ideological consistency is further supported by the fact that the mothers in the present study reported that they made their own choice regarding their employment decision and almost all reported being happy with their employment status choice.

The present study extends our understanding of mothering ideology in several ways. Elvin-Nowak and Thomsson (2001) found that employed mothers in Sweden embraced the maternal accessibility, happy mother-happy child, and separate sphere discursive positions. The employed mothers in that study are similar to the part-time employed mothers in our U.S. sample. This may be because Sweden has a shorter work week and more extensive maternal leave policies, which enable employed women to separate employment and motherhood spheres. For full-time employed American mothers, the difficulty in separating employment and family roles was a significant source of stress and unhappiness.

Perhaps the most troubling implication of these results is that when employment status and mothering ideology are collapsed into a unitary dimension, the expectations of mothering are consequently based on economic and political values about employment rather than on the needs of children. As a result, cultural discourse focuses on the morality of maternal employment in lieu of studies of the parenting needs of children across all maternal and paternal work situations and parenting philosophies. In this way employment-based mothering ideologies constrain *what is possible* in the construction of parenting ideologies that are created to promote the character of parents and children.

REFERENCES

Bailey, N., Brown, G., Letherby, G., & Wilson, C. (2002). The baby brigade: Teenage mothers and sexuality. *Journal of the Association for Research on Mothering, 4,* 101–110.

Baxter, L. (1988). A dialectical perspective on communication strategies in relationship development. In S. Duck (Ed.), *Handbook of personal relationships* (pp. 257–273). New York: Wiley.

Baxter, L., & Montgomery, B. (1996). *Relating: Dialogues and dialectics.* New York: Guilford.

Biernacki, P., & Waldorf, D. (1981). Snowball sampling: Problems and techniques of chain referral sampling. *Sociological Methods & Research, 10,* 141–163.

Boris, E. (1994). Mothers are not workers: Homework regulation and the construction of motherhood, 1948–1953. In E. Glenn, N. Glenn, G. Chang, & L. Forcey (Eds.), *Mothering: Ideology, experience, and agency* (pp. 161–180). New York: Routledge.

Burr, V. (1995). *An introduction to social contructionism.* London: Routledge.

Buxton, J. (1998). *Ending the mother war: Starting the workplace revolution.* London: Macmillan.

Chang, G. (1994). Undocumented Latinas: The new "employable mothers." In E. Glenn, N. Glenn, G. Chang, & L. Forcey (Eds.), *Mothering: Ideology, experience, and agency* (pp. 259–285). New York: Routledge.

Collins, P. (1994). Shifting the center: Race, class, and feminist theorizing about motherhood. In E. Glenn, N. Glenn, G. Chang, & L. Forcey (Eds.), *Mothering: Ideology, experience, and agency* (pp. 45–66). New York: Routledge.

Coontz, S. (1992). *The way we never were: American families and the nostalgia trap.* New York: Basic Books.

Darnton, N. (1990, June 4). Mommy vs. mommy. *Newsweek.*

Degler, C. (1980). *At odds: Women and the family in America from the revolution to the present.* New York: Oxford University Press.

Dill, B. T. (1988). Our mothers' grief: Racial ethnic women and the maintenance of families. *Journal of Family History, 13,* 415–431.

Duncan, S., & Edwards, R. (1999). *Lone mothers, paid work, and gendered moral rationalities.* New York: Palgrave Macmillan.

Elvin-Nowak, Y., & Thomsson, H. (2001). Motherhood as idea and practice: A discursive understanding of employed mothers in Sweden. *Gender & Society, 15,* 407–428.

Foucault, M. (1978). *The history of sexuality* (Vol. 1). New York: Pantheon.

Freeden, M. (2003). *Ideology: A very short introduction.* Oxford, UK: Oxford University Press.

Garey, A. (1999). *Weaving work and motherhood.* Philadelphia: Temple University Press.

Garey, A. (1995). Constructing motherhood on the night shift: "Working mothers" as stay-at-home moms. *Qualitative Sociology, 18,* 414–437.

Gerson, K. (1985). *Hard choices: How women decide about work, career, and motherhood.* Berkeley: University of California Press.

Glaser, B., & Strauss, A. (1967). *The discovery of grounded theory.* Chicago: Aldine.

Glenn, E. N. (1994). Social constructions of mothering: A thematic overview. In E. Glenn, N. Glenn, G. Chang, & L. Forcey (Eds.), *Mothering: Ideology, experience, and agency* (pp. 1–29). New York: Routledge.

Golden, A. (2001). Modernity and the communicative management of multiple roles: The case of the worker-parent. *Journal of Family Communication, 4,* 233–264.

Hattery, A. J. (2001). *Women, work and family: Balancing and weaving.* Thousand Oaks, CA: Sage.

Hays, S. (2003). *Flat broke with children: Women in the age of welfare.* Oxford, UK: Oxford University Press.

Hays, S. (1996). *The cultural contradictions of motherhood.* New Haven, CT: Yale University Press.

Hochschild, A. (1989). *The second shift: Working parents and the revolution at home.* New York: Viking.

Lewin, E. (1994). Negotiating lesbian motherhood: The dialectics of resistance and accommodation. In E. Glenn, N. Glenn, G. Chang, & L. Forcey (Eds.), *Mothering: Ideology, experience, and agency* (pp. 333–353). New York: Routledge.

Macdonald, C. L. (1998). Manufacturing motherhood: The shadow work of nannies and au pairs. *Qualitative Sociology, 21,* 25–53.

Mauschart, S. (1999). *The mask of motherhood: How becoming a mother changes everything and why we pretend it doesn't.* New York: New Press.

Perry-Jenkins, M., & Crouter, A. (1990). Men's provider-role attitudes: Implications for housework and marital satisfaction. *Journal of Family Issues, 11,* 136–156.

Potuchek, J. (1992). Employed wives' orientations to breadwinning: A gender theory analysis. *Journal of Marriage & the Family, 54,* 548–558.

Ranson, G. (1999). Paid work, family work, and the discourse of the "full-time mother." *Journal of the Association for Research on Mothering, 1,* 57–66.

Rich, A. (1976). *Of women born: Motherhood as experience and institution.* New York: Norton.

Segura, D. (1994). Working at motherhood: Chicana and Mexican immigrant mothers and employment. In E. Glenn, N. Glenn, G. Chang, & L. Forcey (Eds.), *Mothering: Ideology, experience, and agency* (pp. 211–233). New York: Routledge.

Shorter, E. (1975). *The making of the modern family.* New York: Basic Books.

Strauss, A., & Corbin, J. (1990). *Basics of qualitative research: Grounded theory procedures and techniques.* Newbury Park, CA: Sage.

Therborn, G. (1980). *The ideology of power and the power of ideology.* London: Verso.

Thurer, S. (1995). *The myths of motherhood: How culture reinvents the good mother.* New York: Penguin.

Uttal, L. (1996). Custodial care, surrogate care, and coordinated care: Employed mothers and the meaning of child care. *Gender & Society, 10,* 291–311.

Wall, G. (2001). Moral constructions of motherhood in breastfeeding discourse. *Gender & Society, 15,* 592–610.

Wetherell, M., & Potter, J. (1988). Discourse analysis and the identification of interpretative repertoires. In C. Antaki (Ed.), *Analysing everyday explanation: A casebook of methods* (pp. 168–183). London: Sage.

Zavella, P. (1987). *Women's work and Chicano families: Cannery workers in the Santa Clara Valley.* Ithaca, NY: Cornell University Press.

GLOSSARY

A

ABBA design Research design in which one order of the levels of the independent variable is presented for one participant, and then the opposite order is presented for the next participant.

abstract A brief summary of the research project; appears at the beginning of a research article.

achievement measure Assesses the amount of material a person has mastered.

action Criterion for evaluation of qualitative research; underlying position is that research is not an end in and of itself, but rather a means toward social change, policy change, problem solving, or program development or evaluation.

action research Study for which the goal is to problem-solve a situation for the betterment of the community participating in the study (Chapter 7); and/or for which goal is to demystify research methods and research results for research participants (Chapter 9).

all-possible-orders counterbalancing Research design in which each level of the independent variable appears in each ordinal and each level precedes and follows every other level equally often.

analysis of a text *See* **textual analysis**.

analysis of variance (ANOVA) Statistical method used to determine if the mean scores of three or more groups or levels of an independent variable differ on a dependent variable.

anchors The two endpoints of a bipolar response scale.

applied research An investigation that has obvious and immediate applications to real-world settings.

aptitude measure Measures a person's potential for success in a given area, such as an intelligence test or the SAT.

artificial immersion Research method in which the researcher interacts, as a researcher, with the group being studied.

attention-getting preface A type of transition that can make the interview more interesting; for example, "The next question is a bit awkward to ask . . . " or "The next question is very personal . . . ."

attrition The dropping-out of participants over time in a longitudinal study.

authenticity Evaluative criterion that investigates how genuinely or closely the data reflect the lived experiences of the participants.

autoethnography A variation of observation research in which the researcher reports his or her own personal experience.

B

background information Includes personal data or information such as demographic (e.g., age, marital status, education level, socioeconomic status), pertinent personal history with the group or program under study, and factual information or data that help the researcher to understand the operations of the culture, group, or program under study.

basic research An investigation that adds to the knowledge of a particular area of study, but may not have obvious or immediate applications to real-world settings.

between-group error variance Error variance due to differences between the groups in the experiment.

between-groups design An experiment in which participants receive only one level of an independent variable.

biographical case study A case study focused on one person.

boundaries The demarcations between self and other of which an interviewer must be continually conscious.

C

caring *See* **emotionality and caring**.

case study Research that investigates a specific, unique, bounded system.

categorical variables Variables that take on values that represent discrete groups rather than quantitative values; for example, married/nonmarried, male/female.

categories Larger classifications for the organization of themes in qualitative data; eventually lead the qualitative researcher to more complex analyses.

causal inference A statement about which variable is the cause and which variable is the effect.

causation The claim that a change in one variable (independent variable) *creates* a change in another variable (dependent variable).

ceiling effect When participants score at the highest level on the dependent measure.

chi-square A measure of association between two nominal variables indicating that the observed frequency distribution of the two variables differs from the expected frequency distribution.

circular Describes the process in qualitative research by which the research design evolves in a feedback cycle from data collection and analysis, and in turn informs subsequent data collection and analysis.

clarity Quality of interview questions; interviewers should strive for this in framing questions.

closing Part of the interview that should bring the respondent back to the present environment.

closing question Used at the end of an interview to provide participants the opportunity to amend, supplement, or redirect the researcher's agenda; use is consistent with the values of qualitative research.

cluster sampling Sampling method that involves randomly selecting or assigning groups of people, rather than individuals, based on membership in a group, geography, or some other variable.

cohort effects At work when a finding that is thought to be due to the independent variable is in fact due to some generational differences in the sample.

collective case study (also called *single-case study*) Research design that involves a comparison of several related cases, such as the comparison of several corporate organizations.

colonialism/imperialism Attitude when the researcher assumes that he or she (or his or her culture) is superior to the people or culture studied.

comparison questions Asked to get at underlying constructions of meaning; for example, to discern the meanings constructed by skaters, one might ask, "How is a set [series of moves] that is 'smooth' different from a set that is 'diamonds'?" "How is a set that is 'sick' better or worse than a set that is 'smooth'?"

complete observer One possible researcher role, in which the researcher is uninvolved in the group being studied.

complete participant One possible researcher role, in which the researcher is an active member of the group being studied.

completely-crossed design A research design in which all the levels of one independent variable are paired with all the levels of the other independent variable.

complex design An experiment with more than one independent variable.

confessional tale A type of autoethnography that helps the researcher make sense of a real experience.

confound A situation in which it is not known whether changes in the dependent variable were caused by the independent variable or by an extraneous variable.

construct validity The extent to which a measure is on target to measure what the researchers are seeking to measure; often assessed by correlating a measure with another measure that is known to be related.

content validity The extent to which the items or behaviors assessed by a measurement represent all the known dimensions of the construct being measured; the extent to which a measure fully represents and captures the construct that the researchers are trying to measure.

context of the case The social, economic, cultural, geographical, and/or historical setting of a case study.

control group A group of participants in an experiment that receives either no exposure to the independent variable or the same exposure that would otherwise occur in everyday life.

convenience sampling A non-random sampling method that involves selecting people for a research project who are available for study.

convergent validity The extent to which other measures of a construct are similar to your measure.

conversation analysis The systematic interpretation of a naturally occurring conversation.

core categories Large classifications for qualitative data; following the identification of these, data are coded to determine category members.

correlation A statistical measure of covariance between two variables.

correlation coefficient The measure of association that is used to assess the covariance between variables.

correlation matrix Set of correlations among the variables in a study.

correlational research Research design that involves identifying statistical relationships between two variables rather than causal relationships.

counterbalancing A method of alternating the order of delivering the independent variable to reduce practice effects.

covariation Occurs when scores on two variables change at the same time.

covert Describes research in which the people or groups being observed do not know that they are being observed.

crisis of representation Challenge of qualitative research to accurately reflect the lived experience of others when the research report is filtered through the researcher's interpretations; term developed during the rise of qualitative methods in response to criticism of quantitative methods.

criterion measure In educational research, measures how much a student has learned in a particular subject.

critical incident study A case study focused on one event.

critical studies Research paradigm founded on the expectation that study should identify oppression in society and the research process and that the outcome should give voice to the disenfranchised, empower the silenced, and ultimately bring about social change.

critical studies perspective Viewpoint that sees texts as sites of power struggle.

critical tale A type of autoethnography that presents the voice of a marginalized person.

Cronbach's alpha The most common way to assess the reliability of self-report items; measures the degree to which the items in an instrument are related.

cross-sectional design Research design in which several different groups of people are measured on a variable at a single point in time; for example, comparisons may be made when different groups represent different ages, or different amount of time on a medication, or different stages of a disease.

cross-tabulation A method of showing how the frequency of responses of one nominal variable relate to the frequency of responses of another nominal.

cultural "maps" of human social behavior One way in which ethnographies are described/defined.

cultural performances One way in which ethnographies are described/defined.

culture-centered criticism Explores the interpretation of a text from different cultural perspectives of meaning.

D

data Recorded measurements on a set of variables from a research sample.

debriefing Meeting or communication that takes place at the conclusion of a study, at which time the purposes of the research are revealed.

deception The practice of giving false information to research participants about some aspect of the study.

deductive approach A process of reasoning that flows from a theory/hypothesis to systematic empirical observation to conclusion.

demographic and factual questions Interview questions that are typically fact-based and easy to answer; beginning with this type of question can help to put the respondent at ease.

dependent variable The outcome the researchers are measuring.

description questions Interview questions that ask the respondent to talk about a scenario or activity. Examples are: "What is your job description?" "You've just walked in the door of your office. Describe what you do first. What do you do next, and next?" "You said you prepare for the morning conference. How do you prepare for the conference meeting?"

descriptive research Describes the attitudes and behaviors observed during the investigation, but does not make predictive or causal inferences.

directory-listed sampling Procedure that randomly selects households with listed telephone numbers.

discourse analytic perspective Viewpoint maintaining that the window to understanding a particular culture, a particular social group, or a phenomenon is through detailed analysis of conversations and stories.

discriminant validity When the instrument being examined is *uncorrelated* with another measure that is presumably unrelated.

discussion section The last section of a journal article, providing a narrative summary of the results, the implications of the study, and suggestions for future research.

documents and material culture Written texts or cultural artifacts.

dominance in emphasis A way to recognize a theme, when one begins to see the same idea repeated within a case and/or repeated across cases; look for words, phrases, or behaviors that meet this criterion.

double-barreled question A survey item that has two distinct components in the stem of the question, thereby making it difficult to interpret the results of a study.

E

emergence A process in qualitative research by which the design and insights arise from the initial observations or research.

emergent design The design of a naturalistic inquiry (whether research, evaluation or policy analysis) that arises, develops, and unfolds as the research progresses.

emotionality and caring A criterion of evaluation for qualitative research that reflects the quality of the relationship between the research and participants.

epistemology The study of knowledge; beliefs about the nature of knowledge and knowing.

error variance The variation in the scores of the dependent variable that cannot be accounted for by the independent variable.

ethnographic observation Research process of observing people enacting culture.

ethnography Research process that involves the observation and recording of conversations, rituals, performances, ceremonies, artifacts, jokes, and stories.

evaluation research Research process that focuses on assessing the effectiveness of a particular program or course of action in solving a particular problem.

event analysis Research process that explores the meaning and interpretation of selected critical occurrences.

event sampling Involves recording all or a proportion of the specific instances of the behavior of interest.

example questions Interview questions that include an example to give the respondent a sense of the type and level of response being solicited.

exit procedures Means of concluding some phases of a qualitative study; should be incorporated in the research design.

exploratory questions Interview questions designed to find out what is salient or important in the culture, group, experience, or text being analyzed.

external validity Refers to the extent to which the findings from one investigation will generalize to other samples, populations, or settings.

extraneous variable A rival explanatory variable that can also account for the relationship between the independent and dependent variables.

F

factor An independent variable controlled by the researcher.

feeling questions Interview questions that solicit narrative descriptions of emotions; for example, "How do you feel about . . . ?"

feminist criticism Analysis that is particularly focused on gender inequalities.

fidelity Refers to the purity of the recorded data in comparison to the actual lived experience being assessed.

field notes Handwritten notes of observations (such as journal entries) made by qualitative researchers; often used in addition to audio and video recordings.

follow-up questions Spontaneously generated interview questions that pursue a line of thought or direction of inquiry opened by the respondent.

frequency across cases A way to recognize a theme in qualitative research when one begins to see the same idea repeated within a case and/or repeated across cases.

frequency distribution Shows how often the different possible values of the variable were selected.

full immersion Condition when the researcher has natural membership in the group being studied.

G

generalizability How much the findings from the current sample extend to the entire population.

grand narrative A story shared by a culture; characterized by a prescribed sequence, required elements, identifiable functions, and a script.

grounded theory Theory arrived at through, or that emerges from, data exploration and analysis.

grounded theory approach Process of discovering a theory through data exploration and analysis.

group communication effect Found in focus groups; occurs when the whole direction of the focus group diverts toward an extreme attitude presented by a particularly outspoken and dynamic person.

guided interview A compromise technique that carries some of the benefits of both informal and structured interviews.

H

Heisenberg uncertainty principle In qualitative research, the recognition that the researcher influences the behavior of those studied (based on the natural science physical postulate regarding observation and measurement of particles).

heuristic value Extent to which a research study generates more research.

historical analysis Analysis of the people, problems, policies, and responses that have defined the past.

history Term for when participants in a study experience some common social or cultural event, not related to the independent variable, that could affect the outcome of the study.

hypotheses Specific predictions, based on theory, about the degree and direction of the relationship between variables to be tested in the research study.

I

identifiable functions The purpose or purposes underlying the perpetuation of a grand narrative for a given community; common functions include helping a community make sense of some phenomenon or providing a moral lesson.

"I-it" A type of communication in which the respondent is treated or regarded as an object, an ID number in a computer file.

impressionist tale A type of autoethnography that challenges conventional thinking about an issue by presenting a nonconventional perspective, such as the perspective of a character in a story.

independent variable The variable that is systematically controlled by the researcher to determine the effect of that variable on the dependent or outcome variable(s).

independent-samples _t_ test A statistical test that compares respondents' mean scores on a dependent variable in a study in which each participant receives only one level of the independent variable.

individual difference variable A measure of some inherent trait, ability, or personality characteristic upon which people differ.

inductive approach A process of reasoning in which observation precedes proposition of a theory, the generation of hypotheses, and interpretation of data.

inferential statistics Statistical analytical techniques used to draw conclusions about significant relationships between independent and dependent variables.

informal interview Type of qualitative research that allows the researcher to create impromptu questions and move in various directions as the interview progresses.

instrumentation error Error that occurs when the scale, survey, or performance measure used to measure the dependent variable changes over time.

interaction error The condition when two independent variables at specific levels together affect the dependent variable in the study.

internal validity The extent to which the claim of changes in the independent variable causing changes in the dependent variable is accurate.

interpretive interactionalism Research based on the experience of the writer; some qualitative researchers assert that it is the only truly authentic research because it is biographical, personal, and focused on self.

inter-rater reliability Extent to which people who are observing a behavior agree on the coding of that behavior.

interval data A measurement that has equal distance between measurement points; for example, temperature is an interval measure because the difference between 10 degrees and 11 degrees is the same as the difference between 80 degrees and 81 degrees.

interview A face-to-face question-and-answer process; a type of qualitative research method.

interviewing The process of interacting with a respondent in a face-to-face question-and-answer process; a skill set that qualitative researchers must develop and practice.

introduction Beginning portion of a research paper; sets the stage for the research by reviewing the literature and describing research questions.

"I-Thou" A type of communication in which the respondent is revered as an individual, not as a representative of some group.

L

Latin Square design Repeated-measures research design in which each level of the repeated-measures independent variable appears in each position.

law of large numbers As the size of a sample increases, the more likely it is that the sample will approximate the overall population.

leading question Type of interview question that suggests the (desired) answer within the question; for example, "I have heard all sorts of stories from students and faculty about problems with this teacher. What problems have you had?"

legitimization A challenge to qualitative research in regard to making claims, in which qualitative research assumes that reality and truth are constructed and variable.

level of significance The probability that a relationship between variables is not real, but rather due to chance factors.

Likert scale A five-point scale anchored by bipolar adverbs (like/dislike; agree/disagree) in which respondents indicate their degree of agreement with a stated attitude or judgment.

literature review Section of a research paper that summarizes previous research in the area to set the stage for the current study.

longitudinal design Research design in which the same people are studied over multiple data-collection periods.

M

main effect A test of whether an independent variable is statistically significant across all of the levels of the other independent variable(s).

margin of error Represents the extent to which repeated random samples will deviate from the population.

Marxist criticism Type of textual analysis that focuses on signs of disparity in wealth and power.

matched-groups design Research design in which participants are placed into groups based on some preexisting characteristic.

matching Involves making experimental groups as similar as possible on a potential rival variable.

maturation Threat to internal validity that arises when the participants change during the course of the experiment.

mean The arithmetic average of a set of numbers.

median The middle score of numbers in a dataset.

metaphors In qualitative research, one way to analyze categories.

method section The "how to" section of a journal article, describing the participants, measurements, and research procedures used in the study.

methods The strategies and processes involved in conducting research studies.

mixed design A complex experimental design that contains at least one between-groups factor and at least one repeated-measures factor.

mode The most frequently occurring number in a dataset.

mundane realism A research setting that simulates actual life events or circumstances.

N

narrative analysis The investigation of naturally occurring storytelling.

natural-groups design Research design in which some difference already present among the participants is used as the basis for forming or selecting the groups.

naturalistic observation Research design in which data are collected where people are ordinarily found doing what they ordinarily do.

negative correlation The opposite of a positive correlation; as the value of one variable increases, the value of the other variable decreases.

neutrality A nonjudgmental attitude on the part of the researcher.

nominal data Data that reflect two or more distinct categories, as opposed to numerical levels.

non-equivalent control group A comparison group that is created by some method other than traditional randomization.

non-participant observation A technique in which the researchers observe a group of people from outside of the group and thus do not embed themselves in the community under study when they conduct their investigations.

non-random sample A sample in which each member does not have an equal chance of being selected as a participant in the study.

normative measure Determines a person's performance relative to the performance of others.

numeric variables Variables that take on quantitative values, as opposed to categorical responses.

O

objectification Construction of the research participant as an unknowing other by an "expert" researcher.

objectivity Epistemological viewpoint associated with positivism and quantitative research; both a criterion for evaluation of quantitative research, and also an assumption of quantitative research that is challenged by qualitative researchers.

observation The process of viewing and recording human behavior; most often associated with qualitative research, but also often a component of experimental research.

one-shot design Research design in which one group of participants is studied only one time.

open-ended questions Interview or survey questions that require more than a single-word response or single selection of a multiple-choice option.

operational definition Working statement specifying how a variable will be measured or assessed.

opinion questions Interview questions that solicit personal beliefs or attitudes; for example, "What do you think or believe about . . . ?"

ordinal data Data that show increasing numerical values that are not equally spaced; for example, the rank order of race finishers.

outcome analysis Focuses on the functions that certain rituals or meanings serve for a community or culture; sometimes yields an evaluation of a program or an action plan for change.

outliers The few cases in quantitative studies that are far above or below the average.

overt Describes research done when people being observed know that they are being observed.

P

p value Chance that a statistically significant difference between variables can be attributed to measurement error or chance.

paired t test Tests whether two means in a repeated-measures study are statistically different.

parallel-forms reliability A form of assessing reliability that involves administering similar, but not identical, versions of the same instrument that have the same measurement characteristics.

participant observation A type of observational technique in which the researcher enmeshes himself or herself in the community under study.

past, present, and future perspectives Perspectives on background, experience, and meaning that should be consciously considered in a research design and report.

Pearson correlation Measures the covariation between two interval variables; most social scientists use it for ordinal data as well.

phenomenological validity The more formal name for the "Aha!" criterion in qualitative research; a term for congruent experiences that ring true for the participants.

phenomenology Research or investigation that focuses on how people experience a particular event or life process.

placebo A non-active or zero-level version of an independent variable; often used in drug trials.

placebo effect When participants behave differently because they *believe* that the independent variable is having an effect rather than because the independent variable is *actually* having an effect.

population The universe of people from which a sample is drawn and to which the results of a study could be generalized.

positive correlation The opposite of a negative correlation; as the value of one variable increases (or decreases), the value of the other variable also increases (or decreases).

positivism Epistemological viewpoint that embraces certain assumptions about truth and reality as existing outside of the self or observer.

post-hoc tests Statistical tests performed on statistically significant ANOVAs to determine how the means differ from each other.

post-positivist Term describing qualitative and more contemporary quantitative research methods that are not based on positivist assumptions.

practice effects Occur when participants' performance in an experiment changes simply because they do the experimental task multiple times, rather than because of the experimental manipulation.

prediction Research that allows one to make predictions about one variable based on participants' responses to other variables.

predictive validity Refers to the extent to which a measure is related to some other measure that the researcher is interested in predicting.

prescribed sequence In a grand narrative, the order of occurrence of elements of the narrative.

presupposition questions Interview questions that use grammatical structure to make an assumption; for example, rather than asking if someone drinks alcohol, a presupposition question would assume that everyone drinks and the question would focus on how much: "How much alcohol do you drink each week?" rather than, "Do you drink alcohol?"

primary observer and secondary participant One possible researcher role in qualitative research.

primary participant and secondary observer One possible researcher role in qualitative research.

probes (also called *follow-up questions*) Typically, impromptu responses to something the interview participant has said that ask for more details and explanation.

process of observation Begins once group access is attained and the researcher's role is determined.

psychological analysis The exploration of people's attitudes, feelings, beliefs, motives, values, and goals.

purposeful sample Comprised of people based on a particular attribute, and often designed to arbitrarily include equal representation of groups that may not be equally represented in society.

Q

qualitative purists Apply post-positivist criticism to quantitative research.

qualitative research Produces narrative or textual descriptions of the phenomena under study.

quantitative purists Attempt to evaluate qualitative research using the standards of quantitative research: sample, variable, measurement, statistics, etc.

quantitative research Specifies numerical assignment to the phenomena under study.

quasi-experiment Research design that involves conducting an experiment, usually in a real-life setting, without the benefit of random assignment of participants to conditions or other controls.

R

random assignment Research design in which all participants have an equal opportunity to be placed in any of the conditions of the experiment.

random-digit dialing A telephone sampling procedure that can take several forms. Because nonlisted numbers are included, the sample will be more representative; this procedure increases the percentage of minority respondents.

random-groups design Research design in which participants are randomly assigned to one of the experimental conditions.

random sample A sample in which each member of the sampling frame has an equal chance of being selected as a participant in the study.

range The subtractive difference between the highest score and the lowest score in the dataset.

rapport Empathy and connection; affirmation and feedback are particularly important to build this with interviewees.

rating scale An observational record in which the observer or participant records his or her own judgment about the nature of an act.

ratio data Set apart from ordinal (increasing order) and interval data (equal spacing) by having the additional property of an absolute lower value (such as zero) that corresponds to the absence of the measure.

reality of consciousness Perspective which suggests that reality resides in the interpretation or consciousness of an experience.

redundancy A criterion met when the inclusion or recruitment of an additional respondent does not significantly add new information and understanding.

reference section A section of the research paper that provides complete and accurate citations of all sources mentioned in the paper.

reflexive inquiry Research design in which interviews are conducted (phase one), then focused follow-up interviews are conducted (phase two), and finally, to assess validity, the researcher goes back to the interview respondents and verifies the analyses.

reflexive validity Determined by asking the research participants if the researcher's interpretations are accurate.

reformed qualitative researchers Accept the value of aggregate data, such as averages and frequencies, to inform their analyses.

reformed quantitative researchers Embrace the richness of qualitative approaches but attempt to make the qualitative research live up to positivist expectations in terms of theory, design, sample, and analysis.

regression to the mean A fundamental law of statistics stating that scores that are way above or way below the mean will, on a subsequent measure, return or regress back toward the true mean.

relational analysis Research that focuses on relationships and the interpretations and feelings associated with those relationships.

reliability The extent to which a measure yields the same scores across different times, groups of people, or versions of the instrument.

repeated independent samples design Research design that studies a different sample of people over repeated trials to track changes in behaviors or attitudes.

repeated-measures ANOVA Procedure used to test significant differences when the independent variable in a repeated-measures design has more than two levels.

repeated-measures design An experiment in which participants receive all levels of the independent variable rather than just one level.

repetition within cases A way to recognize a theme, when one begins to see the same idea repeated within a case and/or repeated across cases.

replication Demonstrating or duplicating the findings of a study in a different place or with a different group of people.

representative How much a participant or group is similar to the larger population.

representative sample A group used in a research study that is similar to the population to which the researcher wishes to generalize findings.

request for proposals (RFP) A call from an organization for researchers to submit a plan to conduct research on a specific question unique to that organization.

required elements Parts of a grand narrative that form the skeleton of the story.

research participants Newer term for "subjects" (those being studied in the research).

research proposal Document that describes the planned research process, including literature review, research questions or hypotheses, and proposed method.

research question A clearly articulated statement about the topic and variables of interest.

research team A group of researchers who work together.

response alternatives Choices of answers on a survey from which respondents select.

response bias Arises when those who do not participate differ from those who do participate in ways integral to the research.

results section Portion of a research article that describes the quantitative and qualitative findings of a study and whether the hypotheses were or were not supported.

rhetorical perspective Viewpoint that focuses on persuasion and influence.

role-playing An interview question in which respondents imagine themselves in the situation or context that you wish to understand.

S

sample The subset of people from the population who will participate in the current study.

sampling frame The members of the population who are eligible for the study.

sampling rationale The selection of a sampling technique (such as random, convenience, or purposeful sampling) that varies according to the nature of the research question.

scatterplot A graphic representation of the relationship between two variables; commonly used with interval data.

script Part of a grand narrative; an order of presentation for required elements.

secondary data analysis Data analysis on previously collected data.

selection bias Arises when there are unintentional yet systematic differences between the people in the sample and the people in the population.

self perspective An active reflection on the impact of self in regard to what is being observed.

self-presentation bias Arises when participants in the study know they are being observed and behave differently because of it.

self-report data Collected by asking participants to answer questions on their own.

self-serving bias A tendency to report one's own behaviors and attitudes in a positive light.

sensory questions A specific type of description question that asks respondents what they see, hear, smell, touch, and taste as part of the experience under study.

set-up Section of a research project that informs the participant of the roles and expectations for the interviewer and interviewee.

silence An important interview technique, by which the interviewer gives sufficient time for the respondent to think about the question, organize a response, and articulate the response.

simple main effect The analysis of one independent variable at a particular level of the other independent variable.

simple random sampling Involves picking a certain number of participants out of the total number of participants in the sampling frame.

single-case study (also called *collective case study*) Research design that involves a comparison of several related cases, such as the comparison of several corporate organizations.

single-issue Quality of interview questions that ask about only one thing.

situated knowledge Information gleaned when the researcher fully explores how he or she interacts with the history, setting, context, culture, and participants, and how the research methods impact the context, culture, and participants.

situational analysis A rich description and interpretation of the situation, context, or problem.

snowball samples Research samples generated by participant recruitment or recommendation.

snowball sampling Research design in which a core group of participants who are initially sampled for the research project recruit or recommend other potential participants.

social construction of reality Viewpoint that assumes meaning arises from communication and socially agreed-upon understandings; in this perspective, there is no objective reality that can be discovered outside of the human interpretive experience. Proponents of this view hold that one cannot analyze and understand an entity by analysis of its parts; rather, one must examine the larger context in which people and knowledge function.

social embeddedness The belief that people are integral parts of a social world and are entwined in social relationships.

social influence Effects of relationships; a focus group is an excellent way to observe and analyze this.

sociocultural perspective Viewpoint taken in a social and cultural analysis of what is being observed.

Solomon four-group design A special case of a mixed design used when the presence of a pretest might create a practice effect.

spiral of silence theory Holds that the articulation of strong opinions by outspoken people can silence those who hold contrary views.

standard deviation The square root of the variance; the average amount by which any observations differ from the mean.

statistical designations Letters or symbols that specify different statistical terms; examples are mean, standard deviation, F, t, and chi-square.

statistical weighting Method that involves overcounting the returned surveys of an underrepresented group.

statistically significant Term for when the level of significance surpasses a threshold such that researchers are willing to conclude that the finding is a "real" relationship rather than due to chance factors.

stories of culture One way in which ethnographies are described/defined.

stratified random assignment sampling Research design in which participants are assigned to conditions based on a preexisting trait.

stratified random sampling Research design in which research participants are selected based on their membership in a particular subgroup; participants may be selected to produce relatively equal sized groups that may not be represented equally in the population.

stratum A particular subgroup in a study that can be used to more precisely select a sample.

structure Refers to the degree of flexibility in adapting methods during the course of data collection.

structured interview Follows a set of prescribed questions; written out, with probes, transitions, and follow-up questions.

subjective Viewpoint associated with post-positivism and qualitative research.

synergistic group effect Refers to the fact that groups can provide information that individual interviews cannot; recognizes that people's behaviors and attitudes are made, not individually in isolation, but in a social context.

systematic sampling Method in which a researcher moves through the sampling frame list and selects one out of every fixed number of entries.

T

t **test** A statistical technique used to determine if two groups or levels of an independent variable differ on a dependent variable.

test-retest reliability A form of reliability assessment that involves administering an instrument two times to participants to determine if scores are similar.

text In qualitative research, refers to spoken words, visual representations, written texts, and other artifacts of a culture or a cultural group.

textual analysis A type of qualitative research method that involves investigation of cultural texts.

thematic units Units of analysis identified in qualitative data after data collection, during analysis; data are coded to determine category members.

theme identification A cyclical process of identifying thematic units that eventually leads the researcher to more complex analyses.

themes Metaphors, words, phrases, essential meanings that emerge in qualitative data analysis; consistent patterns of usage lead the researcher to identify themes.

theories Sets of organizing principles that help researchers describe and predict events; not yet proven, but can be supported by testing specific hypotheses.

thick description Characteristic of field notes.

time sampling Research design in which systematic observations are taken at preset intervals.

tools Data collection techniques, such as interviews, focus groups, or oral histories; can be used across a number of different methods.

traditional research Tries to describe, predict, and control the area being investigated; conducted in controlled environments using mainly quantitative methods, with the goal of generalizing to the larger population.

transitions Comments that help an interview progress smoothly from topic to topic.

treatment group The group that received the independent variable.

triangulation Using more than one methodology to address the same question.

Type I error A probability estimate of whether a relationship is true when in fact it is due to chance factors.

Type II error A probability estimate of whether there is *not* a difference between two variables when there really is one.

V

validity Extent to which a measure actually assesses what it claims to measure (truthfulness).

value questions Interview questions that solicit or probe the respondent's judgments; for example, "To what extent is this good/moral or bad/immoral?"

variable A construct that can take on two or more distinct values.

verbal or nonverbal signs Everything encountered in a culture, from clothing to books to food to architecture; textual analysis involves the identification and interpretation of these.

virtual communities Autonomous groups created on the Internet; they have made the selection of participants for phenomenology much easier.

visual analysis Interpretation of mediated communication texts such as films or television programs.

W

within-group error variance Error caused by random fluctuations in the performance of one group of people due to characteristics of the people in the study.

written representations of culture One way in which ethnographies are described/defined.

INDEX